Sinéad McCoole is the author of two highly acclaimed Irish history titles: *Hazel: A Life of Lady Lavery* (Lilliput Press, 1996) and *No Ordinary Women: Irish Female Activists, 1900–1923* (O'Brien Press, 2003). Other publications include *Guns and Chiffon* (1997); *The Researcher's Handbook* (2000); and *Passion and Politics* (2010). Sinéad has curated exhibitions on Irish history and Irish art at Dublin City Hugh Lane Gallery, including *Society and Politics* (1996); and *Passion and Politics* (2010); Kilmainham Jail's *Robert Emmet Bi-centenary Exhibition* (2003) and *Guns and Chiffon* (1997), which toured in the US in 1998. She is currently Curatorial and Historical Advisor at the 2016 Project Office, and a member of the Expert Advisory Group to the Irish Government for the Decade of Centenaries 2012–2022.

D1424815

EASTER WIDOWS

Sinéad McCoole

DOUBLEDAY IRELAND

TRANSWORLD IRELAND PUBLISHERS
28 Lower Leeson Street, Dublin 2, Ireland
www.transworldireland.ie

Transworld Ireland is part of the Penguin Random House group of companies
whose addresses can be found at global.penguinrandomhouse.com

Penguin
Random House
UK

First published in the UK and Ireland in 2014
by Doubleday Ireland
an imprint of Transworld Publishers
Trade paperback edition published 2015

A CIP catalogue record for this book
is available from the British Library.

ISBN 9781781620236

Typeset in 11.5/14.5pt Baskerville by Falcon Oast Graphic Art Ltd.
Printed and bound in Great Britain by Clays Ltd, Bungay, Suffolk

Penguin Random House is committed to a sustainable
future for our business, our readers and our planet. This book
is made from Forest Stewardship Council® certified paper.

MIX
Paper from
responsible sources
FSC® C018179

1 3 5 7 9 10 8 6 4 2

For Gráinne Blair
who made it her mission to make sure
that I never gave up on writing the 'Widows'

THE DALY AND CLARKE FAMILIES

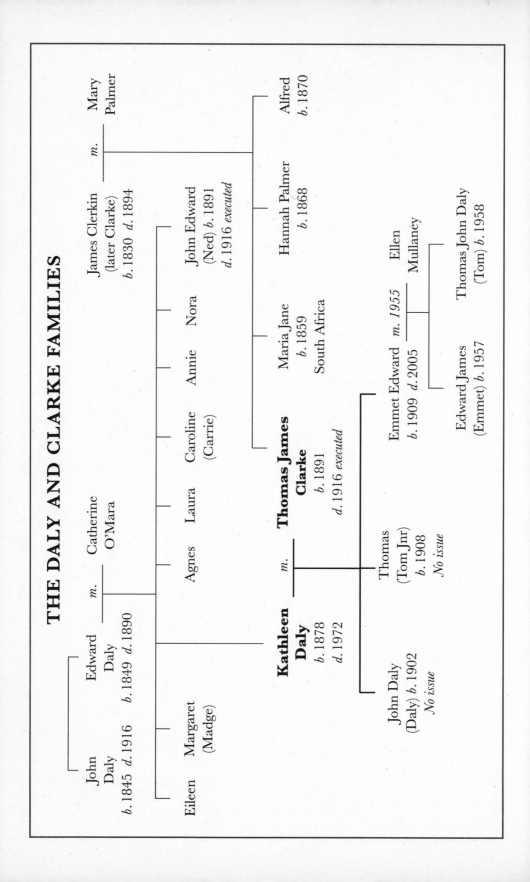

THE GONNE AND MACBRIDE FAMILIES

Patrick *m* Honoria
MacBride — Gill
d. 1868   *b.* 1837

Edith (Edie) *m.* 1865 Thomas 'Margaret
Frith Cook — Gonne ----- Wilson'
b. 1844 *d.* 1871   *d.* 1886   *b.* 1862

Joseph   Patrick   Francis   Anthony   **John**
b. 1861   *b.* 1863   *b.* 1864   *b.* 1867   *b.* 1868
d. 1938   *d.* 1943   *d.* 1916
executed

m.(1) 1893   *m.*(2) 1916
Emmie Elizabeth
Mary   *d.* 1914   Mooney
b. 1862

Lucien   **Edith**   Kathleen   Margaretta   Eileen
Millevoye ----- **Maud**   (Mrs Pilcher)   Rose   Constance
b. 1851   *b.* 1866   *b.* 1868   *b.* 1871   (Daisy)
d. 1918   *d.* 1953   *d.* 1918   *d.* 1871   *b.* 1886

m. 1903

Jean/Seagan *m.* 1926 Catalina (Kid)
(Seán)   Bulfin
b. 1904
d. 1988

Anna   Tiernan
b. 1926   *b.* 1932
      d. 1995

Constance *m.* 1904

Niall   Cleena   Mary   Erc   Úna   Sheila
b. 1905   *b.* 1906   Clodhra   *b.* 1907   *b.* 1910   *b.* 1915
d. 1905   *b.* 1906

Iseult *m.* 1920 Francis
b. 1894   Stuart
d. 1953   *b.* 1902
      d. 2000

Georges
b. 1890
d. 1891

Ian   Kay
b. 1926

Dolores
b. 1921
d. 1921

THE REYNOLDS AND CONNOLLY FAMILIES

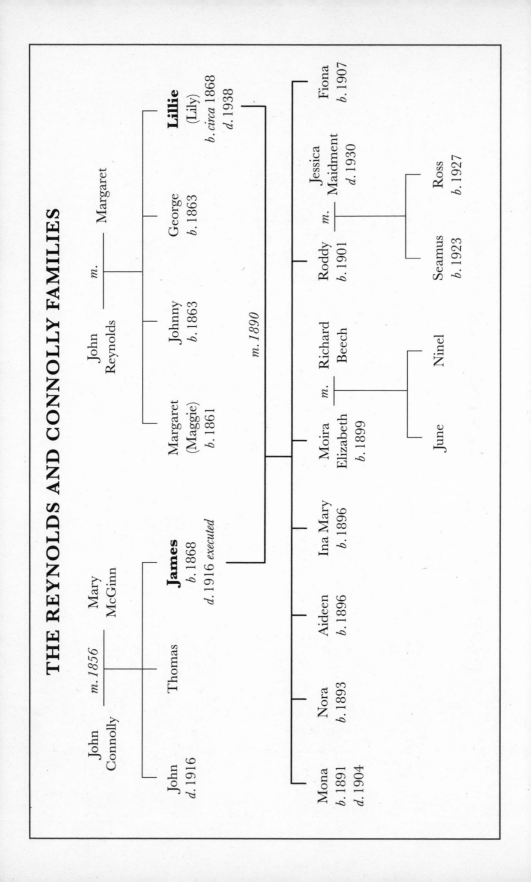

THE O'BRENNAN AND KENT (CEANNT) FAMILIES

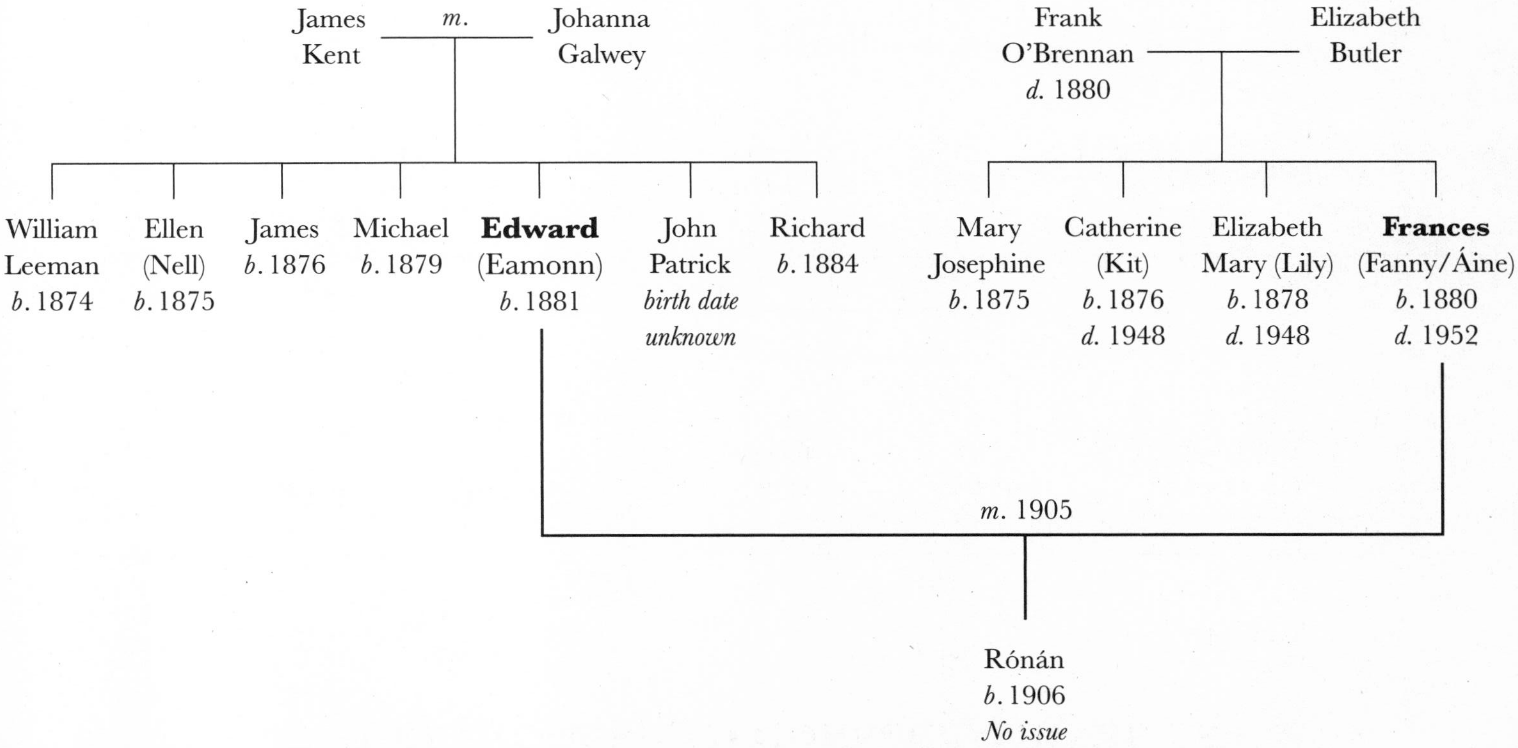

James
Kent

m.

Johanna
Galwey

Frank
O'Brennan
d. 1880

Elizabeth
Butler

William
Leeman
b. 1874

Ellen
(Nell)
b. 1875

James
b. 1876

Michael
b. 1879

Edward
(Eamonn)
b. 1881

John
Patrick
*birth date
unknown*

Richard
b. 1884

Mary
Josephine
b. 1875

Catherine
(Kit)
b. 1876
d. 1948

Elizabeth
Mary (Lily)
b. 1878
d. 1948

Frances
(Fanny/Áine)
b. 1880
d. 1952

m. 1905

Rónán
b. 1906
No issue

THE HICKEY AND MALLIN FAMILIES

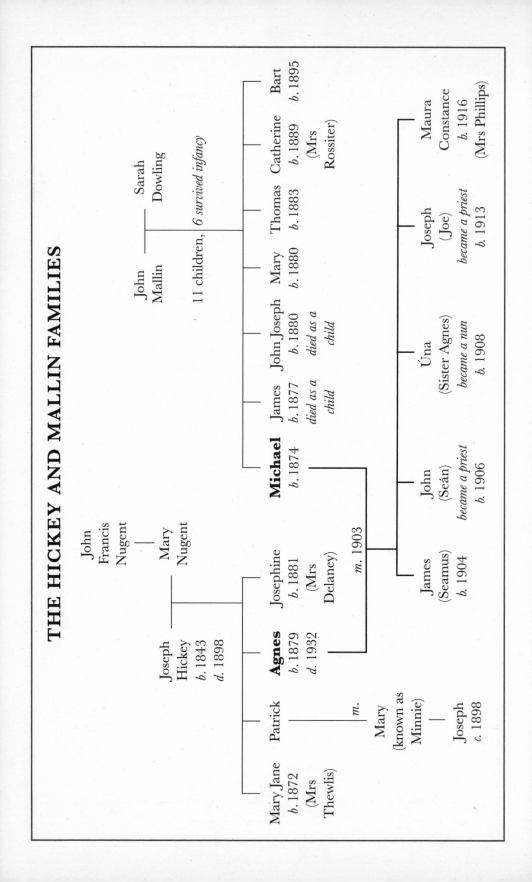

THE GIFFORD AND PLUNKETT FAMILIES

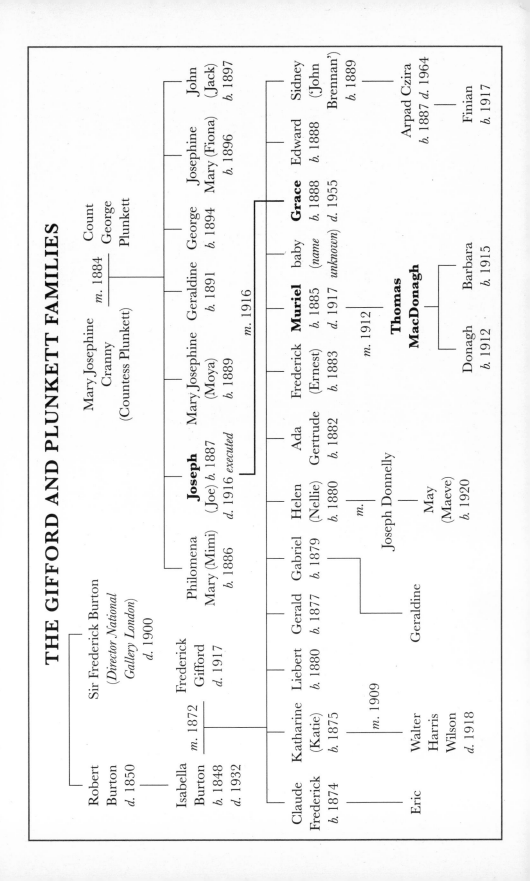

THE GIFFORD AND MACDONAGH FAMILIES

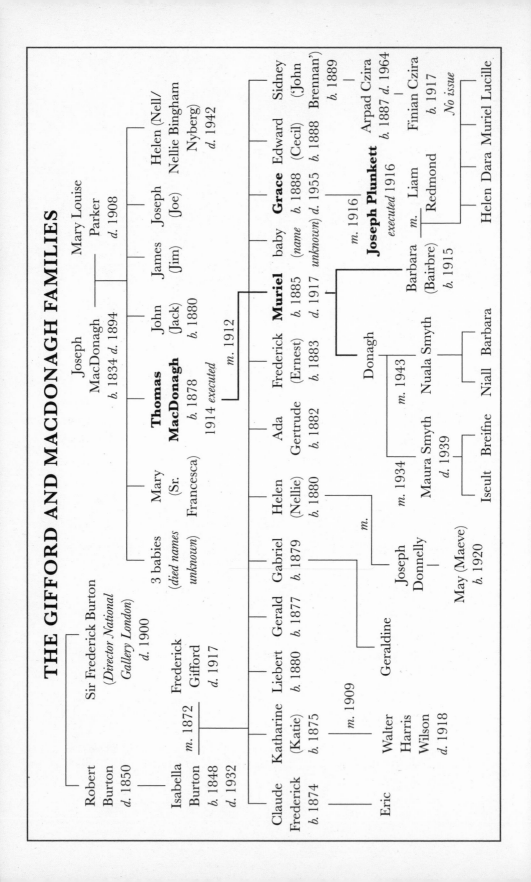

Contents

Acknowledgements

I must begin by thanking my family, Éamon, Eve and Edward Howlin. When work, other projects and family commitments dictated that I could no longer work on this manuscript during the normal course of the year, they accepted that on every holiday, and on every train journey, the 'Easter Widows' came with us.

I am also indebted to the women who assisted me in so many ways over these twenty years – my mother Barbara, mother-in-law Ann, sister Fiona, sisters-in-law Fran, Liz and Sara – and friends Dorothy Davison, Valerie Butler, Kathleen Daniel and Anne Marie Forbes. And for their support of me and my work, I also thank my father-in-law Eddie, and Ray and Ciaran.

I am grateful to my mother, to Carla Briggs, Niamh O'Sullivan and Paul Turnell, who gave me their insights, observations and guidance on the manuscript. Special thanks to Clodagh Ní Mhaoilchiaráin for her translation of the Éamonn Ceannt letters. Without Larisa Sioneriu researching Arpad Czira and speaking to Mr Ciobota, Arpad's son, it would not have been possible to uncover the truth of that story. A special thank you to Dr Margaret MacCurtain for her timely intervention when I was losing interest (and hope) in ever completing the work on this book.

Thanks go to those who assisted with information and location of documents and by giving me their insights over two decades – Ann Clare; Anne Clarke; Anne Fagan; William Henry (who gave me access to his research notes); Alan Hayes; Mike McCormack,

National Historian for the Ancient Order of Hibernians in America; Father Brian Murphy OSB; Carol Murphy; Loretta Clarke Murray; Maire O'Neill; and Honor Ó Brolcháin.

For his kindness in giving me his expertise in editing and captioning the picture section, I am honoured to have had the assistance of Vincent Virga; and thank you, too, to Jimmy McCourt for his hospitality during that work. I extend my gratitude to Dawn Blanquier for her speed and precision in digitizing my own collection. I am grateful to a number of people who have given me items as gifts over the years, especially to Dr John Cowell for the Brigid Lyons Thornton Collection – many of her 1916 items illustrate this book; to Miss Bunty, who gave me her father's 1916 collection when she learned of my interest at the time when, aged four, Eve joined her Irish dancing class in Dún Laoghaire; and to Dr Ledwith from Limerick I also extend my thanks.

I am extremely grateful for help given to me by the following descendants of the 'Easter Widows'. Kathleen Clarke: Helen Litton, her grand-niece; Emmet and Tom Clarke, her grandsons, and their late father, Dr Emmet Clarke; and the de hÓir sisters of Limerick. Maud Gonne MacBride: her grandson, the late Tiernan MacBride; her granddaughter Anna MacBride White; and her daughter-in-law Imogen Stuart. Lillie Connolly: her grandsons Seamus Connolly and Roderick Wilson. Fanny/Áine Ceannt: Mary Gallagher and the late Maírín O'Connor, descendants of the Kent brothers. Agnes Mallin: her daughter, the late Maura Mallin; her son Father Joseph Mallin; Michael's nephew Michael Mallin; their grandsons Michael and David Phillips; and the late Ciss and Lily Thewlis, nieces of Agnes. Muriel MacDonagh and Grace Plunkett: the late Iseult MacGuinness, Muriel MacAuley and Lucille Redmond, the granddaughters of Thomas and Muriel; and Nellie Gifford's daughter, the late Maeve Donnelly. Margaret Wilson: Georgi Särekanno of the Jäneda Manor Museum, Estonia; Sven Tölp of the Estonian Embassy, London; her granddaughter Mary MacBride Walsh; the Alexander family and Tim Souter.

ACKNOWLEDGEMENTS

*

I am grateful to the staff, past and present, of the National Library of Ireland, in particular James Harte, Tom Desmond and Paddy Hawe; the staff of Kilmainham Jail, past and present: Niamh O'Sullivan (so good to me I name her twice), Pat Cooke, Louise O'Hanrahan, Phil Mason, the late Maureen Cashman, Niall Bergin, Conor Masterson (also to Livia Henderson for her assistance with an interview in 2005 – a kindness never forgotten). Thank you to Rosemary King of the Allen Library, and Tara O'Reilly Photography for taking such wonderful images from that collection; Austin Vaughan, and the staff of Mayo County Library; Mayo County Council's Jackie Clarke Collection for source material and so many insights; the National Museum of Ireland, and Sandra McElroy for her assistance; Ann Field, trustee of the Marx Memorial Library in London; Ken Bergin and Sinéad Keogh of Glucksman Library, University of Limerick; Cécile Gordon of the Military Archives; and Vince Hay of the Royal Highland Fusiliers Museum. Thank you also to Susan Reyburn of the Library of Congress.

I wish to thank Peter O'Connell, my agent. To my publishers Doubleday Ireland – it has been a pleasure to work on this book with you. I must especially thank my editor, Brian Langan, who made sure that the book was accessible to those without in-depth knowledge of Irish history, and Eoin McHugh, who believed in the book from the start. I am so grateful to Brenda Updegraff, my copy-editor, Janet Shuter, who compiled the index, and Phil Lord, design manager at Transworld, London, for their contributions to the creation of this book.

For better, for worse, for richer, for poorer
Till death do us part

Introduction

Seven women – Kathleen, Maud, Lillie, Fanny, Agnes, Grace and Muriel – all shared one destiny: they were all widowed at Easter time in the year 1916. In this, they shared the same fate as so many of their contemporaries whose husbands were at war in Europe.

Selecting their widows' weeds was no problem, as many outlets were selling those clothes for war widows. A whole generation of men were dying, in their hundreds of thousands that year alone. Men in uniform had been a common sight for a number of years. Soldiers marching, bands playing, parades and drills.

These seven women came from different backgrounds to be united in a common grief. Maud was the wealthiest. Kathleen's upbringing was considered comfortable due to the support of an uncle who had made a fortune in Australia; she had also established her own dressmaking business. Sisters Grace and Muriel were the daughters of a solicitor and were well off by the standards of the day. Fanny, brought up by a widowed mother, became a clerk, earning her own income as soon as she left school. Lillie had been in service and had become a governess to the younger children of the household in which she lived, and Agnes became a nurse, but marriage had brought both of them down the social scale.

Death had already fractured the lives of some of the women before 1916. Maud was brought up by a faithful servant who fulfilled the role of her parent, as her mother had died when she was four and her father was constantly absent. Fanny and Lillie lost their fathers to early death, their mothers taking charge and shaping their lives. While Agnes and sisters Grace and Muriel had not spent their childhood under the shadow of death, it was to be only a short time before they too would experience the effects of loss.

Maud and Kathleen would both marry against the wishes of their closest friends and family. The others married seemingly conventional men. Edward worked in the heart of the British administration at Cork Hill, next to the entrance to Dublin Castle. James was a British soldier stationed in Dublin when he met Lillie. Michael was also a soldier in the British Army, about to embark for service in British India at the time he met Agnes. Joe was the eldest son of the director of the National Museum of Science and Art, Dublin when he began his courtship with Grace. A poet, playwright and inventor, he was managing director of a theatre along with Thomas, who married Muriel; he was a promising academic, a university lecturer, a poet and a playwright.

These men shared with their women an interest in the arts, literature, music and theatre. Dublin had a wealth of groups, clubs and societies of all kinds, and those interested in Ireland and all things Irish were plentiful, with classes in the Irish language, sport and music. All of them became meeting places for young men and women, facilitating introductions and romance. But there were also early indications of what the future would hold for Kathleen, Maud, Lillie, Fanny, Agnes, Grace and Muriel, hints of what and who these men would become . . .

By 1916, five of their husbands – Tom, James, Edward, Joe and Thomas – had formed a self-styled Provisional Government of the Irish Republic along with P. H. Pearse and Seán Mac Diarmada. John MacBride and Michael Mallin became commanders of outposts, part of an Army of the Irish Republic during the fateful Easter Week.

POBLACHT NA H EIREANN

THE PROVISIONAL GOVERNMENT
OF THE
IRISH REPUBLIC
TO THE PEOPLE OF IRELAND

IRISHMEN AND IRISHWOMEN: In the name of God and of the dead generations from which she receives her old tradition of nationhood, Ireland, through us, summons her children to her flag and strikes for her freedom.

By addressing their Proclamation to both men and women in 1916, a time before women had been granted the franchise, they were taking a progressive step and one that showed their advanced opinions about their women and the women of Ireland. James Connolly's Irish Citizen Army had women drilling on equal terms with men, while Thomas had been an active member of the Irish Women's Franchise League. Kathleen later said that in fact one of those who signed the Proclamation had objected to the inclusion of Irishwomen, but she said she would never divulge who it was, though it was not her husband Tom.

Having organised and trained her manhood through her secret revolutionary organisation, the Irish Republican Brotherhood, and through her open military organisations, the Irish Volunteers and the Irish Citizen Army, having patiently perfected her discipline, having resolutely waited for the right moment to reveal itself, she now seizes that moment, and, supported by her exiled children in America and by gallant allies in Europe, but relying in the first on her own strength, she strikes in full confidence of victory.

These men selected key buildings in the capital city, Dublin, occupied them, and led various groups out to fight, including the men who had joined a Volunteer movement, formed by those who had opted to stay at home to defend Ireland during what was known then as the Great War.

> We declare the right of the people of Ireland to the ownership of Ireland, and to the unfettered control of Irish destinies, to be sovereign and indefeasible. The long usurpation of that right by a foreign people and government has not extinguished the right, nor can it ever be extinguished except by the destruction of the Irish people.
>
> In every generation the Irish people have asserted their right to national freedom and sovereignty; six times during the last three hundred years they have asserted it in arms.

Ireland was one of Britain's oldest colonies and had a long history of unsuccessful rebellions. Previous uprisings – in 1645, 1690, 1798, 1803, 1848 and 1867 – had all ended in failure; exile for some, execution for others.

> Standing on that fundamental right and again asserting it in arms in the face of the world, we hereby proclaim the Irish Republic as a Sovereign Independent State, and we pledge our lives and the lives of our comrades-in-arms to the cause of its freedom, of its welfare, and of its exaltation among the nations.

The authors of this document envisioned a prolonged period of fighting. Their original plan was to take Dublin and then make their way to the country to continue their fight alongside their comrades in other parts of Ireland. They had allocated each other roles in the government that would be established to take over the working of the administration while the war continued. They wrote with a hope for the future of their country:

> The Irish Republic is entitled to, and hereby claims, the allegiance of every Irishman and Irishwoman. The Republic guarantees religious and civil liberty, equal rights and equal opportunities to all its citizens,

and declares its resolve to pursue the happiness and prosperity of the whole nation and of all its parts, cherishing all of the children of the nation equally, and oblivious of the differences carefully fostered by an alien government, which have divided a minority from the majority in the past.

Until our arms have brought the opportune moment for the establishment of a permanent National Government, representative of the whole people of Ireland and elected by the suffrages of all her men and women, the Provisional Government, hereby constituted, will administer the civil and military affairs of the Republic in trust for the people.

We place the cause of the Irish Republic under the protection of the Most High God, Whose blessing we invoke upon our arms, and we pray that no one who serves that cause will dishonour it by cowardice, inhumanity, or rapine. In this supreme hour the Irish nation must, by its valour and discipline and by the readiness of its children to sacrifice themselves for the common good, prove itself worthy of the august destiny to which it is called.

Signed on Behalf of the Provisional Government,

Thomas J. Clarke,
Sean Mac Diarmada, Thomas MacDonagh,
P. H. Pearse, Eamonn Ceannt,
James Connolly, Joseph Plunkett

By signing this document, these men had taken part in armed rebellion and waged a war against the king, the head of the United Kingdom, and for this they faced the ultimate punishment.

Sixteen men in total were executed, including former British soldier Michael Mallin, who was sentenced by court martial to be put to death; and John MacBride, appointed a major by the Boers in South Africa, who, having chanced upon the fighting, also took up arms and as a result was shot by firing squad. According to Maud Gonne MacBride, it was the death he had always desired.

This is the story of the seven Easter Widows.

PART ONE
ROMANCE

1

Kathleen and Tom

In her dream the man had said to her: 'Ah, I knew I would find you. You thought you had escaped me.'[1] Kathleen Daly recalled this when she came face to face with Tom Clarke in March 1899. She was not a believer in dreams and was shocked to discover when she met him that Tom was the man she had dreamed of. Incredibly, she had never seen a picture or a photograph of him, but Kathleen had grown up from the age of six with stories about Tom Clarke, who had been imprisoned with her uncle John Daly for revolutionary activities. One of her childhood memories was sticking stamps on the envelopes of scores of letters seeking amnesty for political prisoners in England. She felt that she was helping 'free Uncle John and of course Ireland.'

John Daly was the national organizer of the Irish Republican Brotherhood, a secret oath-bound organization working for the creation of an Irish Republic. He was arrested in April 1884 for alleged possession of explosives, but he was not guilty of the crime he was charged with. The lack of evidence did not prevent his conviction, however. Even later, when the police chief confessed on his death bed that John Daly had been imprisoned on perjured evidence, it did not bring about his release.

Years earlier, Kathleen's father, Edward, had also spent time in prison, when he was just seventeen, in the aftermath of the Fenian Rebellion of 1867. Now, on hearing of his brother John's imprisonment, he immediately gave up his job as attendant in St George's

Private Lunatic Asylum in Sussex and returned to Limerick. A branch of the revived Amnesty Association[2] was started in Limerick to work for the release of Irish political prisoners.

Edward Daly suffered from heart problems and in September 1890 he died, aged just forty-one. Many people believed that his condition had been affected by his brother John's incarceration and his funeral was used as a protest against John's continued imprisonment. The *Munster News* recorded that several thousand mourners marched 'to show they believed with the dead man in his brother's innocence.'[3] Others blamed Edward Daly's death on the harsh conditions he himself had endured in prison.

Kathleen, who was just twelve years old when he died, said that her father's death ended her childhood, requiring the eldest children, Eileen, Madge and herself, to take on responsibilities 'not normally placed on children's shoulders.' The family consisted of eight girls, and his grief-stricken wife Catherine[4] was pregnant with their ninth child at the time of Edward's death; he didn't live to see his longed-for son, named John Edward (who became known as Ned). At first Catherine struggled to accept her newborn child, who was frail, but soon she became preoccupied with nursing him and in time she came to idolize her only boy.

Following Edward's death a subscription was raised to help the family and a lease was taken on a public house, but it failed within a year. Help came from another of the Daly brothers, James, who had gone to the island of New Caledonia in Australia in the 1850s and had made a fortune in numerous professions, including sheep farming, a racing stables and coastal trading. Kathleen said his return in 1894 was to care for his extended family and 'his wealth certainly made life very easy for us.'[5]

Uncle James, however, refused to pay for music lessons for Kathleen, whose ambition was to become a professional musician. Entirely self-taught, she deeply regretted that she never got the chance to do the one thing that she loved. Determined to have her independence nonetheless, she asked him if she could undertake an apprenticeship with a court dressmaker and he was willing to pay a substantial sum for her to learn this trade. Although it wasn't her first choice, she selected it as a good profession; each season and each activity required different clothes for the well-to-do of Irish society, and while the wealthiest women went to Paris, or visited the London branch of a Parisian salon, to replenish their wardrobe, most ladies used the services of local court dressmakers. Kathleen also knew there were few other opportunities for girls at the time.

In 1893 Kathleen met the charismatic and independent campaigner Maud Gonne, a member of the Amnesty Association, who along with the MP John Redmond and others spoke publicly, petitioned members of parliament, published articles and fundraised for the families of those imprisoned. When Maud came to Limerick it was to assist Kathleen's uncle John, who was still in jail, get elected to the British parliament. Kathleen later recalled: 'I thought her the most beautiful woman I had ever seen . . . She was fascinating as she was beautiful, and the Limerick men went mad about her.'[6] Maud succeeded in persuading the other candidate to withdraw and so secured John Daly's election. He was prevented from taking his seat as a 'treason felon', but he would have refused to take it as he wanted self-government for Ireland.

John was finally freed in August 1896, after he went on hunger strike to demand his release. Following his recovery, he went on a tour of England with Maud Gonne, holding rallies to highlight the plight of those still imprisoned and to campaign for their release. Tom Clarke would be the last to be freed.

Uncle John often spoke of Tom Clarke. Kathleen built in her mind a picture of 'a noble courageous, unselfish character, one that showed unwonted sweetness and restraint under the most terrible provocation during his imprisonment.'[7] In Chatham Prison Tom Clarke and the other Irish political prisoners were known as 'the special men' and held, as Tom recalled, in 'solitary confinement in cold, white washed cells, with a short daily exercise varying the monotony . . . Day after day all alike, no change, maddening silence, sitting hopeless, friendless and alone.'[8] The prison governor devised a system of 'perpetual and persistent' harassing, which included bread-and-water punishments if the prisoner went to bed before the bell rang for supper and the nightly torture of interrupted sleep, all intended to destroy the men mentally and physically. This lasted for seven years. Few fared as well as Tom Clarke and John Daly. Tom later compiled a list; alongside the names of his prison companions he had written their fate – dead, health shattered or insane.

A fellow prisoner acknowledged that Tom 'was almost continuously under punishment',[9] and Tom himself wrote: 'it has been a source of perpetual surprise to me that I was able to get through it at all'.[10] As Kathleen later recorded, Tom's ingenuity played a large part in his survival – 'his keen brain outwitted his jailers'[11] – but he was also sustained by the friendship of two of his fellow prisoners, John Daly and James Francis Egan. To overcome the rule of silence in one cell, Tom fashioned a pencil out of the lead into which the bars were embedded and used this to communicate with his fellow prisoners. Later, in another cell with no lead available, a code for a cell telegraph was devised with Daly and Egan, based on Morse code, with dot and dash replaced by the sound of the dull knock made by the knuckles and the sharp knock of a button or slate pencil. His charge sheet shows that for this tapping he was subjected to solitary confinement on a bread-and-water diet on a number of occasions. Tom later recalled: 'the sterling friendship of manly comrades counted for much.'

As convict J464, Tom Clarke served his sentence with his head shaved and clothed in prison dress: 'I wore that convict garb with a certain amount of pride, and took satisfaction in the thought that with all her laws and with all her power this great England could not force me – one of the mere units of the Irish rank and file – to regard myself as one of the criminal class any more than I could ever be forced to regard myself as English.'[12]

Yet Tom Clarke actually was an Englishman by birth. He was born on 11 March 1858 in the barracks located at Hurst Castle, a fortress built during the reign of Henry VIII as a coastal defence guarding the entrance to Southampton. His father, James Clerkin, had enlisted in the British Army from his native Leitrim in 1847, changing his name to Clarke. James had married Mary Palmer of Clogheen, County Tipperary, whom he met when he was posted to the nearby garrison town of Clonmel; Mary's father, Michael, was in charge of the local jail. They were married in the Church of Ireland chapel of St Paul's in Shanrahan, a mile west of the village of Clogheen. James served ten years in the 12th Royal Artillery regiment and was promoted to the rank of corporal shortly after his marriage and transferred to England.[13]

Their first-born son was named Thomas James Clarke and was baptized a Catholic. He was brought up with his mother's religion but his father always practised his own faith. In April 1859, when Tom was just over a year old, the family travelled with James's regiment to Natal in South Africa, where Mary gave birth to a second child, Maria Jane, in May of that year. Four other babies were born in South Africa but none of these children lived beyond infancy.[14] Tom's early years were spent living in various British barracks in the coastal region, at the Cape of Good Hope and on the Indian Ocean, which had been taken by the British from the Boers in 1842.

Tom did not live in Ireland until he was seven years old, when the family returned from South Africa in March 1865 after James Clarke was appointed sergeant of the Ulster Militia. They settled in Dungannon, County Tyrone, which Tom would always regard as his home town. In 1868, when he was ten, his father retired[15] from the army at the age of thirty-nine, having served twenty-one years. He took up a position as a groom, which had been his profession before he enlisted. Two more children were born to the couple in Ireland, Hannah Palmer in 1868 and another son, Alfred, in 1870.

According to Kathleen, the conditions Tom observed in County Tyrone shaped his character: 'the ruin and desolation, the evictions and injustices he saw all around him drove him mad; it had a terrible effect on his ardent temperament and forced his decision to dedicate his life to Ireland.'[16] This was a period of severe economic depression in which many tenants, lacking fixity of tenure on their holdings, were evicted. Landlords were often not working the land, many of them living outside Ireland. The poor conditions resulted in a Land War that began in 1879 and the formation of a Land League by Michael Davitt and others; their slogan was 'Land for the People'.

Tom's teacher saw his promise as a scholar and when his education was over engaged him as an assistant teacher in Dungannon boys' national school, but his politicization meant that he never studied for a teaching qualification.

In 1878, twenty-year-old Tom was present at a rally at Drumcoo Hill outside Dungannon when John Daly of Limerick addressed the crowd in his capacity as national organizer of the Irish Republican Brotherhood. Later that year Tom travelled to Dublin and was sworn into the brotherhood by Daly. He then returned to Dungannon and set up his own circle of twenty-three men; in the leadership structure of the organization he was known as the 'centre'.

One of the objectives of the IRB was to take military action against the police force, the Royal Irish Constabulary. In 1880 Tom was involved in clashes with the RIC and went on the run to America. When he got to New York he found work in a shoe shop before becoming night porter at the Mansion House Hotel, Brooklyn. By 1883 he had been offered the position of manager of the Brighton Beach Hotel, close to the resort of Coney Island, but once again his commitment to the cause of Irish freedom changed his plans. After arriving in the USA he had joined Clan na Gael, the American auxiliary of the IRB, and the 'bright, earnest, wiry, alert young fellow' was chosen along with other single men for 'dangerous work'.[17]

In the spring of 1883, aged twenty-five, Tom was selected to undertake a mission to England, where he travelled under the pseudonym Henry Hammond Wilson. There he was tutored in the procurement and manufacture of explosives. That April, after correspondence with other known conspirators was intercepted, he was arrested in his lodging at Blackfriars Road in London in possession of explosives and charged under the Treason Felony Act of 1848. At his trial at the Old Bailey, where Tom conducted his own defence, the judge commented that it was a pity such ability was being misused. He was sentenced to penal servitude for life.

Tom's family had known nothing of his whereabouts since he had disappeared from home three years before and his use of a false name meant that his arrest and conviction did not alert them to his whereabouts. He would never see his father again, as James Clarke died in 1894. When Tom's true identity became known his widowed mother was supported by the Amnesty Association. According to Maud Gonne, the news of Tom's imprisonment had caused Mary Clarke to have a breakdown and she had been confined for a time to a lunatic asylum. Upon her release her health was broken and she could not work. Maud sent her money in November 1895, and Mary thanked her, saying that she had received the payment when she was most in need: 'God will bless you for all you are doing for the poor prisoners and their families.'[18]

The final years of Tom Clarke's sentence were served in Portland Prison and he had spent a total of fifteen years and four months in jail when he finally received his 'licence to be at large' from Whitehall on 21 September 1898. On his release his sole possession was a bundle of old letters which he described as 'very dear' to him. Tom was later to write: 'Irish freedom has gone on for centuries, and in the course of it a well-trodden path has been made that leads to the scaffold and to the prison. Many of our revered dead have trod that path, and it was these memories that inspired me with sufficient courage to walk part of the way along that path with an upright head.'[19]

At the time of his release, Tom Clarke was described by a reporter as 'a man of medium height and intelligent aspect. The face and body emaciated from the cruel years of hardship and deprivation while the long enduring of penal labour had left its mark in a slight stoop of the shoulders.'[20]

In March 1899, the year after Tom was released, he went to stay with the Daly family, as John Daly, now mayor of Limerick, had arranged to present him with the Freedom of the City. John was living with his mother and his sister Ellen (known as Lollie), as well as his widowed sister-in-law Catherine and her children, Eileen, Madge, Kathleen, Agnes, Annie, Caroline (Carrie), Laura, Nora and Ned. Their uncle James had returned to Australia.

When she first met Tom, Kathleen was approaching her twenty-first birthday. Since the age of eighteen, she had owned her own 'dress warehouse' and had her own staff, based in Cecil Street. Unlike her sisters, she had refused to work in the bakery Uncle John had opened on his release from prison. This angered him, but Kathleen reasoned that she did not want to be bossed by her older siblings and that she was already earning more money from her business than the bakery would pay her. Her family opposed her, but she had her own capital and continued with her plan. Her enterprise soon expanded, moving into a better address on O'Connell Street, the main street in Limerick. By the time she met Tom her business was fast becoming the largest of its kind in the city.

Kathleen later described seeing Tom for the first time: 'He was then 41 but looked much older. He was about 5ft 10 well built but so thin and spare that he looked as if every scrap of flesh and all material things were burnt away as if only the vital spiritual force of his personality remained.' Within a few days of knowing him, however, Tom's 'appearance receded into the background, and the man Uncle John portrayed was revealed.' Tom Clarke had no intention of falling in love, especially with a girl over twenty years his junior, but he was taken with the young Kathleen Daly. He later wrote: 'You wonder how it came that I took to you – Oh I'll tell you that – I couldn't help it – do you recollect the morning in the dining room I astonished you by tossing your hair – that was done on the impulse and my own astonishment was far greater than your own – even yet when I think of it I can't understand how it came about – I couldn't help it.'

Kathleen and Tom agreed to correspond. The first letter was dated 26 March 1899 and signed 'your very sincere friend Thomas J Clarke'. Kathleen replied three days later, writing to 'Mr Clarke' and signing it 'your sincere friend Kathleen'. Tom replied on 1 April 1899: 'I was indeed glad to get your long and very interesting letter – since I left Portland I haven't received a letter from any one that has given me such pleasure.' He wrote that his visit to the Dalys was 'delightfully pleasant' and that he had not realized how much he was enjoying it until it drew to an end. He later wrote of walks on the Shannon banks and the Circular Road in Kathleen's company. Writing in June 1899, he told her that although he enjoyed political news from others he enjoyed her letters for news of Kathleen herself.

As their correspondence continued, Tom was invited to spend time with the extended Daly family in their rented lodge in Kilkee, a coastal town in County Clare popular with Limerick people during the summer months. Uncle John wanted to have Tom's company; as Kathleen wrote, 'he wanted him with him all the time, he loved him so'. John was unaware that for Kathleen and Tom it was, in Kathleen's own words, 'a golden opportunity' to spend time together. When the news of their romance was announced during this visit, Tom was confronted with objections from the Daly family. Although nobody in the household disliked Tom Clarke, they disapproved of the union – the 'flower of the flock' marrying a man without 'social or financial position'.

Kathleen's mother spent the rest of their stay in Kilkee conspiring to separate them, so they were forced to use their ingenuity to spend time alone. Tom later described their courtship as 'our cliff-climbing and hill climbing and road slapping companionship'. Kathleen sneaked out in her stockings in the early hours to spend time alone with him without one of her sisters chaperoning her. When the family went out as a group, her mother and aunt would walk on either side of her, but under cover of darkness Kathleen would slip away from her 'captors' to be with Tom.

Tom left Kilkee at the end of July, before the Dalys returned to Limerick. When their correspondence recommenced on 31 July, Kathleen became 'My dear Kattie' or 'My dear Girl' and Tom dispensed with formalities to become 'ever yours, Tom'. Kathleen wrote on 1 August: 'Dear Tom, it does seem strange to be addressing you in this way.' He replied on 3 August: 'It does I am sure seem strange at the start addressing me by the "near" name . . . but it does seem very pleasant.' Kathleen became 'Your own Kathleen' and soon began signing her letters 'with love'.

By September, family opposition to Kathleen's choice was such that nobody even wanted to discuss him with her; as she wrote to Tom: 'To tell the truth I get such a hot time of it when I mention your name – either to ask a question or anything else – that I stay as clear of doing so as I possibly can. I tried to pluck up the courage a few times to do so but failed.'

Faced with the Dalys' objections, the couple were forced to postpone their immediate plans to marry and had to fulfil the conditions laid down by Kathleen's family: Tom was to find employment and Kathleen was advised to 'take time to make sure her heart and her head were in unison on the matter.' The passage of time did not diminish her feelings, but Tom's efforts to find employment in Ireland were not successful. He had hoped that he would have the opportunity to embark on a lecture tour in America, but was turned down, delaying his plans for setting up home for himself and Kathleen. Distraught, he wrote to her: 'I built everything upon the tour – hopes, plans and everything for me my hopes of having a home and the means that would justify my going down to see you on my return and ask you to give me your hand and leave your own home.'

Now he had no choice but to go to America to find work. He asked Kathleen to think for herself what the change in plans would mean for their future, accepting that he would be beginning in the US 'at the bottom rung of the ladder.' He wrote in a letter: 'Recollect you have given me no promises – from my point of view you are now as free as if you had never seen me at all – free if you so wish it to stop writing to me even – But Kattie, my darling – I love you and I am cut to the heart wretched – Tom'.

Kathleen did not stop writing, replying: 'It's ridiculous for you to think that because a lecture tour fell through my love for you must change, things may look black at present but if they looked as black again I cannot take back what I gave . . . I have all I care about, your love and so long as I have that I'm all right.'

He replied on 8 August 1899:

> Fate may do its worst, my Kattie's heart is safe in my own keeping for good and all now and I can face the worst and feel confident that I'll succeed – After all, now that I think the prospect for me is not by any means as dark – Oh yes I'm happy and stronger. You have no idea I think what it cost me to write that last letter to you – it wrung my heart lest you might misunderstand me or that misunderstanding me you would do what I apparently wished you to do – But Kattie I'll tell you now, I dreaded you would be 'wise' but in my heart of hearts I had hopes you would do and say just what you have – God bless you for it my brave girl.

Tom was so disenchanted with his life at that time that he is said to have told people he met in Dublin that he was thinking of going to South Africa and fighting for the Boers. There were Irishmen on both sides of the conflict – those who had joined the British Army and those who joined the 'Irish Brigade' fighting alongside the Boers. Instead, in October 1899 he sailed once more to America. Despite his connections, he did not immediately find suitable employment there. Writing on 5 November, he told Kathleen he hoped that friends in Clan na Gael would assist him in setting up a shoe shop, but this came to nothing. Unwilling to accept an offer of a pension from Clan na Gael, he did take a job as a night clerk at the Clan's headquarters and in addition he took a job as pattern-maker in the Cameron Pump Works. He was living with his sister Maria but was anxious for Kathleen to join him.

For Kathleen the first days of the new century were spent adjusting to the idea of leaving for America, but still insufficient time had passed for her relatives, or as she called them 'the criticizing crowd', to give their blessing to the union. The Daly household in Limerick was a prosperous and happy one and Kathleen felt keenly that she had to choose one life or the other. As she wrote on 4 January 1900: 'I sometimes get a terribly sad feeling over me when I'm with them in the dining room, when I think of how soon I may be wishing them all good-bye . . . Yet it is surprising how fast the sadness passes away when I think of who I'll be parting with them for.'

On 20 January she was writing to Tom: 'I'll go if Uncle John and Mama will let me and I don't see any reason why they wouldn't. Uncle John will be sure to consent I think. Mama I'm not sure about, though as she gives way to us in everything she will do so in this case. You may be sure I'll do my best to smooth all objections.' However, Kathleen had underestimated the strength of their opposition. On 10 April she wrote:

> What can I say to you, Uncle John or Mama won't consent to my going out to you so soon. I can hardly believe it I was sure they'd make no objection. Mama does not like the idea of my going at all . . . I told her that sooner or later I would be going she must try and like it . . . I can argue and reason with Mama but there's some kind of reserve on both sides that neither of us can break through.

They wanted her to wait a further twelve months. Tom wrote: 'What makes me feel worse is the thought that only for I feeling so sure and making you feel so you would not have asked them so soon.'

Her elder sister Madge was puzzled as to how Kathleen could contemplate leaving 'everyone I ever knew for what she calls almost a stranger.' As the months passed, however, Madge came to know that Kathleen was in love and promised that she would promote her case with the family. Kathleen was delighted to have her sister as an ally as she had a great deal of influence with Uncle John, but despite this the objections continued. They said that she was not robust enough for the journey but, as Kathleen protested to Tom, that was all nonsense as she was never stronger in her life. Uncle John was surprised that she was willing to leave her successful business. But she was determined to marry Tom, as she wrote on 26 July 1900:

'Tom my darling . . . you are more than all the world to me.'

Finally, the couple's luck seemed to be in, when Tom's name was put forward by the Amnesty Association for work as superintendent of the Dublin Abattoirs, with a good salary and a house. He had the support of John Dillon MP and in September 1900 he travelled back from New York. However, he did not get the job. To compound this failure, he had to return to New York without Kathleen, as 'Mama and Uncle John' had said it was still 'too soon'. On 12 October Kathleen wrote: 'I feel very miserable since you left, more miserable than is reasonable . . . I was so sure of going with you I can't get over it just yet, though Uncle John says I had no right to be so sure . . .' Uncle John then took pity on her 'forlorn state' and asked her to accompany him to Dublin to visit the Egans; James Egan had been in prison with John Daly and Tom Clarke. The visit was to change Kathleen's plans again. While they were there she witnessed a serious accident in which Mrs Egan was knocked down by a *Freeman's Journal* van. Minutes later, as she lay on the ground, she was run over by a second of their vehicles. Kathleen stayed on for a number of weeks to assist Mr Egan with the meals and running the house.

In December the couple began to make plans anew, as they had found a travelling companion for Kathleen whom they thought would be agreeable to the Daly family. Maud Gonne was going to New York early in 1901 to join a lecture tour with Major John MacBride of the Irish Brigade, which had taken part in the Boer War. Tom wrote to Maud himself, telling her all about Kathleen and saying that he would be very happy if she would accompany Kathleen to America. Maud replied that she knew all about Kathleen; she had indeed met her seven years before when Kathleen was fifteen. The couple were still working out the arrangements, however, when the Egans decided to take a case against *Freeman's Journal* and Kathleen had to stay to testify as the principal witness. The case dragged on for months and she still had not arrived in America when Maud Gonne was leaving New York. Maud told Tom on her departure that she was sorry not to have had the pleasure of being bridesmaid at their wedding.

*

It was not until July 1901 that Kathleen finally travelled to the United States. Her misfortunes were not over. During the journey she lost her bag containing all the money she had saved, and the wedding dress and trousseau that she had so carefully made also went missing. She refused to postpone the wedding, however, and was married wearing ill-fitting borrowed clothes.

It was always a matter of intense surprise to Tom that he had won the affection of Kathleen Daly: 'what a girl as young as his wife was, could see in him and find her ready to marry him and face possible poverty with him in a strange land.'[21]

Tom and Kathleen both wanted a quiet wedding. Tom told her that he had a horror of a big ceremony and was delighted that she agreed; he expressed the wish that they would always be of one mind on everything. She had plenty of time to go over the details, including asking Tom for a pen picture of the man who was to be his best man. 'You ask what kind of a fellow is Major MacBride – a small man, reddish hair, high forehead, light moustache . . . His manner is not very taking but the more one knows him the better you like him. He is a first class fellow I find in every respect – I like him.'[22] Kathleen and Tom were married in St Augustine's Catholic Church in the Bronx on 16 July 1901. Married life for the couple got off to a rather inauspicious start. With the loss of all Kathleen's savings, they had to forfeit their honeymoon.

Their first home was in the Bronx, then they moved to Greenpoint in Brooklyn, where their son, John Daly Clarke (always known as Daly), was born at 175 Russell Street on 13 June 1902. In Greenpoint Tom became president of the Clan na Gael club and produced a paper, the *Clansmen*. He also worked as a private secretary to John Devoy, the Fenian leader who had been imprisoned in 1866 and exiled on his release five years later. Devoy said that he never met a man with such energy and enthusiasm as Tom had for national work. He organized lectures, and promoted Irish music, language and dancing classes. When Tom lost his job at the Cameron Pump Works the couple had to rely on the money he got from the Clan. From September 1903 he worked as general manager on the *Gaelic American* while John Devoy was editor-in-chief.

Kathleen, with money from home, bought an ice cream and sweet shop, but persistent ill health prevented the venture from succeeding. During 1903 both she and her new baby were constantly unwell. To recuperate, Kathleen and Daly spent two months in Englewood, New Jersey, with the nuns of St Joseph of Peace, who provided holiday accommodation for Irish working girls. The exact nature of the ailment was not explained beyond her having bouts of neuralgia.

The following year Kathleen and her son were separated from Tom again when they were quarantined for a six-week period after Daly contracted diphtheria, which could have killed him. When he recovered, Kathleen brought him for his first visit to Ireland, setting out in July. Tom urged her to stay at least two months in the family circle. She asked him would he not be lonely, to which he replied: 'Do I feel lonely? Yes, but the predominant feeling in my mind is satisfaction and pleasure at your going away. It will be the means of returning to health and strength and I am already picturing you coming back to me full of health with dancing eyes and rosy cheeks and ready to enjoy life to the fullest.'[23]

However, as the weeks passed Tom struggled with the separation from his wife, writing to her:

Kattie, I miss you very much. Life wouldn't be worth living if I had to face the future 'free and unfettered'. God Almighty! How fond I am of that chain that binds us to each other. Yes you are my first thoughts in the morning and [the] last at night are of you and I will make you laugh when I get you back telling you of the fool things I catch myself doing in my lonesomeness. God bless you darling and send you back safe and strong to me.[24]

After several more weeks had gone by and Kathleen and Daly still had not returned, Kathleen wrote that the stay had made them 'different creatures altogether.'[25] When they had been away over three months, Tom wrote on 3 October: 'Oh Kattie I am getting very tired of being alone and it will be many a long day before I leave you go off all by yourself again. Next time I'll be with you when you go to Ireland.' His wife and child finally sailed from Liverpool and landed back in New York on 5 November 1905.

While Kathleen was in Limerick Tom had become an American citizen. He applied for his citizenship in order to qualify for a job as an inspector for the city with a salary of between $10,000 and $12,000 a year.[26] However, this plan came to nothing. His life in America was still shaped by the Irish cause. On 1 January 1906 he joined the military wing of the Clan, styled the 'Irish Volunteers', and was appointed to the rank of adjutant in the 2nd Infantry. He also dedicated himself to seeking out the graves of Irish patriots buried in the US so that wreaths could be laid on the annual American Decoration Day.

Then suddenly Tom had to distance himself from all these activities when Kathleen's health declined to such an extent that the doctor advised them that she needed country air and could no longer live in New York City. The Dalys sent them money and on 21 November 1906 they purchased a 30-acre farm in Manorville, Suffolk County, New York, from a Henry Waterling. Maple Farm was a small market-garden farm located in the centre of Long Island, known today as the gateway to the Hamptons. It was a very pretty place and Tom described the farm as 'very delightful'.[27]

They planted potatoes, onions, corn, oats, beans and cauliflowers. It was hard work; Tom rose at half past four and worked until after dark and in his free time studied agricultural publications. Unfortunately for Tom and Kathleen, it was an exceptionally bad year for farmers and they had to write to Limerick to ask the Daly family to assist them with the mortgage repayments on the property, although Tom wrote to John: 'I haven't been nearly so badly hit as the fellows who have been farming all their life time.'[28]

Kathleen and Tom were all too aware that they had benefited from the generosity of the Dalys during these early years of their marriage, especially given that Tom's lack of prospects and Kathleen's delicate health had been cited as objections to the marriage. The family had always felt he would not be able to give Kathleen the lifestyle she had been accustomed to in Limerick. Tom wrote that he wanted to 'make good' to show John Daly that he was not 'assisting a worthless dog'. He told John that Kathleen was happy as a farmer's wife in Manorville, that she kept out in the open and was greatly interested in raising chickens, 'the best chickens around these parts'. Daly, now five, was also, according to his father, 'very much in love with the life here.'[29] Kathleen later wrote that 'I certainly would have been content to stay there forever; I loved the land and growing things and the joy of being together all the time.'[30]

In November 1907, after just over a year on the farm, the Clarkes travelled together back to Ireland. Deeds lodged in Suffolk County in December 1907 show that at that time Tom had just doubled the size of his holdings in Long Island, buying a further 30 acres.[31] From Ireland he wrote to a friend back in America that he intended to return in the summer, but as Kathleen was expecting their second child in March they would wait until the baby was a few months old before travelling. He joked that living on the farm had encouraged them to expand their family: 'so there you are – there's what living the simple life "close to nature" – brings on a fellow.'[32]

Shortly after his arrival in Ireland Tom left to go around the country meeting his political friends while Kathleen, approaching the last trimester of her second pregnancy, stayed in Limerick. Tom met James Egan and Major John MacBride, who had returned from France and was now back living in Ireland. He also made a point of meeting, in Derry and Dublin, members of Sinn Féin, the political group established by Arthur Griffith in 1905, which was attracting new members to the nationalist movement. Tom wrote to a friend: 'The young fellows I met there and in Dublin who take the lead in the Sinn Féin movement impressed me very much by their earnestness and ability. I am delighted to find them away above what I had expected.'[33]

By early in the new year 1908, what had appeared at the outset to be temporary had now become a permanent move home. Once again, thanks to Madge's skilful running of the Daly Bakery, she offered to finance her sister and brother-in-law in establishing a business in Ireland. Tom chose to set up in Dublin rather than Limerick and in the early days of 1908 was writing to Kathleen in Limerick, describing how he spent his days walking the streets of Dublin hunting for a good location to open a tobacconist's shop. His sister Hannah, who had been running her own tobacconist's shop in Dublin, offered to assist him with suppliers, and Madge and Uncle John were in agreement that 'no small business paid as well as tobacco and cigars.' Embarking on setting up yet another business was difficult for Tom, and Kathleen could not be there with him; as she wrote in March: 'I wonder when easy times for you will arrive. They look as far away as ever. Sometimes I wonder were we wise to come home.'[34]

In their private correspondence at the time Kathleen told Tom not to discuss their affairs with anyone, not even with his sister. She made reference to them being talked out of 'the Long Island lots and their money' and how they had come to Ireland with 'a lot of debt to be cleared off.'[35] They leased the land to different tenants. However, with the mortgage being paid by her family, the Clarkes got none of the money as their debts had to be paid.

The reality of the situation was that her home-place offered many supports that Kathleen could not do without. Her family in Limerick were helping look after Daly while she was in the care of a doctor overseeing some complications with her second pregnancy. Tom, who was living with his mother and sister in Dublin, wrote constantly to her:

God knows my girl you are never out of my thoughts and I won't try and tell you how lonely I have felt ever since I came to Dublin and the chilly feeling that comes over me when I start to count up how long it will be till we are together again although both my mother and Hannah do everything in their power to make me comfortable they can't understand me sitting for long stretches without a word. Sure my thoughts do be with you but its choked down and no one knows how my thoughts are running.[36]

No matter whose company he was in: 'the loneliness and longing does be over me. At the bottom of it all is my being separated from you – there is no getting away from the fact. I could not feel happy or even easy if you were not by me.'[37]

At the end of January Tom, still unable to go to Limerick to see his wife, wrote: 'Life without you wouldn't be worth living. Daly too has my heart but the love is different to that which centres around your own darling self.'[38] This was the backdrop of a difficult pregnancy for Kathleen and an impending caesarean birth. When news finally reached Tom by telegram on 3 March that a second son had been born to them, 'I dropped what I was doing and went back into the room and burst out crying.'[39] He had feared that his wife would not make it through the birth. It was Kathleen's idea to call the child after her husband, so their son became known as Tom Junior.

Tom had by now located a shop at 55 Amiens Street. After he had it decorated, he described it as: 'outside and inside a perfect gem'.[40] He used the American style of decor, placing the numbers 55 on the front window in large gold letters. Following the birth of their son and days of good trading, he wrote to Kathleen: 'I am a new man . . . this place is going to be a success – at last luck seems to be settling in my direction.'[41]

Kathleen's recuperation in Limerick was long and she did not come with their two boys to live in Dublin with Tom until May 1908. This also allowed them to save on household expenses and pay off their debts. To ease their financial difficulties Kathleen even suggested taking Tom's former prison comrade James Egan as a lodger. Tom was opposed to this, as he believed Egan would disrupt their lives by coming in drunk, and he was fearful that he would be 'quarrelling and running the show'. He concluded that they would be better off with 'a crust in a back room than the misery inflicted on us by his being with us.'[42]

By the summer of 1908 Tom's shop became the central depot for activists who wished to work for Irish freedom, known colloquially as 'the Movement'. From all parts, men, women and boys came to discuss with Tom matters of national concern: 'His work went on from 9 in the morning until 11 at night, everyday, yet such was his indomitable will that in a short time he had gathered around him a group of young men, ardent spirits such as Sean Mac Dermott' – who would later become better known by the Irish form of his name, Seán Mac Diarmada. And all the time Tom was under the surveillance of the police authorities. Having been released on licence in 1898, he lived under the ever-present threat of being returned to prison for involvement in subversive activities.

Madge Daly sent a word of caution to her sister and brother-in-law about mixing politics and business, as she had heard from one of their colleagues in the Movement: 'he'd consider you'd make a big mistake to get your shop known as belonging to any clique, Sinn Féin, Gaelic League, or any other, as those cliques will support you only for a time and then they get tired of it, or for some reason or other drop off – meanwhile they probably have antagonised other people who would have supported you.' Kathleen's reaction to this was that she would not 'accept as gospel all people will say but I think that there is enough in his talk to make you careful in your dealings with all classes who come in and above all keep a close mouth. Our endeavour should now be to make ourselves independent. When that is accomplished we can be anything we like.'[43]

It was difficult for the Clarkes to be beholden to the Daly family. Tom worked long hours at both business and politics until the late summer of 1908, when he became seriously ill with typhoid fever and was hospitalized. On his release he went to Limerick, then on to a cottage in Crookhaven, County Cork, rented by the Dalys, where he recuperated in the company of John, Kathleen's mother and some of her siblings. He was away from Dublin and Kathleen for almost two months while she ran the business. Kathleen herself was taken into hospital in January 1909 due to the difficulties of a third pregnancy. She remained in poor health throughout the spring of that year and was unable to assist Tom in the shop. As he wrote to a friend at the time: 'I have never been more busy in all my life than since I came to Dublin. The business itself would require all my time and energies to look after it but I can't help doing some work in other directions, such as the Wolfe Tone memorial project, Sinn Féin work, etc, and the whole job has kept me going at as strenuous a pace as a rushing New Yorker.'[44]

Kathleen's sister Laura Daly had come from Limerick to assist with the shop, as Kathleen was unable to work and Tom was now increasingly involved in political activities. Amongst his other roles, Tom was president of the Pipers' Club in the North Wall area. In March 1908 Arthur Griffith had wanted Tom to contest the next municipal election as a Sinn Féin candidate for the Corporation but, as he told Kathleen, 'none of that for me'.[45] Instead, early in 1909 he set up the North Dock Ward branch of Sinn Féin and became its president.

Kathleen gave birth to their third son on 13 August 1909.[46] He was named Emmet Edward Clarke, after Robert Emmet, who had staged a short-lived rebellion in 1803. Tom was delighted that Kathleen was 'splendid' after a birth with no complications.

By 1910, following the success of their business, the Clarkes moved to a larger premises on Amiens Street, where they were able to employ a girl to run the shop; in addition, they rented another shop at 75a Parnell Street. The family were now able to move into a substantial red-brick terraced house on St Patrick's Road in Drumcondra on the north side of the city. Kathleen had been advised to stay off work following the birth of her baby and again went to Limerick to rest. Unlike her family there, who always had staff, Kathleen often had no hired help. Their eight-year-old son Daly was frail and prone to sickness, while Tom called his youngest, baby Emmet, an 'obstreperous kid'.[47] He described his namesake Tom Junior as 'bowld' as the devil, who when he had not seen his father for some time would not shake hands or kiss him. Daly was the only one of the family whom two-year-old Tom would treat decently.

*

Even with his young family and expanding business interests, Tom was increasingly involved in committees, commemorations, fundraising and demonstrations. He was the guiding force behind the newspaper *Irish Freedom*, which was supported by those who wanted independence. Its opening editorial on 15 November 1910 read: 'We stand for the complete and total separation of Ireland from England and the establishment of an Irish Government untrammelled and uncontrolled by any other government in the world.'

Tom and Seán Mac Diarmada became close friends and co-conspirators, assuming the key positions of secretary and treasurer in the Irish Republican Brotherhood. They managed the appointment of Denis McCullough as chairman, as he lived in the North, enabling them to take over the core of the work of the Supreme Council uninterrupted. Tom and others worked unceasingly to facilitate their members in infiltrating the different national organizations formed during this period, including the Irish Volunteers when it was established in November 1913 with the primary aim of ensuring independence for Ireland.

According to Kathleen, the formation of the Irish Volunteers gave the IRB the chance they had been looking for; as Tom wrote at the time: 'The Volunteer Movement caught on in great style here in Dublin. Such an outpouring of young fellows was never seen. They filled Rink in the Rotunda Gardens (which holds 7,000) filled the adjacent garden, overflowed into the large concert hall in the Rotunda building and packed the street around the entrances . . . about 4,000 enrolled.' One of the new recruits was Kathleen's younger brother, Ned, then aged twenty-two, who had moved to live with the Clarkes earlier that year. Kathleen never remembered seeing Ned looking so happy as on the night of the formation of the Volunteers. He told her it was what he had been waiting for. He joined B Company, 1st Battalion, and was elected as a captain.

Tom wrote on 8 December: 'from the national point of view it is brighter than it has been in many a long year – certainly as far back as my memory goes – and remember I am no spring chicken and some of the boys here have no scruple about keeping me reminded of the fact by referring to me as "the old chap"'.[48] Tom aligned himself with a new young generation of activists, but he was suspicious of a number of the people involved in the Volunteers, including Sir Roger Casement, a former diplomat in the British Foreign Service, whom Tom thought was a spy.

In April 1914 Kathleen joined Cumann na mBan (Women's Association), the women's division of the Irish Volunteers, which was an autonomous organization with its own constitution. She was active in the Central Branch but was not a member of the executive.

When the First World War was declared in July 1914, the Dublin Metropolitan Police rented a room opposite the Clarkes' shop to monitor those who entered it. In June 1915 Seán Mac Diarmada was arrested in Tuam, County Galway, for making a speech that was deemed to contravene the terms of the Defence of the Realm Act; he was imprisoned for six months in Mountjoy Jail in Dublin. As he had no family in the city, Kathleen undertook to provide him with anything he required and Tom was a frequent visitor for the duration of his imprisonment.

On 29 June 1915, the Fenian leader Jeremiah O'Donovan Rossa died in New York; he had been imprisoned after the Rebellion of 1867 and, as a condition of his release in 1871, had been exiled from Ireland for life. Tom Clarke was cabled to see if the Irish Republican Brotherhood would accept the body to be buried in Dublin. Tom became president of the O'Donovan Rossa Funeral Committee and Kathleen too became a key member of the group, which included men and women from all the nationalist organizations of the day. One of those involved was Patrick H. Pearse, a teacher, barrister, poet and nationalist who had become increasingly active in both the IRB and the Irish Volunteers. Daly was a pupil at Pearse's school, St Enda's, founded to provide Catholic boys with a distinctively Irish education, and Tom facilitated 'Pearse's progress as a public speaker on Republican platforms and as a writer in *Irish Freedom* . . . Clarke made it possible for Pearse's evolution to follow its natural, steady and progressive course.'[49] Pearse was selected to give the oration at the graveside in Glasnevin Cemetery when O'Donovan Rossa's burial took place on 1 August 1915. When he asked Tom how far he could go with the speech, Tom replied 'as far as you can, make it as hot as hell, throw discretion to the winds.'[50] The words of that speech would be long remembered: 'the fools, the fools, the fools! They have left us our Fenian dead . . . Ireland unfree shall never be at peace.'

By the end of 1915 Tom, along with Seán Mac Diarmada, was coopted on to the Supreme Council of the IRB; Joe Plunkett, Éamonn Ceannt and Patrick Pearse were already members. Kathleen, unlike a number of the other wives of the men who formed the council, knew that an insurrection was planned for Easter 1916. As she recalled:

> Tom came home from a meeting of the supreme council of the IRB, and told me that it had been decided at the meeting to select some person whose discretion, silence and capability they could rely upon; one who would be made fully acquainted with all their decisions. In the event of the arrest of all the members of the Supreme Council, the custodian of their plans and decisions would be in a position to pass on the work to those next in command, this preventing confusion and temporary stoppage . . . I was very interested in all he was telling me; it was unusual for him to mention anything that happened at their meetings. So I was very surprised when he informed me that the person selected was myself.[51]

She had been selected by the Supreme Council to be told the identity of the key men throughout the country as a result of the work she had done for the organization over the previous number of years. She was known to be capable and trusted.

In early 1916 Kathleen was to be sent to New York with a message for John Devoy, but it was called off as it was possible she may not have been able to return before the Rising; Joe Plunkett's sister Mimi went instead. Kathleen was delighted, as she did not like leaving Tom even for a short time.

In early April, Tom and Seán asked her to write a list of sixteen girls from Cumann na mBan for despatch work, whose discretion and secrecy could be relied on; she asked Sorcha MacMahon, a member of Central Branch, to help her undertake this task.

On Tuesday of Holy Week, Tom told Kathleen that the Rising would go ahead on Easter Sunday. He explained that a military council consisting of himself, Seán Mac Diarmada, Patrick Pearse, Éamonn Ceannt, Joseph Plunkett, James Connolly and Thomas MacDonagh had drawn up a Proclamation outlining their charter for the 'Irish Republic', and that he had been given the honour of being the first signatory, the president, of the Provisional Government. When he told the other members of the Military Council that he was not seeking honours, Thomas MacDonagh had said 'no other man is entitled to the honour. You Sir, by your example, your courage, your enthusiasm, have led us younger men to where we are today.' Kathleen asked Tom, if they won, would he act as president? He replied: 'If we win through it will take a long time. By then I fear I would be physically unable for the job, but if I am fit I shall certainly act. I have more experience of our enemy, and if necessary the force and ruthlessness needed for the position.'

On Holy Thursday Tom arranged for Kathleen to take a message for the Limerick Volunteers: '[Eoin] MacNeill [chief of staff of the Irish Volunteers] has signed the Proclamation and is quite enthusiastic'. She was to take the children – fourteen-year-old Daly, eight-year-old Tom and seven-year-old Emmet – to stay with her family in Limerick for the duration of the fighting. Tom did not dare to say goodbye to his children, fearing he might break his rigid self-control, though he realized it was possibly a final parting. Kathleen's family did not know that the so-called 'manoeuvres' which were to take place on Easter Sunday were 'really a Rising'. As she spent time with them before catching her train back to Dublin, she joined them in making First Aid outfits and later recalled that 'they seemed to sense a crisis, which made them very anxious and troubled.'[52]

Kathleen arrived home alone late on Good Friday. Tom was in hiding and she was in charge of the shop for the usual opening hours until 2 p.m. on Easter Sunday. She was to behave as normal, as the premises were being watched by the police the whole time, and after the shop was shut she was to return home, where she was to remain to receive communications from the GPO, which was to be a head-quarters for the leaders of the Rising.

While she was in the shop on Easter Sunday Kathleen read in the newspapers of unfolding events. Roger Casement had been due to land in Ireland with a shipment of German arms for the fight, but the ship carrying them, the *Aud*, had been intercepted off the Kerry coast and Casement, who had arrived separately in a submarine, had been arrested. When this news reached Eoin MacNeill, as head of the Volunteers he posted a notice in the *Sunday Independent* cancelling the 'manoeuvres' that were planned for Easter Sunday. Neither MacNeill's countermanding order nor the arrest in Kerry appeared to Kathleen to put the plans for the Rising in jeopardy; however, Tom knew that MacNeill's action was 'of the blackest and greatest treachery.'[53] Tom wanted to maintain the strategy and strike as planned, but he was outvoted and the plan was changed to striking on Easter Monday instead. Female couriers were sent all over the country with the change of plans.

Kathleen and Tom were in their own home on Easter Sunday night when they were disturbed by an old man named Ryan who called to their house after they had gone to bed. He had just heard that there was to be a Rising and that Tom was one of the leaders. He shouted at Tom: 'was he mad, what was going to happen to his wife and family, hadn't he suffered enough for Ireland?' Tom took a while to get the man to go home and he was still protesting as he left. Tom was very indignant, asking, 'does anyone think that I would expect or encourage other men to do that which I was not prepared to do myself.'[54] Kathleen, well aware of his commitment to the cause, asked him to consider her and their children and how they were going to suffer. He replied: 'that can't be helped. My children will have to accept it the same as you. We are going to make a bid for freedom no matter what happens.'[55]

Kathleen was pregnant again, carrying their fourth child. She had taken the decision not to tell Tom before the fight. He was, she remembered: 'Full of hope for the future and admiration of his comrades in arms.' In contrast, Kathleen recalled, 'I was feeling that the world was tumbling around me, though I did not say so . . . As far as I was concerned my happiness was at an end.'[56]

2

Maud and John

They first met at the Gare de Lyon in Paris in the winter of 1900. Maud Gonne stood almost six feet tall, and, in her thirty-fourth year, was considered strikingly beautiful, with masses of auburn hair and strange golden eyes.[1] She was one of a welcoming party that had gathered at the railway station to greet Major John MacBride of the famous Irish Brigade during the Boer War.

When she first saw him, he was 'a wiry, soldierly-looking man with red hair and skin, burnt brick red.' At last she was meeting the man about whom she had read, written and spoken, who had fought so gallantly alongside the Boers in their struggle against British rule in South Africa. John MacBride's actions won him the gratitude of the Boer leaders[2] and a national reputation in Ireland, where MacBride Clubs were formed. Maud had avidly followed the progress of the war, and had fundraised and protested against the recruitment of Irishmen to the British Army.

Maud herself was a prominent campaigner and activist on Irish issues. Earlier that year, she had set up her own nationalist organization for women, Inghinidhe na hÉireann (Daughters of Ireland); one of the group's first actions was to have a flag made and sent to John MacBride. All women of Irish birth or descent were eligible to join her political group. Previously, women could join cultural groups such as the Gaelic League, established seven years earlier to teach the Irish language. Inghinidhe na hÉireann had wider objectives, including the opening of free classes in poor areas of

Dublin to teach children Irish history, language, music and dance. History lessons included the stories of ancient heroes from the Irish sagas, with the idea that these tales would promote a spirit of nationalism and so discourage enlistment in the British Army, whose ranks were filled each year by scores of young Irishmen. The group attracted young women who shared beliefs about social justice and independence for Ireland.

John MacBride was born in 1868 in the coastal town of Westport, County Mayo, on the picturesque Clew Bay. He was the youngest of five sons – the others being Joseph, Anthony, Patrick and Francis[3] – born to Patrick MacBride, the former captain of a merchant schooner from the north of Ireland, and his wife Honoria (*née* Gill), a native of Westport. For several generations John's ancestors had been engaged in Irish revolutionary movements, and his great-grandfather had taken part in the insurrection of 1798.

When John was six months old and Joseph, the eldest of his brothers, aged just eight, their father died and Honoria was left as sole supporter of the young family, running a ship chandler's, general grocer's and a public house. John was educated first at the Christian Brothers School, Westport, and afterwards at St Malachy's College, Belfast, in his father's native Antrim. Following that he worked for two years in a draper's business in Castlerea, County Roscommon. It had been hoped that he would become a doctor like his brother Anthony, but this was not for him, and when he was about twenty years of age he went to work in Dublin at Hugh Moore & Co., wholesale druggists and grocers.

Around this time he entered the secret organization known as the Irish Republican Brotherhood, whose avowed aim was to bring about a separation between England and Ireland and to establish an Irish Republic. He soon gained the confidence of his colleagues and in 1896 he was sent as the Dublin delegate to the Irish National Alliance Convention in Chicago.

On his return he again took up his post at Moore's, but remained working there for only a short time, having decided to seek his fortune in the gold mines of South Africa. This was the height of the Witwatersrand gold rush and his destination was Randfontein, a mine and town established a few years earlier by the mining financier J. B. Robinson in western Gauteng, about 28 miles (45 km) west of Johannesburg. John worked there as an assayer, analysing the quality of the ore. However, he had an ulterior motive for travelling to South Africa: as well as improving his own circumstances, he was also still working for the national cause. There were many Irishmen employed in the mines and he wanted to recruit them to the move-ment for national freedom.

The outbreak of the Second Boer War in 1899 aroused a wave of support from the Irish for the Boers in their fight against the British. At the forefront was John MacBride, who became one of the founders of the Irish Transvaal Brigade, which fought alongside the Boers despite the fact that so many of their countrymen were in the British Army. John earned a reputation for recklessness and daring during the war. According to his own account, the Irish Brigade took part in the actions at Dundee and Ladysmith; they helped to capture the English guns at Colenso; and they were present at Platrand and Petershill. They engaged in all the fighting, as John later recounted, 'from Brandford in the [Orange] Free State of Pretoria in the Transvaal, and from Pretoria to Kompatipoort, close to the Portuguese [East Africa] border.' In the late summer of 1900 the brigade was disbanded, in part, according to MacBride, because the Boers could no longer supply them with horses. He recounted how 'The Boer Government chartered a boat to take them to Europe, giving each of the men a present of a small sum of money'; it is also recorded that many of the dispersed Irish fighters crossed the border into the neutral Portuguese territory of Mozambique.

After the disbandment of the Irish Brigade MacBride was unable to return to Ireland for fear of arrest, so he set off for New York to begin a lecture tour, stopping en route in Paris, where the Young Ireland Society, which had been founded a few years earlier by Maud Gonne, held a reception in his honour. John's mother,

Honoria, as well as his brother Patrick with his wife Mary, travelled from Westport to be with him. He later recalled: 'After their departure at Miss Gonne's request I took up my abode in 7 Avenue d'Eylan until I left for America. Miss Gonne was there all the time . . .'[4] Maud and John engaged in intense discussions, on one occasion even sitting up all night talking. He enthralled her with stories of the war, and she agreed with him that physical force was the only means of defeating the British.

John departed for America at Christmas 1900. Within a short time he was missing Maud and wrote to her asking her to join him; she delighted in telling others that 'he could not get things going unless she came.' He claimed that he put pressure on the Irish-American societies to have her lecture in conjunction with him.[5] She was in fact an experienced speaker who had herself been on the Irish-American lecture circuit in 1897 and 1900. After recovering from a bout of influenza, she set sail from Le Havre for New York in February 1901.

Over the next two months John and Maud lectured at twenty-seven places over forty-eight days, including venues in cities with large Irish populations – New York, Philadelphia, Boston, Chicago, Kansas City, Cincinnati, Pittsburgh and St Louis – as well as in smaller places like the mining town of Calumet, Michigan. She wrote from the Arlington Hotel in Calumet on 25 March 1901: 'Oh the weariness of an American lecture tour! The constant being on show! The receptions, meetings, banquets . . . MacBride is going around with me, and is very good and saves me all the worry and fatigue he can.'[6] John wrote to his mother: 'Miss Gonne astonishes me the way in which she can stand knocking about. For a woman it is wonderful.'[7]

In St Louis, John MacBride proposed to Maud, but she refused him: 'I had replied that marriage was not in my thoughts while there was a war on and there was always an Irish war on.' They parted in Chicago. Maud was anxious to return to Europe: '[John] tried hard to keep me but I was resolute'. John remained in America, travelling out to the west coast while she returned to Paris; among the gifts she brought back with her was a live baby alligator.

*

Maud was an independent woman who had for much of her life done as she had pleased. She was born Edith Maud Gonne in December 1866, in the village of Tongham, near Farnham in Surrey; her father was then stationed in nearby Aldershot. She was the eldest daughter of Colonel Thomas Gonne, who had served in India with the 17th Lancers. An excellent linguist – he spoke French, German, Italian and Portuguese – he joined the regimental staff as a Hindustani interpreter, later becoming interpreter and staff officer for the Cavalry Flying Column. He received the Indian Mutiny medal and returned to England in 1859, remaining with his regiment.

Tommy, as Maud always called her father, was posted to Ireland in the aftermath of the Fenian Uprising in 1867, the year following Maud's birth, and her formative years were spent there. She identified herself with Ireland and all things Irish, making much of the branch of the Gonne family with Irish lineage. The family name began as Gun, but over the centuries became Gonne, and family records mention branches in Kerry and Mayo. In fact, Maud's Irish ancestors were of English planter stock and were loyal subjects to the crown; in the seventeenth century Arthur Gonne was a signatory of the loyal address to King Charles II by the people of Mayo.

Maud's sister Kathleen was born in Ireland in September 1868, while Tommy was stationed in the Curragh Camp, County Kildare. In 1869 the Gonnes moved to Dublin. Two years later, her mother Edith, known as Edie, already suffering from tuberculosis, wanted to return to England for her third confinement, and her husband took a leave of absence to be with her in May 1871. His plan had been to take his wife to Italy to see if the climate could restore her health, but the couple were unable to leave London and on 21 June Edie died, aged just twenty-seven. Her baby survived, a girl named Margaretta Rose, and was baptized on 22 June, but she would not live for long. She died on 9 August and was buried next to her mother in Tongham graveyard, close to the couple's first marital home.[8]

Tommy Gonne, now a widower, took his two surviving daughters, Maud and Kathleen, back to Ireland, accompanied by their nurse, Mary Ann Meredith (known as Bowie), a widow in her thirties. Edie had asked him not to send the girls to boarding school or to give them into the care of her relatives, as she had been when she was orphaned as a young child. When a doctor advised sea air for Maud, Tommy moved them to the Hill of Howth, overlooking Dublin Bay. The Gonne sisters visited the cottages nearby, which Bowie often frequented, gaining a reputation for helping with sick babies. Maud later recalled eating griddle cakes made on turf fires, while barefoot children nimbly climbed rocks and rode the donkeys better than she could in her shoes.

In 1876 a period of separation from their father began which would last for almost a decade, as his army career took him to areas of conflict where it was not possible to bring his daughters.[9] From this time, the girls led a nomadic existence, initially spending time in England with relatives of both their mother and their father, and visiting various resorts. In 1880, when Tommy was posted with his regiment to India, he decided to relocate his family to France, where he rented a villa for the girls and their staff outside Cannes. A French governess took charge, and Maud later wrote: 'I owe her most of the little education I possess.' In 1881, when her father accepted a posting to Russia as a military attaché in St Petersburg, his daughters and their servants went back to England to live at a small educational establishment, Rosemont School, Torquay.[10] Maud never referred to this period of formal education she received.

The years passed and the Gonnes continued travelling in Europe, befitting women of their status and wealth, while their father returned to live in Ireland in January 1885. He was appointed assistant adjutant and quartermaster general based at Royal Barracks in Dublin (now Collins Barracks). According to Maud, when word reached Tommy Gonne in Dublin that she had accepted a proposal of marriage from a young Italian in Rome[11] he sent word that she and her sister were to come to Dublin immediately.

From that time Tommy's beautiful eldest daughter returned to live in Ireland's capital city. Maud played hostess for him to scores of British Army officers. She later recalled that she worked hard for her title of the Belle of the Dublin season of 1885, but that her namesake, Maud Guinness, was more beautiful.

The life Maud had in Dublin changed for ever when her beloved father died of a fever in the Royal Barracks on 30 November 1886.[12] Maud was just twenty-one. Within a year of Tommy's death she was in possession of her share of the family's substantial wealth. Her father had owned properties in Knightsbridge and Piccadilly in London, as well as other monies, and Maud also had access to her mother's sizeable family fortune. Tommy framed the will in such a way that, even if they married, Maud and Kathleen would have their inheritance for their own 'sole and separate use.'

Maud decided to live in Paris. By this time she had met the French politician and journalist Lucien Millevoye,[13] fifteen years her senior. He politicized her and introduced her to a new way of thinking about nationalism, even involving her in an espionage trip to Russia. He gave her a pistol and at another point a monkey, whom she named Chaperone. The Irish artist Sarah Purser painted her portrait with the monkey perched beside her. *Lady with a Monkey: A Portrait* (1890)[14] captures something of the spirit of this young woman, whose unconventional life was made possible by her independent wealth.

Under Lucien's tutelage, Maud began to work for Ireland as a self-styled 'freelancer on the fringes', devoting herself to causes such as evicted tenants and seeking amnesty for political prisoners held as convicts in terrible conditions. While all the time promoting her belief in the right of Irish men and women to rule themselves, she later described that she went to Ireland 'whenever the Irish question took her in an acute form, that is to say when there were evictions of tenants, when there was distress'.

Maud became known in Paris as *la Patriote Irlandaise*. Her first article on Ireland appeared in a French magazine in 1891, launching a successful career as a journalist. She lectured extensively in France, Belgium and Holland on conditions in Ireland, particularly in the poorest regions of Donegal and Mayo. Reports of her lectures and activities numbered a couple of thousand in French newspapers alone thanks to her influential friends. Such was her fame that the '*Femme de Lettres*' had her own card in the Félix Potin collection, a popular series of collector's portraits of well-known public people given away to promote the businessman's retail outlets.[15]

Living between France and Ireland allowed Maud the freedom to become a mistress; even her friends knew little of her personal life, or that Lucien Millevoye was her lover. He was married for the entire period of their relationship, although he was estranged from his wife and their son.[16] Maud gave birth to his son Georges in January 1890, but he died of meningitis in August the following year, aged just nineteen months.[17]

Alongside Maud's relationship with Millevoye, the poet William Butler Yeats feted her for years following their first meeting in 1889. He immediately fell in love with her and was later to write that 'the troubling of his life' began when first they met. She became his muse, the focus of scores of his poems. Yeats wanted to marry her, proposing to her twice during the 1890s, but Maud turned him down, claiming that this unrequited love made him a better poet. She agreed instead to enter into a non-physical 'mystic marriage' – a meeting of minds – in the belief that their spiritual selves would be reunited in the afterlife; it was all that she would offer him. Deeply in love, Yeats contented himself with keeping in written contact with her. Their closeness was belied by the fact that he was unaware of Maud's true private life.

Between the death of her baby son and the conception of another child, Maud took over the arrangements for the care of her half-sister. According to Maud, her father was so inconsolable at the death of her mother that he had never remarried.[18] However, he had had a lover and this woman had given birth to his fourth daughter on 18 July 1886 in County Dublin. Three weeks before Tommy's death, Eileen Constance was baptized into the Church of Ireland, but as his illegitimate daughter she was not given his name. Her father was registered as Thomas George Wilson, a clerk.[19]

According to Maud's own account, when Eileen's mother – whom in her autobiography Maud called 'Mrs Robbins' – discovered that Tommy Gonne was dead, she approached his brother looking for money. Maud later described how she came in on this meeting: 'As I opened the drawing room door, I heard Uncle William's voice, very hard and precise, saying "I tell you, my good woman, I don't believe you. That letter is no proof that the child was his." ' Maud, however, intervened to confirm the truth of the woman's story. She enquired about the baby and the woman replied: 'She is safe, no one shall take her from me.' Afterwards Maud maintained contact with the woman and her child: 'My uncles and aunts were scandalised; but I felt Tommy approved and that was all I cared about.'[20]

Some time after this, Count Ignaty Platonovich Zakrevsky, one of Russia's leading lawyers, met Maud and told her that he was looking for a governess to teach English to his twin daughters, as it was the fashion at that time in Russia to speak English and copy the English way of life. Maud introduced him to a 'tall, very good-looking woman, with a great deal of poise', whom she described as her companion, and who had recently lost her husband. This was Eileen's mother, and she agreed to be nanny to Assia and Alexandria (known as Alla) and their brother Platon (known as Bobik) Zakrevsky for one year. Despite being given the role of governess, Eileen's mother, who was known as 'Margaret Wilson', was not well educated; she could hardly read at all and found it difficult to write a letter. She never learned more than a few words of Russian, but made herself a valued member of the household and was waited on by servants. She spent summers on the family estate in the Ukraine and winters in St Petersburg.[21] Maud, meanwhile, arranged that her own nanny, Bowie (Mary Ann Meredith), would raise her half-sister Eileen in England as her adopted daughter.[22] Tommy Gonne had left Mary Ann £700 in his will and she had retired to the picturesque village of Hartley Wintney, near Farnborough in Hampshire.

While Maud took charge in making all these arrangements, she was still grieving the death of her infant son. When two years later she became pregnant again, it was something she had planned carefully. Believing in the transmigration of souls, she would later reveal that she hoped to conceive again in the tomb in which Georges was buried. Her second child with Lucien, a girl she named Iseult Germaine Lucille, was born on 6 August 1894 at 51 Rue de la Tour, Passy, Paris. For a time after the birth Maud stayed out of public life, but by the end of the year she had taken another speaking engagement.

Maud later said that after Iseult's birth her physical relationship with Lucien was at an end, although elsewhere it was suggested that they were still involved for another five years. Even if that was the case, there was a marked change in their relationship after this date. Politically, Millevoye was no longer anti-English; he also had a new mistress. During that time Maud formed the Paris Young Ireland Society in 1896 and the following year she brought out her own journal, *L'Irlande Libre, Organe de la Colonie Irlandaise à Paris.*[23] But much of the time she spent travelling and was away from France and from Iseult, spending time in Ireland, or lecturing about Ireland in other countries. She left her daughter in the care of her housekeeper, Madame de Bourbonne, as Bowie and Eileen remained living in England. Maud created for Iseult a home full of pets, singing birds, dogs, cats and exotic creatures, but it was a solitary childhood without siblings.

In 1897, according to her own account, Maud averted a famine in County Mayo, travelling out to the stricken areas, encouraging the Board of Guardians to implement relief efforts. She set up a fish-curing station and arranged for the feeding of children at school and for 'rough and ready' nursing. She was proud that she had saved many lives, something that, she later said, all the talking in the House of Commons would never have achieved.

In 1898 Maud worked in Ireland on the commemoration of the 1798 Rebellion and preventing evictions in Mayo. Alongside her work for the poor she worked tirelessly for the amnesty of political prisoners, joining the Amnesty Association that had been founded in

1869 to campaign for the release of Fenian prisoners. Throughout the 1890s Maud petitioned members of parliament, held rallies and fundraised for the men's families. She went on a tour of England with one of the released prisoners, John Daly, to highlight the plight of the men still incarcerated, until in 1898 the last of them, Tom Clarke, was released. In 1900 Maud returned to America to campaign and fundraise for Irish causes. Back in Ireland, she was instrumental in setting up a massive 'Patriotic Children's Treat' for nationalist children as a protest against the one arranged for children during the visit of Queen Victoria to Ireland that year. Since the start of the Boer War she had also been busy campaigning against recruitment to the British Army in South Africa.

By 1901 Iseult was, as Maud described her, 'much too tall and much too clever for her age.'[24] She now had a governess, Madame Dangien (Dan), but when Maud spent longer times away, as she did in America that year, she sent Iseult to live in a convent in Laval. Maud returned after her tour with John, the alligator her present for the six-year-old. Her arrival was timely, as a short time later Iseult became very ill with suspected meningitis, which had killed her brother. Maud nursed her child back to health, but she was still unwell in July when John returned to Paris.

When John arrived in Paris that summer, it was as an exile from Ireland. If he were to return to Ireland he could be convicted of treason and imprisoned with penal servitude for life. It was difficult for him to find work in Paris as his French was so poor; when he spoke, everyone thought he was speaking Dutch. The only money he had was £50 from his American lecture tour. After a while, however, he was given a position by a friend, Victor Collins, Paris correspondent of the *New York Sun*[25] and Laffan's Bureau. Although John was often described as a journalist, in fact he worked as a secretary for Collins.

Over the next year Maud reconsidered John's proposal and in June 1902 decided that she would marry him. She wrote to her sister Kathleen: 'MacBride is a man I know well. I have seen a great deal of him for the past two years and I know he is thoroughly sincere and honest and I can trust him entirely and I think I will always be happy'.

In her reply Kathleen disagreed with her choice, to which Maud replied: 'My mind is quite made up and in these matters no one can decide for another, I do not think it wise to try and influence another much.' She told her sister that she did not understand why she objected so strongly to John MacBride, feeling that her opinion was based on hearsay from prejudicial people. Kathleen would have preferred her to marry Willie Yeats, who she knew adored her sister and could provide a life at high social and cultural levels. Maud replied:

> As for Willie Yeats I love him dearly as a friend but I could not for one moment imagine marrying him. I think I shall be happy with John our aims are exactly the same and he is so good and thoughtful that it makes life very easy when he is there and besides he has a vitality and a joy in life which I used to have once but which the hard life I have led wore out of me, with him I seem to get it back a little . . . I love John MacBride and I am going to marry him.

She reminded Kathleen that she and Kathleen's husband, Thomas David Pilcher, a British Army officer (who had fought in the Boer War) did not get on, but that had not come between them. She assured her: 'Darling my marriage won't change me even one bit – you will always find me the same, and we would not let it in anyway come between our love for one another . . .' As she explained to Kathleen:

> Little sister, neither you or anyone on earth quite knows the hard life I have led, for I never talk of my troubles and I have preferred to be envied than pitied. Now I see the chance, without injuring my work, of having a little happiness and peace in my personal life and I am taking it. <u>Marriage</u> I always considered abominable but for the sake of my work and for the sake of Iseult, I make that sacrifice to convention . . .

Maud went to the convent at Laval to tell Iseult that she was marrying John. It came as a shock to the eight-year-old that 'the red-haired Irishman with poor French' was going to marry her *Amour*, as she called her mother.[26] Maud wrote: 'She was such a beautiful and such a strangely wise child. She had cried when I told her I was getting married to MacBride and said she hated MacBride. I had felt like crying too. I told her I would send lovely things from Spain, where we were going for our honeymoon, but she was not consoled . . . Sister Catherine had to drag her away.'

John had learned shortly after returning to Paris that Maud's name 'was mentioned in a scandalous manner in connection with Millevoye.' She then told him the truth of the transgressions of her past life. She reassured him that she 'intended, of course, to turn over an absolutely new leaf, and she said that she intended to become a Catholic.' Maud had wanted to become a Catholic and a nun during her childhood, but her father had dissuaded her.

In February 1903, at the convent at Laval, Maud received instruction and was baptized. She wrote to Willie Yeats describing herself as an Irishwoman: 'I prefer to look at the truth through the same prism as my country people – I am going to become a Catholic . . . I do feel it important not to belong to the Church of England'. For her confirmation, she took the name Honoria, John's mother's name. Honoria MacBride did not attend and Victor Collins's wife stood as proxy. While Maud was in the convent preparing for these sacraments she wrote to Willie of her forthcoming nuptials, which were about to be announced in the press: 'Marriage won't change me I think at all. I intend to keep my own name and to go on with all my work the same as ever'.[27] She wrote in similar terms to her close friend Madame Avril: 'I expect that with the husband I have chosen I shall be able to more effectively serve the cause of independence.'[28]

John later claimed that by now he had his doubts as to the wisdom of the marriage and was swayed by conflicting emotions up to the very day of the wedding. He described how, when Maud told him she was writing to her former lover the day before their marriage, he was 'amazed and indignant and there was a violent scene and he advised her again to think of what she was doing in marrying him.' Later the same evening he met Victor Collins, who remembered him 'smarting under the irritation caused by the letter to Millevoye.' John told Collins: 'I do not know that I will get married at all; I do not know that I will turn up to-morrow'.

Honoria MacBride had also written to her son warning him against the marriage: 'I have seen Maud Gonne. She is very beautiful; she is a great woman and has done much for Ireland but she will not make you happy. You will neither be happy, she is not the wife for you. I am very anxious. Think well what you are doing.' John's eldest brother Joseph had warned him against it too. He believed that Maud was 'used to going her own way and listens to no one.' He had told his brother 'These are not good qualities for a wife. A man should not marry unless he can keep his wife . . .'

Their mutual friend, Arthur Griffith, who would later found Sinn Féin, also advised against it. He had been in South Africa with John and had been a close friend and collaborator of Maud's for many years, and he had seen from the outset that Maud was attracted to John. He wrote to her: 'For your own sakes and the sake of Ireland where you both belong; don't get married. I know you both, you so unconventional – a law to yourself; John so full of conventions. You will not be happy for long . . . Forgive me, but think, while there is still time.'[29]

Their marriage took place in Paris on 21 February 1903. There was a civil ceremony in the British Embassy, with the marriage rite at the Church of Saint-Honoré d'Eylau. John later wrote: 'We had to go to the British Consulate to have the civil ceremony performed and I kept my hand on my revolver while the deed was being done as I was under the British flag while there and I was not going to allow them any tricks.'[30] As British citizens, they needed this civil ceremony to formalize the marriage, but, indeed, John could have been arrested. Maud wanted a quiet wedding, so she invited no friends. At the reception the priest who had married them, Father van Hecke, former chaplain to the Irish Brigade, toasted the groom as a reliable and brave man, and Maud toasted the complete independence of Ireland.

They did not have their honeymoon immediately. Maud prepared their home, Les Mouettes in Colleville-sur-Mer in Normandy, which she had recently purchased with another inheritance; then the couple explored Normandy for some time before going to Spain and Gibraltar on honeymoon. They wanted to be in Gibraltar when King Edward VII was visiting: Maud later said that they were planning to assassinate him. It was, as she claimed, an adventure in which they could have lost their lives, so in anticipation of this she had arranged her affairs accordingly, giving up her apartment and making a will leaving Iseult to the care of a relative. The British monarch arrived in Gibraltar on 7 April and was due to remain there for five days before travelling on to Malta. John was to go to meet his friends and 'do the deed'. He arrived back late and drunk, having failed to accomplish his task. Next morning Maud, angry and desperately upset, packed her bags, saying she was going back to Paris and that he could come if he wished.

Upon their return, Maud found it difficult to have no contact with Lucien Millevoye. He had moved on and had another mistress, but still she wished to have him in her life. She tried to arrange a meeting between him and her new husband, but John thought this a grossly improper suggestion and it fell through. Still, memories of her long relationship lingered. She had a photograph of her former lover in her house at Colleville, which John made her take down. Her dog, which Lucien had given to her, slept in their bed, even though the mere sight of it upset John.

From the outset theirs was a union of inequality. John left his job a few days before he got married and did not work again in Paris. Maud gave him a sum of money to live on, the amount based on her travelling and clothing allowance, but John's reliance on his wife's income made for a difficult domestic arrangement. Maud continued as before, travelling back and forth to Ireland, taking part in protests and the activities of Inghinidhe na hÉireann, which now had branches in Dublin, Limerick, Cork and Ballina in Mayo.

John found himself in an all-female household, and many of the women in it had never before lived with a man. The servants were in the pay of his wife. Then there was Iseult, as well as Maud's half-sister. When Bowie died at the age of sixty-eight in February 1902, Eileen, then sixteen, was brought to Paris.[31] Her mother was still living in Russia, from where she sent letters and gifts, including exquisite pieces of embroidery; it is not known why she had not returned as arranged after one year. Zakrevsky, her employer, came and met Eileen when he was travelling in France. Eileen's role in Maud's household was as governess for Iseult, but she was treated as a member of the family.

For Iseult, this meant having to share her mother with someone else and Iseult disliked Eileen; on one occasion she rubbed butter into Eileen's hair.[32] John MacBride got on well with Eileen, but the same could not be said of his relationship with Iseult, of whom he wrote: 'I considered my wife brought her up in a very bad way. My wife used to tell Iseult that beauty was all that was required of a woman and that she was the most beautiful child on earth. I naturally warned . . . of the danger of such advice.'

The following year saw another change in the household. While she was in Ireland in May 1903, Maud discovered that she was pregnant. She took to walking in the hills of south Dublin to think over her situation. Her marriage was not going as planned. As her pregnancy advanced, Maud, now aged thirty-seven, was not well. John was distressed that she was not happy carrying his child: 'she was always complaining about the horridness of her condition as if it were something new to her, and tried to induce the Doctor to hasten the birth but the Doctor would not allow it.'

By December 1903 John had convinced himself that Maud and Lucien were arranging meetings at Madame Avril's house, where Iseult met with her father twice a week when he was in Paris. Although John did not object to this, he refused to allow Iseult and Lucien Millevoye to meet at their home. On one occasion around this time, Maud returned and admitted to John that she had met with Lucien. John told her that if there were any other such meetings, accidental or otherwise, when the child was born it would be separated from its mother.

On Christmas night John got so drunk that he had to be restrained and put to bed by the women of the household. Maud was unable to travel out of Paris because of the advanced stage of her pregnancy. Word reached her friends in Ireland that the marriage was in trouble. Willie Yeats wrote to the dramatist Lady Gregory that he had heard a painful rumour: 'Major MacBride is said to be drinking. It is the last touch of tragedy if it is true.'[33]

Maud and John's son, Jean Seagan (later known as Seán), was born on 26 January 1904. There was great jubilation among nationalists; the boy, hailed as the child of heroes, had a 'heroic future forecast for him'.[34] The evening his son was born, John purchased a ring[35] for Maud and returned after the birth to give it to her. He later recalled that she declared the memento to be the most beautiful she had ever received.

Despite their son's birth, relations between the couple continued to deteriorate. A couple of months later, at her husband's suggestion, Maud arranged to take the baby to Ireland to have him christened there. John could not accompany them for fear of arrest. Maud recorded that Seagan 'first breathed Irish air on 8 April 1904'.[36] She went to Ireland for extended periods that year, taking the baby with her, renting a house in Rathgar, where she hosted meetings of Inghinidhe na hÉireann. She brought Iseult with her to Ireland for the first time, too, describing her variously as a kinswoman or a child she had adopted.

At the end of March 1904 John travelled to America to take part in a speaking tour. From there he wrote to Maud saying that he thought he would settle in America and that it would be the best place for them to live; he said that Paris life was not a happy one and his feeling was that the best thing for their future happiness was to sever all connection with her other life, and to begin anew in another country where there would be no revival of past immoral associations. Maud did not agree to this, but she wrote him loving letters, urging him to come home to her and their son.

While John's marriage was in crisis, his eldest brother, Joseph, had fallen in love with Maud's half-sister, seventeen-year-old Eileen Wilson, whom he had got to know when he came to Paris to visit his brother. John was still in America when Joseph – a forty-two-year-old bachelor farmer and harbour official who was described as 'exceedingly smart'[37] – married Eileen in London on 3 August 1904.[38] Maud considered Joseph 'very nice' and well read, and was taken with the fact that he knew all of Yeats's poetry.[39] It is undocumented how much John and Maud knew about the couple's intentions to marry, but this was not a secret marriage. Witnesses to the wedding were another MacBride brother, Anthony, a doctor, and his wife Emmie. On her marriage certificate Eileen claimed she was twenty-one, dispensing with the need for parental consent to be married.[40] Maud was not listed as a witness at the wedding; Eileen had already left for England before John had gone to America. Following their wedding Eileen went to live at Mallow Cottage,[41] a substantial ten-roomed house in County Mayo with Joseph, who 'adored' her.[42]

John returned to Colleville in August after five months away from his wife and son. He returned 'in deference', he later said, 'to the pleading of my wife'.[43] He confronted Maud, claiming he had been told in America that she had had two other lovers. The first paramour was supposedly the writer and painter George Russell (AE), and the second alleged lover was Arthur Griffith, both of them married men.[44] John's jealousy raged on and he wrote that after he returned he 'could not warm to her at all and always felt unhappy and constrained in her presence knowing how deceitful she had been'.[45] John also said of his wife's relations with Yeats: 'There was also a distinguished Irish literary man who was in love with Mrs MacBride before her marriage. How far there were any immoral relations between them cannot be said with certainty.' John had previously written to a friend: 'glad weeping William has retired into solitude he so richly deserves and from which he should never have emerged.'[46]

It became clear that someone in their circle wanted the marriage to end when John began receiving anonymous portions of Maud's letters. He suspected her cousin May Clay, who had herself had an unhappy marriage. In one letter Maud had written: 'It is too horrible to have any more children, but John does not think precautions should be taken and all should be left to God: I call that cheap on his part'. At the time that John was sent this, it served, as intended, to inflame his unhappiness with his marriage.

At the beginning of October, Maud returned to Ireland, taking the baby with her. John urged her to leave their son 'with my people, for it is my determination to go back to my native country'. Maud was still in Ireland in the last week in October when she got an urgent message to return home immediately. The upheaval that she met on her return was, as she described, 'a measure of her husband's acute unhappiness.' According to Maud, he had been drinking steadily with his visiting Irish friends, disturbing the residents of the quiet bourgeois Rue de Passy. Maud later claimed that this was the first time she 'learned the extent of MacBride's infamy of insanity.'[47]

She was in Ireland again in late November when John decided that he was leaving France for Ireland; he had planned it believing that the British authorities, who had him under surveillance, would never dream of his leaving Paris just when he was expecting his wife back. When Maud arrived in Paris she received a letter from John written before his departure. He later recalled that its content was as follows:

That their married life was not a happy one . . . that it was very painful to him to see that she was only a weak imitation of a weak man. He also advised her, in case he was hanged or died in prison, to get married again, as she was a woman who could not live without some man or other behind her. That it was better for her if she were really interested in the cause of Ireland to be married, even if she were a little unhappy, than to live an impure life.

John later wrote that this was a foolish letter and that it had annoyed his wife considerably. 'It was a letter I should not have written: but she had made my life simply intolerable by her complete lack of all womanly delicacy, by constantly lying, and by trying to force her ex-lovers on me.'

John did succeed in getting to Ireland and was not arrested. The political situation was not inflamed at the time, so his presence in the country was tolerated by the authorities. In the middle of December, while he was still in Ireland, Maud travelled to London. She arranged to meet Dr Anthony MacBride, to whom she claimed that his brother had been guilty of indecent behaviour towards Iseult; not an assault but indecent exposure. She told him that 'in addition to the Iseult affair, his brother had acquired drunken habits and was generally acting badly'.

Days later, on 19 December, less than a year after the birth of their son, Maud asked her brother-in-law to meet her for a second time at the Gonne family solicitors. A proposal had been put forward that John should sign a document confessing his guilt towards Iseult and agreeing to leave Europe and to stay for the rest of his life in America. If he did this, Maud would take no further action, but if he did not do so, then he would be prosecuted criminally in the French courts. Anthony expressed his utter disbelief at the charges against his younger brother and sent his wife, Emmie, to Dublin to tell John in person of these accusations. John laughed at the notion of signing the document and said he would start immediately for London to see his wife and meet 'these grotesque charges' at once.

John and his brother then decided to consult Mr Richard Barry O'Brien, the president of the Irish Literary Society in London, who was a lawyer and a journalist. O'Brien told them: 'My interest in the business is Ireland . . . you both have been associated with the Irish cause, and if I can, I will not allow either of you to besmirch the other in public'. On the same evening, 21 December 1904, John wrote the following letter to his wife from the Euston Hotel, London:

My dear Maud,

I learned on Tuesday last for the first time of the scandalous charges you and your English friends have been making against my character. They are absolutely false and of course I will meet and disprove them . . . but I cannot lie under any such accusations as I am told you have been making lately. I can hardly credit you believe in the charges yourself . . . please send me word saying where we can meet to talk matters over without any heat . . . This is an awful blow to me as I was looking forward to a happy time in Ireland. Please make arrangements as to where I can see Seagan each day while I am in London. Any place and any hour you name will suit me. His happy little face is always with me.

    Your husband

      John Mac Bride

On the evening of the 24th, Christmas Eve, John called to see his wife, who was staying with her cousin, May Clay. He later related what happened:

> The door was opened when I got there and I sent in my card by the maid; after a while Mrs Clay came out and I asked to see my wife; she told me that my wife would not see me and I said 'Cannot you ask her?' She said: 'It is no use asking her' . . . Then I asked to see the boy . . . I asked her to go to my wife and say that I wanted to see the boy. I broke down completely this time . . . She came back from my wife saying that my wife said that I could not see the boy; that she could not bear it; I think they were her exact words. So then I left the little toy I had brought for Christmas and left the house.

Up to this event John had had hopes that reconciliation with Maud might be possible, but 'this scene had hardened his heart and had shown his wife to him in a most heartless and unpleasant character.'

After Christmas Maud's solicitor, Mr Witham, informed O'Brien that there was a fear that the child would be molested or kidnapped and a detective was posted to the house where Maud and her son were staying in London. On 26 December 1904 she wrote to Mr O'Brien that she wished to arrange a separation, giving entire guardianship of her son to her. She wrote to him: 'If John could get work and lead a sober decent life during the next seven years' then she would not prevent him from seeing the child and 'having a share of his affection.'

Although Maud had been in agreement that eleven-month-old Seagan be brought up a 'good nationalist and a good Catholic', she could not accept John's request for her to leave Paris and live in Ireland with his child. Then John's side put forward another solution, which exacerbated the situation further: 'I propose that the question shall be left to the arbitration of three Irish nationalists, common friends of us both, of whom John O'Leary (the godfather of the child) shall be one, or let the question be referred to Cardinal Logue or Archbishop of Dublin . . .'

Once the Catholic Church was mentioned, Maud then instructed Witham that she wanted 'full control of the child till it is of age.' Initially she said that this was to be twenty-one years; later she said she would compromise to eighteen. O'Brien saw this as ending the negotiations. He stated: 'I would not advise the husband to agree to any such terms; she must come down and I think the six years quite reasonable, in fact the husband would not agree to this only for me and the pressure I put upon him in the interests of Ireland to avoid public scandal . . .'

The new year of 1905 opened with O'Brien writing to Maud from West Kensington, London: 'Those who undertake public duties have public obligations. Your husband recognises this fact. You will recognise it too if you are true to Ireland.'[48] O'Brien made one last attempt to meet with Maud and appease the situation. He made a written record of their interview, opening with his suggestion that the matter be passed to the Catholic clergy in Dublin:

Mrs Mac Bride: No, I won't.

Mr O'Brien: But why not, he is the head of your church, you are a good Catholic I suppose, you could not have a better tribunal, absolutely secrecy, and his adjudication as binding practically as the adjudication of any Court ... your clear duty is to go before the Archbishop of Dublin, go into the whole case and accept the terms which he will decide for a private separation.

Mrs Mac Bride: I won't do that, he would take my child from me.

Mr O'Brien: Oh, not at all if there is no reason for such a course, why should he?

Mrs Mac Bride: Oh, yes he will (again placing her elbows on the table and putting her face in her hands) they will take my child from me.

Mr O'Brien: Nonsense, they will do nothing which is not right, why should you imagine that your child should be taken from you?

Mrs Mac Bride: No, no, no, I will not go to the Archbishop.

Following this, Maud asked Willie Yeats to contact O'Brien and let him know that John was in Dublin and that there were reports that he was drinking with his friends. Maud wrote to Willie: 'in a short time he will discredit himself so that my position will be vindicated without my saying a word.' However, her lawyer pointed out to her on 16 January: 'the law does not take any notice of drunkenness unless a man knocks his wife about when he is drunk . . .' Maud lamented to Willie: 'Of a hero I had made, nothing remains & the disillusionment is cruel. I am fighting an uneven battle because I am fighting a man without honour or scruples who is sheltering himself & his vices behind the nationalist cause . . .'[49]

At this point Maud decided that the case should be heard under French law, claiming the domicile of both parties. She knew, as she wrote to Willie, that it was always possible for her husband to reopen this question in the English court, where French divorce was recognized but the custody of the child could be contested. Maud lamented that John would not allow the divorce to be pronounced at once and undefended.[50] She then engaged the best lawyer in Paris and threw herself into work on the case, gathering evidence from the neighbours and servants.[51] She knew that she could not allow the charges against her husband 'to be made too light.'

Maud now let it be known to John's solicitors that she had just discovered new information while enquiring into 'other matters'. She recorded that: 'if made public as they inevitably would be, [they] would injure the reputation of a woman whom I should think he has every reason to wish to spare.' Maud asserted that John had committed adultery with her half-sister, Eileen. She assured Willie that she alleged this having obtained 'complete proof.' Her lawyer told her to prepare material on the 'Eileen affair', as she called it, 'so if John gives trouble it will be used'. Maud felt that: 'As the case is tried in camera I hope the Eileen part will not get to Ireland.'[52] John later claimed that Maud had applied for the divorce and proceeded to collect and manufacture evidence, which was supplied 'to order'.[53] Elsewhere, he commented: 'what is the explanation of her keeping the supposed instances treasured up in her mind for six months and then suddenly breaking silence.'

On 3 February 1905 Maud made her written petition: 'That the petitioner ... suffering from the jealous, suspicious and violent temper of her husband, that his intemperate habits, his unbridled licentiousness and his unscrupulous immorality constitute a dangerous environment for the petitioner and rendered life with him insupportable.'

Maud wrote to Willie: 'John is going round with tears to most people saying he is an innocent man and very badly treated'. Before the case even began, she claimed, John had 'talked over several people in Dublin.' She said of him, 'he is quite unscrupulous & very plausible, when sober.' She also asserted that she continued to look 'fearlessly at life', as she always had done, and that she would 'fight it alone', as she explained: 'this is why I have spoken to none of my friends. Why should they who are engaged on noble work be mixed up with a sordid horror of this sort?' Willie offered to come to be with her, but Maud wrote: 'I think it is best that you do not come to

Paris, though I would very much like to see you as my husband is insinuating that every man who has ever been a friend of mine, is a lover.'

When she was told that Eileen was coming from Ireland with her husband to give evidence, she wrote: 'I am sorry for their sakes, as MacBride persisting in his defence & his claim on my son makes it unavoidable to bring Eileen's name forward.'[54]

For John's defence, his lawyers focused their attack on Maud herself. John collected material from his friends in nationalist circles to discredit her. One of them testified: 'She was beautiful and she certainly fascinated not only many young men, but was attractive to all men who met her. However, it may be stated that no secrets were confided to Maud Gonne and the general feeling was that she was playing with politics and nobody sensed trouble.' John's lawyer made a notation on the margin of one transcription which he may have used in his summation: 'She was a born actress and Ireland was her stage.' His side gave the following description:

> While in the National ranks there were certain men who took an amiable view of her, there were others who regarded her as an imposter from the beginning . . . By degrees, however, it became to be whispered that her moral history would not bear inspection; her Irish friends scotched this idea, said that it was an invention of the enemy and did all in their power to protect her fair fame, but the rumours continued and multiplied and soon took more definite shape. A man's name was associated with her, Mr Millevoye . . .

The petition cited four counts of drunkenness. Maud had tried to get affidavits on John's drinking habits in both Ireland and America, but she had been met by silence and opposition.[55] Point 5 on the petition made reference to his 'constant threats while Maud was pregnant that as soon as the child was born he should be separated from his mother.'

Other allegations were to show how drinking affected her husband. It was alleged that he 'went as far as to brutalise the cook

Mrs B. and tried to outrage her'. The evidence of the middle-aged cook, Marie Bosse, was, according to John, 'a tissue of lies'. As he wrote: 'She is dirty, ugly, fat and greasy. I would not touch her with a forty-foot pole. If I wanted a woman I had plenty of money in my pocket and had no difficulty in making a suitable choice in Paris without trying to rape a hideously ugly old cook in my wife's house.' He also questioned why the woman would have lived on in the house if what she alleged had taken place.

It was also suggested that John had made 'obscene propositions' to Maud's close friend Mary Barry Delany, or Barry O, as the family called her.[56] John wrote of this allegation: 'It is absolutely false that I offered to show myself naked to this witness. Her looks would not have tempted any man . . . I would not be seen dead with her in a five-acre field.'

The final allegation was that he had compromised 'a young girl, EW, to whom this petitioner has shown hospitality'. It was stated that when Maud was absent in the summer of 1903 he had adulterous relations with her seventeen-year-old illegitimate sister. John's response was that the 'insinuations about Eileen and myself are absolutely false.' In his notes for his lawyer he wrote in reply to suggestions of impropriety: 'I did not flirt with Eileen at Colleville or elsewhere . . . I never went . . . with Eileen by myself except to go to the village to help her carry vegetables'. He protested that the whole time he was in Colleville without his wife there had been visitors there, including Victor Collins and his two children, as well as a Mr and Mrs Anvil. He also pointed out that Eileen and Iseult shared a room and he was never in Eileen's room for an immoral purpose, and he refuted the accusations that he had been seen embracing and kissing Eileen. One of the witnesses was a dressmaker, 'Madame B'; she had no English, yet she was, as John recorded: 'bold enough to swear that from our facial expressions she believed we were talking about my wife!!!' To charges made in testimony by another witness, John wrote his response in his notebook: 'This woman never saw me embrace Miss Wilson in the drawing room or any other place. I think I kissed her on the day Seagan was born and do not recall kissing her again till she was going to England and then it was in the presence of my wife and Mrs Clay. In fact it was my wife who first got me to kiss her.'

When it was suggested that traces of sperm had been found on her bed linen, John said this was 'a monstrous lie', stating how incomprehensible it was to him that the witness, an unmarried woman, could 'swear' that marks on Eileen's linen were sperm. He pointed out that 'No person but a medical man could take it upon himself to give evidence unto whether the stains were or were not a specific character.' Maud wrote to Willie:

> The only one to make me feel very sad was Eileen, though she has behaved very badly, it was terrible to bring her into it & I regret very much having allowed it. I allowed it at first because I believed it would make John MacBride accept my offer of a quiet separation – leaving me the child – but it did not & I thought her name in any case would not have been made public, but now they have brought her over as a witness there is no way of keeping her name out . . .[57]

When Eileen's husband, Joseph MacBride, took to the stand, Maud wrote to Willie that he 'seems quite convinced of her innocence which is a great thing, & I forbid my lawyer putting any questions to him in cross examination which would shake this belief – he declared that all those who slandered his wife were vile women in the pay of the vilest creature upon earth . . .'[58]

The MacBride family were anxious to highlight what had been referred to as the 'Iseult episode'. It had been agreed by both sides before the judge that it would not be alluded to by either side; however, on the last day of the trial Dr Anthony MacBride raised it. This meant that Maud had to call witnesses, although she fought hard to keep Iseult out of the witness box and indeed the girl was not called to the stand.

Iseult always maintained that her stepfather had made 'advances' on her as a child; when she would recount it afterwards, it would be in a detached way, much as she often spoke on other topics, with a 'cool rather disdainful composure.'[59] The story sometimes included the detail that he had asked her into his room to give her sweets.[60] John's explanation for the incident was that the child had once come upon him when he was about to empty a chamber pot. He said that the doors of all the rooms were unlocked and Iseult entered rooms without knocking or asking permission, whether her mother was in the house or not.

Ultimately, the allegations around this episode did not hold up in court. When the case concluded, Maud wrote to Willie: 'The court thinks the charges of immorality are insufficiently proved'.[61]

It was also raised during court proceedings that Seagan was by now suffering '*nervosité excessive*', which resulted in frequent and sudden loss of consciousness. When this was highlighted it came as a complete surprise to his father, who had been living with him up until the time he was ten months old, in which time he had never suffered from any illness. Maud thought the cause might have been the pre-natal influence of the terrible strain she had gone through before his birth. Seagan would also now cry hysterically when his mother was away from him; Maud described how she felt sometimes as though his life depended on her. Doctors, however, said he would grow out of it before he was seven.

The household had been in a state of siege since the previous year. Iseult was described by her mother as 'a nervous child and used to wake at night screaming that MacBride with his eyes of an assassin was running after her.' She refused to go upstairs in the dark as she was 'always afraid MacBride will be hiding and run after her'. Seagan was never left alone and was always accompanied by a guard dog called Brutus. This was not because of his condition, but in case his father or his father's friends might try to kidnap him. According to Thora, Maud's niece, who claimed to have seen it, Maud kept a revolver under her pillow just in case of a kidnap attempt.[62] Kidnap was in fact a real possibility. Maud was now seen by many of John's associates as highly immoral and therefore not a fit mother for Seagan. At least one family in Dublin discussed the possibility of taking him in.[63]

With the conclusion of the court case, Maud took the decision to keep out of Irish politics for a time, assuring Willie that when the divorce was over she would return and see if there was any useful work she could do. For the moment she decided to study art (in which she had considerable talent) and to wait for the result of her appeal, as so far she had only been granted judicial separation and wanted a divorce. She wrote to Willie in November 1905: 'I worked for Ireland for Ireland's sake, not of my own, I always thought I was an instrument for force working for Ireland's liberty, it may be these forces need me no longer, that they have chosen others for their work – it does not matter, so long as the work goes on.'[64] Maud wrote every week to Helena Molony, secretary of Inghinidhe na hÉireann, and read every Irish publication she could obtain.

The decision of the Civil Court in Paris was announced on 8 August 1906 and, as the Paris correspondent for the London *Times* reported, 'The divorce was refused on the ground that both parties were of Irish nationality and the divorce is not permissible to Irish Catholics.'

The case had been held *in camera*, but details were leaked and published abroad. Maud suspected Victor Collins, who had attended the court case with John. John sued the *Irish Independent* for libel in the reporting of the case and, in the process, the French court noted that he had had to prove domicile in Ireland for the purposes of the case in Ireland. In the final judgment it was because his domicile was Ireland that they were not granted a divorce, as it would not be recognized there: 'A decree of separation was, however, made and the custody of the child, the issue of the marriage, being entrusted to Mrs MacBride.'[65] The father was allowed to see the child once a week and after the age of six the child was to spend one month with his father each year. Maud immediately put in an appeal, because she did not want John to have any access to his son at all.

When she finally returned to Dublin in October 1906, Maud did so without her children. She was greeted by 'Up MacBride!' and hissed at by the audience at the Abbey Theatre when she attended the opening of Lady Gregory's play *The Gaol Gate*.

The appeal case dragged on. By this time Maud was regretting her hasty decision, writing to Willie in the autumn of 1907 that she felt she should have stayed still and let fate work: 'MacBride had to disappear from my life because fate ordered it – I need not have troubled about helping fate by going to the law.'[66] In January 1908 she got the news that she was once again denied a divorce. According to the London *Times*, the court refused to grant a divorce to Irish Catholics, and stated that under British law divorce would require an Act of Parliament. Maud was also refused full custody of the child, with visitation rights awarded to the father once a week for two hours.[67]

John, in fact, had not been exercising his rights, as he was now living permanently in Ireland. Maud wrote at the time: 'as long as Major MacBride does not attempt to interfere with me or my child, I don't think I shall take the trouble and go to law again but it is always well to know I can, if I need to.'[68] She told Willie: 'as he is unlikely to live in Paris I hope these visits will be a dead letter. Still they are always a nuisance & will prevent me from living in Ireland for the present'.[69]

The following year, forty-three-year-old Maud and Willie Yeats consummated their relationship, but it was a brief affair. After this Maud was no longer linked to any man. Her children and her political work became her focus once again.

In the five years following his departure from Paris John had struggled to obtain employment and did not have a fixed address. It was not until 1910 that he was successful in getting a permanent job, when Dublin Corporation employed him as a water bailiff. His duties consisted of collecting dues from ships using the River Liffey. Maud used her influence to assist him in getting this job; when he found out, he resented her interference. The local City of Dublin Union Association tried to have him dismissed from his post because of his inflammatory public speeches, but the Corporation maintained that his own views were his own business.

In August 1910 Maud finally brought six-year-old Seagán on a visit to Ireland, staying in Ballycastle, County Mayo. She took him to see his grandmother in Westport, but John did not meet with them. Seaġan did not speak English in his early years; it was said that this was to prevent him speaking to his father, who had never mastered the French language.

Despite the destruction of their personal relationship, Maud and John still shared a desire for complete independence for Ireland. From Paris Maud kept in touch with the work of Inghinidhe na hÉireann; in 1908 the group brought out a newspaper, *Bean na hÉireann* (*Woman of Ireland*) and continued its education programme with lectures. In 1911 Maud was involved in the organization's protest against a Royal visit, and John MacBride was one of those who ensured that there was no loyal address during that visit. Since his return to Ireland he had been active in the Irish Republican Brotherhood and was given a place on its Supreme Council for his native Connaught. He was still popular in nationalist circles and lodged with Dublin City's mayor, Fred Allen, and his wife Clara, whom John had known since the early 1890s.[70] He was also a member of other nationalist organizations such as the Irish National Foresters.[71]

In 1912 Fred Allen removed himself from the IRB due to disagreements with those in Ireland and their associates in the USA in Clan na Gael, which also advocated freedom of Ireland by revolutionary means. This affected John's position with the movement, as now there was a new generation of political activists. Seán Mac Diarmada, described as an 'up and coming arch conspirator', replaced John as the Connaught representative.[72]

During this time, Maud sporadically returned to Ireland. One of her projects was to organize a pilot scheme for school meals, distributing food in John's Lane school along with women from Inghinidhe na hÉireann and she addressed Dublin Corporation on financing the scheme. She worked closely on this with the labour leader James Connolly, who had returned to Ireland to live after years in America. Maud was back in Dublin in 1913 giving practical assistance in the feeding stations during the widespread strikes of that year, when workers were shut out of their workplaces in what became known as the Lockout.

In 1914, after the outbreak of the First World War, Maud was determined to bring Seaġan to Ireland to enrol him at St Enda's School, located at the Hermitage, a mile from Rathfarnham village. Its headmaster was P. H. Pearse, barrister-at-law, who had been in the Gaelic League for a number of years. The boarding school for Irish Catholic boys had been founded six years previously to provide a secondary education that would be 'distinctively Irish in complexion' and which would be 'bilingual in method'. It endeavoured to create 'strong, noble, useful men'.[73] Maud believed that the school system in France was in decline and that, as she wrote at the time, it would be bad for some years to come, as the schools were being run by old men while all the young men were at war.[74] Seaġan later remembered the meeting he and his mother had with Pearse about his enrolment.

However, he did not travel to Ireland for school, Maud deciding that if she brought her son to live in the country his father might 'interfere', as she later wrote: 'MacBride and the English law make it impossible to me to have him in Ireland until he is old enough to defy both.'[75] Seaġan was sent instead to school with the Jesuits at the Lycée Saint-Louis-de-Gonzague on Rue Franklin in Paris.

Maud was prevented from travelling back and forth to Ireland when she pleased as she could not risk being cut off from her son should the shipping lines be closed down as a result of the ongoing war. 'I am torn in two,' she wrote, 'my love of France on one side, my love of Ireland on the other . . . This war is an inconceivable madness which has taken hold of Europe – it is unlike any other war that has ever been. It has no great idea behind it. Even the leaders hardly know why they have entered into it, and certainly the people do not . . .'[76]

She and Iseult, now a young woman of twenty, nursed wounded soldiers in a makeshift hospital in the small town of Argelès-Gazost in the Pyrenees, with Seaġan acting as an errand boy. Maud had taken Iseult there for her health and at the request of the mayor of the town she had assisted in setting up the hospital, where they worked until they returned to Paris that Christmas.

In Ireland John MacBride still had revolutionary intent, attending a meeting in September 1914 of those who convened to stage an Irish rebellion in wartime. He was also involved in the Irish Neutrality League, which was actively pursuing an anti-recruitment campaign; and he was a member of the Jeremiah O'Donovan Rossa Memorial Committee when the Fenian leader was brought back to Ireland in 1915 for burial.

Meanwhile, during the summer of 1915, Maud moved the family to the Infirmière Hopital Militaire at Paris Plage, near Etaples. Built by the British Army on a narrow strip of land, it was the largest hospital complex of the time – twenty hospitals totalling twenty thousand beds. Casualties were brought straight from the front and Maud wrote that she and Iseult were 'patching up poor mangled, wounded creatures in order that they may be sent back again to the slaughter.'[77] For those who did not survive, next to the hospital complex was the burial ground, which became the largest commonwealth cemetery in France.

Maud and Iseult were given the rank of lieutenants, which allowed them to travel with the French Army to treat the wounded if necessary. When they returned to Paris Maud continued to nurse at a makeshift hospital in Passy. Nursing wounded soldiers and witnessing the death of a generation of young men, including her nephew Toby in March 1915 and Millevoye's son Henri, who died later that same year, turned her into a pacifist.

By Easter 1916 she had already come to see the futility of war when news reached her of 'troubles in Ireland'.[78] Censored newspapers contained information on the leaders of the Rising, all of whom she knew. She wrote at the time: 'The papers say my old friend James Connolly is killed, Pearse is wounded and a prisoner with John MacBride. They were men I esteem and like the best in Irish politics . . . I feel so wretched and powerless. I doubt if I shall be able to get a passport to go to Ireland. I shall try to get one to London and from there try and get over.'[79]

3

Lillie and James

Lillie Reynolds watched as a soldier ran along the length of Dublin's Clare Street to board the tram at the Merrion Street stop. He tried to hop on the step and grip the bar, but failed. Now having to wait for the next tram, he started to talk to her, as she too had missed that one. The soldier noted that she was 'small and fair' and looked 'refined in an unassuming way'.[1] Years later the circumstance of how Lillie Reynolds met James Connolly was often recalled, but the exact date of this chance encounter is unknown.

James was born in Cowgate under the shadow of Edinburgh Castle in 1868, although when asked he would always say he was born in Monaghan, in the north-east of Ireland. This was the home county of his parents but, unable to eke out a living from the land, his father, John Connolly, had swapped the poverty of County Monaghan for the destitution of the tenements of Edinburgh.[2] It was here, in 1856, that he married an Irish-born domestic servant, Mary McGinn. James was their third and youngest son.

At the time of his son's birth, John was working for Edinburgh Corporation as a manure carter, his duties including the removal of dung at night and the carting of ashes on a Saturday. James started work as a child. He was a printer's devil at the age of ten and an apprentice baker by thirteen; he later recalled that as he walked to work he would pray that he would find the bakery had burnt down. At that time he was living with his parents and his older brother

Thomas at 2a Kings Stables, Edinburgh. His eldest brother, John, had already joined the army. When James was fourteen years old, he followed suit and enlisted.

James was posted to Ireland in the late 1880s. Ireland was part of the British Empire, so the major cities and towns had a large army presence. There was always a degree of turbulence because of Irish resistance to British rule and during James's time serving there the country was also experiencing a Land War as small tenant farmers sought a fair rent, fixity of tenure and freedom to sell their holdings. James, who was largely self-taught, later said that he devoured the publications of the Land League, whose members were fighting for a change in the land-ownership system in Ireland. By the end of the 1880s, the young soldier was already consumed with a sense of social justice and the necessity of attaining basic rights for ordinary men and women.

At the time of their first meeting, Lillie Reynolds had prospects. As she was a member of the Church of Ireland, the Girls' Friendly Society – an organization established by the church to help young girls from rural parts of Ireland find employment – had found work for her as a domestic servant with William Wilson, a stockbroker and notary public, and his wife Anne, at 35 Merrion Square East, where she had risen from the position of maid to become governess to the couple's younger children. Mrs Wilson was very fond of Lillie, and they shared many interests and exchanged confidences like mother and daughter. The family's large house in a fashionable quarter of Dublin had a library, conservatory and garden, and the residents of the square had use of the private park. Elsewhere in the city the same red-brick houses, built in the Georgian period and individual-ized by their distinctive doors, were now tenements, occupied by the poor, with several families living in each room.

Lillie (also known as Lily) was born in rural County Wicklow, in 1867 or 1868, the fourth child of a farm labourer, John Reynolds, and his wife, Margaret. Her elder sister Margaret (known as Maggie) was born in 1861, and identical twin brothers, Johnny and George, in 1863. Following the premature death of John Reynolds in a farm accident,[3] his widow brought the family to live in Rathmines when it was still a village outside the city of Dublin.

After their chance meeting at the tram stop, Lillie and James began courting, and when James left Ireland to return to his native Scotland their courtship continued by correspondence. Lillie's letters have not survived, but they were described by James as effusive and affectionate. Following his departure from Ireland his circumstances changed: he was no longer in the army. It has been suggested that he deserted[4] and that the reason he stayed undetected by the authorities was because he had enlisted under a false name. Writing to Lillie at the time, he explained: 'I could get plenty of work in England but you know England might be unhealthy for me – you understand.'[5] An early sign of Lillie's commitment to him is evidenced by the fact that she sent him money. He acknowledged her contribution to what he described as 'the distressed fund'.[6]

Lillie made a fateful decision: to leave her homeland, her family and the security of her job to follow this young man to the town of Perth, where she had been sending her letters. However, when she arrived in Scotland (the exact date is unknown) and travelled to Perth she discovered that he was no longer there, but had moved to nearby Dundee, where he had found temporary employment replacing a man who was ill.

In later years Lillie would recall that she went to Scotland on the promise of marriage: 'when I left for Scotland to be married I was the happiest girl of my acquaintance';[7] but surviving correspondence of the period shows that James was less intent on marrying immediately; indeed her arrival in Perth seems to have taken him by surprise. He wrote to her:

> I was rather amused to see that you treated my proposal to visit me in all seriousness. Do you think me 'daft' or what [?] I am getting vexed you see. I mean to say, I wish to tell you that I cannot bring myself to ask to meet you on Tuesday, or any other day for some time yet. I can not think but that my conduct is rather selfish in imposing on your good-nature as I have been doing and proposing to do . . .

when I do see you next, it will be when I will not be quite so afraid of shaming you, as I have been. So Lillie, although I am very loth [*sic*] to be so [long] without seeing you . . . still I am persuaded it is all for the best, better that it should be so. Don't think it is for any other reason.[8]

He wrote to Lillie addressing her as 'my own sweetheart', yet he failed to travel the short distance (around twenty minutes by train today) between the two towns. In April he wrote: 'So my love, your unfortunate Jim, is now in Dundee and very near to the "girl he left behind him" but the want of the immortal cash and the want of the necessary habiliments presses me to remain as far from her as if the Atlantic divided us.' He hoped to get to Perth before she left the city, he told her, writing: 'But cheer up, perhaps sometime or another, before you leave Perth if you stay in it anytime, I may be available to see you again.'

The only indication of how Lillie felt arriving in a strange town was when she told James that she could not warm to the people of Perth.[9] He still did not arrange to meet her: 'God knows I would like to see you and be with you every night in the week if possible and think myself happy if I would be allowed to do so. But I cannot bring myself to inflict my presence, as I have been proposing to do, upon you.'[10] After they finally did meet face to face, he wrote to her: 'I hardly expected you to come and meet me. And the fact that you did come served to increase my love for the girl who could lower herself to be seen speaking to one who has descended so low in the social scale.'[11] Throughout this period of courtship he signed himself: 'yours lovingly James Connolly'.

The surviving correspondence gives only glimpses of what happened between the couple. There is no indication of when they met for the first time after Lillie's move to Scotland; what is known is that she took the decision not to return to Ireland, but left Perth and went to find work in London. As the months passed, they continued to correspond. James saw a change as her letters became less affectionate. Sometimes they were just a few short lines, enquiries after his health, and instructions for the times and dates of meetings.

Some six months after her departure from Ireland, Lillie and James were still not reunited in the same place, but her letters appear to have grown effusive once more. In a surviving letter dated 17 November 1889, James delightedly described how nice it had been to receive her previous letter, which he described as 'chatty and lively'. He wrote in reply: 'I have told you so often that your letters are always welcomed that I need not repeat, but in truth I was desirous of encouraging you in your letter writing that I am always reminding you that I want you to write whether you will be able to say anything remarkable or not. And let me tell you Lillie, in all seriousness that your letters in reality form a welcome change to the miserable monotony of my present existence.'[12]

Although he described his existence as tedious, James had by now immersed himself in a movement that had already begun to con- sume him and that would influence and affect his every decision for the rest of his life. The previous April he had become a member of the Socialist League. Through this movement he had met with John Leslie, a close friend of his older brother John who, having left the army, was also in Dundee, moving in socialist circles and distinguishing himself in local politics.

James's decision to take part in politics himself was a bold one: any public role, but especially one that was anti-establishment, was quite a risk for an army deserter, as if he were recognized he could be arrested and imprisoned. He appeared to refer to this when he wrote:

Lillie I am in truth dissatisfied and surely troubled in my mind I have been trying hard to recruit myself principally since I came here but the incubus which I have mentioned to you before prevents me most effectually. I have had intentions of, when recruited a little, endeavouring to settle down and trying to realise that ideal of home which I have formed in my mind. With your help Lillie, I had hoped to find happiness. In other words I had intended to ask you if you could find courage to risk your life and welfare along with such a

scapegrace as myself. As far as love could carry me, I would do anything possible to secure such a prize as yourself and to guard it
against harm, but, Lillie, much as I would love to have you in the
near future as, let me say it reverently my wife, the consideration of
my present poverty and the barrenness of the general outlook deter
me. I am in a quandary ... You see, mavourneen you have
conquered me and reduced me to slavery. What will you do with your
prisoner?[13]

By April 1890 James had returned to Edinburgh and, like his
father before him, had taken up work as a manure carter.
Correspondence between the pair now focused on their impending
marriage. He wrote to Lillie: 'How I am wearying to get beside you,
and hear your nonsense once more. It is such a long time since we
met, but I trust this time we will meet to part no more. Won't it be
pleasant?'[14]

Actual marriage plans were finally being worked out and James
wrote of subjects such as choosing a best man. One letter declares:
'This is a <u>love</u> letter written by Jim to the nicest girl between here
and anywhere to tell her that her mistakes, her wilfulness, her
troublesomeness [sic], only make me love her the more'; yet, he postponed the marriage again, as a surviving undated letter attests: 'By
the way if we get married next week I shall be unable to go to
Dundee as I promised as my fellow-workmen in the job are
preparing for a strike on the end of this month, for a reduction in
the hours of labour. As my brother and I are the ringleaders in the
matter it is necessary we should be on the ground.'[15]

James and Lillie finally married on 30 April 1890 at a ceremony
in St John the Baptist Church, Perth. They had been granted dis-
pensation by the Roman Catholic bishop of the diocese of Dunkeld,
enabling James, a Catholic, to marry a Protestant. This decision was
not an easy one for Lillie. James wrote acknowledging her difficulties
and saying that he knew it would be hard for her to meet a priest and
to promise that any offspring from their union would be brought up
as Catholics. Yet she dutifully fulfilled these obligations in order to

marry him. On the eve of their wedding, a surviving letter from James shows how little he knew of Lillie's past life: he did not know the Christian names of her parents, nor her father's profession, nor her birthplace. He wrote: 'I gave your age, I gave it as 22 was I right?'[16]

Following their marriage, Lillie had thought that they were to live with James's parents, but they moved instead into a home of their own at 22 West Port, located on the corner of the Grassmarket, an area of Edinburgh then populated by Irish immigrants. The building was crowded and sanitation was primitive, but despite living in such poverty, Lillie was very happy: 'we were very happy on very little,' she later recalled. 'To be together, and the understanding that we had for each other, made up for a lot of short rations.'[17]

By 1894, James and Lillie Connolly were the parents of two small daughters; Mona, born on 11 April 1891, and Nora, born on 14 November 1893. During their first four years of marriage they moved five times; like so many of their class, they had no security of their tenancy. They lived for a while at 75 St Mary's Street, before moving to 6 Lawnmarket and then to 6 Lothian Street, part of the warren of streets in the Old Town of Edinburgh.

Their home in Lothian Street became a centre for socialist meetings. Lillie had had a better education than her husband and she worked with him on his political speeches and writings, although she shunned the public sphere. On one occasion when James asked her to attend a meeting he was addressing, she did so, but as soon as her husband stepped on to the platform to speak, Lillie became so frightened and nervous that she ran out and never stopped running until she got home.

In October 1894, James agreed to stand as the Scottish Socialist Federation's candidate only a week before the municipal elections took place. With no resources available to promote their candidate, his supporters did what they could, including chalking his name on the pavements. His opponent described him as a 'young man of no business ability advocating ideas repugnant to all right thinking men.'[18] As a carter, he was the lowest of workers in the city, advocating radical policies such as the end of one-room houses. He was defeated at the polls. This did not deter him from contesting the election the following year for the position of Poor Law Guardian. He was once again unsuccessful.[19]

The manure carter was by this time unemployed. During the bitterly cold winter of 1895, with James unable to find work, his friends gave him money to open a small cobbler's shop. His advertisement read: 'Socialists support one another. Connolly, 73, Buccleuch Street repairs the worn-out understandings of the brethren at standard rates.'[20] Later one of his customers recalled that not a single pair of shoes he had repaired could be worn again. Within months it was clear that the shop was a failure.

By now, however, James was so committed to bettering the circumstances of his fellow workers that the only work he was willing to do was as a political propagandist or organizer. Living on a tiny income from the Scottish Socialist Federation, survival was difficult. As Lillie later described, '[it] was alright when we had only ourselves but when the family made its appearance, the picture took on another aspect.'[21]

The financial situation of the family was so dire that they made plans to emigrate to Chile, where the government was providing land. James was not a farmer, but it is said that he had hopes of establishing a socialist colony there. Lillie, who was pregnant for the third time, initially consented to make the move to the remote and unfamiliar country, but when James told her that he would have to carry a gun for protection, she began to feel apprehensive and implored their friend John Leslie to find her husband work. Leslie made a public appeal on James's behalf: 'Here is a man among men . . . the most able propagandist in every sense of the word that Scotland has turned out. And because of it, and for his intrepidity, he is today on the verge of destitution and out of work.'[22] He concluded with a description of Connolly: 'an unskilled labourer, a life-long total abstainer, sound in wind and limb. Married, with a young family, and as his necessities are therefore very great, so he may be had cheap.'[23]

By chance an offer of work came from Lillie's home town of Dublin, as a paid organizer for the Dublin Socialist Club, and James accepted it. Returning to her homeland, Lillie brought with her Mona, aged five, Nora, aged three, and the baby Aideen, who had been born on 3 March 1896. Although her brothers were in Dublin, her sister Margaret had by now moved away to live in Scotland.[24]

Within a month of arriving in Dublin, James had established the Irish Socialist Republican Party. The group held weekly outdoor meetings at the fountain at James Street, or at the Phoenix Park, or in the Customs House. He also organized classes. Their clubrooms at 67 Middle Abbey Street opened every night, and members could access a library of books there. James Connolly's dream of starting a social revolution meant more than mere employment for him; it consumed him. He persisted in his work, writing leaflets to spread the socialist message to an often unreceptive audience. Membership numbers remained small; a recorded list contains the names of just forty-three men. No women are listed, although two women prominent in the nationalist movement, Maud Gonne and Alice Milligan, contacted the party expressing an interest in its work.

The Connolly family lived first on Queen Street, near Arran Quay. For Lillie this part of the city, although only a short distance from her former home in Merrion Square, was a completely different world. The room that became the Connolly home had bare boards with a thin strip of lino between the beds. Food was cooked on the fireplace or on a gas ring, and water was carried in a bucket from the yard. According to her family, Lillie's ingenuity was such that she made this single room look like a cheerful home. The family then moved to another tenement at 76 Charlemont Street. At a time when Dublin's infant mortality rate was one of the highest in the British Empire, Lillie's children, living in one room in a nine-roomed house that was home to six different families, were among the most vulnerable.

From the earliest age, Lillie's daughters were aware that their mother was different from the other women in the tenements. She worked hard not to succumb to the hopelessness of the poverty that surrounded her, and she always kept her appearance as neat as she could, as Nora later described: 'She looked so much nicer than the other mothers in the big house . . . She was always so clean and her brown hair looked so nice piled on top of her head, with the little curls dancing at her neck . . . such a nice face – it was not red and dirty like some of the other mothers – it was white, and soft and clean.'[25] When her work was finished, or when she went out, she wore different clothes than those she used for scrubbing and cleaning at home. Even then, she devised ways to make her work clothes last as long as possible. When she was scrubbing the floor, she would wear hessian bags that she washed and cut to fit over her legs as a type of apron. Her simple attentions to maintaining her appearance kept a degree of self-worth intact for her, which many other women lost during long years of hardship. Her children loved to watch Lillie washing her long hair, which reached down below her hips, and to see her afterwards wind it round her head so that it looked like a crown.

The Connolly family had come to Dublin with the promise of £1 a week. This wage was to be provided by a group that consisted of just eight men. In September 1896, however, after a strike in the building trade, the money stopped. Nora overheard the exchange between her parents. When James told his wife what had happened Lillie was dismayed: 'But they promised it.' James replied, 'I know, Lillie, but they haven't the money, they can't pay me!'[26] Lillie was pregnant again and already they had not enough to eat. She had to ration the children's food and lit the fire only at night.

For weeks James searched for work from morning until night. There was no social welfare, no government assistance for the unemployed. At last he found work as a labourer, but months of living on insufficient food had left him unable, despite his youth – he was still in his late twenties – of doing the job. As he described it: 'I was wheeling barrows of cement. All day long. I felt as if they were pulling the arms out of my body . . . A hundred times I thought I'd give up and go home.' He could not bear the thought of returning to Lillie in such a manner, though, saying: 'Then I thought how happy you were this morning because I had work at last and the hungry days were over. You had pawned everything so I said I must stay.' Lillie still retained one item of value, a tiny gold watch, but now she took the decision to go out and sell it. James looked at her and said: 'your last treasure gone', to which she replied: 'Wasn't I the selfish woman to cling to it so long. But I was so fond of it. But now it is gone I know that everything is going to be all right.' This event was a defining moment. James replied: 'I'll make it up to you, Lillie. I'll make it up to you. God help me, I'll make it up to you.'[27]

Lillie gave birth to a premature daughter at 75 Charlemont Street in November 1896. Lillie chose her name, Ina Mary,[28] but her father called her 'his Irish Mollie', which in later years he shortened to Mollie. Lillie visited her former employer Anne Wilson on Merrion Square with her new baby. For Lillie it was an important occasion, as Mrs Wilson had never seen any of her babies. Anne Wilson was aware that Lillie was now condemned to a life of grinding poverty, something that was all too common in the Dublin of the 1890s. It was the custom of that time to present a new child with a shilling or sixpence, and Anne Wilson placed money in the baby's hand. When William Wilson arrived home, he too gave the child money. Lillie could hardly wait to tell her husband of their windfall. His reaction was not so jubilant: 'This is the last straw!' he exclaimed. 'To use my child for charity is more than I can bear . . . I don't believe we should live on the kindness of others. We have a right to live – a right to be fed if we can't work.'[29] His pride meant that in future Lillie had to be resourceful and secretive about when and where she got assistance.

On another occasion when James queried where she had got money, she simply told him to 'ask no questions and she would not tell him any lies'. In fact she was assisted by a community of women who had developed a means of providing for their families in an age when there was no welfare system. On one occasion when Lillie was in rent arrears a neighbour gave her money and then told her to take it to a house on the South Circular Road to see a merchant and buy a suit length of men's material. Then she was to take the material to the local pawnshop and exchange it for a sum of money, and use that to pay her rent. Lillie came to learn that the women of the tenements worked together, providing money to each other, always giving to those in the most need.

In Dublin James was moving in circles of like-minded people with the twin goals of improving social conditions in Ireland and bringing about the country's self-government. One of these was the beautiful and charismatic campaigner Maud Gonne. James asked her to address a socialist meeting, timed for June 1897 to coincide with the occasion of Queen Victoria's Jubilee Day, marking her sixty years as monarch. Maud's slides of evictions were projected on the gable wall of a building in the centre of Dublin. This public display of disloyalty resulted in the police baton-charging the crowd watching the show. A woman was killed and many were injured and arrested. Meanwhile, James had organized a procession that made its way through Dublin headed by a cart carrying a coffin inscribed 'The British Empire' while a band played the 'Death March'. At O'Connell Bridge, over the Liffey, Connolly ordered the coffin to be put into the river, shouting 'Here goes the coffin of the British Empire'.[30]

In the aftermath of these protests, James was arrested. Maud Gonne had breakfast sent to him in the Bridewell police station and paid his fine, writing to praise him as the only man with the courage to stage a public protest against the jubilee. She also went to tell his wife of his arrest. Maud arrived at their door with her Great Dane, Dagda, while Lillie was bathing Ina;[31] Lillie always recalled it as the arrival of the most beautiful woman she had ever seen. James had told her of Maud's beauty, but as she said: 'I never realized that anyone could look so lovely. And here she was in my own home.'[32] Maud was taken with Lillie's stoical outlook. Once when they were discussing her circumstances, Lillie said of her husband, 'he cares nothing but for the cause', adding that she would continue to be unstinting in her support of him and that she 'would not have him otherwise.'[33] Shortly after their first meeting Lillie requested an autographed picture of Maud, which afterwards she always put in a central place in her home.

The following year the family succeeded in renting a tiny cottage, the last in a long row of identical houses in Weaver Street in the Liberties. There was even a tiny yard. Lillie did not mind the small space of this house, as her own family were its only occupants. James became a well-known figure in the Liberties, speaking at the James Street fountain on a weekly basis. In October 1897 the tenants of the artisan dwellings who were being threatened with eviction asked him to speak on their behalf. When Lillie heard she said, 'Oh James, was that wise, was that wise, just now?' They too could be evicted from their new home. He replied, 'I know, Lillie but when I am asked to help people I can't refuse.'[34] He spoke at the packed meeting in Gray Square, telling the audience of the evils of rack-renting landlords and exposing the profits that the company was making. The demonstration was successful and there were no more evictions.

In early 1898, when a famine once again threatened in Ireland due to the failure of the potato crop, Maud and James joined forces, publishing a pamphlet: *The Right to Life and the Rights of Property*. Using the writings of Pope Clement I, Gregory the Great and others, they argued that it was not a sin to steal if people were starving, and that no human law could stand between the people and starvation. Maud funded the printing of the publication, while James went to County Kerry in April to distribute the pamphlet and report on conditions for *L'Irlande Libre*, the newspaper Maud published in Paris. His business card, which read '*Journalist L'Irlande Libre*', found its way into the possession of a local police inspector. He also submitted articles on his experiences in Kerry to the *New York People*.

James's journalism was to bring the family some prosperity when in July 1898 he spent several weeks in Scotland raising finances for the newspaper the *Workers' Republic*, and this made it possible for the organization to give him an additional payment as editor. Lillie arranged for Mona and Nora to get new dresses, telling her husband, 'I thought I would celebrate by getting new frocks for the girls. Just think it will be the first frocks they'll have made from stuff bought for them.' He replied, 'But when will you be able to get a new frock to replace the ones you cut up? That would be a real celebration.' She replied, 'I don't need new frocks. What do I need a new frock for? I'm too busy looking after the children to go out anywhere.'[35]

Prosperity was short-lived. Due to insufficient funds, the newspaper ran for only eleven issues. James wrote to a friend asking for a loan to set up as a peddler, writing: 'it lowers me in my own opinion to ask this but it would tear my heart to leave Ireland now after all my toil and privation and unless I succeed in this instance the welfare nay the mere necessity of feeding my family will leave me with no alternative.' [36]

As the new year began, Lillie gave birth to their fifth daughter, Moira Elizabeth, on 1 January 1899. Those days were recalled by James himself: 'It makes me shudder even yet when I think of the hard grind of those poverty-stricken years, of the hunger and wretchedness we endured to build up a party in Ireland.' The workers had little money themselves to support the party, so income was inconsistent and unreliable.

During the summer of 1899 James was invited by the Socialist Democratic Federation in Scotland to give a six-week tour. His colleagues in Dublin expressed a wish that he would not go, as the *Workers' Republic* was to be reissued, yet when he asked for an increase in wages to allow him to stay in Dublin this was not forthcoming, so he took up the Scottish invitation, once again leaving behind his young family.

On 11 February 1901 Lillie gave birth to their only son, Roderick James, known as Roddy, at 54 Pimlico, Merchants Quay, bringing the number of children in the Connolly family to six, all under the age of ten. Lillie was delighted at the birth of a son, who would carry her husband's name, as she said, 'through the generations to come.' James was more concerned that the children would have 'sufficient intelligence to work their way through life and leave this world a better place than they found it.'[37] In the Census of that year

James described himself officially as a printer's compositor, but when his son was a few months old he was again away working as a socialist propagandist. He spent time in May and June that year, and later in September, giving lecture tours in Scotland and England. He was a popular speaker, described as 'perfectly intelligible to the ordinary man.'[38] He spoke to large crowds in towns such as Reading in Berkshire, but did not succeed in gaining any recruits to his cause.

When James returned to Dublin he was elected by the United Labourers to be their representative at the Dublin Trades Council, and in November 1901 he was formally adopted as a Labour candidate endorsed by the United Labourers' Union to contest the Wood Quay Ward in the Dublin Municipal Elections. The Dublin Trades Council also endorsed him. In the election he polled over four hundred votes, losing out to P. J. McCall, the candidate of the United Irish League, who had waged a bitter campaign against James Connolly, describing him as: 'a scab printer, a scab painter . . . an ignorant labourer, he wasn't a labourer at all, but a journalist, he was a confirmed drunkard and a bigoted teetotaller.' Despite the unfounded personalized attacks, James was heartened by the fact that he had moved from providing 'propaganda of theories' to becoming 'a political force'.[39]

For much of 1902 James was away from Dublin; he travelled to Scotland and England for several months and spent only a few days in Dublin before embarking at Liverpool for New York on 30 August, primarily to promote the *Workers' Republic*. He was billed as the 'foremost representative of socialism in the Emerald Isle.' In his first address in the Cooper Union Hall, New York, the biggest hall in America, he addressed the crowd saying: 'I represent the class to which I belong. I do not represent the entire Irish . . . The Irish situation is two-fold, political and economic. Politically the people of Ireland are under the rule of another country . . . No person can be economically free who is not politically free and no person can be politically free who is not economically free.'[40]

The tour, on behalf of the Socialist Labour Party of America, took him to New Jersey, Boston, Ohio, Michigan, Kentucky,

Indiana, Missouri, Utah, Arizona, Illinois, Colorado and Canada. Midway through the trip, in Boston in October, he wrote: 'I have not been a single day out of the train since I arrived in America. In fact it is no exaggeration to say that I have been travelling since the 30th of August'.[41] However, when he visited Salt Lake City in October he wrote to his wife: 'Lillie it is worth a lifetime of toil to make this trip.'[42] His children, especially the eldest two girls, had been waiting daily for his return. When their mother was making the Christmas plum pudding she let each of the children stir it and make a wish, which they were to keep secret. Nora later wrote: 'I confided mine to Mona. "I wished Daddy would arrive home". "I did too" said Mona. Then that makes three of us, I said because I am sure that Mama did also.' Stockings had been hung on the mantelpiece and the next morning, as Nora recounted, 'Daddy still did not arrive.' He actually left New York after Christmas, setting sail on 27 December 1902. Nora later recalled that when eventually he arrived 'he made it all up to us'.[43] He brought back a book on China for Mona, an American history book for Nora, Indian moccasins with beads for Aideen, a ball for Ina and a doll for Moira.

When he returned, James immediately began canvassing the Wood Quay Ward for the municipal election of January 1903. Nora recalled being brought by her father to the election rooms, where she saw people writing and volunteered to help, so they gave her the job of addressing envelopes. Again James failed to be elected.

Shortly after his return, James became aware that the Irish Socialist Republican Party had misused monies raised by him, meeting bar debts rather than the payment of rent and printing costs. He resigned, writing: 'I consider that the party here had no longer the exclusive demand on my life which led me in the past to sacrifice my children's welfare for years in order to build it up'.[44] Elsewhere he wrote that: 'when I recall the fact that this party in Dublin has been built on sacrifices – the sacrifices by many members of their time, energy and spare cash, and by myself by the time and energy and the sacrifices of the commonest necessaries of life to myself and family for nearly five years ...'[45] Later, his only regret was that he had not known of these circumstances before he left America, as he had been made some tempting offers to stay.

The *Workers' Republic* ceased publication; James described how this news made him feel 'as if I had lost a child'.[46] By the summer the Irish Socialist Republican Party had virtually collapsed.

Now James focused his thoughts and interests beyond Dublin. He was involved in the setting up of the Socialist Labour Party of Britain, chairing the conference at which the new party was formed in May 1903. During that year he spent a good deal of time in Scotland, undertaking a five-month lecture tour at the invitation of the Scottish District Council. Then in September he accepted an offer from a cousin to pay his fare to New York, where he had decided to seek out a new life. Before his departure he wrote: 'As you say the conditions under which I existed in Ireland were very hard to my family and myself, but hard as they were they were not hard enough to drive me from the country . . .'[47]

James described his move to America as 'banishment to this cursed country'; he wrote at the time: 'My career has been unique in many things . . . Men have been driven out of Ireland by the British Government, and by the landlords, but I am the first driven forth by the "Socialists".' His eldest daughter, Mona, pleaded with him to take her with him, but he told her there was no money to bring her and she must stay to fill the role of little mother, *máthairín*. Ina remembered that he made Mona 'feel big, grown up, older than her years, attaching so much importance to her herself that she finally consented to remain home and travel out with the family'.[48]

When James first arrived in New York he hoped to gain employment as a printer for the *Weekly People*, the organ of the Socialist Labour Party. However, he was unable to get the work as he had no union card, so he left the city for Troy in upstate New York, where he stayed for a time with relatives.

In the middle of 1904 the difficulties of separation from his family intensified when Lillie became seriously ill and was confined to bed for two months. On 22 June James wrote to his friend

J. Carstairs Matheson in Scotland: 'My wife is dangerously ill and may not recover and my children have all had to be taken away into the homes of neighbours and friends.'[49] By the following month, however, he was writing again, saying that his wife was 'a bit better' and that plans had been put into place for the family to be reunited in the middle of August.

A price war between the White Star Line and Cunard Steamship Company had reduced transatlantic fares, so James was able to send home tickets for his family to sail on RMS *Cedric* on 6 August 1904 from Queenstown (Cobh). From their planned arrival date, he met every ship, but they did not appear and he had no idea why. They finally reached New York on RMS *Oceanic* from Liverpool, three days after the expected date.

When the family disembarked they were detained in Ellis Island, held in a wire cage. The Ellis Island records show that Lillie Connolly travelled with ten-year-old Nora, eight-year-old Aideen, five-year-old Ina Mary, four-year-old Moira and three-year-old Roderick. Outside, James Connolly waited for his wife and children, but the reason for their detention was that he was not claiming the correct number of passengers. An official came to them in the waiting area to query if there had been some mistake: 'He said his wife and six children. There are only five children.' Lillie told the man: 'There should be six . . . One died before we sailed. Bring him here and I'll explain.' Nora recalled the arrival of her father: 'He came. The children were all wild with delight jumping around and hugging him. Puzzled, her husband looked at her, asking Lillie what has happened. There are only five of them. Mona's gone, said Lillie, with tears running down her cheeks. Tell me what happened, James asked her. She shook her head. Take me away from here. Take me away. I can't tell you here.' The official who stood by said nothing, but acknowledged their loss by shaking their hands as they left. James gathered the children around him. After the tears of the reunion, Lillie began to come alive again, glad to be once more with her husband, and now she was able to tell him how his daughter had died.

Mona had been alone in the house with only her five-year-old sister Ina for company when her apron caught fire. She ran out of the house into the garden, but she became engulfed in flames before a neighbour saw her. She had an agonizing death; she lived only for twenty-four hours, conscious all the time, before she finally died at a hospital in Drumcondra on Thursday, 4 August 1904. At the moment of Mona's death, Lillie cried out 'James! James!' as if he could hear her. The telegram bringing the news to him had never arrived, and so it was in Ellis Island that James found out that his eldest child remained in Ireland, buried two days after her death in an unmarked pauper's grave in Glasnevin Cemetery.

The grief-stricken family took a boat up the Hudson to Troy in upstate New York, where they were to live at 76 Ingalls Avenue. It should have been a time of celebration that the family was finally to enjoy a better life. Lillie's new home had a sitting room, a dining room, kitchen, pantry, bathroom and three bedrooms. Her greatest joy, though, was to be once more with her husband, and Nora, now the eldest, later recalled how her mother looked at her father a long time, then kissed and kissed him, and held him tight.

Troy was a centre of the textile industry. The main source of employment was in the manufacture of shirts, which were made in factories and also worked on by people in their homes. The Connolly children earned money by bringing baskets of collars from the factory to the homes of workers before school, then they would do another delivery on their way home from school. James worked as a collector for the Metropolitan Life Insurance Company. However, within three months of his family arriving in America, he lost his job. Yet again, the family was broken up when James went to New York City to look for work. It was not until April 1905 that he returned to Troy as the local representative of the Public Mutual Life Insurance Company: 'this job is only a commission job, and . . . in a year if I can hold it so long it will be one of the best jobs in the country'.[50] He did not last the year; the Starchers' Union in Troy started a strike and for the fourteen weeks of its duration James spent this time agitating and collecting for the strikers. As he had not been doing his job, he was fired.

By June 1905 James was writing that he wished to return to Ireland: 'For after all it is to Ireland all my thoughts turn when dreaming of the future. I suppose I will never see it again except in dreams . . . I regard Ireland, or at least the Socialist part of Ireland which is all I care for, as having thrown me out, and I do not wish to return like a dog to his vomit.'[51] Later that same year his friend Matheson in Scotland suggested that James return there, but as he replied, it was not as simple as he proposed:

> But to shift a family across the Atlantic is no picnic, and to return home myself, and leave them in the United States is not as easy as it would have been to leave them in Ireland or Scotland and come here . . . You see I have grown cautious and reserved. At one time if I thought a thing was right I just up and did it, and let the consequences take care of themselves but now I sit down and carefully consider the consequences so carefully and so long that by the time I have made up my mind the opportunity to act will be gone.[52]

The family moved again, first to New York City, where they stayed with friends, and then on to Newark, New Jersey, where they moved into an apartment in a detached three-storey wooden house. James got work in the local Singer Sewing Machine factory when a socialist foreman helped him to get employment as an expert mechanic by using falsified documents and qualifications. He was later transferred to the nearby factory in Elizabeth, but was able to stay living in Newark and commuted to work by special train.

The Connolly children were happy in Newark, with its large public park, libraries and a swimming pool. However, their father's health was suffering from the heavy manual work and he developed headaches and stomach problems from the lack of fresh air in the factory. He often came home and had to go straight to bed, then when he woke up he would frequently leave again immediately for meetings in New York City. Lillie was distressed at his condition and, with tears in her eyes, told him that he was killing himself by working like that. But James would not heed her; he had made promises to his comrades and he would not disappoint them.

In November 1906 the Socialist Labour Party launched a campaign to unionize workers in the factory where he worked and he became involved. As the months passed, tensions increased and James's activism intensified. He left before his boss was forced to fire him.

He continued doing the work to which he was best suited, accepting a position as organizer of the Building Section of the New York branch of the Industrial Workers of the World. For this job he had to move his wife and children into New York City. By this time the family had a new addition, a baby girl named Fiona, who had been born in Newark on 22 August 1907. As they were packing to leave Newark, Lillie was heard saying to James, 'it seems to be our fate James never to spend five years in any one place'.[53] This move would 'deprive Lillie of the quietness of the suburbs and the garden of which she was so fond'.[54] The children had once again to change schools and make new friends. Among the Connolly children, Moira was noted as 'exceptionally clever' and 'always head of her class.'[55]

They moved into a six-storey building on Elton Avenue in the Bronx, sharing a floor with several other families. This was one of the notorious firetrap tenements and while they lived there, there were several epidemics, including an outbreak of diphtheria, during which Lillie assisted officials from the Department of Health in nursing her neighbours. She also worked as a washerwoman, as once again her husband's income, $18 a week, was unstable.

In his role as organizer, James was 'down town' until late nearly every night. The familiar pattern of their lives continued, his political life, his work for the spread of socialism consuming him, while Lillie maintained house and home. But she found it hard to settle in the Bronx. Ina recalled hearing her mother saying at this time: 'what's the use of building up a home when you know that it is bound to be broken up again?'[56]

In February 1907 James decided to 'form a socialist organisation of men and women of Irish race and extraction' in America, which was called the Irish Socialist Federation. In April 1908 he left the

Socialist Labour Party; his disagreements with the founder, Daniel De Leon, had continued unstintingly. James once wrote to a friend: 'I have such an unfortunate knack, as you know, of saying things that turn my best friends into enemies.'[57]

The new Irish Socialist Federation launched its own publication, the *Harp*, and James became editor and did most of the writing himself. Lillie and her children were again left alone as he travelled across America throughout 1908, covering over 3,000 miles as he promoted the *Harp*. On his return after eleven months Nora went to meet him at Grand Central Station. Much to her annoyance, two members of the Socialist Party of America were there to meet him too and accompanied them to the Connolly home. Lillie was anxious for them to leave, telling her husband: 'I thought they would never go, after eleven months we want you to ourselves. Others have had you long enough.'[58] James's present to her was a gold watch to replace the one that she had sold many years before. As he gave it to her he told her he had not forgotten, and she cried on his shoulder; she had not forgotten either.

In May 1909 he set out on a third speaking tour as a national organizer for the Socialist Party of America. He travelled to Ohio, Indiana, Missouri, Iowa, Colorado, Texas and Arizona over the summer months. He was paid $3 a day plus expenses and he was allowed to keep the proceeds from his literature sales. A surviving letter to Lillie from Cleveland, Ohio, written in June 1909, included $12, which James told his wife would pull her through for the week. He occupied his long solitary hours on the train by educating himself, reportedly learning German and Italian to a level of fluency; he could read French too and even knew some Arabic. He also used the time when he was travelling to write, including some poetry, and a volume of his verses, *The Jewels of King Art*, was published in 1906.[59] This tour allowed him to promote his pamphlet *Socialism Made Easy*, which had just been published, and on one occasion he was able to send Lillie $100 from the sales. His tour was so successful, bringing many Irish Americans around to an acceptance of socialism, that it was extended through the winter, with engagements in Montana and California. He left the Pacific coast in April 1910 to return to his family, who were still living in the Bronx, now on East 155th Street. Nora, by now seventeen, was working as a dressmaker.[60]

Within weeks of returning from his tour, James was away from his family again, this time travelling to New Castle near Pittsburgh, where a strike was under way. His 'constant activity, tireless initiative' earned him great respect, yet his work for socialism in America was not fulfilling him. Readers of the *Harp* complained of the paper being preoccupied with Irish affairs. As he described his situation: 'I feel that most any one can do the work I am doing here, but that there is work to be done in Ireland I can do better than most any one.' He wrote to William O'Brien, one of the leaders of the new Socialist Party of Ireland: 'I am not satisfied here, have not near enthusiasm for the fight that I had in Ireland, and want to get amongst people with whom I feel I have more in common.'[61]

When O'Brien sent him news that the Dublin Trades Council was seeking an editor for a weekly paper, he replied:

> I am more than willing to be repatriated (I am extremely desirous for that end) . . . I may confess to you that I regard my emigration to America as the great mistake of my life, and . . . I have never ceased to regret it. Of late I have been studying very attentively the situation in Ireland, as far as it is possible to do so at a distance, and I am very much impressed with the belief that all the conditions are favourable for a forward move in our direction. That thought has filled me with a burning desire to get back, but as an individual the position was hopeless. My family growing and their needs are pressing . . . possibly in six months time I may have the money to spare, but just now I am only painfully recovering from the long financial depression of the winter.

The editorial job in Dublin was given to someone else, but James was heartened by the contact from his former colleagues, writing to O'Brien: 'It has aroused the call of Erin in my blood until I am always dreaming of Ireland, dreaming of going back to fight at home.'[62]

James Connolly left America in July of 1910. He funded the trip himself with the promise of a tour of Ireland, Scotland and England. A farewell dinner was held on 14 July, costing a dollar a ticket, and the advertisement for the event read: 'Don't miss this occasion to tell Connolly what you think of him.'[63]

Despite the fact that he had said he would not leave his family behind, he set off alone. Nora recalled her mother telling him that she did not want him to go, but he persuaded her that it was the right thing for him, saying: 'I love Dublin. I'd rather be poor there than a millionaire here.'[64] But despite the difficulties James's decisions often brought her, she did not resent the circumstances caused by her husband's determination to improve the conditions of his fellow workers, years later writing: 'never did I ask him to consider me or the family. I felt it was his duty to pursue any line of action he particularly wished. It was sufficient to me that I helped not hindered.'[65]

He arrived in Derry on 26 July 1910, travelling on to Dublin where the Socialist Party of Ireland hosted a reception for him at the Antient Concert Rooms a couple of days later, describing him in the publicity literature as 'the well known Irish-American Socialist, Writer and Lecturer'.[66] James's book *Labour in Irish History*, written during his time in America, was published in Ireland that month. He dedicated it to Lillie: 'To my dear wife, the partner of all my struggles and the inspirer of my achievements.'

The political landscape had altered during the years of his absence. In 1909 William O'Brien, Francis Sheehy Skeffington, Michael Mallin and others had come together to form a new Socialist Party of Ireland. There was also a new leader of the Labour movement, James Larkin, who had come to Ireland from Liverpool as an organizer for the Belfast dockers in 1907. He moved on from Belfast to Dublin and within a year had enrolled 2,500 dockers in the Dockers' Union. He then formed his own union, the

Irish Transport and General Workers' Union (ITGWU), in 1908 and strikes took place in each of the next two years. In 1910 Larkin was convicted for taking strikers' money for his own use and was sent to prison for a year.[67] James, who had been in correspondence with Larkin, visited him in Mountjoy Jail shortly after he arrived in Dublin and worked out the terms for his release in October after serving only four months of his sentence.

James had hopes of a job with Jim Larkin, having helped negotiate his release, but did not want to feel that he should 'demand a price for it;'[68] he felt it would be better if he could be employed by the Socialist Party and assist with Larkin's union rather than be employed by them. Larkin thought that James should stay in Ireland and told colleagues that he was willing to help him find employment.

James travelled to speak in Cork and Belfast, as well as addressing countless meetings in Dublin, before going to Scotland for a lecture tour. In September the Socialist Party of Ireland proposed that he be offered a position as an organizer, but he declined because it was for a period of only six months and the pay was insufficient. Disappointed, he wrote to William O'Brien that he would have to resign himself to being 'an American for good or bad'.[69] By October, however, the Socialist Party had worked out an agreement to pay him for a year, and his income would be supplemented by lecturing in Scotland and England.

He now wrote to Lillie:

> This is the fatal letter. I want you to come back to Ireland. Now, after you have drawn your breath, let me tell you the particulars. My engagement is for two pounds a week and most of the money is already in hand. Also, I am sure that I have a more promising future in Ireland than in America, not so often and so long away from home as I would be if we stayed in the US. You are not coming back to the misery you left. Do not be afraid of that.[70]

James was aware what he was asking of her; he had previously explained to a colleague: 'I could not go into the Dublin slums again to live; one experience of that is enough in a lifetime. My children are now growing up, and it is part of the creed once I have climbed any part of the ladder towards social comfort I must never descend it again.'[71]

In New York friends came from long distances to see off Lillie, Nora, Aideen, Ina, Moira, Roddy and Fiona Connolly. As Ina recalled: 'many were crying, as was Mama. Wasn't she coming with us to see father and her brothers so why the tears?' Years later she told Ina that, as they set sail, she felt she was leaving the land where she had spent the best six years of her life.[72] On the ship home they were called the 'millionaire family': they were the only family that the stewards had ever brought back to live in Ireland, so it was assumed they had made their fortune. When he heard this story, James replied: 'they'd probably call you the mad man's family if they knew the truth.'[73] In December 1910 they landed in Derry, from where they travelled down to Dublin. James brought Lillie and the children to Ringsend, in the south of the city, and Ina recalled skipping down South Lotts Road with her sisters and brother, asking which one was their house. When they reached number 70, it was immediately clear that this was their new home, as someone had draped an American flag in the window to welcome the 'returned Yanks'.[74]

No sooner were they settled in Dublin than James was away again, travelling through the country working as the national organizer for the Socialist Party and also assisting with the Irish Women's Franchise League and Maud Gonne's Inghinidhe na hÉireann. They were campaigning to have the School Meals Act, which had just been passed in England, extended to Ireland. During this campaign James attempted to get the backing of the Irish Trades Council for this proposal.[75]

In May 1911 James confided in his friend John Leslie that 'his first mistake was to go to America, my second was to leave it.'[76] The three eldest Connolly girls were of working age, but there was no employment for them in Dublin, so Nora, now eighteen, took the decision to go to Belfast where there were better opportunities. Her mother was very opposed to her going alone, and by the end of May the rest of the family had also made the move to Belfast. According to her children, Lillie was loath to leave Dublin, as there she was close to her twin brothers, Johnny and George. Johnny was married with no children, while George, a clock-maker, was married to his third wife and by 1911 had ten children.[77] Ina recalled an exchange between her parents, in which her mother said that 'she knew it was obvious that they could not go on with such peace and happiness, as they had known in Dublin'. James's reply was reproachful: 'we cannot be selfish and forget that other men and women want a little comfort and happiness too. It's for the improvement of their lives that I devote my time. You know how much I love you, my family and Dublin, but I have my work to do. You will have to come along with me since we have come so far in it.'[78] Lillie left Dublin asking her husband if it would be the last time they would break up their home.

As James searched for a home for his family, he was aware that it must suit Lillie's needs, as it was she who would spend the most time there, and he found a large house for rent at 1 Glenalina Terrace in the Falls Road area. After they had moved in, he left immediately for Scotland. Lillie and her children were once more at the mercy of the Socialist Party for their survival and, yet again, she was left penniless. James wrote from Scotland: 'Mrs Connolly ... has already been three days in Belfast, a strange town, without a penny to buy food and I away in Scotland. Such an impression on her part makes my work in the movement rather difficult.'[79]

In Belfast Ina found work in a laundry, later recalling: 'Mother needed help so urgently to feed the family I was willing to learn any trade or business that would put us on the threshold of brighter days.'[80] Nora, meanwhile, was doing piecework on aprons. Ina later joined her, often doing extra work at home. They concealed their employment from their father, however, as he thought making aprons was a form of slavery. Ina later wrote: 'we were always on the alert for father's footsteps'[81] and scrambled to hide evidence of their work before his arrival. When Nora had once suggested that their father could do his organizing without having to earn a living and that his daughters would bring in the wages, the idea had filled him with rage. He would not live off his daughters, he told her, and the issue was never raised again.

With his family in Belfast, James took a role with the ITGWU as the Ulster organizer. He opened an office on 112 Corporation Street, following a successful strike by the Belfast seamen and firemen working for the Ulster Steam Ship Company, which in turn led to similar pay increases negotiated for timber labourers and men in general cargo. By July 1911 the union had opened a second office at 6 Dalton Street. In October of that year James was approached by a number of women spinners from the York Street area in Belfast, who were striking at the local mills. He set up the Irish Textile Workers' Union, which became a branch of the ITGWU; it was known as 'Connolly's Union'.

Throughout this time, James would go out early in the morning and come back late at night, and he had two public meetings each Sunday and one in the middle of the week. When Nora complained that he was always absent, he encouraged her to join him in his work. She accompanied him in January 1912 when Larkin sent him to Wexford, where workers at the Pierce Foundry had gone on strike after they had been prevented from joining the ITGWU. The dispute had already dragged on for months, and by the time James and Nora arrived in Wexford one of the ITGWU officials had been imprisoned. She recalled that she had many 'lonely walks around Wexford,'[82] but James did negotiate a settlement that enabled the locked-out workers to return to work. The men created an Irish Foundry Workers' Union in February 1912.

At this time James was looking for a woman to assist him in organizing the female mill workers in Belfast. Twenty-four-year-old Winifred Carney (known as Winnie) became his close confidante when she joined the ITGWU in Belfast. She had been an activist in organizations such as the Gaelic League and the suffrage movement and later she took on the role of Connolly's personal secretary, typing articles for him, in particular for the Glasgow publication *Forward*.[83]

James continued to travel, including that year going to speak to striking workers in Liverpool. In May of 1912 he attended as delegate for the Belfast Branch of the ITGWU at the Irish Trade Union Congress at Clonmel, County Tipperary. He put forward a motion that meant that in future there would be two organizations: the Irish Trade Union Congress itself and the Labour Party, which would be a political wing with the aim of securing labour representatives on elected bodies. At the same time James tried to bring the Socialist Party of Ireland, a mainly Dublin-based organization, together with the Independent Labour Party, which was in Belfast, but his efforts came to nothing.

That year James's relative Peter Connolly[84] travelled to Belfast to see him, to sign over the family farm in County Monaghan.[85] Lillie wanted her husband to take on the farm, but James told her it was an impractical idea as he had no money for rents or rates, and besides, he had a 'house full of girls'.[86]

Life in Belfast was difficult for Lillie and her family. She was still a member of the Protestant church and the children were being raised as Catholics. A match at Celtic football ground close to their house resulted in a serious riot between Protestant and Catholic supporters. Stones were thrown, shots were fired and people were beaten. Although none of her family was injured, the episode left Lillie uneasy: 'She just could not understand how people who lived for years as good neighbours . . . should let outsiders work them up into a state of war about football matches or processions.'[87] Traditional tensions were escalating. A Solemn League and Covenant was signed in September 1912 by those who wished to pledge themselves as loyal citizens of the king and resist a parliament being established in Ireland. The Ulster Volunteer Force was founded in January 1913 to oppose by force the introduction of Home Rule to the island of Ireland.

In January 1913 James renewed his bid to attain political office when he contested the Dock Ward in the Belfast Municipal Election on a platform that Ireland should be ruled, governed and owned by the people of Ireland; school meals for children; and advocating new administration of the harbour. In his election pamphlet he described himself as a 'determined enemy of the domination of class over class, of nation over nation, of sex over sex ... vote for James Connolly.'[88] Nora and Ina canvassed on their father's behalf, with Nora doing the talking while Ina carried the election literature. He polled well, gaining 900 votes, 400 fewer than the man elected.

James continued successfully growing the union in Belfast, but in August 1913 he was summoned to Dublin by a telegram informing him that 'Industrial War' had broken out in the city. Employers, led by newspaper publisher William Martin Murphy, who wanted to destroy the ITGWU and its leaders, stated that they would not keep on the payroll any worker who was a member of the union, and that they would employ only those workers who would sign a pledge stating that they would not join the union. The employers were pre- pared to lock out anyone who defied them. James saw the Lockout as 'more than a trade union fight; it is a great class struggle, and recognised by all sides. We in Ireland feel that to doubt our victory would be to lose faith in the destiny of class.'[89]

Tensions grew and there were constant clashes with the police. Workers' meetings were deemed illegal. Four days later, tramway employees in Jim Larkin's union went on strike. Immediately, James joined Larkin in addressing thousands of workers assembled in Beresford Place, Dublin. On 30 August 1913 he wrote to Winnie that the labour meeting to be held on the following Sunday had been banned and that his next letter might be from Mountjoy Jail.[90] He was correct; he was arrested for 'inciting to riot and disorderly conduct', as well as for refusing to recognize the court, and he was sentenced to three months in prison.

Lillie was always anxious when she had not heard from her husband, but in the past had been reassured by the fact that eventually he always did find time to write, no matter how busy he was. This time, Nora remembered 'a sharp ring and a postman's knock resounded through the house. Mama went towards the door. Down the stairs tumbled Moira, crying: "Don't open it, mama; don't open it. I dreamt a telegram came for daddy, and he went to Dublin, and was arrested. Don't open the door, mama." "Silly girl," said Mama, "It was only a dream." She opened the door and received a telegram.'[91]

James wrote to Lillie from prison on 3 September 1913:

> I trust that you and the children are not too much upset over this trouble. It was not entirely unexpected, and it is not so bad as it might be. At least while I am here there is not much chance of getting my head broken as many poor fellows are getting outside. I suppose little Fi cannot understand where her Pa is. Kiss her for me, and tell her I miss her morning visit. For the other children – well, I suppose, they understand, and need not fret. Roddy, and Agna [Ina] and Nono [Nora] should know that many more than I (perhaps thousands) will have to go to prison, and perhaps, the scaffold, before our freedom will be won. Nothing worth while can be won without suffering . . .

He asked that two of his children would inform themselves of what was going on, writing: 'Aideen and Moira must now begin to read so that they will understand what their father is working for, and not think of him as an ordinary criminal.'[92] The eldest girls, Mona and Nora, from the time they had been quite young, had always accompanied their father to meetings and were well versed in all his activities. Nora later wrote: 'I felt so important to know what was being discussed, to hear the different viewpoints put forward by the other socialists. He would patiently explain the finer points to me. He was training my mind, seeing that I would not turn out a vegetable.' He had never excluded the other children, as Nora recalled: 'whenever he was home for the evening, he would read stories to the lot of us as soon as we had our homework done';[93] but, following Mona's death, it was Nora who took the keenest interest. He would recommend books for her to read and he would then sit her down and see what she could not understand. Ina, his 'Irish Mollie', was also completely devoted to participation in her father's interests.

In prison James commenced a hunger and thirst strike to gain his release. He was quoted as saying: 'What is good enough for the suffragettes is good enough for us'. Despite the risks to his life, he told Lillie not to fret. She decided to travel to Dublin to visit him, taking Ina with her as her companion while Nora remained in Belfast with the other children. On the boat to Dublin, Lillie paced the deck with worry. When one of the sailors found out that she was James Connolly's wife he told her that the whole country was talking of the man who would sacrifice his life for his fellow-workers.

When they reached Dublin they went to Mountjoy Jail, where the governor said he would allow them to see the prisoner on condition that Lillie would persuade her husband to give up the strike. Ina recalled that her mother said to her: 'the governor doesn't know what your father is made of, if he thinks I could talk him into giving up a hunger strike or anything else he is convinced is right'. Lillie told the governor: 'I would not interfere in what he thinks is right, but as I do not want to lose him, and everyone says that you will let him die before you give in, I will do my best.'[94] At this point James had been without food and drink for seven days.

Lillie was advised that only the Viceroy of Ireland, Lord Aberdeen, could order her husband's release, so she went to the Viceregal Lodge in the Phoenix Park, walking there rather than taking the tram in solidarity with the tram workers, who had been the first to strike. As a result of their meeting, Lord Aberdeen ordered James's release and Lillie was given the viceregal coach to go back to the prison.

It was arranged that James would recuperate with Countess Markievicz at Surrey House on Leinster Road, Rathmines. James had first met Constance, Countess Markievicz, in 1911. They were both forty-three years old but they had lived very different lives. She had been born into the landed gentry as Constance Gore Booth of County Sligo and had had all the wealth, education and social connections afforded to her by the circumstances of her birth. The actions of Jim Larkin had brought Constance to a realization that she had to play a part in changing the social, economic and political system in Ireland.[95]

Lillie stayed with James at Countess Markievicz's home for a number of days until he was well enough to undertake the train journey home to Belfast. There they were met by a large reception of well-wishers. As her father was still too weak to give a speech, sixteen-year-old Ina was delighted to be asked to address them on his behalf.

As soon as he was well enough, James returned to Dublin and, when Jim Larkin was arrested for seditious speech in October 1913 and sentenced to seven months' imprisonment, James took over as the head of the ITGWU. He travelled to London to address a meeting at the Royal Albert Hall in support of the workers, and writers and activists such as George Bernard Shaw and Sylvia Pankhurst joined him on the platform.

When he returned to Dublin, he lodged for ten shillings a week with Constance Markievicz at her home in Rathmines. She no longer lived with her husband, Polish artist Casimir Dunin Markievicz, whom she had met in Paris in 1900. When they returned to live in Ireland after a short stay in her husband's homeland, Constance and Casimir had gathered around them a group of the artistic set, founding the United Arts Club in 1907 and forming a theatre company. By 1911, however, Casimir was spending increasing amounts of time away from his wife, and had begun boarding with James and Ellen Duncan, co-founders of the Arts Club, at their home in St Stephen's Green.[96] Their nine-year-old daughter, Maeve Markievicz, was living with her grandmother on the Gore Booth estate in County Sligo, and Constance's stepson had left home; in 1914 Casimir would move away from Ireland permanently.

As the Lockout continued, it became all-consuming for Constance: 'For six months she worked day and night and organised a food kitchen and milk depot.'[97] Madeleine ffrench Mullen, Fiona Plunkett, Maud Gonne, and the Gifford sisters – Muriel, Nellie and Grace – were amongst countless other women who joined her, motivated by humanitarian instincts to help those who were affected by the strike. They assisted in soup kitchens and took part in food distribution for the strikers and their families.

In November 1913, as a direct response to the strike and Lockout, the Irish Citizen Army was formed 'as a means by which to bring discipline into the distracted ranks of labour'.[98] A drilling scheme was introduced by James at Liberty Hall and by mid-December a thousand men were being drilled at Croydon Park, Clontarf. The formation of an army without uniform or weapons was a cause of great amusement for Dubliners, but its presence kept peace at labour meetings, prevented evictions and protected strikers from the police, who had been baton-charging the crowds at rallies.

Prolonged absences from his family meant that James felt cut off from them. On 1 January 1914 he wrote to Lillie from Liberty Hall: 'I did expect that I would have got a card from at least one of my family, but no, not one. Please write and tell me how Aideen is, and I am very uneasy about the boy, I have been expecting a letter every hour of the day since I came. Give my love and kisses to the girls and Roddy and tell them not to forget their papa so easy.'[99]

Lillie's own isolation and confinement in her home during this period is underscored by a family story of an argument that resulted from a gift that James gave her, a present of a suit for her to wear. After a few weeks had passed, she decided to cut it down to fit her daughters. When James discovered this, he was angry with her, saying: 'You think of everybody but yourself Lillie! Why should you work from early morning till late at night and have nothing to wear? You are just as important to me as my children. You must have some reward from your toil. You give away everything you have and never stop working. How will you enjoy the good things of life if you don't go out, and you can't go out if you don't have proper clothes?' She replied: 'As long as my family is happy and fed, I'm the height of fashion with a change of dress and a clean overall. What would be the use of me dressing up, and the children with no clothes to go to work in?'[100]

In January and February 1914 the workers began drifting back to work. On 22 March the Citizen Army was reorganized with the aim of arming and training all workers capable of bearing arms in order to create a disciplined force. It had its own constitution and its own flag, and later its own uniform.

In the North, in a bid to resist Home Rule, the Ulster Volunteer Force had been formed and began openly importing arms and ammunition; now the Irish Volunteers did the same in response. In July 1914 a cache of weapons smuggled in from Germany was brought ashore at Howth in County Dublin, and Ina and Nora were involved in distributing them. When they had completed this job they were given some to bring back to Belfast with them. Countess Markievicz, who took part in the incident, told the girls: 'you are the first women to run guns to the North. Show what you're made of.'[101] It is said that it was in the aftermath of the Howth gun-running that James began to contemplate the use of arms.

In August 1914 the beginning of the First World War changed the political landscape on the island of Ireland. In the North, Sir Edward Carson and his Ulster Volunteer movement had been defying the Asquith government for two years, calling for resistance to the Third Home Rule Bill, which was about to become law. Its passage through parliament had been assisted by John Redmond's Irish Parliamentary Party, which now supported the war in the belief that showing loyalty to Britain in this time of crisis would ensure Home Rule when it came to an end. The Bill was passed in late September, but by agreement between the parties it would not take effect until the war was over.

In October, the Irish Volunteers split into two: the great majority, who supported Redmond, broke away to become the National Volunteers and many enlisted in the British Army, while the rest – some eleven thousand men – retained the name Irish Volunteers and remained at home in anticipation of fighting a war on Irish soil. From this point onwards, the Irish Republican Brotherhood, the militant nationalist group that had infiltrated the Volunteer movement, prepared to fight by methods other than politics. It was at this time that James spoke to his friend William O'Brien in Dublin about the 'desirability of acting with all those who would favour organisation for an insurrection.'[102]

In September 1914 James had attended a meeting in the Gaelic League offices organized by Éamonn Ceannt, who was a member of both the Irish Volunteers and the IRB. An outcome of this meeting was the formation of an Irish Neutrality League to ensure that Ireland stayed out of the war in Europe. Those who attended the first meeting also included Seán Mac Diarmada, Joe Plunkett, Tom Clarke, Patrick Pearse, John MacBride, Thomas MacDonagh, Arthur Griffith and William O'Brien. James acted as president of the Provisional Committee, which took a few actions, such as the publication of some pamphlets and some lectures; however, it did not last long. William O'Brien called it an organization of leaders without members.

Jim Larkin went to America in October 1914 and Connolly was appointed acting general secretary of the ITGWU in his absence. He was also nominated by Larkin as commandant of the Irish Citizen Army and Michael Mallin became his chief of staff. Under James Connolly's leadership, the Citizen Army was the first Irish army to admit women to its ranks and give them a role. According to Nora, her father constantly said that 'no movement was assured of success that had not women in it'. When some of the men complained that the women's section would be an encumbrance in the event of an uprising, James responded that if none of the men turned out, the fight would go on with the women.

He also hung a banner across Liberty Hall: 'We serve neither King nor Kaiser – but Ireland'. It remained there from October until December 1914. The lack of action by the authorities, despite the Defence of the Realm legislation, shows that there was some reluctance to engage with James and the Irish Citizen Army.

During the summer of 1915 James took part in the funeral of the Fenian Jeremiah O'Donovan Rossa, which had become a focus for nationalist feeling. In the souvenir pamphlet, James wrote: 'In honouring O'Donovan Rossa the workers of Ireland are doing more than paying homage to an unconquerable fighter. They are signifying their adhesion to the principle of which Rossa till his latest days was a living embodiment.'[103]

James was firmly immersed in activities in Dublin, where he continued living in Constance Markievicz's home. He had never liked working in Belfast, which he found 'stultifying and unproductive'. Winnie Carney kept him informed of all political news in Belfast. He addressed her as 'Miss Carney' and signed his letters 'Yours, James Connolly'. They always met when he came to Belfast, and on one occasion he wrote: 'I probably shall be home on Friday, the usual train.'[104] According to those in the Belfast circle, Winnie would blush deeply when his name was mentioned and 'She had been in his confidence and felt deeply concerned.'[105] There was no suggestion of impropriety between them, but clearly Winnie had become close to him at this time, aware of his plans and aspirations. He in turn valued her opinions, writing to her on 1 December 1915: 'Your criticism of the attitude of the Volunteers is the best I ever read. You seem just to have gone straight to the heart of the matter, and sized up the situation in fine language. I am going to quote some of your letter as a Correspondent.'[106] Letters could pass between them on a daily basis; he wrote to her from Surrey House on 5 December 1915: 'Be sure and write me a good letter, and I will promise a good one in return. Higho, I am weary.'[107] By that time he was not travelling home to Belfast every weekend as before.

The Belfast branch of the ITGWU complained about James's prolonged absences. The branch was almost bankrupt and broken up. At the outbreak of war, relations between James and his colleagues in the Irish Labour Party in Belfast were so strained over his opposition to the war that he claimed only to have three supporters who wished him to continue the meetings. He wrote to William O'Brien: 'I have spent myself pushing forward the movement here for the past three years and the result of this is that my activity is labelled as a desire for "cheap notoriety". I am sick . . . of this part of the globe.'[108] His pamphlet *The Reconquest of Ireland*, published in 1915, was in the main a programme of action for the

Irish Labour Party but by the end of that year, with Larkin in America, the political landscape was changing.

In Belfast, Lillie was becoming increasingly isolated. She rarely left the house. Ina recalled that she felt that by doing so she 'lost out on very little', as Nora and Ina would bring everybody they met home to see her. She would always share what little they had. At the time the family were members of the Co-operative, so when dinner was served she would say 'eat up; the more you eat the bigger the dividend.'[109] Yet the truth was that her visitors were a politicized group. As time passed and the Volunteers became armed, visitors to the Connolly home came carrying military equipment, including gelignite. On one occasion two men came from Glasgow, visiting the Connolly family house before being brought by Nora and Ina to the Dublin train. After they departed, the police called on Lillie, who told them: 'whatever my girls do they would never keep their boyfriends here all night without consulting me and of course I would never put up with that.'[110] She waited anxiously for the girls to get back home, fearing that they would be arrested. She had not brought any of her neighbours into her confidence.

Ina and Nora tried to be in Dublin as often as possible with their father, taking part in political activities at his behest. However, James did not curb his criticism of his own family when political activities were being discussed. He wrote to Winnie on 22 December 1915 about an unknown incident, and his dismissal of his daughter is noteworthy: '. . . I would not ask you to trust Nora on any other basis than on her merits. In this particular case I think she deserved a snub.'[111]

This did not prevent him from getting Nora selected for an intelligence mission and she set out for New York in December 1915, her father accompanying her as far as Liverpool. Her task was to give a message to Count Bernstorff, the German ambassador.[112] Even seventy years later, she refused to talk about what she did: 'I promised the leaders that I would never divulge it . . . I never say, even though all those connected with it are now dead.'[113] The trip caused a long period of separation from her family, which was particularly hard for her mother, who relied on her.

In January 1916 James had secret meetings over a period of days. During this time he was coopted on to the Military Council of the Irish Republican Brotherhood and a date was set for an uprising, for Easter Sunday 1916, under the guise of routine manoeuvres. James wrote that month: 'a defeat of England in India, Egypt and Balkans, or Flanders, would be so dangerous to the British Empire as conflict of armed forces in Ireland, that the time for Ireland's Battle is NOW – the place for Ireland's battle is here.'[114]

When Nora returned from New York in February 1916, before she went home to Belfast she went to see her father in Dublin. He would not hear her news privately, but took her immediately to a meeting at Liberty Hall. She later recalled that it was not until St Patrick's Day 1916, when she was in Dublin for a parade, that her father finally told her of plans for a rising at Easter:

> I think it must have been about March 1916, that Daddy told me definitely that the fight was to take place ... He said: 'Are you coming with me? Will you be with me during the fight?' I was torn, because I had been with the Belfast contingent all the time. As I said, I had trained them. I said to him: 'After all, I should be with them in the North. The girls will have more confidence if I am there.' And I wanted to be in Dublin with him. I did not know what to do. In the end, I decided to be with the Northern contingent . . .[115]

On 4 April 1916 it was suggested to the under-secretary for Ireland, Sir Matthew Nathan, that his administration might consider the possibility of seizing Liberty Hall, confiscating weapons belonging to the Irish Citizen Army and deporting Connolly to Edinburgh, but he rejected all these suggestions as provocative.

On 14 April, Connolly cabled Winnie Carney: 'come to Dublin immediately.'[116] Lillie was also told to 'break up their home and go South.'[117] It is unknown how long she had been aware of her husband's plans to enter into armed conflict. His speeches and writing had for a long time been focused on the inevitability of revolution. Many years before, a woman had asked James, 'how come you know so much about revolutions?' He had replied: 'Madam, my business is revolution.'[118]

On Good Friday 1916, Lillie packed as if she were going on Easter holidays so as not to arouse the suspicion of the police who had them under surveillance: 'Every bit of clothing in the house was packed in trunks. The youngsters bustling in and out constantly asking the time; scrappy meals eaten at odd corners in the kitchen; the range roaring from the letters and papers that must be destroyed before the house was left.'

Lillie stood in the doorway of the kitchen, as Nora stooped over the range, burning piles of letters and documents. Nora later wrote that her mother 'looked sad and wistful' and the two locked eyes for what seemed to Nora a long time. Her mother's lips were tight and she was shaking her head. Nora spoke to her: 'Stop thinking, Mama. You mustn't look sad when you're going on holidays.'[119] In a voice that broke with emotion, her mother repeated the word 'holidays' with such despair that Nora came and put her arm around her. This was a pretence that they must carry through in order that the authorities would not suspect anything, but 'This was not an easy leave taking, for there was a fair chance of the house being sacked and burned.' Lillie 'went about, picking up little things that would go in her trunk but the absence of which would not be noticed if any inquisitive policeman came in to see whether anything suspicious was going on.'[120] As they left, she did not look back or give any show of feeling; she was just closing the door on yet another house. During the twenty-five years they had been married, life with James had been nomadic, unstable and full of want. Every five years they had moved on. Yet again, it was five years since she had come to Belfast.

It was Holy Thursday when Lillie parted with her daughters Nora and Ina at the station in Belfast, tears running down her face as she gave them a pound each. Both girls were to fight in Coalisland, but a message reached them there on Easter Sunday that the manoeuvres had been cancelled. The two of them, along with four other Belfast girls, decided to make their way to Dublin, to Liberty Hall.

When Lillie arrived in Dublin she met with James and went with him to Liberty Hall. There they had an argument when James said that fifteen-year-old Roddy was to take part in the fight. Lillie believed that he was too young. Fiona, who was seven at the time, recalled that her mother looked at her father anxiously, saying: 'but he is only a child, James'. Fiona remembered that her father made a stern reply: 'He is fifteen, Lillie.' James's own career as a soldier had already begun when he was a year younger. Lillie lost the argument and Roddy stayed with his father. Fiona remembered that he was a 'stern, serious and unsmiling father' when they left him.[121]

4

Fanny and Edward

It was on the Gaelic League's annual excursion from Dublin to Galway in June 1901 that Fanny met Edward; 'a day of fate' she would call it. A friend had used her influence for Fanny O'Brennan and her elder sister Lily to sit in the special committee carriage, alongside the teachers and the best Irish speakers. Fanny sat demurely watching and listening to the banter and chat of those on the train. She had just left school and was conscious that she wished to appear as a young woman and not as the schoolgirl that she had been some weeks previously. As the train rattled its way across the country, she found herself transfixed by a dark-haired youth. She would later describe him as 'tall and handsome', recalling how his eyes sparkled as they met with hers. He sought out the attention of his fellow passengers by whistling, as 'sweet as a bird on a bush.' He whistled 'old traditional airs, hornpipes, reels, jigs'; his selection of Irish music seemed inexhaustible. When the train crossed the River Shannon, Edward Kent called for 'three cheers for the people of Connaught.'[1] The division of the country by the Shannon into eastern and western regions was for many not just a geographical division; the west of the country in 1901 preserved a strong link to the traditional way of life that Irishmen and women had lived for centuries. At each station Edward would go on the platform and converse with the locals in Irish.

It was a source of great pride to Edward Kent that his birthplace was the village of Ballymoe in County Galway, in the province of

Connaught. He was born in the Royal Irish Constabulary Barracks on 21 September 1881 to Johanna Kent (*née* Galwey) and her husband James, the local constable, whose role was to enforce the rule of law of the British administration. James Kent, like many other members of the police force, was a native Irish speaker. He was originally from Tipperary but had been posted outside his native county. Two years after Edward's birth James was promoted head constable and the family left Galway for County Louth. Edward's older siblings were William Leeman, born 1874; Ellen (known as Nell), born 1875; James, born 1876; and Michael, born 1879. There was another brother, John Patrick, whose birthdate is unknown. The last of the Kent family, Richard, was born in Louth in 1884.

When Edward (known as Ned) was ten, his father retired from the Constabulary and the family moved to Dublin, where Edward's mother died when he was fourteen. Although her death is said to have affected him deeply, it was also noted that he showed remarkable composure and remained silent for the mourning period. When he did mention her years later, it was to recall that she often called him a 'little weasel' because of his vicious temper. During his childhood he felt isolated within the family, later writing: 'I have so often been described as selfish in the former home circle as to have come to look with wonder on anyone who showed regard for me.'[2]

The brothers who were still of school age when the Kents came to Dublin in 1891 were educated by the Christian Brothers in North Richmond Street – the same school James Joyce attended for a short time in 1892–3.[3] Edward's diary entries from the time indicate that his education broadened his outlook, stirring an awareness of nationalism and his native language. He recorded that one of his teachers, a Mr Maunsell, had 'waxed enthusiastic about love of country'. Elsewhere he notes that he wrote a composition on nationalism entitled 'A good cause makes a stout heart'.

Edward did not opt to learn Irish (known as Celtic in his school), although he was keenly interested in languages and studied French and German. When he went to Dublin port to converse with seamen from different countries, he was very taken with the Breton sailors, impressed by their nationalism and their use of their own Celtic language. Significantly, on 5 April 1897, he signed his school diary with his name in Irish – Éamonn Ceannt.

Edward's final results in 1898 were the highest attained in his class that year and he was asked to address the school. His performance impressed his father so much that he is said to have exclaimed: 'My boy will do something great yet.'[4] Edward had still not settled on a career. He applied for a job as a journalist with the *Irish Independent* but, on hearing the hours required, decided against taking it. He was working as an assistant teacher when he was successful in securing a position as a clerical assistant in the City Treasurer and Estate and Finances Offices, with a salary of £70 per annum plus an annual increment of £5. Although he was now working within the administration, Edward's politics were increasingly against the ruling elite; he justified his decision to work for the Corporation by saying that his wages were paid by the citizens of Dublin, not by the Treasury out of taxation.

His opposition to the British government's foreign policy was demonstrated by his support for the Boers during the Boer War, which began in 1899. Edward's older brother William served with the Royal Dublin Fusiliers on the British side in the conflict,[5] but despite his brother's involvement Edward asked his sister Nell to make a Boer flag, which he flew from a tree in the garden for several days until it was brought to the attention of his father, who had it removed.

Edward had begun a double life, spending his free time amongst organizations and people who shared his interest in Irish nationalism and Irish culture. At the age of nineteen he bought a book, *Easy Lessons in Irish*, and his studies soon led him to join the Gaelic League, one of the organizations in the fledgling Irish-language revival movement. He grew so committed to becoming proficient in the language that he was known to stay in his room studying when his brothers and their friends were 'downstairs dancing and amusing themselves'. His days off were spent in the National Library and he carried a book with him constantly so that he could read in Irish at every opportunity. Within a year he had become a member of the governing body of the Gaelic League and a teacher at the Central Branch. He also established a branch of the organization in Fairview, and was involved in setting up a college for training Irish-language teachers. One account records that 'To his fellow workers and his superiors he was simply another clerk, quiet and retiring, studious and diligent, but his evenings and his thoughts were given more and more to the Gaelic League and Gaelic music.'[6]

A gifted musician, Edward began to play the Irish war and Uilieann pipes, as well as the violin, flute and tin whistle. He and his brothers formed the Kent Brothers band, but by 1900 he severed another link with his family when he stopped playing with them to focus on playing the pipes. In February 1900 he was a founder member of the Irish Pipers' Club, Cumann na bPíobairí, taking on the role of secretary and insisting 'that Irish shall, as far as possible, be the official language of the club'.[7] He purchased a printing press and in the summer of 1901 organized the club journal, *An Píobaire*, the first edition of which appeared on 5 July 1901. As well as instruction in the pipes, the club also provided fiddle, singing and dancing lessons. The committee did not confine its activities to the Dublin region, but invited and paid for pipers from Westmeath, Monaghan, Kerry, Wicklow and Galway to attend the Dublin regional competition, the Leinster Feis. This network grew year by year, including pipers from America and elsewhere who came to Ireland to take part. Edward wrote to a piper in Chicago suggesting that he should visit their club: 'the gaels of Ireland will extend to you a Céad Míle Fáilte [a hundred thousand welcomes].'[8]

In 1902, for St Patrick's Day, Éamonn Ceannt (no longer answering to his given name of Edward Kent) organized a language parade which saw seven hundred people marching through Dublin. Within four years he had acquired such fluency and ability with Irish that he was considered one of the best Irish-language teachers in Dublin. At the Gaelic League Fanny O'Brennan became one of his pupils. She would later write: 'There was no interest in politics by the young folk. There were too many divisions. The Gaelic League, where there were no politics spoken, was a mecca for everyone. The people learned they had a language, they learned the music, the dancing and the games.'[9]

Fanny attended classes at headquarters in the centre of Dublin, where most active young Irish nationalists gathered. The club admitted women and was a 'respectable' way to socialize. There were weekly classes, céilis (dances) and summer holidays in Irish-speaking colleges and Gaeltacht regions – those parts of the country where Irish was still the first language. The young people began to use the Irish forms of their names – Sinéad instead of Jane, Máire instead of Mary and Cáit instead of Catherine. Some of them adopted an Irish style of dress: the men wore kilts and women brats or capes, and dresses with Celtic symbols embroidered on them. Éamonn, who liked to sketch, later made a small drawing of the Gaelic League Headquarters at 24 Upper O'Connell Street as a keepsake for Fanny, recalling the days when he was teaching her *and* falling in love with her.

Fanny's life was completely transformed after she met Edward Kent. The change would be so complete that in time she would even become known by a completely different name. Had he changed her? Or would that transformation have happened anyway? Fanny, christened Frances Mary O'Brennan, came from a more national-istic background than Éamonn. She never knew her father, Frank O'Brennan, who died after a short illness four months before her birth on 23 September 1880. Frank was twenty years older than her mother, Elizabeth Butler, and had been active in the Fenian Brotherhood. The story of his escape to Dublin, disguised as a ped-dler of clocks, in the aftermath of the Fenians' abortive uprising against the British in 1867 was often retold to his daughters. He was adopted and had also lived in America before his marriage, but little else is known of him.

Fanny was the youngest in a family of four girls: Mary Josephine, born in 1875; Catherine (known as Kit, although in later life she called herself Kathleen), born in 1876; and Elizabeth Mary (known as Lily), born in 1878. Their mother, widowed while still in her twenties, put on widow's weeds that she wore for the rest of her life and 'retired from her friends'. Her focus became her 'duty' to secure her girls a good education. The girls attended school at the Dominican convent in Dublin's Eccles Street, known for its progressive education for young women. During her long widowhood, with no widow's pension or welfare system, Elizabeth O'Brennan was the sole provider for her family, save what assistance was available from her own family. She opted for a job with a pension. In 1901 she was working as a ward mistress at the South Dublin Union Workhouse, one of the 115 staff members. The workhouse operated under the Poor Law system, providing institutional relief for the destitute. Elizabeth obtained accommodation in the Union officers' quarters, along with her elderly mother, also called Elizabeth, and her two youngest daughters. The eldest girl, Mary, had become a crèche superintendant and moved to Europe, while Kit was a journalist and no longer lived with her mother and sisters.

It was on Easter Monday in 1903 that Éamonn and Fanny became a couple. They were on an outing with a party of friends, walking in Shankill, in the countryside overlooking Dublin Bay, when they became separated from the group, leaving them alone. Writing a year later Éamonn recalled:

> Do you remember the first kiss I gave you, darling? You thought it was a sin and you went to Confession and asked the priest, my poor girl! Well you know now that I was in love with you and I wanted to marry you. And I was the first man to kiss you. Well, girleen, I don't think you regret it now. Please say you don't and that you never will. What will you do Easter Monday? You can't go out to Shankill again? We had peace that day last year and I remember well the kiss you gave me then, under the sky. It's not a cause of embarrassment, not at all.[10]

By June 1903 Éamonn had settled on using the Irish name of
Áine for Fanny, rather than Proinseas, a more literal translation
of Frances.[11] The earliest surviving letters between the two were
written in Irish by Éamonn in 1903, two years after their first
encounter. None of Áine's correspondence survives. One of
Éamonn's first letters is signed 'Do mhúinteoir cráite [Your
harassed teacher].'[12] Others relate to their committee work. In April
1903 he asked her to join Cumann na bPíobairí and later to serve
on the committee with him; shortly afterwards she was appointed
treasurer.

Throughout 1904 Éamonn remained Áine's secret admirer, as he
did not make public his feelings for her to his family, friends or their
wider circle. In his youth he had been known to his schoolfriends as
shy and bashful, and according to his more sociable brother
Richard, Éamonn 'was "no good" at a party, he didn't dance or flirt
or romp about like others of us. He looked on in his quiet way.'[13]

Áine and Éamonn worked near to each other in the vicinity of
Dublin Castle, the centre of the British Administration. Éamonn
worked at the rates office in Cork Hill, from where he could see
Áine, who was working as a clerk, going to and from her office. He
would not go to speak to her, but often watched her from his office
window, writing to her in Irish: 'I think you looked very well when I
saw you today. I hope you are well.' In the same letter he wrote: 'It
will be a long time till I see you and it will seem longer now that I
have become accustomed to seeing you every day. Little as it seems,
I like to see you at dinnertime even if I don't venture to speak to you.
I thought you looked in good form today.'[14] He also watched her in
the distance at the club, writing: 'You were dancing last night and
you looked in good form. Were you, my little darling?'[15] She became
his 'little Darling' or 'little Áine', as she was small in stature and he
was very tall. Áine accepted his terms for their courtship, understanding that he reserved his private side, and his sense of humour,
for those closest to him.

In his new circle, Éamonn was described as 'extremely reserved',
and it was commented that 'you never knew his full mind.'[16] He

spoke little, but always to the point; his face was usually grave and rather expressionless. In one of his earliest letters to Áine he closes with: '*An fear ta I ngrá leis féin – má'is fíor do na daoine – sin é. Éamonn Ceannt. An Rúnaire Bocht.* [The man who is in love with himself – if people are to be believed – that's it. Éamonn Ceannt. The Poor Secretary]'.[17] He set himself apart with his single-minded and focused approach. He never smoked or drank, and it was clear even in his appearance that he was a man of strong principles. He wore a moustache in defiance, he claimed, of laws enforced in the fourteenth and fifteenth centuries, which sought to compel those dwelling in the county of Dublin and the surrounding areas to wear their clothes and beards in the English manner. Later Henry VIII went as far as outlawing the *croiméal* (moustache), as well as other clothes and fashions used by the native Irish. Éamonn claimed that this law had never been repealed, so he delighted in breaking it. He also liked to have a moustache because he felt it gave him a military appearance.

Éamonn's life now centred on concerts, teaching and competitions; he was in demand as a player and an adjudicator at both pipe and fiddle competitions and also at competitions for teaching Irish. In June 1903 he travelled with fellow musicians to London, where they stayed at the Temperance Hotel at Ludgate Hill. It was his first experience of London, and he wrote: 'We saw a little of the town already, but believe me, it's bigger than one would think at first.'[18]

His holidays were spent in County Galway, where he felt at home and seemed to find his voice in the Irish language. He expressed his kinship with the people of Galway and revelled in speaking the language for four days without using English at all. He perfected his musical technique by spending time with other musicians, such as the blind piper Martin Reilly. He also enjoyed boating and hunting. His surviving letters are in Irish, although he often used a mixture of both Irish and English.

During his stay in the summer of 1903 he corresponded with Áine from various hotels. Writing on 21 July, he told her that he missed her:

Áine, darling

Tell me you have been a good girl and sent me a letter?. . . At the
Feis, a man sang a song and here is 2 lines from it 'if you are to be
with me, be with me night and day, if you are with me be with me
in every inch of my heart'. It reminded me of my girleen Áine, up
in Dublin. Are you lonely for me? I think of my 'bright love' often
since I left her that night. That we may be together again soon! . . .
Don't be afraid. Whatever you want to say, say it Áine darling, and
it will please me. Blessings to you, darling.

Éamonn

And so the romance with his pupil continued, often by letter,
during periods of separation. In December 1903, when both of
them were confined to their homes because of ill health, Éamonn
wrote that he was content that their relationship was based on a
compatibility: 'Somehow, I have a great faith in this lovemaking of
ours. I can look back on no time when we depended for mutual
pleasure on the trifling and flattery upon which flirtations are built.
It seems to me that at all times we found simple companionship sufficient . . .'[19] Their companionship took the form of long walks in
the town and countryside in all weathers and seasons. Éamonn provided wonderful entertainment in the countryside, as he could
imitate the call of any bird. He wrote how he cherished his
memories of Áine: 'running down a mountain side in summer
costume or seeing who'd walk faster on a long snowy road on a frosty
night in moonlit winter.'

As their affections deepened, Éamonn mused:

I wonder does she ask herself all the cross-questions he asks himself
questions about the intensity of our present affections – whether the
severest stress of circumstances will strengthen or diminish it . . . I
really pity you at times when I think of the brute that you love – you
of whose goodness I am only beginning to see the depth . . . Yet you
love me and give me your tender heart and your individual affection.
No wonder I can scarce believe it.[20]

For Christmas 1903 Éamonn's present to Áine was a brooch. He wrote: 'I'm glad you like the brooch the oftener you wear it the better twill please me.' They also discussed exchanging photographs.[21] Then, in the week before Christmas, he proposed. It was as if he had taken himself by surprise: 'I suddenly found my glib tongue halt in an unaccustomed manner and there I was putting my whole heart in four words "*An bposfaidh tú mé* [Will you marry me]."' He had made no plans and there was no ring. After he proposed he reflected that it was Áine who hoped that he had made the right choice in her: 'poor little Áithne, gentle, merry . . . unselfish Áithne, consented to become some day my little Áithne, my dearest wife. You say you hope never to do anything, which will make me regret the step. Well, well, sweetheart I believe you. I would trust my life to you freely, knowing that you would willingly do me no injury . . . I never forgot that you and I had entered upon a new path since last Sunday night.'

Over that Christmas period Éamonn had lots of visitors who asked him to play for them; he wrote to his sweetheart with amusement that they were 'admiring my bachelor bliss' while he only felt lonely for her, but still he told no one he was engaged. Being Christmas, they could not meet at their 'usual' spot. He wrote to her on Christmas Eve:

And yet at times I feel proud to see my dear girl looking up to me so. It gives me the feeling of a protector, of a guardian, to see your dear, childlike, innocent, trustful look at me and to know that some day in any case I shall be your acknowledged protector, your husband. People say that 'sweetheart' and 'lover' are more inspiring and romantic and poetical than 'husband' and 'wife'. But for me since you gave me the right I have never tired of repeating to myself 'Áithne-little-wife-that-will-be'. And every time I find an added pleasure.[22]

He also wrote to her that he would give her her own home, adding: 'we shall share with no one . . . What do you think of wanting the luxury of a servant – of dainty fare – of grand furniture . . . I fear my miserable salary put these things all out of our reach,

119

little one. Will you mind?' Even as he asked this he would have been aware that such luxuries were not part of the upbringing of the O'Brennan family, who had lived in staff quarters at the South Dublin Union workhouse. Áine would have witnessed first hand the separation of families – 3,637 men, women and children lived in the segregated sections of the workhouse complex. She had been exposed to the hardship of that institution and, although her thoughts and feelings are undocumented, she would have been well aware of the hatred amongst her fellow countrymen and women for these workhouses. The family had just recently moved from it; they were now living on the South Circular Road.

Éamonn wrote about future furniture-buying and a prospective venue for their wedding breakfast, speculating that the marriage would be in a few months' time, but no public announcement was made, no news of their engagement shared and no date set, and the clandestine nature of their engagement was uppermost in his mind; he wrote to Áine on St Stephen's Day, 26 December, reminding her to keep his proposal secret: 'You won't tell anyone that Éamonn is in love with you and that he asked you to marry him. You won't tell yet. But that said, you know that Éamonn has given you his heart's love. You know that it is of you I think day and night.'[23] Elsewhere he wrote: 'Do you know I haven't the slightest doubt or fear of committing my happiness to you Áine and I think a wife makes or mars a man's happiness just as a husband can make his wife happy or miserable.'[24] Áine had grown up without a father or brothers; she had been educated by nuns in an all girls' school. She would have had no experience of men, nor any comprehension of the norms of married life.

Throughout 1904, the letters continued to discuss their future life together:

No news to tell at all little girl but to remind you that in a few months time, with the help of God, you will have become my prisoner for ever more . . . I can then for the first time look at you with the eye of ownership. How will you like that girleen? A new little wife you'll be that first day, owned by a man,[25] 'bossed' by a man, loved by a man. You won't forget that last word. No you won't . . . Be 'good' and have a nice smile for me at one and I'll have one for you. I could not give you then what I send you now a 100 kisses. *Beannacht agat a stor* [Goodbye and good luck for now, my darling].[26]

The fact that Éamonn was not making their engagement official was not the norm and Áine showed considerable tolerance in complying with his wishes for secrecy. Indeed, the fact that Áine allowed Éamonn to dictate the terms of the courtship shows a remarkable degree of acceptance of him; he constantly remarked on her unselfish nature. During the Victorian era, once an engagement was official it would commonly last up to two years, and couples could hold hands in public and spend time alone. Failure to follow these rules could ruin the reputation of the woman. Now, at the start of the Edwardian era, independent young working women, such as Áine was, were changing society, but a woman's respectability was still of vital importance in the conservative Catholic society of Dublin in the opening years of the new century. Áine was also a practising Catholic, adhering to rules of the religion regarding intimacy before marriage.

There was a potential setback to Éamonn's plans when on 14 February 1904, Valentine's Day, an unidentified suitor made himself known to Áine, as neither he nor anyone else was aware that she had an understanding with Éamonn Ceannt. It is not known how she rejected him, but even this did not spur on Éamonn to make their relationship public. He responded:

I think today's affair will teach me a lesson – to appreciate you at your real value. I try to put myself in some one else's place and Lord what a world this would be to face. It's hard enough without that awful deprivation. I don't know what to write sweetheart but hope you'll be satisfied with this. I feel as a rich man would who has watched a poor man's agony. I can't dare enjoy my riches – calling you my own sweet darling. God help him, child and bless you. Just an embrace from Éamonn.[27]

By March 1904 Éamonn had moved again, to 2 Windsor Terrace, Fairview, from where he wrote on St Patrick's Day:

> Wait till I have you in our house. I wonder what you'll say to my practising and tuning and similar annoyances. Eh sweetheart, I wonder how will my little wife behave then. Pull my hair and say comical things or maybe smile and be pleased. Aye, that's what she'll do I'm sure. In fact, I can never reconcile my conscience to the fact that I have got such a sweet, yielding, good, kind girleen for my future wife. Instead of harshness and rudeness and all the ugly things I deserve, I get gentleness and love . . . I hope to make you happy all the same . . .[28]

Their engagement had been a secret for four months when Éamonn wrote on 1 April 1904 that he could not wait to be married: 'I often think of the day when we will be married. We will always remember that day. May God give us a long life. O Áine, darling, isn't it a pity we can't marry soon. There is nothing I would prefer than to be together in our own home, my darling near me, I can't wait for the day'.[29]

He teased her in a letter later that month that her mother and her sister Kit still did not know about their marriage plans, although he had relented and agreed that she could confide in Lily. 'I wonder what will your mother think of her son-in-law when she comes to hear of it eh? I must prepare the way by telling Cathleen [Kit] if she doesn't know or guess already. Lily may have told her. What will your life be worth then girleen? . . . Your Éamonn.'

There is no record of when the couple finally broke the news of their betrothal, nor of Mrs O'Brennan's and Kit's reactions, but presumably they raised no significant objections because, a year and a half after their engagement, Éamonn and Áine finally became man and wife. On 29 May 1905 he collected the wedding ring and keeper[30] – he always retained the receipt – and the couple married on 7 June 1905 in St James' Church in James Street in the centre of the Liberties in Dublin. The celebrant was Father Anderson, who had returned from France to conduct the ceremony in Irish. Since there was no Irish coinage, Éamonn used five French francs of silver and gold for the symbolic ritual gift.

Shortly after their marriage, Éamonn brought Áine to meet a friend, who later wrote: 'I could understand her appeal for Éamonn. Her gentleness, her sweetness would appeal to his chivalry, and she seemed to be loved and protected, from every rude wind of fate.'[31] Áine may have been perceived in this way, but beneath her exterior was a steely strength of character that would come to the fore later, when she became the protector and not the protected.

Following their marriage the couple moved to a house that Éamonn had begun renting in May 1905, at 44 Reuben Avenue on the South Circular Road. Despite his desire that they should live alone, Áine's mother and her older sister Lily came to live with them (their grand-mother had died). It was in this house that Áine gave birth to their only child, a son named Rónán, born just after the first anniversary of their marriage, on 18 June 1906.[32] Éamonn insisted on the bap-tismal ceremony being in Irish and he also registered the birth in Irish. 'This created a furore, and many letters passed between the Registrar and himself,' Áine remembered, 'but Éamonn held to his point and insisted on the Irish.'[33] From the moment of his birth, he spoke to his son only in Irish.

Little is recorded of Áine as a young mother, though it is known that when Rónán was five months old she almost died from septic poisoning (which without rapid diagnosis could be fatal). She made a full recovery, however, and after this event life took on a regular pattern for the couple. Unusually for the time, they had no other children.[34] Éamonn still continued to work as an official in Dublin Corporation and served on internal committees working to improve conditions and pay for his fellow workers, but he considered leaving to take up other occupations. He tried his hand at market gardening on a small scale, and even for a while considered opening an advertising agency.[35]

Éamonn's exceptional ability as a piper was recognized when he won a gold medal at the Oireachtas (the annual cultural gathering), in 1906. He studied the history of piping and collected Irish music, and he later spoke on the subject of Irish pipes and pipers at the National Museum of Ireland.[36] In September 1908 he went to Rome to play the pipes, accompanying athletes from the Catholic Young Men's Society in Ireland who were taking part in an international athletics competition being held in the Vatican gardens. A large number of countries were represented, but England was not. The idea of having the Irish piper with the team was to illustrate the cultural difference of the Irish people, and to show that Ireland was a separate nation. When Pope Pius X heard of the Irish piper, he asked him to play for him in a private audience. Éamonn wore a replica of an eleventh-century Irish costume and throughout the trip was determined not to use English. He succeeded in his aim by speaking in French and Irish; he also tried a bit of German and a few words of Italian.

Áine later said that it was during 1908 that Éamonn's mind became fixed on the idea of fighting for Irish freedom. The previous year he had joined Sinn Féin, the political group formed by Arthur Griffith in 1905. According to Áine it advocated a policy of self-reliance, the election to parliament of men who would not sit in the British House of Commons but would sit in Ireland. As Áine recalled, the organization 'did not take on very well throughout the country, but Dublin was a strong centre, with some of the most advanced thinkers in the city among its members.'[37] Éamonn became a member of its Central Branch and was quickly co-opted as a committee member of that branch, then later elected to the National Council. As well as his involvement in Sinn Féin, he also served on a committee supporting the sale of Irish-made goods, which set up An Aonach (The Fair) to allow Irish manufacturers to sell direct to the public.

Éamonn's involvement in Sinn Féin exposed him to ideas of more advanced nationalism, but the fact that his father was still alive prevented him from fully advocating physical force as a way of gaining Irish independence.

In 1909 the Ceannt family, along with Mrs O'Brennan and Lily, moved to Bloomfield, Herberton Lane, Dolphin's Barn in Dublin. By this time Elizabeth O'Brennan appears to have taken the place of the mother Éamonn had lost in childhood. The O'Brennan sisters, known as 'that cultured family', remained closely involved with the activities of the nationalist movement. Kit was still working as a journalist, writing for a number of papers including the London *Times*, while Lily wrote plays and stories but earned her living as a clerk.

For the rest of her life, Áine used the title 'Bean Éamonn Ceannt'. Throughout this period her husband was involved in lengthy correspondence with the post office, the office of the Registrar and the bank about the use of the Irish language in his business transactions. In 1911, details for the entire household were inserted in the Census in Irish.

In the same year, Dublin opinion was divided on the subject of King George V's visit to Ireland that July. Éamonn managed to stage a small protest, using his position in the Corporation to get a permit for the erection of two poles in Grafton Street. They were not festooned with words of welcome, however, but with a banner which read: 'Thou are not conquered yet dear land.'[38] It was in place for only a short time before the police removed it, but it was depicted in a cartoon issued as a souvenir postcard illustrating this protest.

In 1912 Éamonn commissioned the artist Grace Gifford to illustrate a broadsheet to encourage ballad singers to use Irish in the Gaeltacht. He also contributed to an Irish-language newspaper published by P. H. Pearse, the schoolteacher who was becoming central to all cultural and nationalist activities. The paper, *An Barr Buadh* [The Trumpet of Victory], ran for eleven issues from 16 March of that year. On 17 March 1912, the day after the first issue was launched, Éamonn's father died.

Later that year, Éamonn joined the Irish Republican Brotherhood, the secret organization that advocated securing Irish independence by force if necessary. His diary entry for the 12th of the 12th month of 1912 recorded: '*Is Iongantach an lá é seo, is iongan-tach an lá dom-sa freisin é* [This is a wonderful day and a wonderful day for me also].' Áine believed that this entry marked the day he was sworn into the Brotherhood. He was sworn in by Seán Mac Diarmada, who had joined the IRB himself in 1906, with the words:

> In the presence of God I Éamonn Ceannt do solemnly swear that I will do my utmost to establish the national independence of Ireland, and that I will bear true allegiance to the Supreme Council of the Irish Republican Brotherhood and Government of the Irish Republic and implicitly obey the constitution of the Irish Republican Brotherhood and all my superior officers and that I will preserve inviolable the secrets of the organisation.[39]

At the Sinn Féin National Council, Éamonn put forward a proposal that all Sinn Féin members be trained in the use of firearms, stating that he believed the time had come for rebellion and that nationalists should avail themselves of military training. Áine had been aware for some time of her husband's desire for armed conflict; among his possessions were a book called *How to Shoot* by Ernest H. Robinson and an American pamphlet on the Mauser self-loading pistol, and he set up a firing range at their home at Dolphin's Barn.

In March 1912 Éamonn gave a lecture to the Socialist Party of Ireland on 'Constitutional Agitation'.[40] In November 1913 he wrote of his belief in the extension of the Volunteer movement to nationalist Ireland.[41] He attended the formation meeting of the Irish Volunteers in Wynn's Hotel and the subsequent meeting at the Rotunda. He joined the 4th Battalion, which was training in Kimmage, and afterwards was appointed captain of A Company. At the outset, the battalion to which he belonged had 2,500 men.[42]

At the outbreak of the First World War in 1914 the Ceannts were at the centre of a group of Irishmen and women who looked on this as a time for the Irish to fight for their freedom from the British

Empire. John Redmond, leader of the Home Rule Party, wished to place twenty-five of his own nominees on the Provisional Council of the Volunteers, but when it came to a vote the proposal was opposed by eight men, including Éamonn Ceannt.[43] In August 1914, when Redmond's call for men to join the British war effort brought about a division in the Volunteer movement, with the National Volunteers splitting off, Éamonn Ceannt became the officer in charge of the 4th Battalion of the remaining Irish Volunteers, which consisted of about three hundred men.[44]

Áine attended the first meeting of Cumann na mBan (the Council of Women) in April 1914 along with her sister Lily and Kathleen Clarke. This group formed the first branch, Central Branch, and they rented rooms from the Gaelic League in Parnell Square for their meetings. They lost some members in November 1914 when the group declared support for the Irish Volunteers. Members became efficient in drilling, marching and first aid, and Áine and Lily were among the most active members of the organization.

Áine was also a founder of a short-lived organization for boys, Buachaillí na hÉireann (literally 'Boys of Ireland'). A small committee, which also included Kathleen Clarke, undertook to launch this movement and Áine later recounted: 'We progressed sufficiently far to hold one large meeting . . . which was addressed by PH Pearse.' However, there were objections to the new venture, as there was already an organization for boys called Na Fianna Éireann and Áine said that she and the committee decided that 'sooner than have trouble or dissension, the idea of Buachaillí na hÉireann was abandoned.'[45]

Áine and Lily continued to play an active role in Cumann na mBan with their first aid classes and fundraising for the Defence of Ireland fund. Kit was not involved in this development, as she went to America in October 1914 for a brief stay but had to remain there because of wartime travel restrictions. She tried to find work as a journalist, and in time moved to California, where she spoke at various clubs on Gaelic customs and arts.[46]

The Ceannts, along with the O'Brennans, moved again in 1914, this time to another house in Dolphin's Barn – 2 Dolphin Terrace. The following year Lily decided to set up a private preparatory school there for Catholic boys and girls, which she called Scoil Naoimh Rónán. Rónán, her nephew, was not one of the pupils. At the age of eight he attended P. H. Pearse's school, St Enda's, at its new location in the Hermitage, a historic demesne a mile outside Rathfarnham village. Guest lectures were given by the scholar and founder of the Gaelic League Douglas Hyde in Irish language and literature; classes in Irish history and archaeology were given by Professor Eoin MacNeill; W. B. Yeats gave talks on literature. Professor David Houston taught science lessons, which included instruction in 'the presence of nature itself' by means of object lessons conducted in the school grounds or in the course of country walks.'[47]

On 5 September 1914 it was agreed at the IRB Supreme Council that a rising would take place and that they would accept any assistance that Germany could offer. Action would be taken if conscription was imposed, if Germany invaded Ireland or if it looked as if the war was coming to an end. Éamonn organized a Nationalist Conference on 9 September in the library of the Gaelic League offices; those in attendance included P. H. Pearse, Joseph Plunkett, Seán Mac Diarmada, Tom Clarke, John MacBride, Thomas MacDonagh, Arthur Griffith and James Connolly.

Éamonn remained on the committee of the now reduced Volunteer organization following their convention in October 1914. He was financial secretary of the Irish Volunteers in their newly formed separate organization, while Pearse was press secretary and Joe Plunkett was co-treasurer. Eoin MacNeill was chairman. The following March, the heads of battalions were promoted to commandant, and Éamonn was also in charge of communications.

In May 1915 he was appointed a member of the Irish Republican Brotherhood's Military Council and so was intimately connected with preparations for a rising, which it was believed would happen in the near future. Throughout 1915 he gathered maps of towns such as Nenagh in Tipperary, Borris and Edenderry in Offaly, Naas and Maynooth in Kildare from members of the Volunteers, and he enquired about the communications used by the organization in these areas. He gave a lecture in May on 'street fighting'.

Every summer Rónán accompanied his parents to the west of Ireland to be among native speakers; as Áine later recalled, 'Éamonn was a Connachtman and his heart was there'.[48] However, in August 1915 there was a change in the holiday routine. Éamonn did play the pipes as usual in the country houses and at small céilís with the locals and students from the Irish College, but now at nights Áine and Rónán witnessed his involvement with the Volunteers. That summer he trained the local County Galway Volunteers, which involved drilling them and giving them instruction in all sorts of athletics. He also gave them advice on the use of guns.

By the late winter of 1915 Seán Mac Diarmada had sent a man called Francis Daly to Éamonn, who instructed him to make bombs. Daly later recounted that he was informed that 'in the Spring something would be doing.'[49]

In January 1916 the Military Council began to meet regularly at the Ceannt family home. It was only at the first meeting that Áine came in direct contact with the Council; she remembered seeing Tom Clarke, Seán Mac Diarmada and Patrick Pearse; some time later, James Connolly joined the meetings. Éamonn was naturally secretive about his activities and she remembered joking with him about this time: 'Give me some money before the Rebellion starts.' She was taken aback when he replied: 'It might start sooner than you expect.'[50] On 7 January 1916 Éamonn wrote in his notebook: 'In case of death I leave all my possessions present and future to my wife: failing her to my brother Richard in trust for my son Rónán, failing my son Rónán to Miss Lily O'Brennan, my sister-in-law.'[51]

During those early months of 1916 Áine worked together with the other members of Cumann na mBan making sleeping bags and providing provisions for men who had left England to escape conscription and had joined the 4th Battalion of the Irish Volunteers at Larkfield in Kimmage.

Áine remembered a change in her husband as Easter approached, with Éamonn refusing to go out to social events. He explained to her on the Sunday before Easter that the Military Council had met and arranged the roles the men would take in a new government of the Irish Republic; he was very pleased that he had been chosen to become minister of war. He told her some of the other posts, but Áine said she did not pay much attention to any of this, because she 'did not take the matter seriously.'[52]

The next day, Éamonn took a week's holiday from work; he had asked for and received a salary advance of £16 18s 6d on 19 April 1916. He said he took the holidays as, if the rumours of arrests proved to be true, 'he did not want to be caught like a rat in a trap' in his office.[53]

On the first day of the holiday he asked Áine and their son to accompany him to St Enda's School – a strange request, as Rónán's school was closed for Easter. Áine recalled: 'It was a glorious morning; the sun was shining, birds singing, fruit trees in full blossom and everything was promising peace and plenty . . . we had a pleasant lunch, the conversation roaming from books to music . . .' After lunch she and her son were sent out to wait in the garden, while her husband conversed alone with Pearse. She remembered how 'That wait in the grounds seemed an eternity', and it was only then that the reality dawned on her that the visit had not been social but business.

She was told by Éamonn on the Tuesday that a document had come from Dublin Castle to disarm and arrest Volunteers. This caused her some surprise, as she did not believe that the role of the Volunteers was to go out to attack but rather that they would go out to fight in defence. That night Éamonn placed his Mauser pistol beside the bed, remarking, 'we are living in stirring times'. Áine was relieved when she woke next morning that the night had passed peaceably. On Wednesday she occupied herself by going into the city to buy stores for knapsacks, as Éamonn and her sister Lily were, as she understood, going on manoeuvres that Easter weekend.

On Thursday there were constant callers. Áine convinced herself that her husband would tell her what was happening when the time was right. On Good Friday they were at church attending three o'clock devotions when a man entered and gave Éamonn a message. Later she recalled that they went to Phoenix Park for a walk that night; while there they clearly observed the British Army weapons store at the Magazine Fort being emptied by Volunteers. Éamonn made no mention of what they were witnessing; all that he told her was 'you can almost over-organise things.'

About six in the evening on Saturday, Éamonn finally told her that the Irish Volunteers were going out to fight the next day; that they had to strike a blow while England was at war or they would be a 'disgrace to the next generation'.[54]

It was not safe for her husband to spend the night in his own home; when he left at 10 p.m. Áine told her sister Lily the facts. Lily, like so many other members of the military organization, had believed that manoeuvres only were being planned. This had been a deliberate ploy by the leaders; they were well aware that before the Fenian Rising in 1867, when the participants were told they were to fight the next day, so many had attended churches to have their confessions heard that the authorities had been alerted that something was afoot. Ned Daly was the exception to this: he told his men that they were going out to fight on Easter Sunday and they went en masse to have their confessions heard in Mount Argus.

During the middle of the night Éamonn returned home and told Áine that when Eoin MacNeill realized what was being planned, he had cancelled the 'manoeuvres', which had been the cover for the start of the Rising. As the leader of the Volunteers his action was hard to overturn, and Éamonn said: 'MacNeill has ruined us – he has stopped the fight.' Áine later recalled: 'I immediately started to make suggestions, but Éamonn replied: "The countermanding order is in the hands of the [news]paper. I am off now to see if anything can be done."' He returned at 4 a.m., however, to say he had failed to contact anyone. Áine gave him some hot milk and suggested he should sleep. He joked that if he could sleep now then he could sleep on dynamite, but he took her advice and slept.

On Easter Sunday morning at 7.30 a.m. a note came from James Connolly: 'MacDonagh and I agree that it is important we have a conference immediately as various messengers are awaiting decision.'[55] Éamonn immediately took his bicycle and went to Liberty Hall, where it was decided to go ahead with the original plans for the Rising, starting the following day, 24 April.

When he returned home his older brother Michael and his sister Nell had come with news of the death of their aunt. Michael later recalled that it was a 'lovely sunny morning'; as they approached the house they saw a large number of bicycles along the railings in the front garden. The owners were in the front parlour of the house and 'appeared to be mere boys, we thought very little indeed of them, for I said "look what's going to free Ireland."' When Éamonn arrived they all stood to attention, while Michael looked on: 'I had the feeling, the whole thing was a jest: that they were boys playing at soldiers.' He wanted an opportunity to tell his younger brother to give up the Volunteers, for he felt sure there would be trouble and, like the vast majority of Irish people, he believed physical force against England, whose super-dreadnoughts could blow up Dublin City from nine or ten miles out to sea, would be utter madness. Éamonn did not take time to speak to them, however, even after they gave him the news of his aunt's death; instead he told Michael that he had written him a letter, which arrived later that day. It read: 'All well here – on the defensive. If the friends of small nationalities should decide on interfering with our inspections tomorrow I would advise you to make yourselves scarce . . . Come what may we are ready.'[56]

Later that day Éamonn asked Áine to accompany him as far as Howth. He did not speak much. She recalled him standing silently staring at the pier, where two years previously the famous gun-running had taken place. When they returned home she asked if she could help him; he gave her mobilization orders to fill in and when she asked him what she should insert he said 'Emerald Square

11 O'Clock'. It was then that he realized he had not told her that they were going out to start the rebellion the following day.

Éamonn slept at home that night, joking that thanks to MacNeill he could sleep in his own house; the British would not suspect anything now that the manoeuvres had been cancelled.

On Easter Monday morning, as the couple were alone in their room dressing, Áine asked her husband how long he expected the fighting to last. He replied, 'if we last a month they – the British – will come to terms.'

At quarter to eleven on 24 April 1916 Áine said goodbye to her husband at their home. She would have wished to go to Emerald Square to see the men march off, but Éamonn asked her not to. She embraced him, bade him God speed and he went out. His last words to her were: 'We'll trust in God.'[57]

Leaving her married home, Áine wore two dresses and carried all the money she possessed. She was accompanied by her mother and her ten-year-old son. They had a basket of food – a pretend picnic basket, in case anyone was watching their house. She locked the door and exited the life she had been living since her marriage a decade before. She later wrote: 'I crossed the threshold of that house, which would never mean home to me again, and closing the door I said farewell for ever to my ten years of happy married life.'[58]

5

Agnes and Michael

Michael Mallin was a British soldier in the 1st Battalion of the Royal Scots Fusiliers when he first met Agnes Hickey at the close of the year 1895. It was a chance meeting that brought them together. Michael was on leave and had been asked by a friend, Joe, who served in the army along with him, to deliver a letter to his relatives, the Hickey family, at their home in the Strawberry Beds, on the banks of the Liffey, the fruit-growing area on the outskirts of the city of Dublin.

They met a second time, and he later wrote to Agnes that when he pressed her hand to say goodnight, he recalled that she smiled at him as if daring him to kiss her. He had longed to snatch that kiss and said that if they had met again he would not have been able to resist.

Michael tried to get an extension to his leave so that he could spend more time with Agnes, but he failed. He had gone out to the Hickeys' home, never thinking that he was going to fall in love with one of the daughters of the family, just at the point where his regiment was due to depart for five years' service in India. Michael would later tell Agnes that he would give his friend Joe 'a good telling off' when he saw him for not letting him know that he 'had such a nice cousin years before he did'.

Despite just two brief meetings, Michael Mallin made a good impression on both Agnes and her mother Mary, though he did not meet her father. He would later write that Mary Hickey's good opinion of him was 'more than he deserved'.

Although enlistment in the British Army by Irishmen was common, it was the army of an occupying force. Agnes's maternal grandfather, John Francis Nugent, was a well-known Dublin printer who had moved in nationalist circles in his day and had been active in the fight for the independence of Ireland.

Agnes had been born in exile, as her father, Joseph Hickey, had spent eleven years in England, having been active in the short-lived Fenian Rising of 1867. Like many of the Fenians, he had previously served in the British Army.[1] He was in his late twenties when he went with his wife Mary to live in Liverpool, where his profession as a tailor meant that it was easy for him to find work. The couple had three children whilst living there: a boy, Patrick, and two girls, Mary Jane and Agnes, who was born in 1879. During the previous decade an amnesty had been granted to the Fenian leaders who had been imprisoned, and the key activist Jeremiah O'Donovan Rossa was released on condition that he would be exiled from Ireland for the rest of his life. As a result of these changes, Joseph, a member of the rank and file, felt that he and his family could return to Ireland. They came back to live in County Dublin, where another daughter, Josephine, was born in 1881.

Michael Thomas Mallin was twenty-one when he met seventeen-year-old Agnes. He was born on 1 December 1874 at 1 Ward's Hill, in the congested medieval centre of Dublin City known as the Liberties, in the shadow of Christ Church Cathedral. It was an area known as the Tenters, after the 'tents' of flax fibres stretched out to dry on frames across the fields in the days when weavers were based in the locality, and in the 1870s many weavers and their descendants still lived in this part of the city. Michael's mother had married from number 5 Ward's Hill, where her family were living.

Michael's mother, Sarah Dowling, a silk winder, had worked in a silk factory in Macclesfield, in the north of England, in her youth. There she had witnessed an attack on a police van in September 1867 when a number of Irish Fenians attempted to rescue Thomas J. Kelly and Timothy Deasy, who had been arrested and charged with involvement in the failed Fenian Uprising earlier that year.

During the attack a policeman, Sergeant Charles Brett, was killed. William Philip Allen, Michael Larkin and Michael O'Brien were hanged for this, although their conviction was questioned. They became known as the Manchester Martyrs and when Sarah expressed sympathy for them in her workplace she was asked to leave. Returning to live in Ireland, she met and married John Mallin, a 'strong nationalist'. John was a carpenter; his father Michael had had a small boat-building yard in Dublin, at 14 City Quay, which had been in the family for five generations, and where he made water pumps and blocks for sailing ships.

Of the eleven children born to the Mallins, only six survived. Michael was the eldest. A second boy, James, was born on 20 February 1877 but died in childhood. After this Michael and his parents lived for a number of years in the USA, in New Bedford, Massachusetts, where they had travelled in the hopes of locating Sarah's brother Bart, who had left his training for the priesthood to marry a girl from Connemara, then vanished with his new wife to America. Sarah and John did manage to find him, after which John returned to Ireland, while Sarah stayed on with Michael for a year or two. Eventually they followed John back home and the birth of another child, John Joseph, is recorded on 8 February 1880; again he died young.[2] Michael's surviving siblings were born in the 1880s and 1890s – Mary in 1880, followed by Thomas three years later, Catherine in 1889, John in 1892 and Bart in 1895.

Michael maintained close contact with his mother's family. He was very close to her brother James Dowling who was in the British Army and had served in India, where his wife and two children had died. When he returned to Ireland he lived with his second wife in a comfortable house close to Christ Church Cathedral, a short distance from Michael's home. The couple had no children, so Michael spent his holidays with them. When he was fourteen he was holidaying with them in the Curragh, where his uncle was then stationed, and one day he was taken by his aunt to hear the army band, as he had great musical ability and was eager to learn more instruments. He made up his mind to enlist and was recruited on

21 October 1889, delighted to be joining the band. On 24 October he reported for duty at Crinkill Barracks, Birr, County Offaly, which was then known as King's County, and for his first six years he was stationed at various barracks in Ireland, England and Scotland. In June of 1891 his rank was changed from 'boy' to 'drummer'; he became a marksman in 1894. He described his army life as quite uneventful until his departure – immediately after first meeting Agnes Hickey – for the North West Frontier of India.

The journey to India was the longest of Michael's life. He wrote to Agnes: 'I was very tired with the voyage but I seen some grand sights and fine places but none I like as well as Dublin you may be sure of that or a finer sight than Old Ireland.'[3]

For his first year he was stationed at Sialkot in the present-day Punjab province of Pakistan. His first surviving piece of correspondence[4] with Agnes, on 19 January 1896, began formally: 'My dear friend I received your very welcome letter as you say it takes a very long time to come you may depend I feel a little home sick and lonely it is a very long time to be away from home and friends but you know absence makes the heart grow fonder . . .'

Michael was anxious to maintain contact with Agnes: 'you must write often now don't forget indeed it was very kind of you to answer my letter five years is a long time to be away from home I will be an old man when I come back. I will see a great many changes when I come back if I am spared I hope I shall.'[5] He had promised to send his photograph, which she had requested, but it was not possible to get one taken in Sialkot.

Although he would later recall that Agnes had captured his heart the moment he saw her, he did not show his feelings for some time. 'I had made up my mind as soon as I came out here to keep my love all to myself,' he later told her, 'and if you were free to try and win you when I came home.'[6]

Michael was not a natural writer; it would be three months before he would write again, a letter dated 11 April 1896 that was very similar to the one he had written before, full of misspellings and a lack of punctuation: 'I was very much put about leaving home I did not think it would be so hard I hope you will not punish me for not writing to you before this . . . good by [sic] for five long years I sopose [sic] I shall see a great many changes by that time if I am spared good by [sic] again. I remain your Affectionate Friend.'[7]

From that point onwards Michael began to write to Agnes of his life at a frontier station, which he described as 'a very dangerous place', though he felt that Sialkot was 'about the best one of the lot'.[8] The brutality of life was evidenced in his experiences during the month of March 1897, when he and his fellow soldiers got lost in the woods, which he described as belonging to the 'Rajha of Jumus Domaine'. As he wrote to Agnes: 'the natives about there do not like us very much of course a crowd of them got around us and started beating us with sticks.' They would not have got away but for the fact that they had trained dogs with them: 'Natives are very frightened of dogs at least our dogs because the soldiers train them to hate natives.' Michael and some of the others were injured in the incident and their horses were cut. The drum major refused to allow any retaliation by the soldiers, however, as he said the area they were in did not belong to the British government and that the men had no right to be there.[9]

Michael's feelings about his own country's independence were not expressed at this time, but he recorded his delight when, for St Patrick's Day 1897, Agnes sent him a sprig of shamrock. His Catholicism was much more to the fore in his sense of identity. He was a member of the League of the Cross and as part of this organization he took part in an army concert on St Patrick's Night. He would spend his evenings at the Catholic Library set up at the camp, playing draughts and cards and talking about 'the Old Country'.[10]

By the summer of 1897 Michael was still addressing Agnes as 'my dear Miss Hickey' and signing his letters 'I remain your affectionate friend Michael Mallin'. He was also still anxiously waiting for her picture to be sent to him. Then Michael's letters ceased for a time, and when he did write to her again it was to tell her that there was a lot of fighting going on close to them but he believed that 'everything would quieten down very soon'.[11] He was mistaken, for by October he would be at the centre of the fighting and engaged in combat.

Michael was part of the Tirah Field Force, which consisted of over thirty thousand British and Indian troops. The Tirah region of British India was a key position in what was the traditional trade route of the Khyber Pass, an important mountain route into Afghanistan. A collection of tribes known as the Afridi had guarded the pass over the previous decades with monetary compensation from the British Indian government, but now, as a result of general unrest among the tribes, warfare had broken out between the tribes and the British Army.

In October 1897 Michael's battalion was posted to the Kohat Fort in the Ublan Pass, on the Punjab frontier. They had received orders to clear the enemy, the Bizotis tribe, from the hills about six miles from the fort. Michael joined the battle as a bugler, telling Agnes that they marched for six miles along the bed of a dried-out river and spent fourteen hours without food or drink, and that there were fatalities and injuries. In his words: 'it is a horrible sight to see the men coming down from the front they are coming down on an average one hundred sick and wounded per day we have lost one thousand three hundred and fifty nine men killed and wounded and goodness knows how many have died from sickness and how many are in Hospital . . .'[12] Others who were sick were invalided home. Michael himself received only a small wound in the neck from a piece of rock, which had been struck by a bullet.

During this campaign the troops slept outside their tents in case of attack and it was at this time that Michael contracted his first bout of malaria, the chronic form, with his spleen being affected. He was taken to hospital in Sialkot and recovered, but he lost two and a half stone in weight.

Michael's involvement in direct combat changed the tenor of his and Agnes's relationship. In October, a year and ten months after their correspondence began, he wrote to her for permission to use her first name, adding: 'it would also be a pleasure if you would call me Mike or Michael as you choose now don't forget.'[13] As fighting continued into December 1897, he wrote from Sialkot, addressing her as 'my dear Agnes', letting her know that he had to return to fighting: 'Just a few lines to let your [*sic*] know I have to go to the front at once we have lost a lot of men this last few days some of them are married it is very hard to see the women running about almost mad especially the married ones that have lost their husbands.'[14] As for the fight, he wrote: 'it is very near all over now I don't think I shall have to go up again.' He confided in her that 'his people' were very anxious about him. His own concern was that if he did not return to the front he would not get a medal.[15]

In mid-December 1897 Michael was posted to the Khyber Pass. He wrote to Agnes: 'we have to watch and not let Russia come down through India'.[16] Christmas Eve was spent lying under the walls of the Jamrud Fort, stationed at the entrance waiting for orders to proceed to the pass.

Agnes's Christmas gift from Michael was a shawl he had been knitting for her; before he departed from the fort for his march up the Khyber Pass he gave it to one of his friends to complete. His Christmas dinner was a piece of bread and a drink of water. There was some firing going on in front of him as he was marching up the pass and, although Michael himself was not wounded, there were many injuries and deaths. He recorded that one regiment lost three officers and thirty-one men wounded; the Yorkshire Regiment lost eight officers and fifteen men; while the 36th Silkes lost two officers, three men killed and two men wounded. There were also twelve men missing.

From the beginning of 1898 the couple were exchanging letters by return. Michael agonized about sending kisses, even if these were merely strokes of a pen on paper: 'Agnes I hope you will forgive me for taking the liberty of sending you kisses in my letters but if I were at home I would close up any angry words by kissing them away from your mouth.' He replied to her anxious enquiries about him, saying that he attributed to her prayers his safe return from the front and he hoped that her prayers would also 'fetch me home please

Kathleen Daly's family protested when the twenty-year-old wanted to marry Tom Clarke (**right**), twenty years her senior. He had just spent fifteen years in prison.

IRISH REBELLION, MAY 1916.

MAJOR JOHN McBRIDE
(Born in Westport, May 7th, 1868).
Executed in Kilmainham Prison, May 5th, 1916.

Above: Iseult, photographed during the period of her mother Maud Gonne's (**left**) brief, ill-fated marriage to Major John MacBride, whom Iseult hated. Her hatred was a key factor in the destruction of all their lives.

Below: Featured as 'Three Irish Irreconcilables in Paris' in the *Tatler*, February 1904, this photograph shows Maud and John with their new son Seaġan. Note John's guns at the front of the table.

Lillie Reynolds' photograph, taken in Perth, Scotland,
April 1890, during her courtship with James Connolly.
This picture is thought to be the one he carried in
his wallet during their twenty-six years of marriage.
It was returned to her after his execution.

IRISH REBELLION, MAY 1916

JAMES CONNOLLY,
(Commandant-General Dublin Division).
Executed May 9th, 1916.
One of the signatories of the "Irish Republic Proclamation."

She was known as Frances O'Brennan when Edward Kent first met her. He was her teacher at an Irish-language class when he fell in love with her. He changed his name to Éamonn Ceannt and she became known as Áine.

Agnes Hickey first met Michael Mallin (**left**) when he was a soldier about to embark for British India, where he would spend the next seven years. These are the photographs they exchanged during their courtship by correspondence.

IRISH REBELLION, MAY 1916.

JOSEPH PLUNKETT (son of Count Plunkett),
Commandant-General Irish Republican Army,
Executed May 4th, 1916.
Who was married a few hours before his execution.

In London in 1907, long before Grace Gifford had any involvement in Irish politics, William Orpen chose his art student to sit for a painting which he entitled *Young Ireland*.

Inside the newspaper clipping:

Above: Muriel Gifford in 1911, before her marriage to Thomas MacDonagh.

Below: Muriel, Thomas and their son Donagh MacDonagh, photographed in 1913. Thomas is wearing a Celtic outfit, favoured by those who supported the nationalist movement. He would replace this costume with a military uniform. Ultimately his participation in the Easter Rising would destroy his family.

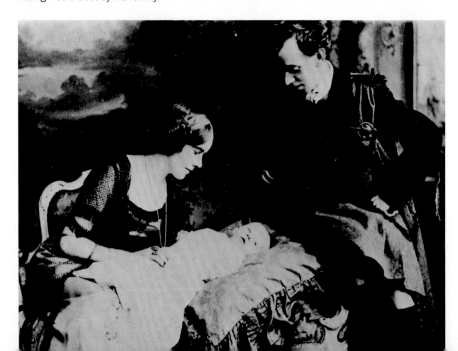

God.'[17] In fact, Michael's own ability was keeping him alive; he had been one of the best shots in his company for the previous two years, for which he had won a cash prize.[18]

In March of 1898 Michael writes for the first time of Ireland: 'I wish it was for Erin that I was fighting not against these poor people.' He was concerned by news from home; crop failures and adverse weather conditions in Ireland had resulted in famine conditions in parts of the country, in particular in Counties Kerry and Mayo. This was all the talk among the Irish soldiers. A fund was set up and Mallin's unit sent £13 to Carraroe in County Galway. He wrote to Agnes: 'the poor people is [*sic*] starving and they have to give in through [*sic*] that but we did not beat them by fair fighting.'[19]

Two years into his posting, Michael wrote to Agnes that the time seemed to be getting longer rather than shorter: 'it must be on account of thinking that makes it as long but it has made a better man of me out here. I was not as good as you thought of me . . .'[20] At this time it was recommended that he should be sent to 'the hills' for his health due to his ongoing bouts of the malaria he had contracted during the Tirah campaign. He described the torment of the flies and the prickly heat, telling Agnes that the soldiers were not allowed outside between 10.30 in the morning and 5.30 in the evening as the sun was so dangerous. He wrote of how beautiful the nights were: 'the moon is so bright you could almost read a paper by it you may take the full benefit of the nice nights if you were here you would be surprised to see the amount of men walking about . . . these are the nights which makes one think of home and friends.'[21]

In May 1898 Agnes's father, Joseph Hickey, died, aged just fifty-five. Michael read of it in the newspaper. When Agnes wrote, she told him that she had been ill from the shock of getting the message of her father's death and that she wished she too had died. In his return letter he tried to console her, and it was her bereavement that prompted him to declare his love for her and ask her to become his sweetheart: 'Agnes give me permission to call you sweetheart for you have been one to me since I first saw you and I think you care a little for me. I love you with all my heart your face is constantly in my mind no one could love you better than I do my Colleen Dhas [lovely girl]. Mike.' He added a postscript: 'the thought of you keeps me good out here Agnes.'[22]

Agnes wrote of how the loss of her father had left her with the feeling that she would never be herself again. Although he had left the family 'comfortable', their circumstances after his death meant that Agnes, her mother and her seventeen-year-old sister Josephine were now planning to move into the city. She was now carrying on her tailoring business, which she was finding hard. Michael wrote to her: 'remember your Father had left you a duty to perform that is to look after your poor Mother and I know you will do it to the best of your ability.'[23]

Michael confided in her in July that he had been through more of the war than he had previously told her, and that his father and mother did not know of his part in the fighting:

> I hope you will forgive me for telling you a couple of little lies about the front . . . you had enough to think about than to bother your head thinking about my chances of an ounce of lead or a couple of inches of steel you said I should not wish to go up to the front again after been sent down but you know an Irish man would get rusty if he did not get a fight with somebody . . .[24]

He recorded the details of one skirmish that took place in June 1898 when, following an attempt by the British Indian government to impose new taxes, soldiers were attacked by tribesmen. According to Michael, the troops had spotted what they believed to be an attempted attack in the village they were patrolling, so they changed direction to investigate this. It was, in fact, a trick by the tribesmen, who were using the old men, boys and women of the village as a decoy. The tribesmen's 'ruse succeeded': armed men of the tribe were hiding in a number of dried-up waterways, from where, knowing every foot of the ground amongst these channels, they were able to outwit and ambush the soldiers, inflicting serious casualties. Michael does not record his own involvement, but later wrote: 'the retreat became a headlong panic-stricken flight, and thus ended the attempt to collect taxes by force.'[25]

Along with other members of his regiment, Michael was awarded the India Medal of 1895 with the Punjab Frontier clasp 1897–1898 and the Tirah clasp 1897–1898. He wrote to Agnes on 7 September 1898 that he would have been happier to have got it for fighting for Ireland:

> Proud to have a medal but far prouder if it was for Ireland. I earned it it is the likes of me that keeps mine and your country down God help her it made the Irish men very bitter out here while we were fiting [sic] for England's Queen and Government they were letting our poor people starve not only that Agnes the British Army is Hell on earth I wish I were well out of it but I did not think it was so bad until I came out here.[26]

That summer he had started a small band in his unit, with a violinist, a mandolin player and a guitar player. He had managed two dances a week, which paid 45 rupees a month, earning him over £3. These dances ran for six or seven months and the extra money allowed him to send some home to his family as well as to save some for his future life with Agnes.

Then there was silence from Ireland. Michael records his disappointment when the mailbag arrived with no letter from Agnes in August 1898. And again two weeks later he wrote: 'I feel very lonely dear Agnes when I get no news from you how lonely I cannot tell you, you will try and write to me very often wont you dear.'[27] He was writing with every post: 'it gives me so much pleasure writing to you that I cannot miss a mail now.'

Agnes's silence was probably caused by a period of upheaval at home. The Hickey family had decided against their planned move into Dublin City and instead went to live in the village of Chapelizod, near the Strawberry Beds, where Agnes's siblings had already settled. Her sister Mary Jane had married Christopher Thewlis five years previously and at first had moved into the city, but when she became unwell the doctor advised her to return to her 'native air' and she now lived in Gambles Buildings in the village with her three children.[28] In 1898 Agnes, her mother Mary and her sister Josephine took up residence at number 5 Hibernian Terrace, the home of Agnes's older brother Patrick, a tailor, and his wife Mary (known as Minnie), who had just given birth to their first child, a boy named Joseph for his grandfather, to whom Agnes became godmother.

After a short time Agnes's letters resumed. In them she told Michael of life in Ireland and he also read news of home in the newspapers that found their way to him. The centenary commemorations of the 1798 rebellion were reported in the papers, once more stirring in Michael a desire to fight for his own country. He wrote of the demonstration that had taken place in August in Dublin to mark the centenary, in which Agnes's brother Patrick had taken part: 'it must have been a splendid sight but how much grander it would have been a demonstration to selebrate [sic] our Independence but God is good and it will come to pass . . . a day will come when we will be able to pay England back with Interest all she has done to us and I hope I am alive and in Ireland I will help to pay it . . .'[29]

Michael also wrote of 'bad Irish men like me that keep poor unhappy Ireland down in the gutter.'[30]

Agnes was unsettled in Ireland and wrote to Michael that she was thinking of going to America. He replied saying that she may not like America, obviously basing his opinion on his family's experiences there during his childhood; he concluded that there was 'nowhere like Ireland no matter where you go.'[31] However, within a short time she had secured a position at home. According to her family she had always had an interest in medicine[32] and in September 1898 she began working at the Stuart Institute, located at Palmerstown House, a forty-acre estate that had been transformed some years earlier into a home for those with mental disabilities.

In mid-October Michael's company moved to Landi Kotal, the westernmost part of the Khyber held by the British. The fort consisted of a keep and an outer fort with accommodation for five British officers and five hundred British and Indian soldiers. It was only eight miles from Kabul, the capital city of Afghanistan. Writing that month, Michael told Agnes that Kabul had two feet of snow. In their station it was so cold over the following weeks that they had to break the ice in the water to wash: 'No chance of getting black up here frost bitten is more like the thing.'[33] He was in a state of readiness for attack, but as he commented to Agnes: 'everything is quiet now the people do not like us up here and they are right dear don't you think so it is their country.'[34]

His time in this camp was not without incident. In November one of his fellow soldiers accidentally shot at another; the bullet lodged in his throat and proved fatal. Michael also confided to Agnes that, during a spate of night raids by a party of Afridi, an intruder in the camp had been shot. His health was bad while he was in Landi Kotal. Conditions were very poor; there were no beds and some men had to sleep on the ground. He was fortunate, as he had a wooden frame with four legs and a straw rope tied across it which he could lie on. A friend who left to go home gave Michael all his warm clothes.

As the new year began Michael was writing: 'Agnes I don't think in fact I will never [*sic*] see a girl as good or as nice as you it is my wish night and day to be with you and I am looking forward to the day when I will get a thousand kisses you have promised to me you must care for me a little dear or you would not trouble to write to one so far away when you could find someone better at home.'[35] He had suggested to one of his fellow soldiers when he was in Dublin to call on Agnes and he teased her 'don't be running away with him'. She wrote in reply that he should do penance for being so bad as to think that she would run away with his chum.

In February 1899 Michael was on the move again, this time to Peshawar, which he described as a very dangerous place. He hoped that this would be his last station in India, but he was happy that he was living in a bungalow and had a church to attend. For the first time in five months he had a bed to sleep in and a table to sit at to eat meals.

Early in the new year of 1899, back in Ireland, Michael's brother Tom and his sister Mary called to visit Agnes for the first time. It may have been Michael's intention to put their relationship on a more formal footing, as Agnes was still writing to him that she wanted to travel, and he was keen for her to remain in Ireland. He also asked her to call on his mother, giving her address as number 12 Cuffe Street, a side street off St Stephen's Green.

In May 1899 Michael began a six-month stint in Cherat. At an elevation of 4,500 feet on the west of the Khattak range in the Peshawar district, the army outpost had a hospital, a church and a few bungalows. He thought it was the most 'beautiful hill station'. During his time there one of the Irishmen in the regiment who had been drinking native whisky fell off a cliff and was killed. The tragic nature of his death was compounded by the fact that he had been due to return home that month. Michael expressed his sadness that the young man's mother would be watching the boat that was to bring him home and 'no son will come, poor woman'.[36]

There were many dangers for the soldiers in the region. On another occasion, when his company got lost in the darkness during an expedition, surrounded by the enemy, their captain told them it was 'every man for himself.' Michael's life was spared, but four men and an officer got lost, and only one of them was recovered. While he was there the regiment also suffered a smallpox epidemic and in November his friend Murphy, a drummer, died. It fell to Michael to break the news to his family: 'I have to write to his people I do not know how to tell dear it is a very hard thing to have to do.'[37]

While he was at Cherat the drum major recommended Michael for lance corporal of the drums. His superiors thought that he was a career soldier who would sign on for twenty-one years and attain the rank of sergeant major, but Michael confided to Agnes that he would not, as he 'hoped be home for his Christmas Dinner in 1901.'[38] When his superiors were unable to persuade him to lengthen his term in the army, he was not promoted. However, he was chosen for other positions of authority, which also earned him more money.

In mid-November he wrote to Agnes: 'the War is lasting a very long time dear we aught [*sic*] to leave the poor people alone for I am sure they will never give in and they have prooved [*sic*] brave men God help them if I were not a soldier I would be out fighting for them.'[39] From 1899 onwards, posts in the Khyber were garrisoned by the Khyber Rifles, an irregular corps of militia recruited from the tribes of the Khyber Agency. At this point members of the regiment were selected for deployment to China, but Michael was not amongst them.

While he was stationed in Cherat there were once more long periods of silence from Agnes, and he worried that she was ill. He had finally got his photograph taken after many years on the field, but still she did not write. Her silence in the summer of 1900 was compounded by the fact that Michael was unable to write for a period after he crushed his hand when a large stone fell on it, leaving a gap of a few weeks.

Agnes had in fact become romantically involved with a family friend, who had now expressed his wish to marry her. Later that summer she wrote to Michael that he was to forgive her. He replied saying that: 'what have you done that you should ask me for forgiveness you cannot help any man loving you but Agnes dearest I know you would not let the man you mention in your letter go on expecting you to marry him knowing you already love me and I love you.'[40] He told her that she must tell this man as gently as she could that she could never be his. Michael asked her to marry him, and said that, with her permission, he would ask her mother for her hand; he declared that if she was not going to be his he would go to China and leave his body there. Later, she admitted that she had had a flirtation with this man. Michael was pleased that she had been honest with him: 'you have kept no secrets from me and that proves the true woman . . .'[41] He told her that her admission had given him pain, but he was resolute in his intentions. He was reassured by Agnes, writing to her on 10 October 1900: 'you could have had the love of a good man but you preferred to wait for me for five long years and you have said to me Mike I love you . . .'[42]

That summer Agnes applied for a job in the Isle of Man, although Michael urged her not to leave Ireland: 'be brave do not run away from danger bow your head to the storm.' However, she still chose to leave home, with the knowledge that Michael had promised her that all the money he had saved was hers: 'remember', he wrote, 'you are my love and everything I have is yours.'[43]

She took up a position as a female attendant at the Ballamona Asylum, at Union Mills in the Strang on the Isle of Man. Known locally as Dr Richardson's Asylum, after its head superintendent,[44] at the time it was a small institution with twenty-six patients. Despite her move, Agnes was still troubled by her rival suitor, and Michael wrote in reply: 'you are never much at home so you do not see much of this man and he cannot trouble you very much.'[45] Agnes was homesick, however, and it was causing her to be unwell. Although she liked the Isle of Man itself, she told Michael the asylum was not a very nice place.

In these same letters, Michael confessed that all his thoughts were of Agnes and, as he described it, of 'poor Ireland'. He described how he and the other Irish soldiers would come together and speak in the Irish language, the 'grand old Celtic tongue'.[46] He had no faith in the politicians: 'In poor Ireland God save her she is in a bad state is there no good and true men to lift her up and strike out for strong and hard if I had my way I would take all our members of parliament out into the Bay put a rope round their necks with a stone at the end of it and throw them in they are only using the poor people for their own ends.'[47] He was kept informed by Irish papers sent to his regiment, delighting in accounts of the Patriotic Children's Treat that had been put on by Maud Gonne in Clonturk Park for those who had not supported the equivalent treat put on in honour of Queen Victoria.

In October Michael moved to the hills. There they would live in small mountain tents, with no bed coverings. He felt at first that these 'manoeuvres' helped him get rid of a small fever, yet in November he was hospitalized again with another bout of malaria, with unremitting fevers that lasted over ten days. While he was still in hospital he wrote to Agnes's mother from Peshawar Punjab on 7 November:

My dear Mrs Hickey:
I am writing to you on a very delicate subject to tell you the truth I hardly know how to go about it, well the fact of the matter is this, your daughter Agnes and, I, Michael have fallen in love with each other and I am about to ask you for her. I want her to be my wife, give her into my care and I promis [*sic*] it will be my whole object in life to make her happy I am very fond of her and I am sure she is as fond of me . . . I cannot give you any proofe [*sic*] as to my character but my word. All that I can say is that I am not a bad one. I have a little money in the bank thirty pounds and thirty pounds reserve pay to come and a war medal if that is any use I can get work with my father and I do not drink now. I have stated my case and I have myself in your hands, but your answer must be yes, I am twenty-six next December. I will be very impatient until I get an answer from you and last remember your own courting days. Good night give my kind wishes to all your children, I remain yours, Michael Mallin, No 2723 1st Royal Scots Fusiliers.[48]

It would be two months before he got her reply. When it arrived he wrote to Agnes: 'I have been made the happiest man in the world . . . how can I thank your mother in giving such a treasure to my care there is only one way I can show her how thankful I am to her that is by showing her how much I love you my darling.'[49] Following this letter Michael corresponded with Mrs Hickey, addressing her as 'Dear Mother' and signing himself her 'affectionate future son'.[50] He sent Agnes a ring of rubies set in a thick gold band, and wrote to her that he was glad she liked his engagement ring: 'I am so glad you are pleased with my ring. I am so glad you like it I only wish it were better but the next one will be the best one although it will be a plain one it will be the most beautiful one.'[51] On the practical side, he was saving money to set up in business, although he had no idea what business he would undertake, asking Agnes in one letter what she would recommend.

Finally, in January 1901, Michael and his regiment were on the move, after all the years on the Afghan Frontier, to a station known as Maja Road Camp, about twenty-five miles from Allahabad in central India, a journey of 'one thousand and thirty miles.' On the journey he saw all sorts of animals and birds – wild pigs, foxes, lynx, jackals, dogs, a tiger – and crops such as tea, tobacco, date and peach trees.

Their new station was described by Michael as 'the nicest Barracks'. There were bedrooms, a large dining hall and two covered verandas where the soldiers could play cards and draughts, plus football and cricket grounds, a handball alley, a swimming pool and a garden. Close by there was a large lake for fishing and a nice little chapel, as well as the 'great river Ganges'. Michael filled his time with all the activities of his regiment, winning medals for cricket and hockey. He studied Pushto, also known as Afghani, an Indo-European language spoken in Afghanistan and western Pakistan. Michael described it as the 'hillmen language'. He was being instructed by a native schoolmaster and took the lower standard. He undertook this task over a period of three months rather than spending the usual six months, and passed his examination, which earned him £12. During this period he was marksman, 2nd grade, which entitled him to wear an emblem of gold guns and a star on his arm. He was also part of the Drummers Minstrel Troupe and worked in the carpenter's shop. He received his good conduct pay following his twelfth year of service in 1901.

While Michael was in Allahabad he had the opportunity to attend Mass during the Easter ceremonies of April 1901, recording his attendance at Benediction and the Stations of the Cross. Later, responding to a report that King Edward VII had made disparaging remarks about Irish Catholics, he wrote that Agnes had no idea 'what Irish-men and Catholics had to put up with in the Army . . . I only hope the day will come when I for one will be able to pay them back for all their insults and I think there are thousands who will do as I would if there was only a chance . . .'[52] He brought his defiance to a new level when he refused to give his subscription to the Queen's Memorial after Queen Victoria died in January 1901. He said he would not pay until the oath sworn by the monarch at the Coronation to uphold the Protestant Faith was changed.

By June 1901 he was finding the inactivity of the camp difficult, writing to Agnes: 'I would like to be back on the Frontier the danger of having your head blown off made it nice and exciting here it is safe and easy.'[53] Michael's plans for celebrating the Christmas of 1901 in Ireland were dashed and in November he told Agnes that she 'must keep up a brave heart for a little while longer.'[54] He began to focus his expectations on being sent back in January 1902.

Michael made a formal application to return home. His commanding officer told him that if he signed on for twenty-one years he would ensure he got home, but Michael had no intention of agreeing to this. His brother Thomas later recounted that Michael was asked to remain in the army as a band sergeant but refused, telling his adjutant 'he wanted to go home as he wanted to forget that he was ever a soldier'.[55] To Agnes he wrote of his disillusion-ment in fighting the people of British India: 'such a brave people getting ruined . . . if I was only a free man I would fight for them'.[56] The previous May he had written: 'The chance of being killed fighting for a robber flag . . . is over . . . if I am to die by bayonet or bullet I hope it is against it for Ireland.'[57]

In January 1902 the government had called for 140 men from Michael's regiment to go to South Africa to fight in the Boer War. They wanted men with over seven years' experience in the army and this included Michael. At first it appeared that there would be a roll call of those who were being sent, but instead the commanding officer decided to put names in a basket and the men had to draw lots; those who drew the papers marked with an X would go to South Africa. Much to Michael's relief he did not get selected. He knew that if he was sent it would delay his return to Agnes, and he also did not want to fight the Boers. 'I think the Boers are in the right and we are in the wrong,' he wrote, adding that, if he had been sent, 'I would have done my duty but thank God the danger is past . . .'[58] Keeping the men beyond their contracted time was affecting all of them. Michael wrote that his friend Dempsey was drinking and in late January another of the men, after a massive drinking session, committed suicide.

Agnes was still in the Isle of Man, where she was more settled than she had been, enjoying amateur dramatics when she was off duty. She was still restless for new opportunities, however, and had applied for a similar position in England. Her younger sister Josephine was now engaged to be married to a Mr Delaney and Michael felt that this was hard on Agnes, as she was still waiting for him to come home, and had been waiting so long to be married.

One of Agnes's attractions for him was that she was 'a good holy and a pure girl'. He assured her at that time that he had shown favour to girls and they had shown favour to him, but he had never loved any of them, and he told her that he had never kissed a girl or a woman since he saw her for the first time.[59] In April 1902 she worried him when she wrote that sometimes she thought that she would like to remain single. Michael replied immediately: 'I am a little angry with you Agnes for saying such a thing only that I know you love me dear it would make me think you were getting tired of waiting . . .'

This was particularly alarming as he had just heard from the adjutant that he would not be getting home until October 1902 and meanwhile he had been sent back to 'the hills', this time to Chakrata, a beautiful hill town in a region called Ultarkhand. This move was designed to acclimatize him to the weather at home. Since getting there Michael had started a choir, a minstrel group of natives 'for the amusement of the troops'.[60] The concerts he put on were sold out and became the talk of Chakrata. During his time at the hill station his loneliness was compounded by the death of his dog Biddy, his constant companion for three years.

Michael remained at Chakrata until 15 July 1902, then travelled the four hundred miles from the snows back to the sweltering heat of

Allahabad with all the other 'time expired men' to await his boat home. He dislocated a knee playing football, then no sooner had he recovered from this injury than he was back in hospital with a bad flare-up of malaria. While he was in hospital 'Orders for Trooping' were issued, and Michael's name was on the list to sail on 19 September. However, there was not enough room on any of the boats as the places allocated were now filled with prisoners from the Boer War.

Michael had collected a 'box of curios' for their future home. Among the items was a sword he had picked up on the battlefield, which he described as an 'Afriedy sword', and he had made a wool picture of the insignia of the regiment.[61] He asked Agnes if she would like him to bring something back, suggesting 'a nice case of flies', a model of the Taj Mahal and a talking parrot. While he did manage to take back two cases of butterflies, there is no record that he succeeded in bringing back the model or the parrot.

Finally a new date for sailing was set and Michael wrote: 'I shall be an Irishman again.' His last letter from India, dated 21 November 1902, more than six years after their first meeting, was addressed: 'My dearly beloved Agnes' and signed 'from your own true loving future husband Mike'.[62] He landed at Fort Brockhurst, Gosport, on the south coast of England, on 16 December 1902 and was discharged two days later.[63] He planned to go directly to the Isle of Man to see Agnes; however, he had to report to Dublin Castle three days after leaving Fort Brockhurst in order to claim his money. He remained in Dublin, in Cuffe Street with his family, until two days after Christmas, then made his way to the Isle of Man for a three-day visit where he was reunited with Agnes for the first time in seven years. Returning home to Dublin after his brief stay, he wrote on 5 January 1903:

> now that I am at home my Agnes, I feel so lonely I cannot get you out of my head and your dear sweet face is always before me . . . what pleasant memories, my darling they will live with me all my life my wilful Irish girl, oh how am I to get on without you this next couple

of months, I don't know, it is very unfair that we should be separated again help me darling beare [*sic*] our seperation [*sic*] for a little while, it must be harder for my own true darling than it is for me . . .[64]

Agnes remained in the Isle of Man because of the unrelenting attentions of the other man who wished to marry her. Michael was in agreement that it was the best course for her to stay there until their own marriage date was set, writing to her: 'now darling I am going to give you a strict order you must remain in the Asylum until I send for you and if that man writes to you, you must send back his letters unopened . . .' He also urged her to write to the rival suitor and tell him that she was going to marry the man she loved. If he replied, Michael told her, she must not open his letter. He said: 'if you love me truely [*sic*] you will do this for me as you are my promised wife, the girl I love so much.'[65]

During their separation Michael visited Agnes's mother and filled his time, as he wrote to Agnes, by practising the flute and talking business with his father. He had worked with his father before he enlisted, and now he began working with him on house renovations until he found work at Jacob's Biscuit Factory close to his family home. His job was as a case-maker, making wooden packing cases for the biscuits. His sister Catherine was a biscuit-packer. Within weeks of being home, he also began teaching music to the Boys' Brigade Drums. On 30 July he joined the Confraternity of Our Lady of the Sacred Heart and became involved with the abstinence movement, joining the Workingmen's Temperance Society. He wrote to Agnes that it was 'delicious being in Dublin'.[66] During these weeks back in his native city, he eagerly awaited her letters, but sadly they have not survived. He repeated back to her what she had written: 'all my love is yours'. In reply he told her: 'how I shall treasure those words, no sweeter words were ever said.'[67]

Agnes finally returned from the Isle of Man to be reunited with Michael in Ireland in early April. Having been prevented from marrying during Lent, their wedding took place in Chapelizod Church on 26 April 1903.[68]

Their first child, James (known as Seamus), was born on 21 February 1904 in 24 Upper Wellington Street. They were still living there when they had a second child, John, in June 1906;[69] he was later known by the Irish form of his name, Seán. The family remained in Wellington Street – where one of Michael's brothers, Bart, also lived – until the following year. Music students came to Michael to learn how to play the violin and he also worked with his father as a carpenter, though he later wrote of his regret over his shortcomings in managing his father's business.

From the time of his return from the army, Michael had 'put in my claim to the silk trade', as his grandfather on his mother's side had been a Silk Master. His mother's family, the Dowlings, had been members of this ancient trade, which had flourished in Ireland with the arrival of exiled French Huguenots in the seventeenth century, although a weavers' guild had been established in the country as early as 1446. It was a tightly controlled business, with the right to join the trade limited to those who had a familial link to the profession. Michael's mother had been a silk winder and his uncle James, who was retired from the army, now worked for Richard Atkinson and Company, poplin manufacturers in College Green.[70] Michael began an apprenticeship as a weaver with Atkinson's and after a year and a half he secured the post of journeyman, a qualified weaver, although normally it took seven years to achieve this.

The popularity of Irish poplin ties meant the number of weavers had been growing steadily: in 1890 there were twenty looms in the Liberties; by 1903 the number had increased to 117; and by 1911 there were 193. Irish poplin was a mixture of pure silk and wool and was made by hand. In the past weavers had worked in their own homes; now workers were located in factories and there were four firms in Dublin. Atkinson's had two factories during this period. Michael and the other weavers were paid according to the amount of material they produced.

Michael was joined in the trade by his brothers John and Bartholomew; he even signed the indenture allowing Bartholomew

Mallin to become an apprentice silk weaver in his capacity as secretary of the Weavers' Union, in 1908.[71] Attaining this position within five years of becoming an apprentice is significant, indicating Michael's ability to organize and his standing among his fellow-workers.

He also maintained his interest in the activities he had undertaken as a soldier. British Army Major General Robert Baden-Powell published *Scouting for Boys* in 1908, and the previous year had held his first scouting camp using his own army experiences in India and South Africa. From this he created the Scouting movement. Michael was at the same time using his training from the British Army to form a small group of boys into his own scouting unit, which was set up 'in opposition to the Baden Powell scouts'.[72] The group consisted of twelve to fourteen boys who were training in signalling and scouting, and Michael often brought them to the Dublin Mountains on Sundays to practise.

Evenings in their home were filled with music. Dublin was a city of many bands and they played in public parks and on piers. Michael gave lessons to bands and also put on concerts in different parts of the country.[73] They were not profitable, however, and he lost a lot of money. Undeterred, he founded an orchestra of thirty men, who entered *feiseanna* (Irish cultural competitions) and won gold medals.

In 1908 Michael, Agnes and their two boys went to live in Blessington Street in the north inner city and after a short time moved again to 111 Capel Street, where they opened a shop. This constant change of address was not unusual in Dublin at that period, as there was no security for those who rented. Most of the accommodation in which the Mallin family lived was over shops, but before the end of the year they were renting a little red-brick house at 40 Hamilton Street. It was in this house on the last day of October that their third child, a daughter named Úna, was born.

Michael's son Seamus was later to write that his father was 'forever planning things in his mind. There was no end to his planning, but it was seldom any of them succeeded once he put them into practice.'[74] One of his schemes included the opening of a cinema[75] at the intersection of Mary Street and Jervis Street. It was probably an unlicensed premises, as no record of it has survived. Michael acquired the equipment and the films and began to show them using an electric arc as a means of lighting. Seamus remembered films with American policemen running about. There was little support for the scheme, however, and the family lost a great deal of money. Agnes learned to be a good manager; 'were it not for her skills and her thriftiness,' wrote Seamus, 'things would have been very difficult for the Mallin family.'[76] Money was found for family holidays and Seamus recalled visits to the Isle of Man.

In 1909 an article by James Connolly, who was then living in America, was featured in the *Nation*. This prompted a group of 150 people to come together in the Trades Hall, Capel Street, Dublin, to form the Socialist Party of Ireland, with the purpose of having independent labour representation on elected bodies, as well as supporting the national language and holding democratic discussion to promote socialism in Ireland. Michael was elected as one of the committee members. This, along with his role as secretary of the Silk Weavers' Union, placed him at the centre of unfolding events.

In 1910, Michael, Agnes, Seamus, Seán and Úna moved to 65 Meath Street, in the Liberties area of Dublin, where they ran a small tobacconist and newsagents. From this shop Michael sold *Irish Freedom*, the publication of the Irish Republican Brotherhood. This was tolerated by the authorities, but in 1911 his support for the newsboys who were on strike brought him into conflict with the police, and he lost all his customers from the nearby police station.

The children remembered their father's habit of reading aloud to their mother during this time: 'It was history that he was most interested in, mainly South America'.[77] They even discussed the possibility of moving to live in South America or Australia. It was during this period that Michael told his friend James O'Shea that 'he would never be able to stick Ireland as she was at the time.'[78]

However, his loyalty to his native land remained paramount and although Agnes was keen to move, in the end Michael did not agree. He would later write to her: 'if only I had taken your advice and left the country we might have been so happy but Ireland always came first.'[79]

In March 1913, when Michael was secretary of the Silk Weavers' Union, there was a strike, described as a 'technical' dispute, at Atkinson's poplin factory on Hanbury Lane, where he was one of about 130 employees. This strike was restricted to members of the union and at first there were hopes of a satisfactory settlement within a few days. On 5 April a notice was issued by Atkinson's stating that the firm would accept applications for reinstatement from the men on strike and that 'all suitable weavers will be taken back at the full Trade Union rate of wages, as heretofore paid' and 'Boy Apprentices over 18 years of age will be taken on as men'. Michael responded that this offer was to 'sell your trade union for an increase in wages'. By mid-April he was claiming the striking workers 'would beg from door to door before they would surrender'. Atkinson's were, at this point, equally defiant and neither side seemed willing to concede to the other.

The dispute continued throughout the month and divisions between employer and employee grew. Michael maintained a strong hold over the men, none of whom applied for reinstatement. New employees were taken on at the factory and, as it was not the busy season in the trade, those weavers still working were able to meet all the orders. The dispute, meanwhile, was growing more intense and the chances of a settlement seemed remote.

However, by the end of April the employers and employees of the company began negotiations to settle the strike. The two sides opened a dialogue, with the Lord Mayor of Dublin, Lorcan Sherlock, acting as arbitrator. The union members objected to the hiring of the new employees; according to Michael's account: 'It would be three years before those scabs could be trusted to do anything for themselves, and only half of them would be likely to become weavers.'[80] It was an issue on which the union remained defiant, but finally, after thirteen weeks, the strike was settled.

The weavers' strike was one of thirty major disputes in Dublin in 1913, most of them involving members of the Irish Transport and General Workers' Union formed by Jim Larkin, who was able to mobilize thousands of workers in unified strikes. The Lockout of 1913 changed the lives of many Dubliners, including the Mallins. As Seamus recalled, previously their family had led 'a life that up to that had been content'.[81] By the end of the Lockout the Mallin family were forced to close their shop 'owing to the poverty of his working class customers'.[82]

Agnes was eight months pregnant with their fourth child when the family moved home yet again in August 1913. Michael had decided to invest in a chicken farm, so they relocated to the country-side. It was a massive change from the centre of the city to living in a little house half a mile outside the village of Finglas, just outside Dublin. The plans were to build hen houses and breed Rhode Island Reds.

However, while in Finglas, Michael was taken ill. The children overheard discussions that it was Bright's disease, whispers that it could kill him. After numerous doctors and a selection of medicines he was cured, but the cost meant that there was no money for the farm, so the family, including the new baby – whom Agnes had chosen to call Joseph, after her father[83] – moved back to the city.

Once they returned to Dublin, Michael resumed work as a weaver once more. He maintained his association with the unions, and during this time he also conducted a quartet, known as the Workers' Orchestra, which played on Sunday nights in Liberty Hall, headquarters of the ITGWU. He was also the conductor of the City of Dublin Fife and Drum Band up to 1914.

Agnes and Michael attended concerts and plays and would bring their older children with them. Seamus recalls attending Edward Martyn's *The Heather Field*, performed in the hall in Hardwicke Street by the Irish Theatre Company set up by Thomas MacDonagh and Joseph Plunkett. Michael also now moved in the circle of Count and Countess Markievicz, who had established the United Arts Club in Dublin and were running a dramatic society. Seamus once saw his father on stage playing a part in a play written by Constance Markievicz.

In the spring of 1914 the family opened another shop, this time at 46 Upper Kevin Street; they later ran another, on Francis Street in the Liberties. In May 1914 Michael took over as conductor of the ITGWU's Emmet Fife and Drum Band, which met every Tuesday and Friday in Emmet Hall in Inchicore, where the members of the Irish Citizen Army drilled. Michael was not a member of the ICA at this time, despite the fact that during the Weavers' Strike there had been some altercations with the police.

However, in 1914 there was a new development in his relationship with the trade union movement when he was removed as the secretary of the Weavers' Union. The exact circumstances are unknown, but Michael refused to return the union's books and he was taken to court in July. The union chairman Charles Farrell claimed they had been unable to get the books audited and that the affairs of the union were 'in a state of chaos.' The result of the court case was that the union should proceed with the claim for 'legal detention of the books.'[84] This ended Michael's involvement with the Weavers' Union, and from then on he was to become closely associated with the ITGWU.

The ITGWU owned the Emmet Hall and, following Jim Larkin's departure for America in October 1914, Michael was approached by James Connolly, who had become acting general secretary of the ITGWU, to take the role of manager of the hall. The job had been vacated by William Partridge, who had been appointed by Connolly as an organizer who would travel to branches in various parts of the country. It may have been Partridge who suggested Michael might replace him, as he later described Michael as: 'One of the finest – most kindly hearted – and clean minded men it has ever been my good fortune to meet.'[85] The position gave the Mallins the use of an apartment and shop attached to the hall. They moved into the apartment and established a newsagent's.

In May 1915 Connolly appointed Michael as the organizer of the

Inchicore branch of the ITGWU. This was not just a branch of the union but also a company of the Irish Citizen Army. One of the members, James O'Shea, recalls Michael's enthusiasm, even as the number of recruits dropped: 'The smaller we became the more active Mike Mallin became. He used to give us lectures and we were becoming real soldiers. He lectured us on outpost duty and brought us out to the Park at night'.[86] This branch was Michael's first real involvement in the drilling and training of men in a more military capacity.

When James Connolly became head of the ICA after Larkin's departure for America his aim was to turn it into a military force capable of participating in an armed revolution. Michael seemed to share Connolly's desire and 'regarded the Citizen Army as a practical military force for use in the near future'.[87] Under Connolly and Mallin, both former members of the British Army, the training of the ICA became increasingly efficient. It was well known that James Connolly was 'not going to play soldiers'.[88] Drilling increased, with Sundays and Bank Holidays being used for outdoor exercises in the mountains. They lectured the men on different forms of guerrilla warfare.

Soon Michael was appointed as chief of staff. He led the ICA to the grave of Theobald Wolfe Tone on 21 May 1915, a commemoration in which both the ICA and Irish Volunteers took part. The *Workers' Republic* reported: 'Mr. Mallin, as Chief of Staff of the Citizen Army, carried out his duties in a manner that earned the praise of all.'[89] Mock battles and attacks on buildings also took place, including a midnight mock attack on Dublin Castle in late 1915.

There was a garden at the back of Emmet Hall, with a firing range that Michael used to train the ICA, instructing the men to fire at an image of a man placed 200 yards away. In another room in the hall, the Volunteers were being trained under Con Colbert. The four Mallin children would sneak in to watch. Seamus recalled curly-headed Joe: 'Although my brother was only two and a half years old at the time, he would slip into the room and mimic Colbert behind his back, which caused the men to smile. But Colbert never looked behind him and could never understand what the men were smiling at.'[90]

As drilling took place on a Sunday, Seamus would go with his father to watch the men. They regarded the eleven-year-old boy as a mascot and often on the long journey home he would sit on a rifle carried between two men. Seamus was at a camp at Croydon Park, Clontarf: 'I was there a few times and once, it was arranged that I would stay over night and go the following day a Sunday to Tullow where there was to be a big fair.' That day Seamus was accidentally shot in the foot. The men regarded him as the first casualty of the war.[91]

Emmet Hall was adjacent to Richmond Barracks, enabling Michael to befriend soldiers from whom he could obtain arms. The wall at the back of the premises was also part of the barracks. James O'Shea recalled how, one evening, he went to Emmet Hall where he was told that Michael was in the back garden and that he should wait for him. O'Shea knew Michael was looking for rifles and became more and more anxious as he was taking a long time. Upon hearing a crash, he grabbed Michael's sword and ran to the back wall. He was about halfway there when, with the sword in his hand, he fell over something. 'It was poor Mallin!' he later explained. Michael had been hit over the head and knocked unconscious by something thrown from the barracks. Undeterred, he also went to buy rifles elsewhere and hardly a night went by without him bringing one home. Maeve Cavanagh, who contributed poetry to the *Workers' Republic*, wrote: 'Mallin used to come a lot to our house. He was always collecting rifles and he told me he got a lot from the soldiers in Inchicore barracks. He often came in exhausted after these expeditions, and my sister used to make him a meal.' Michael got a .22mm revolver and ammunition for Maeve.[92]

Michael Mallin spent more time at Liberty Hall as 1915 progressed. Sometimes he would take his young sons with him. Gradually he devoted more and more time to training with the men and less time to his music, which was a source of sadness to him, although he was known to play his piccolo on the way back from manoeuvres. Agnes was during this period living with her four small children in what was effectively a military barracks, with her husband stockpiling arms for an inevitable conflict. Samples of different types of materials for the making of bombs were also brought there.

On Wednesday, 19 January 1916, James Connolly left Liberty Hall at lunchtime. Michael came home in a distressed state and told Agnes: 'Connolly is missing. We got a telegram from him about an hour or so ago, but we cannot make proper sense of it. It was handed in at Lucan Post Office ... I would like you and Dr Kathleen Lynn to go to Lucan and try to find out any definite information.' It was raining heavily that same night, Seamus remembered, 'so I expect my mother and the doctor had a difficult enough journey'.[93] Michael felt that James was being held against his will, and recorded that he had visited the Military Council of the IRB to demand his release or else the ICA would go ahead with their own plans for rebellion. When Éamonn Ceannt sarcastically remarked, 'What could your small number do in such a situation?' Michael replied, 'We can fight and we can die, and it will be to our glory and your shame if such does take place.' At that, Pearse is said to have banged on the table and said, 'Yes, by God, that is so, and here is one who is with you.'[94]

On his return, three days later, James Connolly told Michael and others that he had been coopted on to the Military Council of the IRB and had agreed that the ICA would join the Irish Volunteers in an insurrection. From that point on, several people later attested to the fact that Michael Mallin told them there was to be a rising in the coming weeks. Even Seamus, who had just turned twelve, knew a rising was to take place at Easter 1916.

In the days leading up to Easter Week Michael brought a loom into the workroom at Liberty Hall and in his spare time he worked on weaving a piece of material. His plan was that Agnes could sell it to help to tide her over the period when the fighting was taking place in the city.[95] Michael had told her that the leaders would escape from the city and fight in the countryside using guerrilla tactics.

Michael had arranged that Agnes and the children would be at Liberty Hall for breakfast on Easter Sunday morning; Seamus wrote: 'I think that my father knew while arranging the breakfast that the Rising had been postponed.'[96] His reaction to MacNeill's cancellation of the manoeuvres was that it was the 'worst day's work that had ever been done in the history of the unfortunate country.'[97]

On Easter Sunday night the usual recital took place at Liberty Hall, so as not to arouse the suspicions of the authorities that something was about to happen. Michael Mallin played the flute and Maeve Cavanagh played the piano. The next day James O'Shea met Agnes, now noticeably pregnant with her fifth child. He remembered that 'She appeared as if the weight of the world was on her shoulders – and so it was – she was pale and very shaken but I admired her courage . . . she knew all.'[98]

6

Grace and Joe

Theirs was a whirlwind romance, a love affair that was brief and intense. It should have been a match celebrated in the social circles of Dublin, as two families of similar social standing came together to be unified in marriage.

Joe had always suffered from poor health, and now he was dying of glandular tuberculosis, although Grace never seemed to accept the inevitability of his early death. Following their engagement, he described the new year 1916 as 'Grace 1'.[1] But when their marriage took place just after Easter, it was not the wedding they had planned. Within hours, Joe would be dead.

Joseph Plunkett was born on 21 November 1887, the second child of George Noble Plunkett and Mary Josephine Cranny. George was a cultivated man, multilingual, his abilities nurtured during a childhood spent in part in Nice in the south of France, where he became fluent in both French and Italian. His mother had taken him to the continent to improve his health, as both his siblings had died. George studied law at Trinity in 1873, but he had no real interest in this as a career, so after university he worked as a journalist.

At this time he also became attracted to his second cousin, Mary Josephine (known as Josephine) Cranny, the daughter of Patrick Cranny, a successful builder with considerable wealth.[2] Patrick and his wife, Maria, were keen to make a good match for their only surviving daughter and did not approve of her being courted by a journalist. However, Maria relented in her opposition to the marriage when in 1884 George Plunkett received a papal title, Knight Commander of the Holy Sepulchre, which meant that her daughter would be entitled to use the title Countess Plunkett.

Josephine's dowry, a large number of properties, facilitated the newly married couple in undertaking a honeymoon that lasted two years, during which time they travelled over ten thousand miles in North and South America. When they returned home, one of those houses, 26 Upper Fitzwilliam Street, had been made ready for them. That year George was called to the Bar, but chose instead to continue writing for nationalist publications. He also stood unsuccessfully for parliament. Outside Ireland he was known for his work on the history of art, which culminated in his publishing the definitive account in English of Sandro Botticelli and his school.[3] He became an honorary member of the Academy of Fine Arts in Florence.

Despite the couple's wealth in properties in Dublin, the seven Plunkett children[4] – Mimi, Joe, Moya, Geraldine, George, Fiona and Jack – lived in cramped conditions on the top floor of the Fitzwilliam Street house with their nursemaids. Their mother saw them only a few times each week when she was in Ireland. She was often away, travelling without her husband. While not interfering with how his wife ran the household or providing the necessities of life, when he was at home George Plunkett was very attentive to the amusement of his children, taking them to the zoo, the opera, plays and the circus; his daughter Geraldine remembered: 'He had no idea about things being suitable or unsuitable for children.'[5]

Joe was aged eleven when he first became ill. In March 1899 he contracted pneumonia and pleurisy. His mother nursed him back to health, but the following year he was 'still terribly weak and susceptible after his long illness'[6] and Josephine decided that she would take him to Rome for further recuperation. However, when they got to Paris one of the international exhibitions was on, so instead of continuing on to Italy the countess decided to send him to a boarding school in Passy in northern France while she attended a round of social events in the French capital. The climate of that region of France is said to have had a detrimental effect on his health. Joe returned to Ireland showing visible symptoms of TB, with a scrofula or growth forming on his neck. The following year his uncle Jack Cranny, a surgeon, lanced the growth, but when he was fifteen the scrofula came back. This time he was operated on by an army surgeon, Dr Swan, who tried to burn off the growth with copper-sulphate crystals and 'savagely hacked' away the flesh; as was the norm at the time, this was performed without an anaesthetic. Another doctor used medication made up of anti-toxins extracted from turtles, without success.

Between his numerous periods of sickness Joe was educated at the Catholic University School and Belvedere College, Dublin, as well as for a short period of time at St George's School, Hove, on the south coast of England, along with his ten-year-old brother George and seven-year-old Jack. Joe managed to persuade his mother that this school was unsuitable. She took the boys out after a short time.[7] By then Joe's ill health was so acute that he needed a home tutor and a Mr Greenan from Sandyford School came to teach him.

As well as being a gifted mathematician, Joe had also shown an interest in chemistry and had been experimenting since the age of thirteen. He read everything he could on inventions such as Marconi's wireless, even building his own set. When he was eighteen, having heard favourable reports of Stonyhurst, the Jesuit school in Lancashire in England, his mother enrolled him for the 'Gentlemen Philosophers' class. The course included the arts, science, classics, mathematics, law and medicine. For the next two years Joe had access to 'a splendid library', which gave him 'access to all the information and ideas that he had wanted for so long.'[8] While he was at Stonyhurst he set up a dark room and experimented with the first colour photography process, which had just been sold to the public. He also acquired military training from an Officers' Training Corps in the school, with summer manoeuvres on Salisbury Plain. There he was educated with people from different countries; one of his closest friends was Taffy Asphar from Malta.

On leaving Stonyhurst in 1907 Joe was awarded a prize of £5 and he spent all the money on books of poetry. His siblings noted that when he returned to Dublin his mind was filled with ideas on philosophy, physics, poetry and mysticism.

The following year, the National University Act was passed, but it did not come into effect until 1909. In June Joe decided to sit the matriculation to study medicine or science, and, as he wished to include Irish among his subjects for matriculation, he asked his mother to find him a teacher. His father, Count Plunkett, was president of the Society for the Preservation of the Irish Language, but despite the count's connection to Irish scholars it was his mother who located a tutor by placing an advertisement in the paper. It was answered by Thomas MacDonagh. The man who became his tutor also became his greatest friend. Despite Thomas's instruction, Joe failed to gain access to university that year.

Joe, now twenty-three, spent time at the Irish College in Gortahork in Donegal, staying at the summer home of old family friends, the O'Carrolls. Dr O'Carroll, an eminent surgeon, had been a former suitor of his mother Josephine. She had rejected him when he proposed to her at sixteen, but she had kept up her friendship with him. Joe had known the six O'Carroll children, who lived near them on Merrion Square, all his life, but that summer he realized he was in love with one of the girls, sixteen-year-old Columba, who was pretty as well as intelligent. She had tanned skin and dark eyes, and was considered glamorous, with many admirers. She was fond of Joe, but she 'did not like sick people', and according to Joe's sister Geraldine, she was not interested in the poems he wrote for her. Despite this, he would continue to have feelings for her long after the summer ended.

Joe now took the opportunity to travel, first visiting his friend Taffy Asphar in Malta and then travelling with his mother to Sicily, Naples, Orvieto, Florence, Venice, Bologna and Milan. In the autumn of 1911, to escape the winter weather, he went to Algiers in North Africa, where his sister Moya joined him. As well as taking lessons in Arabic he perfected his skating at the local rink.

While he was away, Thomas MacDonagh arranged for Joe's first book of poetry, *The Circle and the Sword*, to be published by Maunsell & Co., financed by Countess Plunkett. Joe wrote to him: 'of course I know that I have no right to shirk my responsibilities and throw all the onus on you, but the weak have always oppressed the strong in our country!'[9] When he was proofreading it, Thomas wrote to Joe in Algeria: 'You are at such a safe distance now that I can venture to congratulate you. The book will be fine . . . the poems are better to me, now printed, than before. I do not know why it should be so, but it is.'[10] Many of the verses had already been published in magazines. As Thomas had brought the work to publication, it was dedicated to him.

Joe had wished to extend his stay abroad and was keen to travel on to Egypt. He was a keen Egyptologist and had painted Egyptian figures on the door of his bedroom and once had told his family that he thought he was, as his sister Geraldine recalled, 'a reincarnation of Rameses the Second because the outline of the back of his head was the same as Rameses's skull'.[11] However, his mother would not allow him to go to Egypt as it was too expensive.

When he returned to Dublin the weather was bitterly cold and Joe contracted influenza, which caused lung haemorrhages. He spent weeks recovering in a nursing home, and while he was there he was visited by his literary friends, including Thomas MacDonagh, with whom he shared a love for 'good company, good talk, good food and wine, a jolly party, singing and music, interspersed with witty joking and every kind of nonsense.'[12]

While Joe was still in North Africa, Thomas had married Muriel Gifford and it was in their flat that Joe met her sister Grace, although at the time they were merely acquaintances, as Joe pursued his romantic attachment to Columba O'Carroll.

Grace Eveleen Gifford and her twin brother Edward Cecil were born on 4 March 1888 at 8 Temple Villas in Rathmines, Dublin. Her mother, Isabella, had given birth to ten other children, one of whom had died at birth, before the arrival of her twins. Despite the fact that she was their fifth daughter, Grace was her parents' favourite child and, according to her siblings, was absolutely spoilt as a youngster.[13] Her position in the family was unaffected by the birth of another younger sister, Sidney. It may have been that Isabella saw something of herself in her second youngest daughter, as she too had had a twin brother, John George, who had died in 1849, aged just five months. Grace had an inherited artistic ability from her mother's branch of the Burton family.

The Burton family had settled in Corofin, County Clare, in 1610.[14] As well as coming from the privileged world of the landed classes in Ireland, Isabella's family had achieved considerable success in the world of art. Her uncle was Frederic William Burton, painter of *The Meeting on the Turret Stairs* and later knighted for his work as director of the National Gallery in London. Following the untimely death from typhus in 1850 of Isabella's father Robert, at the age of just forty, his brother Frederic, who was unmarried, financed the upbringing of Robert's eight surviving children.[15] The boys were educated at Trinity College and the girls, including Isabella, were able to live for a number of years on the invested money.[16] Isabella's education largely consisted of learning languages; she knew a little French, German and Italian. After her marriage to Frederick Gifford she was estranged from her siblings for marrying a Catholic, but she remained proud of her lineage and her famous uncle Frederic. A vivid childhood memory of the Gifford children was the death of their great uncle Sir Frederic Burton in 1900. In order to ensure that their neighbours knew of her distinguished relative's death, Isabella dressed the children in black, inviting questions about the cause of their mourning attire.

Among their parents' circle of friends was John Butler Yeats, who, like Frederick Gifford, had studied law but was now making his living as an artist and, on occasion, Isabella would give him an unsolicited critique of his work. Yeats would later become better known as the father of the poet William Butler Yeats and the artist Jack B. Yeats. The Yeats family contributed to the Gifford family journals, which were written in old exercise books, with names such as *The Magazine* and *The Barrel Organ*. One edition had a sketch by Jack B. Yeats of an Aran islander and he also wrote a piece entitled 'Mícháil' for their magazine.[17] The Giffords also wrote plays and performed them. Gabriel, who was a gifted artist, made toy theatres for his younger siblings.

In 1904 Grace, at sixteen, went to study at the Metropolitan School of Art in Dublin. As there was then no entrance examination, people of all abilities were admitted. Grace indeed showed talent and won a prize in her first year for 'drawing on the blackboard and freehand drawing', which was presented by the Viceroy in February 1906. At the school she was taught by one of the most gifted Irish artists of the day, William Orpen, who returned from London annually to teach there.

Grace was 'described by all who know her as a particularly handsome and attractive girl',[18] and while she was a student she was transformed from artist to sitter when Orpen chose her to sit for a portrait study. He began by sketching her, then reworked the composition into a full-scale oil on canvas,[19] which he called *Young Ireland*. She was depicted in an Edwardian lace dress, as favoured by young ladies of the time, her striking red hair styled in the fashion of the day, her individuality captured in its untamed nature. She wore rings on three fingers and one on her thumb, defying the rules of conventional dress. Eight of the Gifford children had red hair, the colouring coming from their maternal great-grandmother, Emily.[20] It was a source of shame to their mother and she liked them to keep their heads covered, but now Grace's flame-red tresses were captured on canvas.

The painting was exhibited at the New English Art Club in London in 1907 and the following year it was selected by art dealer Hugh Lane as one of the works to be featured in 'an Irish Gallery' at the Franco-British Exhibition in Shepherd's Bush in London. The colonial villages were a popular attraction at the exhibition. They included an Irish one with 150 'colleens' who demonstrated various forms of domestic industry. The art gallery was located in the village. Lane – whose brothers Ambrose and Eustace were frequent visitors to the Gifford house, as they studied law with Grace's brother Gerald – promoted this event to highlight the 'distinctive temperament, which gives promise of the successful establishment of a recognized Irish school of painting'.[21] Grace represented for Orpen the idealized epitome of an Irishwoman. The bond between pupil and teacher was such that they posed together for a formal portrait photograph. Orpen considered her to be one of his most talented students.

Following Grace's receipt of another award in 1907, she began tuition at the Slade School of Art in London, taking a course in Fine Art and living close to the school at 113 Gower Street. When she returned to Dublin she was anxious to be independent of her parents and to make a living from her work. She even considered emigration. Her siblings Ada and Gabriel had already left Ireland to find work in the United States following their time in art school, while Grace's twin brother Edward had left Ireland at seventeen, travelling to Portland, Maine, before moving on to Toronto in Canada in the spring of 1905. He was in New York in 1908 before returning to Ireland, but he did not settle in Dublin, setting out for New York once more in April 1909. It would be the last time Grace saw her twin, as he never returned to Ireland.

Apart from an occasional job for publications such as the *Shanachie*, in which Grace's cartoons were featured, there is no record of her making any money from her work, although hand-coloured versions of her best-known cartoons survive which may have been copies offered for sale. Her preferred medium was pen and ink, and she specialized as a cartoonist and illustrator. For most of her career her source material was the Irish theatre. The subject matter was produced for a select audience of Dublin society, in the main those who were patrons of the new nationalist plays then being produced.[22]

The artistic coterie of Dublin was very small. Grace was a guest of Count Markievicz at the United Arts Club at 44 St Stephen's Green, which he and his wife, Constance, had founded. The club was 'not bookish or intellectual', and it gave Grace another place to meet people with the same artistic temperament. Her pastime, like many other Dubliners, was to attend the theatre. As well as the professional companies, numerous theatre societies formed at this time.

Members of the wider 'Irish Ireland Movement' also set up their own theatre groups, including the Gaelic Amateur Dramatic Society and the Benson Company.[23] William (Willie) Pearse, a sculptor, formed a group called William Pearse and Miss Mary FitzGerald and Company, and they produced *The Cricket on the Hearth* and *The Chimes*, performed on 6 May. A few years later, in April 1911, Willie's brother P. H. Pearse would bring pupils from his bilingual school, St Enda's, to perform a passion play in three acts in Irish on the Abbey Theatre stage.

In 1904 the Irish National Theatre had merged with the National Dramatic Company and with a donation by a wealthy patron facilitated the transformation of the Dublin Mechanics Institute on Abbey Street into a theatre. One of Grace's earliest cartoons depicts the founders of the Abbey Theatre – Lady Gregory, W. B. Yeats, and the playwrights J. M. Synge and Edward Martyn.[24] Another of her works was an ink drawing of Lady Gregory's play *The Rising of the Moon*, which was first performed in March 1907; the play told the story of the patriot Hamilton Rowan and, although a popular success, it was condemned by nationalists because of its sympathetic portrayal of a policeman. Grace attended plays put on by the different companies and her work documents her attendance at scores of productions throughout these years.

On Joe Plunkett's return to Ireland following his travels, he once again began to indulge his love of theatre, having always been interested in amateur dramatics. He acted in a double bill staged at 6 St Stephen's Green on 22 August 1906. In *A Pair of Lunatics*, a comedy written by W. R. Walkes, Joe played the lunatic Captain George Fielding and his sister Mimi took the role as the second lunatic, Miss Clara Manners. The second part of the double bill was *A Quiet Family*, and Joe, Mimi and other friends again featured in the cast.

Joe studied the revolutionary theatrical ideas of Edward Gordon Craig, son of the actress Ellen Terry, who was a pioneer in stage lighting and design, and of Konstantin Stanislavski, founder of the Moscow Art Theatre. He wrote a number of plays at this time, including a comedy entitled *Tolerance* and another called *The Shroud of Hymen*. Joe played Prince Robert in the first production of *The Spurious Sovereign* by Harry Morris, a production by the Theatre of Ireland at the Molesworth Hall at Easter 1910. He began using the stage name Luke Killeen, and the following February he was again on stage, this time in the Theatre of Ireland's production of Aleksandr Ostrovski's *The Storm* at Molesworth Hall.

The Theatre of Ireland was founded in 1906 and specialized in the cultivation of Irish drama through the production of plays by Irish authors, both in Irish and English. Constance Markievicz acted in several of their productions. Grace made a sketch of the play *The Shuiler's Child* by Seumas O'Kelly, with Mary Walker, using her stage name Máire Nic Shiubhlaigh, playing Moll Woods the Shuiler, while Constance Markievicz played an inspector. These women were members of Inghinidhe na hÉireann, which Grace's sister Sidney had joined the previous year. Getting involved in theatre productions was part of the work of that organization too. Their founder, Maud Gonne, had once acted the lead in the first production of *Kathleen Ni Houlihan*, which W. B. Yeats had written especially for her. It was a historic play with a mix of pathos, comedy, and 'the right shade of national feeling' for members of the organization. Mary Walker recalled: 'How many there that night will forget the Kathleen Ni Houlihan of Maud Gonne, her rich golden hair, willow like figure, pale sensitive face, and burning eyes . . . She was the very personification of the figure she portrayed on the stage.'[25]

The Theatre of Ireland moved its entire 1911–12 season to a new theatre on Hardwicke Street. The previous year, Joe's mother, Countess Plunkett, had purchased a property there which had been advertised as 'suited for lecture hall or public institution being very spacious and in proximity to the centre of the city.'[26] It was 'just one degree better than a slum' and described as 'a large, ugly, rambling

174

old building'.[27] Inside was a stage with rows of the 'commonest chairs', 'no footlights' and 'practically no scenery'.[28] Countess Plunkett had the hall converted into a theatre and it was leased to a number of amateur organizations, as well as being used by the Plunketts for private entertainments. In his diary Joe described it as 'our hall'. From 1912 onwards the Plunkett family discussed offering membership of their theatre with a guarantee of a reserved seat for five performances a year. At this time there were many theatres in Dublin, including the Queen's, the Gaiety, Tivoli, Empire, James's Theatre, Samuel's Theatre and the Abbey. Joe was already formulating plans to start his own company, and later created it as 'Mr Killeen's Company'.

Thomas MacDonagh's play *Metempsychosis: or, a Mad World*[29] was performed at the Hardwicke Street Theatre on 10 May 1913 as part of a double bill with Joe's play *The Dance of Osiris*. A critic remarked that a 'knowledge of Egyptology' was not required to enjoy this play, which was described as coming from 'the easy pen of Joseph Plunkett'.[30] One of the key scenes involved a dance by the Priestess Anhai Maat Ka Ra. Kitty McCormack played this part, impressing the avid theatregoer Joseph Holloway; she also designed the set. Kitty worked for the Dun Emer Guild, a cooperative that in the autumn of 1912 had taken rooms at the rear of the theatre[31] from which it produced handmade books, metalwork and textiles. Its workers shared common interests in the arts, making scenery or designing Irish craftworks, all expressions of a new nationalism among these young Irish people.

Joe had once studied bookbinding with the McCormacks, but now showed more interest in writing, including poetry. Some of his poems appeared in the *Irish Review*, a journal founded in 1911 for 'the application of intelligence to Irish life'.[32] Other contributors included Thomas MacDonagh, as well as Pádraic Colum, P. H. Pearse and W. B. Yeats. The journal also featured Grace's work. Her life and Joe's were still running in parallel. Grace at this time was seeing a Mr Moore and may have even accepted his proposal, but nothing else is known of this relationship.

In July 1913 Joe became editor of the *Irish Review* as Pádraic Colum had departed for the United States the previous month and David Houston, professor of Bacteriology in the College of Science, was looking for a buyer for the magazine who would pay off its debts. Joe wrote to his mother, who agreed to purchase it, as the 'idea of owning a magazine' appealed to her. Like the Giffords, the Plunketts had made family magazines for their own amusement years before; one of their publications, *The Morning Jumper*, contained stories, limericks and illustrations.

When Joe took over the *Irish Review* he changed its focus to concentrate on history, economics and politics. All this was done as his illness confined him to the house and often to his bed, where he would 'study anything and everything, philosophy, biography, mysticism, history and military history'.[33]

In August 1913 Joe headed to Donegal to be with Columba, but he 'came back depressed because Columba showed no sign of caring'.[34] His sister Geraldine long thought that his love was 'unreal', as he had no money to take Columba out. He wrote a poem for her, 'white dove of the wild dark eyes', which was published in the *Irish Review*, but most of the poetry he wrote to her was printed on his own hand-printing press, which he called the Columba Press[35] in her honour. He collected some of the poems in a volume entitled *Sonnets to Columba*, of which he printed a limited edition of twenty-five copies in 1913.[36] However, Columba had no interest in his poetry and refused to accept the little amethyst ring he bought her. Even this did not deter Joe, who still was in love with her.

Although there was no romance at this time for Joe and Grace, they were constantly meeting. Grace and her sisters were involved in a number of the plays at the Hardwicke Theatre, where Grace, though she had no acting ability, helped out with the scenery. It was considered 'a fun thing' to get a walk-on part. Sidney Gifford and her friend Máire Perolz got minor roles, while Nellie Gifford also got some 'bit' parts, using the stage name Helen Bronsky.

Nellie's biggest role, however, was not on the stage; it came when she posed as the niece of an elderly clergyman, Reverend Mr

Donnelly, on the afternoon of 31 August 1913, in a ruse concocted to get Irish Transport and General Workers' Union leader Jim Larkin – disguised as the clergyman – on to the balcony of the Imperial Hotel on O'Connell Street where he could address a gathered crowd, as workers' meetings had been banned. He managed to make his speech before the crowd was dispersed by the police in a baton charge that left fifty people dead and three hundred injured. It was a key moment of the Dublin Lockout of 1913.

Through his editorship of the *Irish Review* Joe was also meeting more activists, including James Connolly. He asked the Labour leader to write about the Lockout and strike, but with the inclusion of articles by Connolly and others the content of the magazine became more radical and the circulation and subscriptions dropped. Joe joined a peace committee,[37] seeking to arbitrate between the employers and the workers. Jim Larkin, however, denounced him publicly, saying that his family owned 'rotten tenements'. Joe's mother had indeed purchased a tenement in 1912 in the Abbey Street area but she had kept it secret from the family and, according to his sister Geraldine, Joe had not realized that it was his mother who owned the building.

On his twenty-sixth birthday, in November 1913, Joe saw a notice of the meeting for the formation of an Irish Volunteer force. He went to see Eoin MacNeill, a professor of Irish History in University College Dublin and a founder of the Gaelic League. In volunteering his services, Joe told MacNeill that his health might not allow him to be much of a soldier but that he would use the *Irish Review* as propaganda for the Volunteers. MacNeill encouraged him to go to the meeting at Wynn's Hotel and, much to Joe's surprise, he was nominated to the Provisional Committee as Volunteer committee director of military operations. Other members included Thomas MacDonagh, P. H. Pearse, Bulmer Hobson, Eoin MacNeill and Michael O'Rahilly, who called himself The O'Rahilly.

The following summer, as the Irish Volunteers began to arm and a large quantity of weapons and ammunition was successfully landed at Howth, Joe hid guns in Larkfield, but the house was under surveillance so they were transferred instead to his childhood home in Fitzwilliam Street.

When the Volunteers split in autumn 1914, the majority – the National Volunteers – followed John Redmond's call to join the war in support of small nations, while those who remained in Ireland were under the leadership of Eoin MacNeill as chief of staff. The Irish Volunteers began to train in the grounds of Sandymount Castle, another property owned by Joe's mother, Countess Plunkett. Éamon de Valera's battalion was one of those to use its facilities. She had acquired twelve acres at Larkfield in Kimmage, an old mill, which had a manager's house, cottages and other buildings, and this also became a location for Volunteer activities.

When the Third Home Rule Bill, granting Ireland a separate parliament, was postponed until after the war, Joe took a secret oath and joined the Irish Republican Brotherhood, espousing their ideal of an Irish Republic and their plan to use the opportunity of the war to stage an armed uprising.

For some time Joe had been filling the empty pages of the *Irish Review* with his own poetry and now he wrote: 'I must get rid of it or let it die.'[38] However, he continued to produce the magazine until, in the first months of the war, it was suppressed after an article was published called 'Twenty plain facts for Irishmen'[39] which encouraged Volunteers in methods of protest against British rule in Ireland. This final issue also contained a cartoon by Grace Gifford entitled 'Cupid and Psyche'.

Despite his increasing involvement in nationalist activism, and his continuing TB, Joe had finally fulfilled a long-cherished ambition when, on 30 June 1914, he joined forces with Thomas MacDonagh and playwright Edward Martyn to form the Irish Theatre Company, to be based at the Hardwicke Theatre, although the first performance took place in 40 Upper O'Connell Street. It was the first staging of Martyn's *The Dream Physician*.[40]

Grace Gifford designed the postcard announcing the company's opening at Hardwicke Street. She depicts an oddly shaped man with a bowler hat and a walking stick held behind his back, reading the playbill of 4–9 January 1915, which lists works by Anton Chekhov, Villiers de l'Isle Adam, Rutherford Mayne and Eimar O'Duffy.

In April 1915 the IRB asked Joe to go to Berlin to meet with Roger Casement, who had been in Germany for six months trying to raise an Irish Brigade from prisoners-of-war to return to Ireland and fight for independence while Germany was at war with Britain. Casement, who was not a member of the IRB, had entered into an unsanctioned agreement with German officials for their assistance in an Irish revolution. Joe spread the word that he was going to Jersey for his health, but he actually made his way to Switzerland and got a permit in the German Embassy in Bern. He then made his way to a prisoner-of-war camp at Limburg, near Frankfurt, but even with his efforts they secured the assistance of only fifty men who would be willing to go back and fight in Ireland. He also worked on an agreement with Germany for the purchase of arms, which would be delivered to Ireland the following year. Joe travelled back via Switzerland, France and England.

Shortly after his return, in August 1915, he attended the funeral of the Fenian Jeremiah O'Donovan Rossa, who had ended his life in exile in America and whose burial back in Ireland was used as a platform to show the strength of numbers of the armed organizations in the country. Immediately following this event, Joe travelled to America to inform Clan na Gael, the secret oath-bound society, of plans in Ireland. The Clan had sent money to Casement, so the members needed to be kept informed of the progress of revolutionary intentions in Ireland and the contents of the German agreement.

While his political interests were all-consuming, there was another reason Joe wanted to be away from Ireland. Even as he departed for New York he remained consumed with love for Columba O'Carroll. Geraldine, his sister, did what she could to show him that it was useless to go on. While he was in America he wrote to Columba implying that he had left Ireland for Germany and was now in New York, not just for political reasons but also as an escape, as a bid to purge his feelings for her: 'Is it not six months since I left my country, home, friends and for your sake? Have I not even abstained from writing to you?' He told her: 'Only in my poems is there anything worthy of your love, and even the celestial glories of which I have written I seem to have obscured with my own murky personality. But I can at least praise God that I have seen his glory in you and have not kept silence.'[41]

When Joe returned to Ireland in mid-October 1915 Columba came to see him at Larkfield. Now aged twenty-one, she was no longer a schoolgirl and was focusing on her career. Her father had been appointed professor of medicine at University College Dublin and she was a medical student. She may have valued Joe as a friend, but she now told him directly that it must end. No longer could she be his muse and the focus of his affections.[42]

Just at that moment, Grace came seeking Joe's guidance. She later recalled: 'I was desperately interested in the Catholic Church. I did not know a single person, to whom I could talk to about the church until I discovered him and then I talked to him . . . we practically talked about nothing else.'[43] She had chosen to approach Joe as she had listened to him arguing with Thomas MacDonagh about religion and thought Thomas was 'irreligious' while Joe was a strongly religious man. He read widely on all religions and made a study of mysticism. The first surviving piece of correspondence to Grace from Joe was an essay on mysticism as the 'practice of perfect love', sent to her on Sunday, 28 November 1915:

> Mysticism is the practice of perfect love . . . Mystical illumination follows the way of perfection and gives the inner understanding to the lover.
>
> Love follows understanding . . . Love is an act of will. Passions are the raw material upon which the will is to act . . . It follows that love is something greater and deeper than an emotion . . . To love is not necessarily to like – at first, but as love is the true child of will it is

not always under restraint but as it grows and ripens comes to command the servant in all things . . .

It is often said: I cannot force myself to love. The answer is: you need only choose to – if you do not choose it may be impossible . . .

Divine love evident in creatures is what we call beauty . . . now all things are in some way beautiful but of all things on earth the most beautiful are the human soul and body for these are the likest [to] God.[44]

Given this level of communication, and perhaps enacting this idea of love, their connection quickly moved to another stage and they began a courtship. 'I did not know him intimately until late 1915', Grace would later tell others.[45]

And so on 29 November 1915 Grace received from Joe a message that he would come to visit her the following Wednesday. He wrote that he was glad to be able to tell her that she had made a mistake; it was not what she thought – he said it was 'something quite different'. He did not want her guessing, as it was serious. He concluded with 'This letter is deliberately colourless . . . I am afraid of giving you the wrong impression.'[46]

Within days Joe had spoken to Grace, expressing his feelings for her, and from his letter of 2 December 1915 it is clear that she reciprocated. While her side of the correspondence has not survived, it seemed she too was expressing her love:

Dear Dear Grace,
Since yesterday everything is different . . . But I only told you part of the truth even then I did not dare to tell you how much I cared for you for fear of saying more than I meant. You know what my sort of love is. It is a poor thing beside the splendours of your heart. But such as it is you have it. I do love you. I hope to become more worthy of loving you. Will you marry me? Joe.
Postscript: By the way, I am actually a beggar. I have no income and am earning nothing. Moreover there are other things desperate, practically speaking to prevent me marrying. J.

His health was indeed an impediment, although he had consulted an unidentified doctor at this time who told Joe that he did not have TB.

Later that day came another note:

2 December 1915

Darling Grace,
You will marry me and nobody else. I have been a damned fool and a blind imbecile but thank God I see. I love you and will never love anyone else.
Your lover Joe.[47]

Grace later said that they became engaged that day, with no immediate plans for marriage.[48] Later on the same day Joe arrived at Larkfield, where he found his father and his siblings Geraldine, Mimi, George, Fiona and Jack all together. When Joe came in, Geraldine said he was in 'high good humour' and told them: 'I am going to marry Grace Gifford.' Geraldine recalled: 'It was a bombshell for all of us – we didn't know they took that much interest in each other nor did we know that he had given up the idea of Columba . . . Mimi was shocked and almost said so but I managed to stop her in time.'[49]

Joe wrote to Grace in the middle of the night, heading his letter: 'This same night written at 2 in the morning':[50]

Darling, Darling, Darling,
I can't believe it. It's crazy. It's impossible. I was never meant to be so happy. I can't believe what I know. I mean I daren't think about it. I know it's true. It is true, it is, it is – if it wasn't I'd go mad. You do love me I hav[e] to keep telling myself that you do. You do don't you, say you do – swear you do . . . Listen I love you love you love you altogether body soul and spirit – every thing and every bit of you I love and worship. I love you. I love you. I love you a million million times. Joe.[51]

Two days later he told Grace in a letter that his family could not make out his strange behaviour or what had taken him over:

4 December 1915

Well I suppose – no I don't this is what I mean (I hope it is now). I can't, I mean partly I can't and partly I mustn't dip my pen in blood and fire and write deep into your heart (by the way don't forget I have it and go looking for it – also don't give mine away by any chance – not that I suppose there's any possibility of my recovering it from where it is now. Don't you find it rather jumpy? It's not used to heaven yet.)[52]

They decided to announce their engagement formally. On 5 December Joe wrote a note to Columba to tell her the news before it became public.[53] He wrote to Grace that Seán Mac Diarmada had told him that he had heard an 'absurd' story that Joe and Grace were engaged. Recounting this to her, he wrote: 'So I take the chance of humour I said Yes, wasn't it? And the funny part of it was that Grace believes it too.'[54]

Over those final weeks of 1915, the couple had difficulty in meeting. This was highlighted in a letter written from Kimmage at midnight on St Stephen's Day, 26 December 1915. Joe wrote that it had been so difficult not to see her and the reason she had not come to see him was because it was a Sunday: 'Listen darling Grace I can't live without seeing you – it hurts too much. There I didn't want to say that but you will not misunderstand me. I love you and I know you love me and so everything is all right.' He signs the letter with fifteen kisses.[55]

He wrote frequently from Larkfield, which in his usual lyrical fashion he described to Grace as 'the field of larks'.[56] His living there had an impact on their meetings. Even courtship by correspondence had some difficulties, as he described in one letter, written at midnight: 'I must tramp about half a mile to post'.[57] They did occasionally meet to socialize, but mainly they had to be content to meet at Larkfield whenever possible.

Illness was not the only reason for their occasional meetings. Joe wrote a note on 19 January 1916 making plans to attend a Percy French show with her. In this note he told her nothing about the secret meeting he had been at when a number of men from the IRB met with James Connolly to inform him of their plans for rebellion. Joe later said that they talked to Connolly almost continuously for three days.

This was followed by a period of illness for Joe that left him unable to move from the house and he had to content himself with speaking to Grace by telephone or sending her letters. Grace later said she knew nothing of his military activities, but by the beginning of February it was dominating his life:

Larkfield, 1 February 1916
Sweetheart,

Just a little letter to say how much I miss you and that I want you very much. It is late and I'm afraid this won't go tonight because I was kept all the morning talking against my will and in the evening I had to go fifty places and then a staff meeting and then more talk till all hours – and with it all I was not very chirpy today I should have had to go out. But I am better now curiously enough.[58]

Weather in early February also hampered Joe's plans, as it was snowing and he was ill again and could not go out. On 7 February he wrote: 'When shall I see you? I will never attempt to write the things that can only be said. I will not tell you the torment of not seeing you.'[59] This pattern continued over the following weeks. When Grace visited him at Larkfield, she was visiting a patient. Joe would content himself with wandering around the house in pyjamas looking for books. At other times he demonstrated to her his athleticism by jumping 'six chairs at a time'. Grace always maintained that she thought he was suffering from bronchitis.

He wrote to her:

I am so happy when you are with me because I feel your love besides knowing it. I want to feel how much I love you. I want us to be together for always. Listen sweetheart – will you come and see me the very first minute you possibly can? Do – but I know you will because you know you are the life of my heart and all the sweetness and the beauty there is in this world. Oh if you could only know how I love you . . . you would understand so many things – perhaps you do know perhaps even better than I do myself.[60]

The fact that they knew each other so little troubled Joe. He felt that if she came to know him fully that she would not care for him:

I want so badly to talk to you. I am afraid I am not able to write what I want to say. I need your prayers. I am so unhappy at seeing what kind of a fool I am and how poor and mean my character is. If I hadn't been so conceited I would have seen it plainly long ago . . . This is not humility – it is just facing realities and it hurts so much to have to tell you because I am afraid it will hurt you to know that I am no good, and I do so want you to think well of me because I cannot do without your love. I know it is foolish to expect you to love me when you know what I am like but I must tell you that it is my only hope. Bad as I am I love you beyond everything and I simply cannot face losing you – I cannot think of it – it is just black misery.[61]

He wrote a poem to her called 'New Love', which opened with:

The day I knew you loved me we had lain
Deep in Coill Doraca down by Gleann na Scath

Unknown to each till suddenly I saw
You in the shadow, knew oppressive pain

Stopping my heart, and there you did remain . . .

And I swore I would not rest

Till that mad heart was worthy of your breast
Or dead for you – and then this love awoke.[62]

Joe's sister Geraldine was not pleased with his romance. Her opinion of Grace was not flattering. She later wrote: 'I do not think that I have ever met anyone who put on more airs and graces – she patronised all other women, she thought anything serious was stuffy and dull and then presumed that we were all like that. She was a dreadful bore.'[63]

At this point the newly engaged Grace questioned Joe's affections and showed a trait that was a family failing: jealousy. Someone had obviously told her of his affections for Columba. Without referring to any incident or anyone, he replied:

There is one other thing that has hurt me though you did not mean it to, and I am sure I deserve it . . . You suggested seriously and repeatedly that I might think of someone else. I suppose you were right to doubt my love for you . . . Sure if I didn't feel that you are the only person in the world for me my love would be a very queer sort of thing. I know I am a queer sort of thing myself but my love is the only good thing about me and quite different and beyond me [sic] ordinary self. There is no one in the world I could be happy with but you. There is no one good enough to make up for my badness but you – there is no one I can love but you, no one who has ever loved me but you . . . I can only devote myself to your services by working to improve myself and increase my love for you – and meanwhile to trust altogether in your love. Write to me sweet sweet heart. JP.[64]

Following this series of letters the couple issued their engagement announcement in the *Irish Life* magazine of 11 February 1916. Plans were put in place for a wedding that Easter, a double wedding with Joe's sister Geraldine, who was to marry Tom Dillon, with whom she had studied chemistry in university. He had been advising the Volunteers on the production of explosives.

In early March 1916, Joe withdrew abruptly from the theatre

world. It was made known that he had disagreed when the company decided to produce the Swedish playwright August Strindberg's *Easter*, and by the time it opened on Friday, 3 March, Joe's name was missing from the playbill as manager of the Irish Theatre Company. Grace Gifford wrote to Joseph Holloway on 7 March: 'Isn't the play at Hardwicke Street horrible!' He agreed, replying to her: 'I thought *Easter* a crazy play, by a crazy author, for crazy playgoers.'[65]

Other issues were now dominating Joe's mind and taking up his time. It was said that the Dublin Metropolitan Police were about to arrest the leaders of the Volunteers. At the end of March police surrounded Larkfield, where drilling had been taking place and where a number of young men were being housed in anticipation of the Rising. However, for some unknown reason, the police withdrew abruptly.

Joe's sister Mimi had gone to the US with a message regarding the Rising, and his father was sent to Italy to have a meeting with the Pope, which was made possible by his status as a Papal Count. Grace was aware there were secrets, but said she knew nothing of what was evolving. She explained this by saying that she knew Joe was bound by oath to say nothing, and she understood that.[66]

Grace's focus was her conversion to Catholicism and her instruction for her baptism with Father James Sheridan, her spiritual director, who was curate of Our Lady Seat of Wisdom, known as the University Church, St Stephen's Green.[67] It was there on 7 April 1916 that she was baptized a Catholic by him, with Joe's youngest sister, Fiona, as her sponsor. All was now in place for the wedding at Easter. Joe wrote Grace a poem for the occasion:

> The joy of Spring leaps from your eyes
> The strength of dragons in your hair
> In your young soul we still surprise
> The secret wisdom flowing there;
> But never word shall speak or sing
> Inadequate music where above

Your burning heart now spreads its wing
In the wild beauty of your Love.

Joe had suggested that they get married during Lent, which was
not the norm for Catholics. When Grace suggested Easter, she later
recounted that he said 'we may be running a revolution then'.[68] At
this point he told her that they would be 'going into the Rising
together'. This shows how little they knew of each other – if he
wanted someone to fight alongside him, he had chosen the wrong
sister! Nellie Gifford was a member of the Irish Citizen Army,
committed to the role of women fighting as equals alongside the
men. Joe had suggested that Grace become a member of Cumann
na mBan, one of the organizations of women activists who would be
taking part in the fighting, but she never joined. She had no intention of taking part and told Joe: 'I knew nothing about it and
wouldn't have been any good as a soldier.'[69]

Joe's own preparations for the approaching Rising were
hampered by his illness. Dr Charles MacAuley, who had been giving
first-aid instruction to Cumann na mBan, saw him and told him he
needed an operation for the growth on his neck; the doctor booked
him into Mrs Quinn's Nursing Home on Mountjoy Square. As well
as being a physical reminder of his condition, the abscess on Joe's
neck also indicated how ill he was. It is likely that he would have
been suffering other symptoms of TB: chills, tiredness and weight
loss. The operation was performed, the swelling was removed, but
he was still critically ill.

On 19 April, while Grace was with Joe at the nursing home, she
assisted him in transcribing a document in code. It had allegedly
been leaked from Dublin Castle and concerned the arrests of key
members of the Volunteers. This so-called 'Castle Document' was
printed on Joe's hand-press and distributed to the newspapers. A
small number were printed by *New Ireland*, with the statement that if
the Volunteers were attacked it would lead to armed resistance, and
a copy was read at a meeting of Dublin Corporation.

At other times different young men visited Joe, with their notebooks and pencils at the ready for instruction. His doctor quipped that it was like Napoleon with his marshals – a comment that was not well received by those present. He also joked with Joe, asking if he slept with a revolver under his pillow; to his immense surprise, Joe replied 'I do' and pulled it out to show him. It became clear as the days passed what was being planned and Joe told his doctor that there was going to be bloodshed.

When he left the nursing home, against the doctor's wishes, Dr MacAuley made a point of visiting him in the Metropole Hotel, where he was staying on Easter Saturday. He tried to persuade Joe to go back to the nursing home, as he still had an open wound on his neck, but he refused.[70]

Grace was at her parents' home on Saturday when a young man, Michael Collins, who had returned from London to take part in the Rising, called to the house with a message from Joe:

Holy Saturday 1916

I got your dear letter as I was going out at nine this morning and have not had a minute to collect my thoughts since 2.45pm . . .

Here is a little gun, which should only be used to protect yourself. To fire it push up the small bar under the word 'safe' and pull the trigger – but not unless you mean to shoot. Here is some money for you too and all my love for ever. Joe.

Collins also passed on the message that Grace was to go in to meet Joe at the Metropole Hotel, but she misunderstood him and got there just as he was leaving. 'He was coming down the stairs. His uniform looked like a new one, his hair was completely shaved and he was wearing a wide-awake hat. He looked awful and he said "I have waited all afternoon for you".'[71] He had to go at that moment, so rather than leave each other immediately they stole a few more minutes travelling together in a cab to Gardiner's Street where Joe got out.

Grace continued on to her sister Muriel's house, where she was to spend the next couple of days. Geraldine Plunkett and Tom Dillon had continued with their plans to be married but Grace and Joe had not posted their banns, so even when the fighting was postponed from Easter Sunday to the following day it was not possible for the ceremony to go ahead. Joe wrote to her on Easter Sunday 1916 at 9 p.m.:

> My dearest heart,
> Keep up your spirits and trust in Providence. Everything is bully. I have only a minute. I am going into the nursing home tonight to sleep. I am keeping as well as anything but need a rest. Take care of your old cold, sweetheart. All my love for ever, darling darling Grace. Joe.[72]

7

Muriel and Thomas

Thomas Stanislaus MacDonagh was described as having curly brown hair, handsome features and the 'most humorous and friendly expression in his grey eyes.'[1] He was a published poet and writer and a teacher at a boys' school when introduced to sisters Muriel, Grace and Sidney Gifford. The story of their meeting was often retold. The journalist and suffragist Nannie Dryhurst had brought the three siblings to see an experimental school for Irish boys, St Enda's, where the Irish language, history, drama and games were being taught. Dryhurst urged MacDonagh to 'fall in love with one of the girls and marry her', to which he replied: 'that would be easy to marry one of them – the only difficulty would be to decide which one!'[2]

The Gifford sisters were 'noted figures in the social and artistic life of the capital – not less for their good looks and smart dressing than for their many gifts.'[3] There were in fact six sisters: Catherine Anna (known as Katie), born in 1875; Helen Ruth (known as Nellie), born in 1880; Ada Gertrude, born in 1882; Muriel Enid, born in 1885; Grace Eveleen, born in 1888; and Sidney Sarah, born in 1889. There were also six brothers: Claude, born in 1874; Gerald, born c.1877; Gabriel, born c.1879; Liebert, born in 1880; Frederick Ernest, born in 1883; and Grace's twin, Edward Cecil. In 1908 Muriel Gifford was twenty-three and was considered the most beautiful of the sisters. She was described as 'the quiet one' in a family of great talkers.

Her father, Frederick Gifford, was a solicitor, who worked as a land and law agent. Despite his respectable façade, Frederick Gifford was illegitimate, brought up by maternal maiden aunts. Officially, he stated that his father was William Gifford, a surgeon;[4] however, the family story was that his unmarried parents had died young in County Tipperary. His father was known to have been an aristocrat who had left instructions and money that his son would be educated in the law, but despite this level of involvement in dictating his son's future, he did not publicly acknowledge paternity.[5] It is even unclear if his father had given him his surname of Gifford, which had a long lineage; the family had come to Ireland in the twelfth century. Their motto read: 'I would rather die than be dishonoured'. Frederick was also assisted with his education in the law by the Solicitors' Benevolent Fund and was apprenticed to James Swazy, whose offices were on the Liffey Quays.

Isabella Burton may not have been fully aware of the background of the man she was marrying, but she showed herself to be un-conventional enough to marry outside her own religion. Isabella Julia Burton had been born in Clonagoose and was twenty-four years old[6] when she married Frederick Gifford, who was twelve years her senior, at St George's Church of Ireland in Dublin on 27 April 1872. Her Protestant faith was important to her and she married in her own church. Her father had been, as she described, a 'clerk in holy orders'. It is said that when she left home to marry, Isabella climbed out of a window because her family objected to her marrying a Catholic. The rift seems to have been long-lasting,[7] as she was 'removed' from the official Burton genealogy and her name was omitted from her uncle Frederic Burton's memorial, which was erected by her siblings in gratitude for his kindness to their family.

The Gifford children were initially educated in private houses; one such establishment was run by two ladies, 'the Miss Fitts'. Later, they attended a Mrs Harden's Dame School on Ormond Road. The sisters then attended Alexandra College in Dublin. The youngest, Sidney, would later write: 'It was a well kept secret in my school that we lived in Ireland, or had any history of our own at all.' Sidney felt they were 'trained' there 'to look down upon the people of Ireland and of all countries as "natives", you were taught to regard every language but English as a jargon.'[8]

Muriel never recorded her own memories of school, but she seemed to have enjoyed her schooldays and won prizes. While Grace also later made reference to poor education standards there, Alexandra College was in fact the first women's college in Ireland to prepare pupils for degrees, and the eldest Gifford sister, Katie, a gifted linguist, attained entry to the Royal University, from which she earned an honours BA in languages before going to Germany to teach. Nellie left school early and was given the role of junior assistant housekeeper at home in 8 Temple Villas, Rathmines. She was entrusted with the key to the larder and, amongst other duties, assisted at her mother's formal 'at homes'. Ada followed her brother Gabriel[9] to art school.

By 1901 all the family were still living together in Temple Villas, with the exception of Liebert, who had enlisted in the Merchant Navy and moved to Canada. Frederick junior was studying engineering; Claude was working with their father, Frederick, who now had his own practice, Gifford & Son, in Dawson Street (originally at number 46 but now at number 5), and was still living at home; and Gerald was also studying law. However, he had just completed his final exams when he contracted meningitis and died later that year.

Following her schooling, Muriel moved to England, where she began training to be a poultry instructress. The British government was promoting the poultry industry, and the role of the instructresses was to travel to farms to give training in egg fertilization, information to encourage the introduction of new breeds and other ideas in an effort to improve poultry production. Muriel did not settle, however, and moved back home. When she returned to Ireland she began nursing in Sir Patrick Dun's Hospital, but poor health meant that she had to give it up and afterwards she did not hold down any employment.

By the time of their first meeting with Thomas MacDonagh,

Muriel, Grace and Sidney were the only family members still living at home with their parents in Rathmines. By 1909 most of the surviving Gifford siblings had decided to make a life outside Ireland, some in Canada, others in England or America.[10] Nellie, having studied domestic economy, was travelling to various parts of Ireland working as an 'itinerant cookery instructress'.

Sidney, who had finished her schooling and was determined to become a journalist, had already had her first article published. She used the pseudonym 'John Brennan', as she felt her opinions would be more valued if they were thought to be written by a man. She became known to her closest friends as 'John'. Sidney was politicized early and joined Maud Gonne's Inghinidhe na hÉireann.

The sisters enjoyed being social; if they spent an evening at home, their father would quip: 'What is the matter? I hope you are not ill.'[11] Some of their activities – attending lectures and political meetings – were concealed from their mother, because she would have completely disapproved.

Muriel, together with Grace, Sidney and Nellie, joined the Irish Women's Franchise League, which was founded in 1908 advocating 'Votes for Women'. It had its own publication, the *Irish Citizen*. Muriel once admitted she attended these lectures because she was interested in the social aspect rather than the lectures themselves. On one occasion she was 'chaperoned' by Helena Molony, who, at twenty-five, was two years Muriel's senior; she was a leading member of Inghinidhe na hÉireann and editor of the women's paper *Bean na hÉireann*, as well as being a trade union organizer and labour activist. Helena brought many people into political and socialist organizations, but it appears that Muriel was not one of them.

One of the lecturers at the Franchise League was Thomas MacDonagh. He spoke with a strong Tipperary accent, as he had been born in Cloughjordan, County Tipperary, in February 1878, one of nine[12] children of Joseph MacDonagh and Mary-Louise Parker, schoolteachers who had come to the village some years before to open the first Catholic school in what had been a Cromwellian settlement.

Mary-Louise was the daughter of a printer, Thomas Burroughs-Parker, a compositor in Greek, who had come to Ireland from England to work at the Trinity College Press. Privately educated, she wrote stories and poems and filled notebooks with religious meditations. Though born a Unitarian, she converted to Catholicism and wrote articles, among them one entitled: 'The daily life of a convert by a true Catholic'. She was a very different character to Thomas's father, Joseph, who was born in 1834 in County Roscommon. He was a jovial, kind-hearted man, but when his salary arrived each month he often went on long drinking bouts. Mary-Louise's religious outlook dominated the MacDonagh household; religious pictures covered the walls and the family prayed in the evenings and listened to readings of texts such as Thomas à Kempis's *The Imitation of Christ*.

In August 1892 Thomas was sent to Rockwell College, County Tipperary, on a scholarship with his fees paid. The school was run by a French Order, the Fathers of the Holy Ghost, and had a French curriculum. In 1894, at the age of sixteen, the year of his father's death, Thomas wrote to the superior of the Order: 'I have concluded that I have a vocation for this Congregation, and a decided taste for the missionary and the religious state. It has always been my wish to become a priest and now that wish is stronger than ever, and it is to become, not only a priest . . . a missionary and a religious.'[13]

His request was granted. He wore the soutane and broad hat of the Order. He also began tutoring the most junior students at the school and over the next few years he became a full-time teacher.

By 1901, however, Thomas had changed his mind about becoming a priest and wrote to the superior general of the Order on 22 June that 'I have no vocation to religious life, with sorrow I request you to release me from the obligations contracted by me at my reception'.[14] This marked the end of his time in County Tipperary and he left Rockwell after almost a decade. He went to teach English, history and French at the Catholic College of St Kieran's in Kilkenny in autumn 1901.

While he was in Kilkenny, Thomas joined the Gaelic League. He said later that he went to one of their meetings for the first time just 'for a laugh'.[15] However, he quickly became immersed in the activities of the organization, becoming one of the secretaries and an organizer of the Kilkenny Feis (Irish cultural competition). He later described receiving his 'baptism in Nationalism' at the Gaelic League in Kilkenny. Thomas also continued to expand his knowledge of the Irish language. During the summer of 1902 he visited the Aran Islands, attending classes at the Inishmaan summer school.

From childhood onwards, Thomas had been writing poetry and fiction, and would gift his verses to those whose friendship he valued.[16] In 1901 he sent a manuscript of poetry that he was preparing for publication to W. B. Yeats. In his reply Yeats urged caution, pointing out that Thomas's proposal for a thousand copies of the book was far too large for a first collection. He wrote:

> Now about the verses themselves ... They show that you have a thoughtful and imaginative mind – but you have not yet got a precise musical and personal language. Whether you have poetical power or not I could not really say – but I can say that you have not found yourself as a poet ... I strongly advise you not to publish for the present ... If after this, you still care to dedicate the book to me, you are certainly welcome to do so.[17]

Despite this reply, Thomas went ahead with his planned publication, *Through the Ivory Gate*, published by Sealy, Bryers and Walker in 1903 with a dedication to W. B. Yeats. It is a lavish production for a poet's first published volume, and it placed him in considerable debt. In the preface to the book he wrote of his regret that he could not write verse in the Irish language: 'Deep in my Irish heart I grieve that I know not to sing my lays in Irish tongue.'[18]

With the suddenness and intensity that seemed to characterize him, Thomas now deemed his position at St Kieran's School untenable because of the college's decision not to teach the Irish language, and he resigned. He was offered a post at St Colman's

School in Fermoy, County Cork, moving there in September 1903 and choosing to live in a small cottage outside the college. Shortly after his arrival he wrote: 'Fermoy is a good place; college splendid; up-to-date; billiards and hurling.' He described the president of the school as 'a very clever man, progressive'.[19]

While he was there, in April 1903 his second book of poetry, *April and May with Other Verses*, was published by Sealy, Bryers and Walker, again at the author's expense; he had written so many poems in Rockwell that he decided on another publication. This second volume failed critically and financially and later he would destroy a number of copies in frustration.

In Fermoy, Thomas joined the local branch of the Gaelic League, giving Irish classes twice a week as well as attending a teacher's class on other nights. The Gaelic League also introduced him to a world of singing and dancing evenings, lectures and theatrical events. He learned to sing in the traditional *sean-nós* style and appeared in many concerts. He accepted the role of vice president of the Fermoy branch, but within months the commitment became too much and he resigned. He remained a dedicated member of the organization, however, describing himself as 'a pretty fluent speaker of Irish'. On one occasion he wrote a story in Irish to read to the branch.

Thomas continued to focus on his literary works, spending his spare time 'licking my latest book into shape', as he wrote to a friend.[20] One of his greatest successes came in 1904 when he wrote the lyrics to a sacred cantata called 'The Exodus', with music composed by an Italian, Benedetto Palmieri, a voice professor of the Dublin Academy of Music, which was submitted to the annual music competition, the Feis Ceoil, in 1904. Its performance at the Royal University on 19 May was a critical success for Thomas, but it was not well received by his peers in the new movement of Irish nationalists. In the nationalist newspaper the *United Irishman*, edited by Arthur Griffith, it was argued that as the music, lyrics and general subject matter had nothing to do with Ireland, it should not have been submitted to the Feis Ceoil.[21]

The year 1907 saw the completion of another book of verse,

entitled *The Golden Joy*; Thomas's previous failures had not stopped him from writing poetry and wanting it published. When he was in the final stages of preparing this book, he wrote to a friend that three English publishers were willing to take it, but in the end it was brought out by an Irish publisher, D. J. O'Donoghue, who liked Thomas on a personal level, describing him as 'most amiable and charming'. He thought him supremely confident in his own ability as a poet: 'he lost no opportunity of expressing his belief in his literary work'.[22] Yet Thomas was dissatisfied by his verse even when it was finished and published; the copy of the book he gave to his brother Joseph contains so many corrections it looks like an author's proof copy.[23] In other signed versions, more corrections can be found. He blamed his publisher for the poor sales of his book, writing: 'He mismanaged that book of mine hopelessly. I paid him ten pounds, and he got nearly as much more in orders, and that is all that I know of it. He never probably put it on sale at all'.[24]

Thomas MacDonagh now added playwright to his accomplishments when, in February 1908, he completed a drama, *When the Dawn is Come*, and sent it to Fred Ryan, honorary secretary of the Abbey Theatre. He was also at this time in the midst of writing a novel, the story of a man unjustly sentenced to death. He had planned to have it complete by the autumn and 'the whole thing finished in less than a year.'[25] However, this novel was never finished as events in his own life took over and he moved again.

It had been five years since he had come to Cork and Thomas was dissatisfied and unhappy there. He even discussed the possibility of leaving Ireland, believing that it would be easy for him to get work in London. But it was to Dublin that he travelled in the summer of 1908, where he met with J. M. Synge, who had already established himself as a leading Irish playwright. His work *The Playboy of the Western World* had been staged the previous year at the Abbey Theatre. Thomas was drawn to him despite the controversial aspect of the playwright's approach to writing, which many nationalists believed showed the Irish people in an unflattering way. Synge gave guidance to Thomas on getting his own play ready for the stage.

That summer Thomas was asked to join a newly established school at Cullenswood House in the Dublin suburb of Ranelagh, which was being established by P. H. Pearse, with whom he had been corresponding on Gaelic League matters since his days in Kilkenny. Pearse had trained as a barrister-at-law but by then did not practise, although he used this title in his advertisements for the school, which he was setting up to counter the practices of the education system that operated under the British administration. The school was described to prospective pupils as 'an Irish standpoint and atmosphere with a direct method of teaching modern languages; all other instruction bilingual; special attention to science and "modern" subjects'. It assured pupils that there were 'homelike surroundings'.[26] In September Thomas took up residence at St Enda's, where he was appointed assistant headmaster and instructor of language and literature.

It was not just the draw of working in a bilingual school that brought Thomas to Dublin; it was the lure of the literary world, the chance to mix with those who shared his creativity. St Enda's attracted many from the literary and artistic world, including the dramatist Edward Martyn, the Irish scholar and founder of the Gaelic League Douglas Hyde, artist and writer George Moore, as well as other writers and poets such as Ella Young, W. B. Yeats and Seumus MacManus. The ethos of the school allowed for both teacher and pupil to have a creative and artistic outlook, with school visits to museums, or Dublin Zoo; in addition, the pupils took part in Irish language demonstrations at the Abbey Theatre. The school was a hub of emerging Irish culture, its walls decorated with paintings of Irish heroes and legends by artists such as Jack B. Yeats and George Russell (AE). The names of great Irish patriots were written in Gaelic script on the walls. The boys played Irish games such as hurling.

From the time that he lived in Fermoy, Thomas had been in weekly correspondence with the writer Padraic Colum. Although he disagreed with his friend's 'views on most things literary', Thomas thought him 'the most lovable, unspoiled, generous friend',[27] and when he came to live in Dublin, Colum became his close companion.

Thomas's play *When the Dawn Comes* opened at the Abbey on 15 October 1908. The reviewer from the St Enda's publication *An Macaomh* wrote that the students who had seen the play came back 'yearning for rifles'. Another sympathetic reviewer in *Bean na hÉireann* claimed it held the audience 'spellbound'; however, this review went on to describe the staging as 'simply appalling', the use of orange sateen shorts and cycling stockings and breeches 'shockingly absurd'.[28] Thomas's reaction to the production of his play was that it had been 'badly performed' and 'misunderstood'.[29] Following this, he set about rewriting it in everyday prose and began planning a new production.

Meeting a future wife was not at the forefront of Thomas MacDonagh's mind in late 1908. On 26 November his mother died following an operation and it was around this time that the Gifford sisters came to visit St Enda's. When he first met Muriel he was more taken with the woman who introduced her, the journalist and suffragist Nannie Dryhurst.[30] She was in Dublin in November 1908 and on the 14th, in her capacity as 'Honoured Secretary of the Subject Races International Committee', had given a lecture, 'The Small Nations of the Near East and the Importance of Co-Operation', with slides of a visit she had made to Transcaucasia (an area that today covers Georgia, Azerbaijan and Armenia), in the hall of the National Literary Society to raise money for the Industrial Development branch of Sinn Féin. Thomas wrote at the time that he admired her 'sincerity and wonderful enthusiasm'.[31]

Nannie Dryhurst had met Muriel's brother Frederick Gifford in London when he joined a literary group, mixing with Nannie's daughter Sylvia and her future son-in-law, the writer Robert Lynd. Frederick told her of his sisters' interests and of Sidney's writings on Irish politics and urged her to meet up with the girls when she visited Dublin.

Following his first meeting with them, Thomas corresponded with three of the Gifford sisters – Sidney, Nellie and Muriel. Muriel soon became the self-appointed spokesperson of the family as she issued invitations and made arrangements to meet him. Her first surviving letter dates from the following year, 7 August 1909. It is addressed to him in Irish as *a chara* (friend): 'We are asking a couple of friends tomorrow morning at 10 30am for breakfast. I hope you will ... and be sure to wear your kilt'. It is signed '*do ċara* [your friend], ME Gifford'.[32]

Muriel attended Irish classes at the Gaelic League and used little Irish phrases in her letters, but did not seem to have reached any level of fluency. She liked Thomas to wear a kilt, which was considered part of the native dress and was seen as a public statement of Ireland's right to self-rule and its own identity, yet for Muriel it did not appear to go beyond its visual appeal. She wrote to Thomas in similar terms on several occasions: 'Don't forget that you've got to wear your kilt – if you only knew how much nicer they look than ordinary dress you would never wear anything else.'[33]

Her obvious interest in Thomas as a prospective suitor was not immediately reciprocated. In fact, his affections lay elsewhere. He had fallen in love with Mary Maguire, whom he had met shortly after his arrival in Dublin. Mary, who taught in Patrick Pearse's girls' school, Scoil Ita, had befriended both Thomas and Padraic Colum and spent a considerable amount of time with them. Thomas had misconstrued her friendship with him as feelings of love and in the spring of 1910 he decided the time was right for him to propose. Mary's version of events was that she was proposed to at regular intervals by various male friends, but she saw marriage as 'monotonous domesticity' and 'the dreary commonplaces', so would laugh it off. Of Thomas she wrote:

> One of them, however, declined to listen to me and kept assuring me that he was the person that Heaven had destined me to marry and that I could not escape my fate ... he made one final determined effort before dropping me. He called to my little flat, armed with an engagement ring, and told me in a very caveman manner that he had arranged everything, that I was to marry him on a certain date in a

certain church and that I better accept my destiny. The argument that ensued reduced me to a state of panic such as I had never known, for I was afraid I might be unable to hold out, especially as he said I had encouraged him and ought to have some sense of responsibility about it. But I managed to be strong-minded, and the harassing interview ended with tears on both sides, with his throwing the ring in the fire and leaving in a high state of emotion.[34]

The smoke-damaged ring that survives correlates Mary's negative response.[35] When asked about his engagement, Thomas gaily told friends: 'well that's over. We decided I was not good enough for her.'[36] His poem 'After a Year', believed to be written about his un-requited love for Mary Maguire, opens with the lines: 'After a year of love, Death of love in a day', and ends with: 'Into her eyes I looked, Left her without a kiss.' It was included in his book of verse *Songs of Myself*, which was published by Hodges Figgis in 1910.

The second surviving letter in the correspondence between Thomas MacDonagh and Muriel Gifford is dated February 1910. She writes in reply to an invitation from Thomas to the Gifford family: 'my sisters have much pleasure in accepting. My brother [Frederick] unfortunately cannot come at present as he is at present in California and I am afraid even a cablegram would not bring him over in time.'[37]

Muriel Gifford's kind letters were not Thomas's focus, however; rejection from Mary had hit him hard. He resigned from St Enda's on 15 June, writing two days later to Gertrude Bloomer, housemistress at the school, that Pearse had reluctantly accepted his resignation, telling her: 'we had grown so intimate we shall miss each other'.[38] He left for Paris on 26 July in search of freedom, a 'desert, where I could begin again, without shackles'. He set himself a course of study in French literature and philosophy,[39] staying at Hotel Jacob, Rue Jacob, on the left bank of the Seine, a fashionable district within easy walking distance of the museums and galleries, where he lived 'silent and free as a hawk in the sky.'[40]

Without any explanation of why the freedom of Paris was no

longer what he required, Thomas returned to Ireland at the beginning of September 1910. Pearse wanted him to return to the school, but there was no money to pay him a proper wage. Gertrude Bloomer had kept Thomas in touch with the school with questions about timetables for the girls' school, which had moved into the vacated Cullenswood House, while the boys' school had moved a great distance away to the Hermitage in Rathfarnham.

By January 1911 Thomas was back giving occasional lectures at the boys' school. He lived off the North Circular Road until March 1911, when David Houston offered him the use of the gate lodge of his home, Grange House, which was by coincidence in the neighbourhood of St Enda's. Professor Houston came to the school to take the boys on nature walks and became a close friend to Thomas, even standing guarantor for him on a number of bank loans.

In Grange House Lodge Thomas found the solitude that he had been seeking. He wrote to his close friend Dominick Hackett, who had moved to New York: 'I have found a desert here . . . I am in striking distance of the life I want.'[41] Within a short space of time his home of solitude became a place of pilgrimage for a literary circle, according to the writer James Stephens: 'He was a recluse who delighted in company'.[42] Thomas was described as 'full of wit and friendship, and his greatest delight was to discuss poetry.'[43] He would occasionally recite his poems while plucking a stringed instrument, in the style of an old Irish bard.

Despite the fact that Padraic Colum had gained the affections of Mary Maguire, he remained one of Thomas's friends. Other visitors included AE (George Russell), Arthur Griffith and Joe Plunkett, whom he had been tutoring in the Irish language since 1909. Thomas described Joe as being 'great at genealogy and the like; he knows Egyptian and out of the way things and has studied philosophy at Stonyhurst . . .' Elsewhere he met James Connolly. During the winter of 1910 and into the spring of 1911 Thomas also attended twice-weekly classes with Professor Robert Donovan, professor of English Literature at University College Dublin, taking a course of study towards an MA degree.

Upon his return to Dublin, Thomas looked anew at one of the Gifford girls. When he met Muriel, he would always exclaim, 'isn't she beautiful!' Muriel craved such attention, writing to him later that year: 'I cannot agree with you in thinking that I am beautiful . . . as for my hair I have always regarded the colour to be rather ashamed of . . . that is the best (or worst) of being one of a large family you get all the conceit knocked out of you.'[44]

On the morning of 17 October 1911 Muriel woke up, set Thomas's picture up before her and, as she described to him, 'gave you a very serious talking to about the folly of having anything to do with me – I'm afraid my dearest that you will be utterly disappointed with me when you get to know me better – I am not at all the person you imagine – in fact I am utterly ordinary – you should have fallen in love with someone thoroughly different – but please don't darling.'[45] He would often enquire of Muriel why she loved him, a question which caused her unease.

Muriel had no idea of Thomas's romance with Mary Maguire. She had a great sense of inferiority in relation to her more active and vocal sisters, and this manifested itself in her fear that Thomas would prefer Sidney, Grace or Nellie over her. Muriel never referred to Sidney, her youngest sister, by her given name, but rather by her pen name 'John Brennan': 'Please please – for Heaven's sake don't make love to John Brennan or anyway don't in my presence you make me so miserable and jealous this evening. You'll break my heart if you fall in love with her. Why did you arrange for her to come tomorrow evening? I suppose it is so absurd to write this – but I feel it so much. Yours Muriel.'[46] Thomas replied 'I like John and Nellie and Grace very much – Nellie, I think, the most, but my liking for them is as different as the spheres from my love for you, Muriel.'[47]

Later she reasons why she is so jealous of her sister Sidney:

I think I have at last got at the <u>real</u> solution of why I am jealous . . . it is because I love her very much myself and admire her – and then I think that every man should fall in love with her – I was thinking all the time she was speaking the other night, what a much better comrade she would be for you, than I am – I am afraid my own darling, that you must sometimes feel disappointed with me, especially when I hear you talking to clever women – but I do appreciate you my darling . . . I love you with all my heart.[48]

On another occasion she claimed that his love was for her other sister Grace: 'were you ever in love with Grace? Maybe you are now – God Forbid.'[49]

Muriel continued to be tortured by self-doubt, writing to him days later: 'I love you darling, do you really really love me as much as I love you?' Again, in another letter: 'when you are away from me I keep wondering all the while if your love for me will last – it somehow seems too good to be true . . . I am not really dreaming and going to wake up and find that you are only a distant acquaintance. God forbid.'[50] She worried about a horoscope reading given to him by the writer Ella Young, who told him that he would be in love for only eleven months. Muriel wrote of this: '[if] it comes true, darling, don't tell me anything about it, but get a dagger or a pistol and kill me before I find out anything about it.' She wrote to him how she slept with his photograph under her pillow and how she looked at it and kissed it.

She loved his sense of drama and treasured a single sheet on which he had written to her a testimonial of his intentions: 'In earnest of this I have freely given of my beloved, the said Lady Muriel, a lock of my hair (lack-lustre brown) and a penny (with a hole therein) . . . it is my set intention . . . to wed, marry and spouse the said lady.'

The relationship that Thomas conducted with Muriel was a clandestine one because when they first got to know each other, she had another suitor to whom she had been engaged. She had recently broken off with him to commence her relationship with Thomas. When she rejected the other man, 'he wrote me such a terribly despairing desolate letter that if it hadn't been for the thought of you darling I would have felt like taking my life.'[51]

In the early stages of their courtship, accompanied by one of her sisters, Muriel would meet Thomas secretly in art galleries such as the Municipal, where Muriel liked to look at the paintings while she waited for him, or in the National Museum, an ideal location for a discreet rendezvous. They also met in places where they had mutual friends. One note arranging a meeting was written on a bank slip from the Sinn Féin Co-op People's Bank at 6 Harcourt Street, in which Muriel asked Thomas to return there for a meeting later.

As this illicit romance continued, Muriel wrote: 'I must commence by telling you that my mother did see us meeting yesterday . . . So I had my [story] ready when I came into the room – Your name is Mr Homan. I really feel ashamed of myself that I should deny you . . . anyway the incident passed off alright.'[52] Later in the month she tells him 'my father never saw you, it was a false alarm.'[53] Their arrangements now included a new strategy: Thomas would walk along the road outside the house in Rathmines at a certain time and Muriel would go out to meet him.

Three years after their first meeting, the couple became privately engaged. Thomas gave Muriel an engagement gift of a cross with blue enamelling, silver and moonstones. Muriel wrote on 25 October 1911: 'How happy I feel – your beautiful ring is like the clasp of your fingers on mine – I can never be lonely now that I have this link connecting you with me.'[54] At this time he also wrote a poem for her entitled 'A Song of Muriel'.[55] On 28 October she described it as 'your song of me' and told him how she read it over and over again. 'It is beautiful my darling . . . it will always be my most precious possession – outside of you.' She now wrote addressing him as 'dearest': 'How happy you made me tonight – more happy than I have ever felt in my whole life by talking to me about our future and our cottage – ours – yours and mine – it seems almost too good to be true darling.'[56] Muriel's former suitor was still writing to her in mid-October; indeed, she received a 'bitter and cynical letter' just at the point that she accepted Thomas's engagement ring.

Although they had not officially announced their engagement or informed Muriel's parents, her father by this time suspected the seriousness of the relationship. One evening he told a story of a sister who stole off to be married and never said anything until she and her husband came home and announced it. Muriel recounted this story to Thomas, stating that she could never be married because her 'nosey poker' eldest sister (Katie) was keeping an eye on the Registrar General's returns as her husband worked in that office. Katie had questioned Nellie about the 'man with the kilts', telling Nellie that she had it on good authority that Muriel was married or engaged. Muriel told him that she thought the news was out and speculated on how long it would be before it would come to her mother's ears. She wondered why Katie had not told, thinking that it was 'her duty.'

Katie had married Walter Harris Wilson, a Catholic six years her junior, in 1909 and, according to Muriel, her mother feared 'that some more of her daughters may marry Catholics' – a surprising opinion, given her own mixed marriage. Isabella was always suspicious of the activities of her daughters; Muriel claimed that their mother believed even their 'most impossible lies' while the true stories were never believed.

Muriel remained unaware of Thomas's previous entanglement; in November 1911 she refers to Mary in a letter she wrote to him: 'I think that it is splendid of Miss Maguire to write such nice things. I have very few women friends, although as a general rule I take more trouble to be polite to women than to men'.[57] Thomas still spent a considerable amount of time with Mary. She worked as an assistant at the *Irish Review*, and he had become involved in the journal the previous March as his friend David Houston was the financier and Padraic Colum an editor. When Muriel and Thomas attended a function later that month, she witnessed flirtation between the two. Thomas reassured her, but disingenuously did not tell her of his proposal to Mary. Muriel's reply survives:

> I know my darling I have not the faintest reason to be jealous and yet
> I keep on making you miserable by my bad temper – I curse myself
> all the time for it and sometimes feel like killing myself so I could

never trouble you anymore . . . I will never again be jealous of Miss Maguire – I admire her and think she is a grand girl really – but what is the use of talking I'll be the same again without the slightest provocation – I know you have never given me any reason my own love . . . I tried tonight to conceal it and overcome it . . . you observed it – I didn't want to make you unhappy – and I knew in my heart that there was no need to be jealous.[58]

Within days, Muriel suggests that Thomas invite both Miss Maguire and Padraic Colum over to visit, writing that she would like very much to know her better. She had been warned against Mary by the artist Estella Solomons and others: 'do you know that I had quite the wrong impression of her . . . they gave me the idea that she was a disagreeable sort of girl – so now I have been boosting her terrifically to the others . . .' [59]

Thomas wrote to Dominick Hackett in November before he told his siblings about his engagement: 'I have been for just five weeks now engaged to be married, to Muriel Gifford, sister of Grace the artist and of "John Brennan" of Sinn Féin and "Irish Freedom" and of sisters and brothers in America artists too, whom you probably, however, have not met. I have not yet told my kith here, as she is soi-disant Protestant, and so Mary, would be troubled, I fear.'[60]

Thomas's sister Mary Josephine had joined the Sisters of Charity in April 1895, taking the name of Sister Francesca. As he wrote at the time, he did not want to 'fall out with Mary, who was the decentest sister that anyone ever had . . .' He was in fact himself not practising; he put a line through the section for religion on the Census form that year. As he wrote to Hackett: 'Muriel and I are of the same religion, which is neither Catholic or Protestant nor any form of dogmatic creed, neither of us go to church or chapel, but for the sake of several things and people we are willing to conform for a marriage ceremony.'[61]

When Sister Francesca was told of his engagement, Thomas wrote that 'she took it most sedately. She is troubled about the religious difficulty but otherwise is of course delighted by it . . . and glad too we were going to get married right away.'[62] She had asked that Muriel would visit her alone, but Muriel went to the convent with her sister Sidney, and in fact the youngest Gifford got on very well with the nun. When they visited the school at John's Lane attached to the convent, the children put on a singing display and an exhibition of jumping through hoops decorated with flowers. Muriel told Sister Francesca that she did not want to become a Catholic. When she returned she wrote to Thomas: 'she was nice about the whole thing and I really love her very much.'[63]

As part of Maud Gonne's school meals initiative, Muriel became involved in cooking dinners for hungry schoolchildren at Sister Francesca's school at John's Lane, alongside her sisters Nellie, Grace and Sidney, as well as Countess Markievicz and members of Inghinidhe na hÉireann. On one occasion in mid-November, when Muriel was absent, Maud Gonne herself was giving out dinner and asked Nellie if it was true that Muriel was engaged. Muriel recounted the story to Thomas:

> I don't know whether this is true or not but Nellie swears it is – she says that she told her it was not announced yet, but she believed it was so . . . I think that one of the things that I like best . . . is her way of boosting you – she really likes you more than anybody I know, and always takes pains to praise you up – I love talking to her for that reason – I know she will say something nice about you darling and I am waiting all the time with impatience until she talks about you – I wonder did she hear who I am engaged to . . .[64]

By late November Muriel decided the time had come to tell her parents that she was engaged. Her sisters Nellie and Sidney were there to support her. As she wrote to Thomas, 'I threw the bomb last night . . . my mother took it very badly – much worse than I could have imagined – what about it – I suppose she'll get over it sometime – my father kept perfectly silent over the whole thing . . .'[65] In time, Muriel brought Thomas to meet her parents. Sidney 'likes you immensely – she agreed with me that my mother could not possibly dislike you once she had met you – nobody could darling.'[66] In the event, Thomas managed to charm Isabella Gifford to such an extent that he became a go-between for the sisters when they wanted permission for an outing or some new scheme. Indeed, as Sidney later wrote: 'because of his personal charm and kindness he became a great favourite of my mother.' When Isabella objected to her daughters smoking, Thomas devised a plan, inviting a professor to the house who was primed to speak in medical terminology on the virtues of tobacco. After this eminent scholar advised Isabella that tobacco was one of the greatest safeguards against 'microbes', and so was an unspecified protector against diseases, her objections ceased. Despite this amicable relationship, however, Isabella and Thomas had arguments on religion. According to Muriel, her mother considered Jesuits to be 'worse than demons'. The depth of her anti-Catholic feeling is remarkable given that she had herself married a Catholic.

During their courtship Thomas had worked on his MA and in October 1911 he obtained first-class honours for his thesis on 'Thomas Campion and the Art of English Poetry'. He then set about putting it into publishable form, to help secure him a post lecturing in a university. His idea was to marry as soon as he secured a university job; he had many plans to make a decent income.

Thomas wrote to his brother that the couple intended to live in his bachelor home at Grange House Lodge: 'Muriel is quite willing, indeed wants, to join me here in my cottage. I think we shall add . . . to it to make it more than twice its present size and start out life together here alone in the mountains. It is far more attractive to the two of us than red brick suburban life with the tyranny of conventional furniture.'[67]

However, Thomas came to have reservations about Muriel's isolation, especially after she wrote to him: 'I don't allow myself to think of the lonely house in the daytime I only picture the time when you are with me and the time that I am looking out for you and listening for your step.'[68] He also feared that the cottage would be inadequate given the comforts she was used to. She responded:

'don't talk to me about our bungalow . . . as if it was not good enough for me – you know how much I love you – I adore you my love, and if you were actually destitute I would a million times rather tramp with you than marry the wealthiest man in the world . . . so please don't talk of my making sacrifices.'[69] Despite her willingness, the plan to live there was eventually abandoned in favour of the city, and they found a flat above Findlater's shop on Upper Baggot Street. When Muriel brought her mother, who was now more favourably disposed to the idea of the marriage, to see it, Isabella was 'charmed with the rooms', promising spoons, forks and items from her china closet.[70]

In November Muriel urged Thomas not to go into marriage with debts. However, his fortunes changed when he was asked to take a temporary position at the Department of English Literature at University College Dublin. No sooner had he received the new post than he expressed his hope that he would take over the position as head of the department in a number of years, with a salary of £600 a year.

The marriage took place in January 1912. On the eve of their wedding Thomas wrote to Muriel: 'Tomorrow begins life for us. My Darling, you do not know what you have brought to me and what you make me look forward to. I have lost years and years. Now we'll make up for that . . . I'm getting sentimental. You must be hard on me all next week, darling, and keep me on the straight and sober . . . I'll kiss you good night in future, always, always.'[71]

As this was a mixed marriage, the couple were wed on Wednesday, 3 January in a temporary structure on a site at Beechwood Avenue in Ranelagh, where the Catholic Church of the Holy Name would be built. The priest, Father Sherwin, wrote to Thomas in advance of the ceremony: 'if you intend publishing the marriage – leave out church & place.' In attendance were Muriel's parents; her sister Sidney and brother Claude were the witnesses. P. H. Pearse had been asked to be the best man but forgot to turn up for the wedding; the story told was that a man who was cutting the hedges outside the church took his place. Thomas wrote of the wedding: 'we completed the thing with a most informal wedding on Wednesday last, the third. I went through it quite alone without a best man or other aid, Muriel had only her family.'

Thomas MacDonagh saw this as a new era in his life: 'My marriage has been a wonderful thing to me, a new lease of life and new interests and hopes.'[72] He and Muriel established their own literary salon at 32 Baggot Street on Saturday nights, with his friends David Houston, AE and James Stephens often in attendance. Padraic Colum would frequently join them, with his new wife Mary – the former Miss Maguire.

Thomas continued to write poetry but, as he told Muriel in a letter of 1912, he wanted a public persona in his poetry while retaining a private version for them to enjoy. Explaining why he had changed a poem for publication, he wrote:

> I love to be working on something that has to do with you. I could not and would not, try to write poems that did not come naturally. This poem did. Others could define only something of my love but would fail to express it. Indeed the best of my love is not expressed in poems or letters or words at all – you know that. Well, I have finished this poem, and now have two editions, one for publication and one for you and me.[73]

While expressing his desire to keep publishing his verse, he was also working towards the establishment of a new theatre company with Joseph Plunkett. Thomas believed that his own experience producing plays with the pupils at St Enda's School and his brother John's time working in the commercial theatre in America would facilitate them in the venture. Plans were hampered in 1912, however, by Joe Plunkett's ill health. Plunkett's involvement was essential, as it was not possible for the theatre company to go ahead without the use of Countess Plunkett's building in Hardwicke Street. Also, Muriel was pregnant and complications manifested themselves just before they set out on holiday to France on 13 June, so, although she recovered slightly, Thomas felt that 'things will be precarious this side of Christmas.'[74]

During the summer Muriel was given over to the care of Dr Kathleen Lynn, who had her placed in hospital in July. There were fears that the baby would be born prematurely due to what Thomas called 'clampsa [pre-eclampsia] caused by kidney trouble'. She was hospitalized again in September. Her husband wrote that he was relieved to know that she was safe: 'If you were here I would be afraid something might happen to you . . .'[75] At first he planned that when she was discharged she would be put under the care of a nurse at home, but when she was released from hospital on 1 October she went to live at her parents' home at 8 Temple Villas, where she gave birth to a son on 12 November 1912.

On 2 December the birth announcement appeared in *Sinn Féin*, written in the Irish language. They decided on Donagh, which was a play on Thomas's surname in Irish, MacDonagh, meaning Donagh son of Donagh. Thomas was interested in genealogy and had traced his family to County Sligo in the fifteenth century.[76] At this time Thomas also had begun to sign his letters simply using his surname.

Throughout Muriel's stays at the Rotunda Maternity Hospital and then with her family in Rathmines, Thomas continued to live at their home on Upper Baggot Street. By the time of Donagh's birth, their forced separation had stretched from weeks to months. From her parents' house, Muriel wrote: 'We are coming home to you soon . . . I am so delighted that you love him so much – I am never so happy as when you are here with him in your arms talking to him.'[77]

Despite Isabella taking her into her care, Muriel continued to have a difficult relationship with her mother. Thomas wrote to her expressing his concern, but Muriel replied to his enquiries: 'don't imagine I am always unhappy here, dearest – really Mother is most decent to me when you are away.'[78] Isabella would not permit him to visit Muriel in her room and at times Thomas was frustrated by this restriction, but he wrote to his wife that as he could not take her away he would avoid quarrelling with his mother-in-law: 'Really she is very decent, but somehow she and I jar sometimes. I suppose I am too critical.'[79]

In the aftermath of the birth, Muriel's insecurities resurfaced. Thomas wrote reassuring her:

> Nothing happens to me or around me that I do not tell you of. We have lived so intimately together this last year that there is no revelation for me to make. Our having a son is so new to me that I can yet hardly express . . . how I feel towards him and now towards you in your new position . . . You know well my love for you, my confidence in our happiness to be, in your love for me, in our lives for our child and him for us – what more is there?[80]

Muriel was bedridden for three months with phlebitis, an inflammation of the veins of her legs, which meant that she could not mind her new baby. In a letter of 5 December 1912, Thomas wrote: 'my poor poor suffering girl, I love you more than I knew I did ever. There could be no life for me without you, not ever with or for Donn. Get better and come home to me soon with him.'[81] On 17 December he wrote focusing on their future: 'we shall be well the baby growing before us with baby's mind opening gradually and wonderfully. Look forward to tomorrow twenty years when you and baby and I shall be merry old souls. We are in for a great wonderful life, my love.'

Thomas wrote again the following day that she would 'be well and up before Christmas', but she still had not returned to live with her husband by Christmas Day, when he wrote:

> My poor darling. In spite of all I am troubled this evening about you – not about your health. I know well you will be soon better. The thing is tedious and all that but not dangerous or even serious – but about you having depressions and dread of things. Darling, do not fall into that bad mistake of self-blame you know as well as I do that you did all for the best at all times, that you did nothing through

impatience . . . So that it is nonsense to talk of anything happening through your fault. It's all unfortunate, but it is no good to make it worse by blaming yourself or anyone. I know, darling, that you have suffered a lot, that it must be hard not to be despondent and depressed. But still, my love, do not, for all our sakes, for me, for the baby, for yourself, give in to depressions. I would not know where I should be if you did, if I thought you were despondent. Darling, you want to be here at home with baby and me. Fix your mind on that, make it come to pass soon, soon, soon, I want it, I want you to be better, to be here, to have baby here . . . how could you let yourself ever despair of a [long] life with us? . . . Do not let the shadow of such a terrible thought come to us . . . I hope to God you and baby are asleep now, and that you will be better tomorrow. You must be quite better soon. I want you here. With all my love . . . MacDonagh.[82]

As the weeks passed with no sign of Muriel returning home, on 28 December, over six weeks after his son's birth, he wrote: 'I am terribly lonely every time I let myself stop and thinking of your getting better soon. If I think of myself at all, I know how lonely I am . . . when I wake in the night or in the morning.'[83] The following day he wrote again: 'My dearest Love I hope you have now taken final leave of the glooms. You must think of baby as a joy and remember so that you have our own private joy in the room with you. He will be that to you darling and I shall always play second fiddle to him . . .'[84]

Thomas remained at Upper Baggot Street to study. He wrote to her on 4 February: 'My poor darling, in spite of me some things keep me from spending time with you. It makes me unhappy to think of you worrying and fretting there by yourself. But darling I never stay a moment longer from you than I have to. You know that.'[85] He confided in her: 'I have been working – not at exams, as I ought to be, – but at a book of poems. I must get that out of the way next by publishing it.' By mid-February Muriel was feeling better. Thomas wrote on the 15th of the month: 'I am delighted that you are really getting better at last.'[86] Their correspondence then ceased, which indicates that Muriel had returned home to Thomas again.

Thomas Campion and the Art of English Poetry was published on Thomas's behalf by Hodges Figgis & Company in February 1913 and in London by Simpkin in March. Thomas paid for the Irish publishers to print 1,124 copies with 500 bound. The book did not succeed as he had hoped, partially because of the lack of material available to contextualize the work in the Elizabethan period. It was published to further Thomas's chances of obtaining a chair in one of the universities.

From March to June 1913 Thomas was once again living alone, writing to a friend that, while Don was 'thriving wonderfully', Muriel continued to be ill for three months with inflammation of the veins in her legs. He wrote in June: 'She is still with her mother and I am living en garçon at 32 Upper Baggot Street.'[87]

Thomas filled his time with numerous activities, many of which meant that he was away from home. He was always looking for ways to earn more money, as his family were having difficulty living on his income. He may have worried about money, but on one occasion when he thought Muriel was '*too* inclined to economy' he went out and bought her four new dresses at once. The cost of publishing his work and his studies had left him with many debts, yet he continued to invest in furthering his ambitions as a writer and an academic. One of the ways he earned extra money was as an examiner and superintendent under the Intermediate Education Board for Ireland. For this work, he spent weeks in different parts of the country. By the summer of 1913, with Muriel once more living at home, the couple had moved to a small red-brick house with a garden opposite the old St Enda's School in Ranelagh, within walking distance of Muriel's parents' house. Muriel did not travel around the country with Thomas, and as the mother of a small child she would have spent many nights at home alone, as there was no money for a live-in maid.

As well as his work, Thomas attended events such as the

production meetings and performances of his play *Metempsychosis: or, a Mad World*. This one-act drama was performed at the Hardwicke Street Theatre on 10 May 1913,[88] produced by Joseph Plunkett's own company, known as Mr Killeen's Company. Plunkett himself, as his thespian alter-ego Luke Killeen, played the role of Lord Winton Winton de Winton. As the characters' names indicate, the play was a farce.

While Thomas was indulging his passion for the theatre, in July 1913 the *Irish Review* published another volume of his poetry, entitled *Lyrical Poems*. In his letters he constantly wrote of his future ambitions; at that point he was hoping that by 1915 he would be a 'D.Litt and will be publishing book after book, please the Lord.'[89]

However, Thomas's focus on literary and educational pursuits would abruptly change that year when in August Dublin became a city in turmoil during the Lockout. He became a member of the Dublin Industrial Peace Committee, an organization that took a completely neutral stance in the hope of resolving the situation. He was present when the police attacked the crowd that had gathered to hear Jim Larkin speak from the Imperial Hotel, and later gave testimony before a tribunal investigating police brutality during the strike. When he was asked about the role of his sister-in-law Nellie Gifford, he said it should be 'treated as a rumour' that she had been the young woman with Larkin when he gave his speech from the hotel balcony. Nellie had not been identified with enough certainty to be arrested.

Thomas was still trying to get into the established world of academia in the city and seemed unconcerned that presenting evidence at a tribunal in favour of the striking workers, coupled with his Catholicism, might preclude him from getting a job in Trinity College. Regardless of these things, in autumn 1913 he applied for the late Edward Dowden's chair in English Literature in Trinity College Dublin. His application was unsuccessful.

While Thomas was away earning 'pennies', as he wrote in one letter, or indulging his interests, the MacDonagh family's life was complicated when Muriel became ill again. Now the true nature of her 'delicate' constitution became apparent.[90] She spent much of October and November 1913 not in her parents' home as before but in nursing care. Initially she stayed in Mrs Forde's nursing home at 122 Lower Baggot Street, and her surviving letters are filled with her frustration at being so confined. She makes endless plans on paper for excursions as a family: 'won't it be great when the Don is able to go with us, we must bring him up sometime to our lane, and another time we must take him to Woodenbridge . . . or we could all buffet the billows in Aran.'[91] In another letter she wrote of being worn out by simple tasks: 'the bathroom is up three flights of stairs and I felt rather wobbly by the time I got to the top of them and coming back I lost my way and got into the other houses and nearly wandered into the street – however I called a nurse and one of them came to my rescue.' In the same letter she wrote: 'I have been feeling a little lonely and depressed. I somehow don't seem to have seen you at all today – hardly a kiss and not five minutes alone all the time. But I am getting stronger dearest. I wish this was Monday week – I am going to return to you and the Don in bully form.'[92] The next day she felt recovered enough to write to Thomas, who had just left after a visit: 'It was your confidence that pulled me through so well; I am sure of that – I feel that the cloak of my life is wrapped firmly and tightly around me and securely fastened. Thank you darling for never losing trust, I will always feel confident in future.'[93]

She delighted in Thomas's description of Don waking up like a 'fluffy little owlet', but wrote that her son would not know her when she returned home. There was to be no immediate return, however, as she was moved to a seaside location, the Plaza on Sandycove Avenue, on 11 November. She began her convalescence by going for a walk shortly after her arrival: 'Already I feel better, darling, though when I was out this morning I felt blurred and dazed like a drunk person.'[94] In another letter she wrote: 'I wish to heaven I get rid of the dizzy, dazed feeling. I have it again – a kind of swimming of the head and dullness. This morning we were in Kingston [Dún Laoghaire] and all the time we were out I felt it – I was ashamed asking for things in shops for fear they should think that my manner was strange – I wonder if I will ever feel perfectly lucid again.'[95]

Thomas wrote to Muriel at this time: 'When you come back to me now in some days, darling, we shall begin a new stage in our life.' He dated the first stage 'from before the 30 September 1911–3 Jan 1912'[96] – that is, from their engagement to their marriage day. Thomas tried with the stroke of a pen to wipe out all the period of their married life during which Muriel had suffered so profoundly with depression.

Ominously for Muriel and her young son, on 3 December 1913 Thomas was formally enrolled as a member of Regiment I, Company C, 2nd Battalion, in the newly formed Irish Volunteers. Friends such as Joe Plunkett were central to this organization and Thomas wrote at the time: 'We are going to have a tremendous organisation, I hope.'

At the outset, the actual aims of the Volunteers were different for many of its members. There were those who wanted to bring about the complete freedom of Ireland by revolutionary means. However, many who joined saw it as a way of ensuring Home Rule through legislation. Thomas wrote to his friend Dominick Hackett about his observations of the new organization, with men from societies such as the Ancient Order of Hibernians as well as Arthur Griffith's 'Sinn Féiners' and 'Gaelic Leaguers, Irish Freedom men, Parliamentarians, GAA men and University men'. In reply to Dominick's questions about legislation for Home Rule for Ireland, Thomas wrote:

> We know no more here than you do about Home Rule. Some of us are prepared whatever happens. If it passes, good, we shall be in a better position to stand for the full right. If not, we shall have a splendid opportunity of getting a strong following in the demand for the full right. We should be able to get Redmond and the others to withdraw from Westminster and set up a government here. If only they had the courage they could do it successfully.[97]

His Volunteer activity was distracting him from his work on a new book, *Literature in Ireland.* He wrote in January 1914 that he was struggling to submit this manuscript, and as the months went by his political life took over and he did not finish it. Thomas said that the Volunteers gave him a 'new direction and purpose to his life.'[98]

During 1914, as Thomas's involvement with the Volunteer movement grew, he became a member of the Provisional Committee, taking on a role in organizing and recruiting members. Despite his numerous commitments, he travelled to Charleville in Cork and to Derry for recruiting rallies. In March, when Thomas took part in a meeting of the Volunteers in Kilkenny with Roger Casement, Muriel wrote to him, wishing him success – 'the best one so far'. Her letter suggests, however, that she had protested when he left the previous evening: 'I hope the meeting was a success ... I love you darling and I want you to do fine things for the Volunteers – I hope you didn't think last night that I was standing in the way of your going.'[99]

Thomas was known for his theatrical gestures, such as drawing a sword at a rally. His speeches were inspiring and he was a good recruiter: 'We are concerned directly with the present legislative proposals now before the parliament in so far as they relate to the rights and liberties of the country ... We have thousands of men and young, of all classes, of all parties, of all religious denominations, drilling constantly ... All over the country corps have been formed, and have taken up the work of preparation with earnestness and determination. To-day Kilkenny joins the work.'[100] He was delighted with his new role, writing after another public meeting: 'The meeting was a great success, and I spoke to my perfect satisfaction. I am now expecting seven delegates from the different corps of Volunteers in the city here to consult with me about local affairs.'[101]

As a director of training, Thomas studied British military training manuals. During the summer of 1914 the Volunteers were being armed and on 26 July guns obtained from Germany were landed at Howth. Thomas wrote to Dominick Hackett of 'march[ing] the Volunteers down the road from Clontarf on the heels of the British

IRISH WAR NEWS

THE IRISH REPUBLIC.

L. I. No. I   DUBLIN, TUESDAY, APRIL 25, 1916.   ONE PENNY

"IF THE GERMANS CONQUERED ENGLAND."

In the London "New Statesman" for *April 1st,* article is published—"If the Germans Conquered England," which has the appearance of a very clever piece of satire written by an Irishman. The writer draws a picture of England under German rule, almost every detail of which exactly fits the case of Ireland at the present day. Some of the sentences are so exquisitely appropriate that it is impossible to believe that the writer had not Ireland in his mind when he wrote them. For instance :—

"England would be constantly irritated by the petty moral utterances of German statesmen who would assert—quite sincerely, no doubt—that England was free, freer indeed than she had ever been before. Prussian freedom, they would explain, is the only real freedom, and therefore England is free. They would point to the flourishing railways and farms and colleges. They would possibly point to the contingent of M.P.'s, which is permitted, in spite of its deplorable disorderliness, to sit in a permanent minority in the Reich-

stag. And not only would the Englishman have to listen to a constant flow of speeches of this sort ; he would find a respectable official Press secretly bought over by the Government to say the same kind of things over and over, every day of the week. He would find, too, that his children were coming home from school with new ideas of history. . . They would ask him if it was true that until the Germans came England had been an unruly country, constantly engaged in civil war. . . . The object of every schoolbook would be to make the English child grow up in the notion that the history of his country was a thing to forget, and that the one bright spot in it was the fact that it had been conquered by cultured Germany."

"If there was a revolt, German statesmen would deliver grave speeches about "disloyalty," "ingratitude," "reckless agitators who would ruin their country's prosperity. . . . Prussian soldiers would be encamped in every barracks—the English conscripts having been sent out of the country to be trained in Germany, or to fight the Chinese—in order to come to the aid of German morality, should English sedition come to blows with it."

"England would be exhorted to abandon her own genius in order to imitate the genius of her conquerors, to forget her own history for a larger history, to give up her own language for a 'universal' language—in other words, to destroy her household gods one by one, and put in their place

---

Above: One of the propaganda postcards published after the Rising. Ireland, like Belgium, was a 'small nation' seeking its freedom, and many believed that taking up arms against the British would allow Ireland a place at an international conference at the end of the Great War.

Left: *Irish War News*, 25 April 1916, Volume 1, No. 1, produced by P. H. Pearse in the General Post Office during its occupation by the Provisional Government of the Irish Republic, Easter Week, 1916. Female couriers brought it to a printer located nearby.

Above: The ruins of the GPO, Dublin. It was the headquarters of the Provisional Government formed at Easter 1916.

Below: The ruins of Middle Abbey Street, Dublin, following the bombardment of the city by the *Helga*, a British gunboat, which had sailed up the River Liffey to shell the GPO and Liberty Hall.

Above: Major John MacBride under arrest, still dressed in the suit he had worn on Easter Monday to have lunch with his soon-to-be-married brother, Anthony. He was to be his best man that Easter Week, but he did not turn up because he chose to fight for Ireland instead.

Below: The ruins of Henry Street, Dublin, in the aftermath of Easter Week. The city was placed under martial law.

The Irish Rebel Leader Joseph Plunkett was married in prison to Miss Grace Gifford a few hours before his execution. The ceremony was performed by a Roman Catholic priest.

Grace Gifford said she had to get married to Joe Plunkett. Permission was granted hours before his execution by Major Lennon, Commandant of Kilmainham Detention Barracks. Joe was handcuffed throughout the service.

A SAD ROMANCE OF THE RISING

JOSEPH MARY PLUNKETT.
Author of "The Circle and the Sword."

MRS. JOSEPH PLUNKETT.
The original of Mr. W. Orpen's picture, "Young Ireland."

J. M. Plunkett was one of the Provisional Government and a signatory of the Proclamation of the Republic. In the first hour of Thursday morning, 4th May, Miss Grace Gifford was married to Joseph Mary Plunkett, eldest son of Count and Countess Plunkett. A few hours later the bridegroom was shot in Kilmainham Prison and the young wife became a widow. Every Irish Rebellion has had its love romance, Lord Edward Fitzgerald and Pamela, Robert Emmet and Sarah Curran, Joseph Mary Plunkett and Grace Gifford. Mrs. Joseph Plunkett was born 1888, and is the daughter of a well-known Dublin solicitor. A graduate of the Metropolitan School of Art, she is an excellent black-and-white artist, and has gained distinction as a caricaturist in the Max Beerbohm style, many of her cartoons having been reproduced in " The Irish Review," "The Bystander," and other publications. Her sister, Muriel, was married in 1912 to Thomas MacDonagh, another of the executed leaders.

Iosep Ophunnseéad
Spáid mic uí Uilug ndézaup 26
i mbáileáza cliaz

Autograph, with address of Joseph Mary Plunkett.

Above: A photographer from the *Morning Star* newspaper came to Belvedere Place the morning after James Connolly was shot. Lillie posed with her youngest child, Fiona.

Below: Before the Rising, James Connolly had placed a banner across Liberty Hall: 'We Serve neither King nor Kaiser'. After his death the banner was replaced with the one shown here.

Kathleen organized this commemorative postcard featuring her uncle John Daly, her husband Tom Clarke and her friend, Seán MacDermott (Mac Diarmada) (**below**). She also issued a memorial card for her uncle, her husband and her only brother, John Edward (Ned) Daly (**right**). They all died within weeks of each other in 1916.

In Memory of
John Daly,
FENIAN,
AGED 70 YEARS,
Who Died 30th June, 1916.

Thomas J. Clarke,
FENIAN,
AGED 53 YEARS,
First signatory to the Declaration
of Independence of the Irish Republic.
Shot, Kilmainham Jail, 3rd May, 1916.

John Edward Daly,
AGED 25 YEARS,
COMMANDANT OF THE IRISH
REPUBLICAN ARMY,
who was shot by the British Forces
at Kilmainham Jail, Dublin, 4th May, 1916

"JOHN DALY."   "THOMAS J. CLARK."   SEAN McDERMOT."
COPYRIGHT.

IRISH REBELLION, MAY, 1916.

EOIN MacNEILL, B.A.,
(President Irish Volunteers),
Sentenced by Courtmartial to Penal Servitude for Life.

De Valera   Photo; Keogh

IRISH REBELLION, MAY 1916.

COUNTESS MARKIEVICZ,
(Who took a prominent part in the Rebellion, Stephen's Green Area),
Sentenced to Death;

Nearly one hundred people were condemned to death following the Easter Rising. Postcards were printed of key people, including Eoin MacNeill (**above left**), the leader of the Irish Volunteers, who had issued the orders cancelling the manoeuvres that were to be a cover for the Rising. Éamon de Valera (**above right**) and Countess Markievicz (**left**) also had their death sentences commuted. They all played major roles in the Rising and its aftermath.

Above: An artist's impression of the sixteen men executed for their part in the 1916 Easter Rising.

Below: Memorial cards for seven of the sixteen men executed in 1916 for their part in the organization of the Rising. These are the husbands of the women, the 'Easter Widows', who are the focus of this book.

soldiers', but there is no evidence to show that he was involved in the planning of this event; however, he did engage with the police – who had been alerted by the harbourmaster to the illegal arrival of the weapons – when they blocked the re-entry of the Volunteers into the city at Fairview. They argued with Assistant Commissioner Harrel that they would assume legal responsibility for the importation of the arms and would even submit to being arrested. While this was happening, the men were able to disperse with the arms and ammunition. According to Harrel's account to the Royal Commission on the gun-running at Howth, he allowed this situation to happen as he did not want any serious consequences. Thomas wrote his account of events in the *Irish Review* as 'Clontarf, 1914': 'At Clontarf in 1914, as at Clontarf in 1014, has been won a national victory. For the Irish Volunteers now: discipline, vigilance, confidence.'[102] Later that year, he put his literary talents to work again when on 26 December he composed with O'Brien Butler a 'Marching Song of the Volunteers'. Thomas also issued a training programme in the organization's newspaper the *Irish Volunteer*, but there is some suggestion that this was the work of his second-in-command, Éamon de Valera.[103]

Alongside his teaching at University College Dublin and his Volunteer activities, in the first week of January 1915 the Irish Theatre at Hardwicke Street opened with four new plays. The first night had an international flavour with works by the Frenchman Auguste Villiers de l'Isle-Adam and the Russian Anton Chekhov.[104] It was reported in the press that the promoters deserved encouragement, but after the third night the censor objected to Villiers's play, *The Revolt*, and the production was cancelled.

Thomas now had his own theatre company and actors to produce his work, and his drama *Pagans* was staged by the Irish Theatre Company from 19 to 24 April 1915. It told of an unsuccessful marriage between a society lady, played by Úna O'Connor, 'who looked charming', according to one critic, and a bohemian man played by Thomas's brother John. There is no suggestion that art mirrored reality or that Thomas was using his own experiences of marriage.

Muriel was pregnant again. There is no surviving correspondence to draw conclusions on her state of mind, but her last confinement had been 'so difficult'. Her baby girl arrived on 24 March 1915. Born in a time of war, they named her Barbara (she would later use the spelling Bairbre), after the patron saint of artillerymen, and Thomas penned a seventy-two line poem for her that June:

> You come in the day of destiny,
> Barbara, born to the air of Mars
> The greater glory you shall see
> And the greater peace, beyond these wars

With Britain at war and mass enlistment under way, Dublin, as elsewhere, was full of men in uniform – both British Army and other organizations who chose to dress in uniform, including the Volunteers. In May 1915 Thomas wrote of the self-confidence 'the movement' was giving to the Irish people. When he brought himself to consider where all this activity might lead, he could say to Hackett only that 'the country will see its way plain.' He wrote to him on 19 May 1915:

> I work hard every day at Volunteer work. I am a member of the General Council of the Central Executive, of the headquarters Staff. I am Commandant of the Second Battalion of the Dublin Brigade and second officer of the Brigade Council. In addition to the work to be done in all these capacities, I am Director of General Training for the whole country and have to keep a staff working to direct that department. But the work, half like that of a cabinet minister and half of that of a regular military officer, is wonderfully interesting and exhilarating. I am ten years younger than I was when you saw me last.[105]

When the Fenian Jeremiah O'Donovan Rossa died in New York, Thomas headed the committee set up to organize the funeral in Dublin and was given the title of acting commandant general. The date was set for 1 August 1915 and Thomas, along with his staff in the executive, controlled all the arrangements, according to the organization's newspaper the *Irish Volunteer*. It was here that Pearse gave his now famous graveside oration: 'the fools, the fools, the fools! They have left us our Fenian dead. While Ireland holds these graves, Ireland unfree shall never be at peace.' Thomas's contribution in the commemorative booklet was as follows: 'Most Irishmen have grown up with the feeling, whether vague or clear, that the most noble thing for them in life after the service of their God would be to battle for Ireland.'[106]

In October 1915 the governing body of University College Dublin reappointed Thomas to the position of assistant in English for the session 1915–16 at a salary of £180. His lectures began on 12 October. He gave his students fiery and inspirational talks, and many remembered him coming in wearing his Volunteer uniform, with a sword and on occasion a revolver buckled on. Once he took out a large Colt and told them force was necessary. He inevitably attracted criticism from the college authorities and he was forced to stop dressing like this.

The poet Austin Clarke remembered seeing Thomas in the spring of 1916 looking worried, as if his mind was elsewhere. Thomas wrote to Dominick Hackett:

> Well, our work is going on strong and steady. The only opposition we meet is the good old British opportunists of the Castle. Our own people are nowhere against us. The Redmondites give us arms and ammunition knowing that they do not want them. The young priests are with us. We have given an ideal and an enthusiasm to the young boys and girls of Ireland . . . I have here, in this road, forty boys from ten to sixteen years, who would do anything for the country at my bidding.[107]

Things were changing. Thomas's close friend Joe Plunkett had been on the Military Council that had been planning a rising since May 1915 and had been out of the country on different missions for months; he had not been involved in their theatre company for some time. In March, Joe and the other directors had clashed over the Irish Theatre's decision to produce the Swedish playwright August Strindberg's *Easter* and Joe had resigned. When the play opened on Friday, 3 March 1916, in his pre-curtain speech Thomas MacDonagh did not refer to the resignation of his friend, though it was clear to the audience that Joe Plunkett was no longer involved, as his name was missing from the playbill. Was there a rift, or was it a cover for something else?

Rumours of a planned rising were now common. Éamon de Valera said in 1915 that 'some members of his battalion knew more about the plans of the Volunteers than he did. They had information, which he, as battalion commander, should have been given.' When he complained to Thomas MacDonagh, as his commanding officer, he was told that this was because 'de Valera was not a member of the IRB and those who had the information were. If he wanted to take the oath there would be no further difficulty.'[108] On another occasion, Thomas was witnessed on his bike holding on to a tram near Rathmines, with de Valera inside, unsuccessfully trying to talk him into joining the IRB.

Eoin MacNeill, the head of the Volunteers, later recalled a conversation with Thomas in which he had asked him if he knew of plans for a rising: 'From what I knew of him, I am sure he told me what he believed to be the truth, but MacDonagh himself was not in the inner councils of what was going on.'[109] The writer James Stephens met Thomas just weeks before the Rising:

> We walked together for nearly an hour . . . But I can find nothing in his speech with the implication of a rebellion. I think if he had meditated this he would have emphasised some phrase with his tongue or his eye, so that afterwards I could have remembered it. Indeed he was so free from all idea of immediate violence that he arranged to ask me later on to talk to some of his boys about the poetry of William Blake.[110]

It was in fact just three weeks before Easter when Thomas was informed by the Military Council of what was being planned. Éamonn Ceannt said Thomas was 'surprised but very enthusiastic'.[111] It was said by some that he was brought into the inner circle in order to persuade Eoin MacNeill when they needed him to mobilize the Volunteers.

From mid-April onwards Thomas MacDonagh did not sleep in his own home. Detectives had been watching the house for some time previously. During that time, according to Muriel, he would 'just run in in the morning and say that he would not be able to stop for breakfast'.[112] She saw him for some time every day, but he never stayed. On Holy Thursday P. H. Pearse came to their house, but Muriel told him that Thomas was not at home.

On Saturday, as Muriel later described: 'my husband took a whole suitcase of things with him, including his uniform and emergency rations.' There was nothing remarkable about that, as manoeuvres had been planned for the Easter weekend.

On Easter Sunday Thomas did not spend the day with his family and only returned to the house at eight that night. He had just got there when the Pearse brothers arrived; they stayed with him for twenty minutes. Still Muriel did not see him alone, only in the presence of friends. He left after about two hours, at ten o'clock. As he got into the waiting taxi, he said to Muriel: '"I may or may not be back to see you to-morrow – if possible I will come in the morning." He did not say anything about the Revolution. I never saw him afterwards.'[113]

PART TWO
PARTING

8

The Rising

Easter Monday

It was Thomas MacDonagh who issued the order to all four of the
Dublin battalions of the Irish Volunteers to 'parade for inspection
and route march at 10 am on Easter Monday'. In his directive he
stated that the commandants would arrange their locations. They
were to bring full arms and equipment and one day's rations. The
British authorities later concluded that many of those who received
this communication did not know that they were taking part in a
rebellion.[1] Thomas had also chosen to keep Muriel ignorant of what
lay ahead.

Kathleen Clarke begged Tom to let her go with him as he
prepared to leave the house on Easter Monday morning. Surely now
that the Rising was to be short-lived, she did not have to stick to her
orders to stay out of the fight? But Tom told her she must stay, and
she decided not to insist any more, as it would make things more
difficult for her husband.

Lillie Connolly had made her way with twenty-year-old Aideen,
seventeen-year-old Moira and eight-year-old Fiona to a cottage used
by Countess Markievicz at Three Rock Mountain, in the area of
Ticknock, which overlooked the city. It was one of three slate cabins
on a remote lane, which Constance had rented at weekends when
she went on painting excursions. Bare and sparsely decorated, it was
not a home, but it had been selected as a place for Lillie and her
younger daughters to see out the fight. Cut off from news, all Lillie

knew was that her husband and three of her other children – Nora, aged twenty-two, Ina, aged nineteen, and her only son Roddy, just turned fifteen, were actively involved in the Rising.

Although the participants still identified themselves by their old groupings, they were now known collectively as the Irish Republican Army of the newly formed Provisional Government of the Irish Republic. Tom Clarke and Seán Mac Diarmada, along with Joseph Plunkett and James Connolly, were all assigned to headquarters at the General Post Office, along with P. H. Pearse.

Nora and Ina, who had returned to Dublin when the Easter Sunday plans had been cancelled, saw their father on Easter Monday in Liberty Hall before the leaders left to occupy their positions and the girls headed back to Belfast with news that the Rising was going ahead that day. James told Nora: 'God Protect You, Nora. We may never see each other again.'[2] Thomas MacDonagh joked with them that they were about to start a rebellion and all that the Connolly sisters were thinking about was leaving the city. They were shown the Proclamation of the Irish Republic, which had just been printed, and told to memorize it; it would have been too dangerous to carry an actual copy. Ina wanted to stay with her father, but he told her: 'It is not what you want or what I want, but what is wanted of us that counts. You would not desert your countrymen in the north that need you more than we do here. There are plenty of women here to do your work . . . but if there is any fighting taking place up north, then that is your place.'[3]

Eighteen hours after the proposed beginning of the Rising, at 11 a.m. on Monday morning, Éamonn Ceannt met his men at Emerald Square, Dolphin's Barn. The original plans were in disarray and when the expected numbers of Volunteers did not turn up, it was only possible to make small modifications to plans. Éamonn, with just forty-two men under his command, took up position at the South Dublin Union, a short distance from his marital home, entering by the Rialto gate. His sister-in-law Lily did not get her orders from her own Central Branch of Cumann na mBan, so she joined the Inghinidhe Branch which was attached to the 4th Battalion.

Éamonn had worried that their home in Dolphin's Barn would be in the line of fire, so he had arranged for Áine to bring her mother and their son Rónán to a safe house, the home of Cathal Brugha, his second-in-command. They needed to take three trams to make their way across the city to their destination in Dartry. They were welcomed by their host, Cáitlín Brugha, who was pregnant, had a number of small children and was already sheltering two other women.

The Irish Citizen Army was mostly split between the General Post Office, St Stephen's Green and City Hall. The original plans to take Trinity College and Dublin Castle were abandoned; instead approaches to the castle at Cork Hill and City Hall were occupied. It had been James Connolly's idea to occupy St Stephen's Green as a central point with a fresh water supply. Michael Mallin took over command, clearing the park of Dubliners enjoying the late spring weather. It had been planned to take the major buildings over-looking the green, but due to the lack of men this did not happen.

Thomas MacDonagh, as commandant of the 2nd Battalion, took to the west of St Stephen's Green, as far as Jacob's Biscuit Factory, a fort-like building with two towers, which gave a view over a vast area of the city. Small outposts were also set up, including at Delahunt's Pub in Camden Street and Barmack's Buildings in Fumbally Lane. Other sections took over Boland's Mill and Bakery under Éamon de Valera, who had men positioned in Love Lane and Cork Street.

Other outposts included Westland Row Station, Davy's Pub at Portobello Bridge, and a house in Haddington Road at the entry into the city from the harbour at Kingstown (now Dún Laoghaire) via Ballsbridge. At the outset it was said there was a small number of British Army troops in the city, but over the days of the Rising hundreds more would be drafted in, some redirected from travelling to France in order to fight in Dublin.

Thomas was joined in his garrison by John MacBride. There had been reports that John was in Tom Clarke's shop and also at the first battalion headquarters on Easter Sunday morning when the plans for Easter Monday were being discussed. Elsewhere it was claimed that John received an urgent communication from Seán Mac

Diarmada on Easter Monday at his office on the quays. John's own account was that he had been on his way into town to meet with his brother Anthony, who had come up from Castlebar in County Mayo; they had planned to meet at the Wicklow Hotel, just off Grafton Street, for lunch. John had told his landlady, Clara Allen, that he would be back at five o'clock.[4] Anthony, now a widower following Emmie's death some years previously, was to be married again the following Wednesday and John was to be his best man.[5] John was dressed in a blue suit, with a grey hat, and carried a malacca cane. He had no uniform and his landlady testified later that he did not possess one. John said:

> I left my home in Glenageary with the intention of going to meet my brother who was coming to Dublin to be married. In waiting round town I went up as far as St Stephen's Green and there I saw a band of Irish Volunteers. I knew some of the members personally and the Commander told me the Irish Republic was virtually proclaimed. As he knew my rather advanced opinions and although I had no previous connection with the Volunteers I considered it my duty to join them. I knew there was no chance of success, and I never advised or influenced any other person to join. I did not even know the positions they were about to take up.[6]

When John MacBride volunteered his services to Thomas MacDonagh on Easter Monday, an eyewitness heard him say: 'Here I am if I'm of any use to you.'[7] After he had been in the Jacob's Factory garrison for a few hours he was appointed second-in-command, later saying: 'I felt it was my duty to occupy this position.'[8] His appointment 'to be commandant' was written by Thomas MacDonagh on a Jacob's receipt.

Thomas's post also included women. Mary Walker (also known by her stage name, Máire Nic Shiubhlaigh) said that when she volunteered Thomas told her he had made no provision for women, but he let her and some others join the garrison to cook and take care of the wounded.

Kathleen Clarke spent all of Easter Monday working unstintingly in the garden of her house in Richmond Avenue in Fairview, aware that Tom was at the headquarters of the Rising at the GPO. She later recalled that she planted a hundred cauliflowers. There was brilliant sunshine, but neither the heat of the sun nor tiredness would make her cease her task. She waited impatiently to hear gunfire, and when it came it was 'rather like an explosion'.[9] Later she heard that there had been fighting on Ballybough Bridge nearby. On Monday night Seán T. O'Kelly came to Kathleen with a message from Tom, but she never divulged the contents of this communication to anyone.

That same evening, while out shopping for provisions, Áine Ceannt met a Volunteer who told her that Davy's public house had been blown up. He told Áine and her companion that he was 'clearing out'. When they asked him 'Will you not wait and give a hand to your comrades?' he replied 'Not likely.'[10]

Easter Tuesday

On Tuesday Sorcha MacMahon, a member of Cumann na mBan who had been on the O'Donovan Rossa Memorial Committee with the Clarkes, came with messages for Kathleen from Tom; she had been on despatch duty since the Rising began and had been bringing messages 'as well as good cheer and great hope'.[11] Sorcha had been in the Four Courts where Ned, Kathleen's younger and only brother, had led members of the 1st Battalion, as their commandant, at noon on Easter Monday. The battalion's ranks had been reduced considerably, with only one in three of the men showing up, as a result of MacNeill's countermanding order. Ned set up his command centre in the Father Mathew Hall in Church Street and also sent men to the Mendicity Institution, Jameson's Distillery and buildings in North King Street.

On Tuesday, as Kathleen continued working in the garden, a shot was fired that punctured her watering can. She never found out where it had been fired from or if she had been the target of a sniper. Despite the fact that fighting was under way, there were still many people moving about the city.

Muriel MacDonagh remained at home in Oakley Road with her children, Don and Barbara, with the sound of the fighting within a mile of her home. According to one account, 'early in the week' she made her way to the GPO at great personal risk to look for Thomas, unaware that he was posted at Jacob's Factory. At the GPO she met with Joe Plunkett, who told her that if he was arrested he wished to be married to her sister Grace in prison. There is no record of Muriel getting to see Thomas in Jacob's.

On this second day of fighting Agnes Mallin went to Whitefriar's Street church but, finding it closed, she knelt in prayer on the pavement, where she was found by her brother-in-law Tom Mallin, who was also out looking for Michael. It was an area of intense fighting and sniper fire. A small unit had taken over Little's Pub on Cuffe Street, one street away, and Jacob's Factory, occupied by Thomas MacDonagh's battalion, was behind the church. Michael had originally been stationed at St Stephen's Green, where his men had dug trenches, but earlier that day, when the British military occupied the Shelbourne Hotel and fired down upon them, they had moved to the College of Surgeons alongside the Green. Agnes had in fact knelt down to pray less than a four-minute walk from where her husband was stationed. Tom Mallin brought her to his house in Rutland Avenue, Dolphin's Barn, and the next day he went and collected the youngest of her four children.[12] Her two eldest sons were spending Easter Week with her sister, Mary Jane Thewlis, at her house in Chapelizod at the foot of Guinness Hill.

Kathleen Clarke continued to have many callers, including some Volunteers from the North looking for directions to headquarters. On Tuesday evening two of her sisters, Laura and Nora, arrived from Limerick. Thanks to a friend in the ticket office in Limerick, they had travelled to Dublin on a special train for the relatives of British soldiers, where they met up with Éamonn Dore, a Volunteer from Limerick who was on his way to Dublin to take part in the Rising. Nora in particular struck up a great rapport with their travelling companion, and so began their romance, which would develop over time.[13]

Kathleen considered disobeying her orders and going to the GPO with her sisters but, as she was in the early stages of pregnancy, she felt unable to walk that distance and did not want to hamper them. She did not tell them that she was pregnant, but instead said she could not break orders. Her sisters managed to get to the GPO, where they were given orders to go to Cork with a message for Terence MacSwiney. Following their departure from Dublin Nora Daly made her way to Cork and got in touch with MacSwiney, but he and the Cork Volunteers did not take part in the fight.

Easter Wednesday

On Wednesday, 26 April 1916, the British Cabinet declared martial law in Ireland. That morning Kathleen heard the sound of shelling but knew nothing more about it until Sorcha arrived to tell her that a British gunboat, the *Helga*, had come up the River Liffey and was shelling Liberty Hall and the surrounding buildings. When Sorcha left, Kathleen set herself to making a shirt for Tom to pass the time, hoping to drown out the sounds of the big guns with her sewing machine. She also knew, as she later wrote: 'In doing the shirt I was filling myself up with the hope that Tom would be back to wear it.'[14]

Meanwhile, Tom was preparing to die. That same day he talked to Dr James Ryan, who was in charge of the makeshift hospital in the GPO and later recalled: 'For no apparent reason [Tom] launched into a full history of the I.R.B. from the time of his release from prison . . . The talk lasted two hours and at the end I was aware of the reason for it. I was now Red Cross and so he said I might be spared by the enemy in the final bayonet charge.'[15]

Roddy Connolly had spent the previous two days in the GPO assisting his father and Pearse with messages and meals. On Wednesday he was taken by his father to a room in the building and given a suitcase of documents to bring to William O'Brien's house in Belvedere Place. As they parted, Roddy saw his father with 'tears dripping down his cheeks.' James had engineered a reason for his son to be removed from the fight without having to tell him to go. Roddy later wrote: 'it was actually our last goodbye. I never saw him again.'[16]

By Wednesday evening the Mendicity Institution garrison, headed up by Seán Heuston and some twenty men, had held off a large contingent of British troops for about fifty hours. Finally, 'without food, dog tired and trapped', the garrison surrendered.

Tom Clarke sent Seán T. O'Kelly with another message to Kathleen on Wednesday night.[17] He arrived very late, about 11 p.m., and as he talked with Kathleen a complete cordon of troops surrounded the centre of the city to the north of the Liffey, preventing his return to the GPO.

Easter Thursday

Éamonn Ceannt's garrison at the South Dublin Union had been under constant attack from troops from nearby Richmond Barracks. The small force of Volunteers held them off successfully, however, much to the amazement of Sir Francis Vane, the British officer in command of the area for the duration of the fighting. On Thursday there was a full-scale gun battle at this outpost, with British troops using improvised Guinness lorries as armoured vehicles. Cathal Brugha was wounded.

During the week of fighting Thomas MacDonagh was cheerful and optimistic, but lacked any drive or decisiveness, issuing orders and then retracting them. The British troops did not attack Jacob's Factory directly, and most of the fighting undertaken by his garrison was by those on cycle patrols and raiding parties. Unlike some of the other men, Thomas did not send messengers to keep his wife informed of what was going on, although he allowed men from his garrison to leave their posts and go to their own homes to get some sleep. Thomas himself never returned home.

Kathleen Clarke was still able to receive word from Tom on Thursday, 27 April, but, as she later described, the news from the GPO was not cheerful: 'I ached to join them all there, and to be near my husband but hesitated, fearing that by disobeying orders I would only add to their worries.'[18] A number of women who had been stationed at the GPO were asked to leave, as it was felt that the building could not be held for much longer. Nineteen women refused to leave.

As the bombardment of the GPO continued, James Connolly was wounded when he went out to inspect barricades. He wrote the following day: 'I was wounded twice yesterday and am unable to move about, but have got my bed moved into the firing line, and, with the assistance of your officers, will be just as useful to you as ever. Courage, boys, we are winning . . .'[19]

The location of the cottage where Lillie Connolly was staying offered a bird's-eye view of the city. As the week wore on, she watched as smoke rose from burning buildings. Her daughter Fiona later recalled: 'We stood on a large rock someway from Madame Markievicz's cottage and could see the reflection of fire in the sky. I overheard them say, "That is Dublin burning". My mother clasped her hands and looked towards the city and her lips moved silently.'[20]

Easter Friday
Major Sir John Grenfell Maxwell assumed command of British troops in Ireland at 2.30 a.m. on Friday, 28 April.

When Friday morning came, Kathleen Clarke was now isolated and knew nothing of what was happening. The suspense was terrible. A woman who lived on Richmond Hill, whose nephew and niece were in the Rising, called on her to see if she knew what was happening. Kathleen told her what she knew, easing some of the woman's anxiety. The woman told her: 'You're a fit wife for a revolutionary', but Kathleen knew she did not intend it as a compliment. An elderly man also came to their home and asked her to hide a weapon, telling her she was so deeply involved 'a rifle more or less found in my house would make little difference.'[21]

Early that morning Áine Ceannt recalled: 'we were awakened by the military raiding the premises.'[22] The house in Dartry where she was staying became the focus of military attention as it was full of so many women; along with Cáitlín Brugha, Cáitlín's sister, and a friend who had been stranded in Dublin, there was Áine, her mother and a number of children. However, Cáitlín convinced the troops that her husband was a commercial traveller who was stranded in the country, and no one was arrested.

By Friday the GPO was on fire and the evacuation began. Sixteen women left under the protection of the Red Cross Flag, with just Elizabeth O'Farrell, her friend Julia Grenan and Winnie Carney of Belfast remaining with the men. Joe Plunkett was witnessed telling the men as they made their way from the GPO to Moore Street: 'Don't be afraid . . . On! On! On!'[23] The Provisional Government had relocated to a house on Moore Street and it was there that they decided to surrender. When Seán Mac Diarmada asked Elizabeth O'Farrell to provide a white flag, Tom Clarke turned his face to the wall and openly wept.

Kathleen Clarke spent Friday night watching from the upper windows of her house. It appeared as if the whole city was in flames: 'it seemed to me no-one could escape from that inferno. The picture of my husband and brother caught in it was vividly before me, and their helplessness against that raging fire appalled me.' By Saturday everyone had some account of what had taken place, and Kathleen felt 'one rumour more horrible than another.'[24]

Áine could also see the fires in the city from the Brughas' house. News had reached Cáitlín that her husband, Cathal, had been wounded in the South Dublin Union. As shooting was now only sporadic, Áine made her way to Rathmines, closer to the city. News there was that there was a truce, but nothing more was known. On Friday afternoon Áine, as she herself described, 'piloted Mrs Brugha to the Union' to see her husband, who was in hospital recovering from his wounds.[25] Áine was familiar with the surroundings of her old home at the SDU, and she was able to get them there without being stopped. During their visit to Cathal's bedside, Áine said nothing, as she did not want to draw the attention of the other patients. She and Cáitlín managed to get in and out without attracting the notice of the military.

On Saturday, 29 April 1916, from 'somewhere in Moore Street', Joe Plunkett wrote to Grace Gifford:

My Darling Grace, This is just a little note to say I love you and to tell you that I did everything I could to arrange for us to meet and get married but that it was impossible. Except for that I have no regrets. We will meet soon. My other actions have been as right as I could see and make them, and I cannot wish them undone. You at any rate will not misjudge them. Give my love to my people and friends. Darling, darling child, I wish we were together. Love me always as I love you. For all the rest all you do will please me. I told a few people that I wish you to have everything that belongs to me. This is my last wish so please do see to it. Love XXX Joe.[26]

9

'Not Like This'

At 4.45 p.m. that Saturday, P. H. Pearse's handwritten surrender was presented to Brigadier General Lowe, in command of the British troops. It read:

> To prevent the further slaughter of unarmed people, and in the hope of saving the lives of our followers now surrounded and hopelessly outnumbered, the members of the Provisional Government present at headquarters have agreed to an unconditional surrender.[1]

By Pearse's side was Elizabeth O'Farrell, who had joined Maud Gonne's Inghinidhe na hÉireann at the age of sixteen. She now stood with Pearse at the moment of surrender and thereafter made the treacherous journey to the garrisons, in the midst of ongoing sniper fire, with the surrender documents.

When Elizabeth arrived at Jacob's Factory with Pearse's instructions to surrender, Thomas MacDonagh argued that his garrison could hold out for some weeks. He assured her he had ample provisions and ammunition and felt their location was well protected. He was under the impression that the country was 'up' and the British intention was to 'quell Dublin' before attacking the rebel forces in the rest of the country. He claimed he had information that a peace conference for the war in Europe 'was being held or was on the eve of being held', and he believed that holding out for a week or two more would assist the Irish in being able to attend this conference.

In one of his despatches on 30 April Thomas wrote: 'Good news on the International situation. England is down and out. Enemy officers are uttering Proclamations full of falsehoods.'[2] However, when it was made clear to him that those located at the headquarters – including Tom, Seán and James – had surrendered, and he had verified the surrender note, Thomas capitulated. Elizabeth asked him if she should try to get Muriel, but she said he looked around at the troops and said, 'Not like this.'[3]

The men from his garrison assembled at the corner of Bride Street and Ross Road. However, before reaching the British to surrender their arms and ammunition, some of the men simply blended into the crowd. Thomas had asked the women in the garrison to leave, and this was reiterated by the British officer, who simply told them, 'I'll see you over the roadway, ladies.'[4]

It was later said that Thomas and the other leaders could easily have escaped. As he was being arrested, John MacBride told those who could get away: 'Many of you may live to fight some other day. Take my advice – never allow yourselves to be cooped up inside a building again.'[5]

It would be Sunday night, 30 April, before the South Dublin Union garrison surrendered. When news came to Éamonn Ceannt that the GPO leaders had called a general surrender, he told his men that if Tom Clarke had surrendered, it was no shame on them to do so too. That day Áine learned for the first time of the Proclamation that had been issued and that Éamonn's name was on it.

Outside Dublin there had been some limited fighting, including a significant assault in Ashbourne, County Meath, led by Thomas Ashe. In the Wexford town of Enniscorthy, a group of Volunteers had made their headquarters in the Athenaeum under the command of Robert Brennan. In Galway actions led by Liam Mellows included an attack on the Royal Irish Constabulary at Oranmore. When news reached Mellows of the surrender in Dublin he abandoned a plan to march to County Clare with members of the Volunteers and Cumann na mBan. He disbanded his force in Galway and evaded capture along with many others in the county.

*

The rumours of surrender were confirmed to Kathleen Clarke by their local milkman, who came at about nine o'clock on Sunday morning. She refused to believe him, telling him it was nonsense: they would not surrender. He became annoyed and told her he had seen them rounded up in the Rotunda Gardens with his own eyes. He walked away from her saying, 'It's damn cool you take it, anyhow!'[6] Kathleen's icy exterior covered her quiet agony. She did not know if her husband or brother were dead or alive. She was not able to eat or sleep.

Tom wrote to Kathleen on Sunday, 30 April, from Richmond Barracks, where he was being held captive. He gave the note to a British soldier along with his old watch, hoping it would be smuggled out. He wrote the message in the belief that he and the others would be shot immediately without trial: 'Dear K – I am in better health and more satisfied than for many a day – all will be well eventually – but this is good-bye and now you are ever before me to cheer me – God bless you and the boys. Let them be proud to follow the same path . . . I am full of pride my love.'[7] Unfortunately, the letter did not reach Kathleen for some weeks. On that Sunday and into Monday, she remained in suspense. She once again returned to her gardening to help pass the hours.

On Monday, 1 May Nora and Ina Connolly returned from the North, without having taken part in any fighting. They made their way back to Dublin, then from the city to the cottage at Ticknock, a distance of ten miles. On the way, Nora later recalled: 'I saw a poster of the *Daily Sketch*, an English illustrated daily. The poster had a photo of my father on it with the inscription, "*James Connolly – The Dead Rebel Leader*".'[8]

Her first reaction was that she was delighted that her mother had not seen it, but 'when we arrived at the cottage, the half door was open. We crept in quietly, hearing the sounds of sobs and crying from within. Our mother sat on the side of the bed with a copy of the paper . . . Some kind neighbour had brought it to her, not knowing who mother really was.'[9]

They brought news that James had been injured but not killed. Lillie told them: "'I'd given up all hope of ever seeing you again. Now I have you and know that your father is not dead.'"[10]

Lillie and her daughters then made their way to the centre of Dublin City. 'But they will shoot him,' Lillie told them. Nora tried to reassure her, but Lillie said she knew the authorities would not let him live. Through her sobs she said: 'They fear him. They know they can neither bribe or humble him. He will always fight them.'[11]

Kathleen was outside in her garden on Tuesday when a large detachment of British soldiers arrived to raid her home. As she recalled, the soldier in charge had come 'to question me about my men. He wanted to know where they were. Were they out in [the] Rising? When had I last seen them? Was I in sympathy with them? I could have refused to answer, but I felt it would be letting my men down not to show I was with them, so I said that they were in the Rising and that I was in perfect sympathy with them, and very proud of them.' Her defiant answers and demeanour resulted in her arrest.

Kathleen was taken to Clontarf Police Barracks before being transferred to Dublin Castle, where she was to be imprisoned with others the military had rounded up. Her companion en route was Arthur Griffith, founder of Sinn Féin. He had not been out in the fight but had been arrested. When Kathleen saw men being marched along and jumped up to salute them, Griffith grabbed her, saying 'Are you mad? You will be shot before you know where you are.'

Inside Dublin Castle, she was questioned again about her involvement and she gestured that she was up to her neck in it. When asked where her men were, she replied: 'I don't know, they are either dead or in your hands.'[12] With this, the soldier directed that she be locked up. Griffith remained silent when asked about his role. The authorities thought he was a key player in the Rising and that Sinn Féin was behind its planning; it was already being called 'the Sinn

Féin Rebellion'. He was imprisoned along with scores of other men and a small number of women who had played no part in the Rising.

On Monday, 1 May, Áine still knew nothing of Éamonn. She finally located a priest who told her that those who had taken part would be interned and the leaders were to be tried by court martial under the Defence of the Realm Act. This came as a shock to her; seeing her reaction, the priest then tried to make light of it: 'He knew how deeply I was involved.'[13]

On 2 May Joe sent another message to Grace at 8 Temple Villas, this time from captivity in Richmond Barracks:

> My Darling Child,
> This is my first chance of sending you a line since we were taken. I have no notion what they intend to do with me but I heard I am to be sent to England. The only thing I care about it is that I am not with you – everything else is cheerful . . . Listen – if I live it might be possible to get the church to marry us by proxy – there is such a thing but it is very difficult I am told. Father Sherwin might be able to do it. You know how I love you. That is all I have time to say. I know you love me and I am very happy.[14]

In the past, following the Irish Rebellions in 1798, 1848 and 1867, the British government's response had largely been deportations, transportation, long prison sentences and, in 1798, huge numbers of executions. Now the authorities were in the process of drawing up a list of men – close to a hundred of them – to be sentenced to death. The executions were to take place in a disused prison, Kilmainham Jail, which was being used by the British Army for soldiers who had broken the law. On 2 May the military issued internal instructions that those condemned to death would be segregated and asked if they wanted to see family members or chaplains, and these people would be sent for as required by the prisoners. A number of cars were to be stationed at Richmond Barracks for that purpose. The visitors would be taken back to their homes before 3.30 a.m. (which was dawn in early May 1916), when the firing party would 'parade'.

The first to be executed, on Wednesday, 3 May, was P. H. Pearse, who was – as was reported to Prime Minister Henry Asquith – commandant general of the Army of the Irish Republic and president of the Provisional Government. Pearse had wanted to see his mother, but she did not make it to Kilmainham Jail as the military car sent for her was unable to complete the journey. P. H. wrote her a letter, telling her he was 'to die a soldier's death for Ireland and for freedom.' He did not see his only brother, Willie, who was also imprisoned, but he sent him a letter too, telling him: 'No one can ever have had so true a brother as you.'[15]

Muriel got word on Tuesday, 2 May that Thomas was to be shot. She was told by the messenger that if she rang the barracks she would be allowed see him. The only neighbour on the road who had a telephone refused to let her use it, however: Muriel was now the wife of a rebel. Father Aloysius, a Capuchin who was called in to give the last rites to the prisoners, tried to reach her, but without the proper paperwork he was turned back from one of the numerous road blocks that had been erected across the city; the decision was then taken that another relative would be selected instead. Thomas's sister Mary – Sister Francesca – was living in a convent in Basin Lane close to the prison, so it was she who saw her younger brother before his execution.

At midnight on 2 May 1916 Thomas wrote to Muriel from his prison cell in Kilmainham Jail:

> I am to die at *dawn*, 3.30 a.m. 3rd May. I am ready to die, and I thank God that I die in so holy a cause. My country will reward my deed richly . . . For myself I have no regret. The one bitterness that death has for me is the separation it brings from my beloved wife, Muriel, and my beloved children, Donagh and Barbara . . . Never was there a better, truer, purer woman than my wife, Muriel, or more adorable

children . . . It breaks my heart to think that I shall never see my children again, but I have not wept or mourned. I counted the cost of this, and am ready to pay it . . . My wife and I have given all for Ireland . . . My dearest love, Muriel, thank you a million times for all you have been to me. I have only one trouble in leaving life – leaving you so. Be brave, darling, God will assist and bless you. Goodbye, kiss my darlings for me. I send you the few things I have saved out of this war. Goodbye, my love, till we meet again in Heaven. I have a sure faith of our union there. I kiss this paper that goes to you. I have heard that they have not been able to reach you. Perhaps it is better so . . . God help and sustain you, my love. But for your suffering this would be all joy and glory. Goodbye.[16]

Tom Clarke asked to see Kathleen that same night. She was in custody in Dublin Castle and was easy to locate. She was locked up with a number of other women, members of Cumann na mBan and the Irish Citizen Army and others, all accused of being 'Sinn Féiners'.

Kathleen later wrote: 'my mind was in too great a tension to sleep. I could think of nothing but my husband and my brother. Were they blackened corpses in the smouldering city, or prisoners in the hands of our enemy, perhaps being tortured?' Sometime after midnight the door opened and a sergeant asked, 'Which of you is Mrs Tom Clarke?' He handed her a piece of paper directing her to Kilmainham Jail where her husband was a prisoner. One of her fellow detainees, Máire Perolz, asked her what the message meant. Kathleen replied: 'It means death . . . surely you do not think the British are so good and kind as to send for me to say goodbye if they were sending him on any shorter journey than to the next world?' She was driven to the jail in an open car with one soldier driving and two others with rifles and fixed bayonets beside her. Upon arrival, she had not yet been officially told that Tom had been sentenced to death; she just knew.

When she entered his cell he was lying on the floor, but he jumped up when he saw her. She rushed to him, saying, '"Why did you surrender? The last thing you said was no surrender" . . . He was very gentle with me, and said, "I know Katty, and I meant it. Had it rested with me there would have been no surrender . . . I was out-voted. I hoped to go down in the retreat from the GPO, but it was not to be."' Kathleen spent an hour with Tom while a soldier stood by with a candle in a jam jar; the gas supply to the jail had been destroyed during the Rising. Kathleen told her husband: 'I don't know how I am to live without you. I wish the British would put a bullet in me too.' He replied: 'It is not British policy to shoot women . . . God will help you and your own courage, also the children's need for you.' He told Kathleen not to let his death be a shadow on the lives of their sons: 'They have been so far such happy children, but train them to follow in my footsteps.' She replied that she would carry out his wishes to the best of her ability, 'but his death would shadow their lives no matter what I did, and I thought it was a hard road he had picked for them, to follow in his footsteps, children did not always carry out their parents' wishes.'

Thereafter, Tom talked only of the success of the Rising. All through their last meeting, Kathleen recalled: 'I was conscious of the exalted, very exalted state of mind he was in.' He entrusted to her a message for the Irish people: 'we have struck the first blow for Freedom. The next blow, which we have no doubt Ireland will strike, will win through. In this belief we die happy.' Throughout their conversation, Kathleen focused on not breaking down. 'I knew that if I broke, it would break him, at least I feared it would, and perhaps leave him unfit to face the ordeal before him in a way he and I would like.' When they were told their time was up, Kathleen stood by as the door was locked on her husband's cell. In old age she said, 'the sound of that key in that lock has haunted me ever since.'[17] She chose not to tell Tom about her unborn baby.

Later that day, Kathleen's sister Madge arrived from Limerick. She said of Kathleen: 'I hope never to see in any human face such absolute desolation. She looked as if life could do no more to her, as if some vital part of her was dead, and yet she was calm, but most violent grief would have been easier to look at.'[18]

The very next day, Wednesday, 3 May, Kathleen was back at the jail, this time to say goodbye to her only brother, Ned. The police sergeant who collected her sympathized with her, telling her: 'I was very sorry to hear of her husband's death that morning that I knew him well and never expected that he would meet such an untimely end.' She replied that there was nothing to be sorry about; Tom had died as honourably as he had lived.[19]

At twenty-five years old, Kathleen's brother was the youngest man to be executed for his part in the Rising. General Maxwell described him to Herbert Asquith as 'one of the most prominent extremists in the Sinn Féin organization.'[20] While Ned had been commandant of the Four Courts Garrison, the other men who were executed along with him on 4 May were not so involved. Willie Pearse had been his brother's close companion and this gave the authorities the impression that he had a more central role than he actually had, and he pleaded guilty at the court martial. Michael O'Hanrahan had been in Jacob's Garrison and had taken part in no direct combat, but he was well known as he worked at the Irish Volunteers headquarters. His family had received a message to come to the jail as he wanted to see them before being deported to England; in fact, they had discovered on their arrival that he was to face the firing squad at dawn the next day.

On the Wednesday Muriel made her way after curfew to Belgrave Road to tell Geraldine Plunkett, now Mrs Dillon, that Thomas was dead and that Joe was to be shot the next morning. She spoke to Geraldine at the gate, while Geraldine's mother-in-law shouted over and over again 'Don't let her into the house.'[21]

Muriel later said that she had known nothing of Tom's death until the news was flashed to her in an evening paper. Don, then aged three and a half, later recalled how he learned of what had happened: 'I was playing in the rockery and fled in terror from the bogeyman who came riding on a bread van with news which terrified.'[22] This was Father Aloysius, who had come to give Muriel his account of Thomas's last hours. He had prayed with Thomas in his cell between 2 a.m. and 3 a.m., then administered the last rites, saying that Thomas had 'died as he lived with no rancour in his heart.'[23]

On Wednesday, 3 May, Grace entered a jeweller's shop on Grafton Street and asked to be shown some wedding rings. The jeweller, Mr Stoker, later described her as 'a young and attractive lady, evidently of good social position'. She was wearing a veil but the jeweller noted that she had been crying. Surprised at her 'evident distress, Mr. Stoker gently enquired if she was in trouble.' He told her she should not cry 'when you are going to be married.' Then she revealed to him 'the whole tragedy, saying she was Mr. Plunkett's fiancée, that he was to be shot the next morning, and that she was to be married to him that night. "For that moment I was thunder-struck," said Mr. Stoker, "and didn't know what to say or do. Somehow I managed to express my sympathy with her terrible posi-tion, she thanked me very quietly." [Then] she selected the most expensive of the rings, paid for it in notes, and left the shop.'[24]

Later there were rumours that Grace was pregnant.[25] She herself may have been responsible for starting them, as she had told a priest, Rev. Eugene McCarthy, that she had to get married. This may explain the benevolence of Major William Sherlock Lennon, the temporary governor of Kilmainham Jail. A Dubliner and a former member of the Royal Irish Constabulary, he had been invalided out of the war and now found himself in charge of the British Army detention barracks while the executions were going on. He was known to have done many small kindnesses for the prisoners in their final days. Had he thought that allowing the marriage would prevent an unborn child being illegitimate?

Grace arrived at Kilmainham Jail on 3 May at 6 p.m. and finally, at about 11.30 p.m., she was brought to the prison chapel. She did not see her fiancé until she entered the chapel. There were no extra concessions for the couple, such as the presence of friends or family, even though Grace's sister Nellie, who had taken part in the Rising, stationed in the College of Surgeons, was a prisoner in the jail. A number of armed soldiers were in the chapel and the marriage certificate records that two of them, John Smith and John Carberry of the 3rd Battalion of the Royal Irish Regiment, acted as witnesses to the marriage. During the wedding ceremony Grace and Joe were not allowed to speak except to recite the words of their vows.

In the days following the Rising Joe's mother, Countess Plunkett, had visited a number of officials seeking information about him and her other sons, George and John, who had also taken part in the fighting. She was brought to Kilmainham Jail and held there. Her husband had also been arrested in the round-up following the Rising; he had volunteered his services at the GPO, but Joe had sent him home.[26] Although they were both in Kilmainham Jail in the hours before Joe was shot, they were not allowed to see him, as the final visit was now allocated to his next-of-kin, his new wife Grace.

Immediately after the marriage ceremony, Joe was taken back to his cell and Grace left the prison. Lodgings were found nearby for the new bride; as she was now Joe's next-of-kin she would be permitted to see him again before his execution and at 2 a.m. she received a letter granting her permission to return to Kilmainham Jail. Later she recalled her last meeting with Joe in his cell, and that he had to kneel beside her during their ten minutes together: 'We who had never enough time to say what we wanted to each other found that in that last ten minutes we couldn't talk at all.'[27]

The Connolly family were taken in by the O'Brien family. James's friend William O'Brien lived with his sister Sissy and his mother at Belvedere Place and Roddy Connolly had been staying with them. On the previous Saturday he and William had left the house looking for news but had been arrested and were now in prison. After the executions began, Lillie grew more anxious about her son, confiding in Nora: 'Willie Pearse was executed because he was P. H. Pearse's brother. He was not a leader, he was only a soldier.' She reasoned that Roddy was a soldier too. 'How can I be sure that he won't be shot?' At times an awful terror took hold of Lillie that all her children would be taken from her and she could not be comforted.[28]

Roddy had been taken to Customs House and afterwards to Richmond Barracks. Having already been warned by his father to give a false name, he called himself Alfred Carn. Only fellow-prisoner Seán Mac Diarmada knew who he really was. Seán taught him chess and they spent their days in captivity playing on a board scratched out on the floor, with pieces of fruit peel as chess pieces.

On 3 May Ina Connolly went to Dublin Castle looking for news of her father. She was directed to an area that had been converted into a Red Cross Hospital, where the officer in charge took the address where the family were staying and said he would send word when visitors would be permitted. Days passed and they dreaded looking at the newspapers following the newsboys' calls of 'one more execution.'

John MacBride was executed on Friday, 5 May. He did not have any family visit him in his last hours. Prisoner number 34 had been found guilty of 'waging war against his Majesty the King', acting in a manner 'prejudicial to the Defence of the Realm'. In his assessment of MacBride, General Maxwell, who had served in the Boer War, noted to the Prime Minister that 'This man fought on the side of the Boers in the South African war of 1899 and held the rank of Major in that Army, being in command of the Irish Brigade'.[29] When John had met Seán T. O'Kelly in Richmond Barracks some days earlier, he had told him: 'Nothing will save me, Seán. This is the end. Remember this is the second time I have sinned against them.'[30]

In Paris, Maud and her son separately heard the news of those who had been executed, including John MacBride. Maud was later given an account of his death by the priest who was with him at the end; Father Augustine said John knew no fear. Maud then wrote to Willie Yeats: 'He made a fine heroic end, which has atoned for all. It was a death he had always desired.'[31]

*

When Áine Ceannt read in a newspaper of the first of the executions she also read an inaccurate report that a sentence of three years' penal servitude was to be imposed on her husband Éamonn and three others. Áine wrote to the House of Commons requesting confirmation of a reprieve.

Up until 4 May Éamonn had been held in Richmond Barracks, but once his court martial was complete he was moved to Kilmainham Jail. He wrote to Áine: 'I am cheerful and happy and hope Áine and little Rónán also are so . . . I shall try to accept my fate like a man and commend you and Rónán to the sympathy and support of our relatives and friends . . . Do not fret.' On 5 May he wrote again: 'I am well but expecting the worst – which may be best . . . Tell Rónán to be a good boy and to remember Easter 1916 forever. I'm in excellent form . . . Don't expect you'll see No 2 [Dolphin Terrace] as you left it. Probably looted by this. Adieu or au revoir – I don't know which.'[32]

Later the same day he wrote again, this time to say the trial had closed. He told his wife: 'I expect the death sentence which better men have already suffered. I only regret that I have now no longer an opportunity of showing how I think of you now that the chance of seeing you again is so remote. I shall die a man for Ireland's sake.'[33]

Following his sentencing, Éamonn wrote a separate note detailing what should be done with his property. During those days in captivity he also wrote a statement for the Irish people:

> guidance for other Irish Revolutionaries . . . never surrender . . . but fight to a finish . . . the enemy has not cherished one generous thought for those who, with little hope, with poor equipment, and weak in numbers, withstood his forces for one glorious week. Ireland has shown she is a Nation . . . I bear no ill will against whom I fought . . . I wish to record the magnificent gallantry and fearless, calm determination of the men who fought with me.[34]

Áine set about locating any friends who could assist her in

preventing Éamonn's execution. One of them, Johnny Foley, who had been secretary to the Lord Mayor for many years, suggested that they go to Richmond Barracks where the men were being held. On Saturday, 6 May, she met the Provost Marshall, Viscount Powerscourt, who was, Áine remembered, 'very amiable' and said he did not know what sentences 'the gentlemen' got but gave her a note for the governor of Kilmainham Jail which permitted her to see her husband.

She was brought to a cell on the upper floor, up the big iron stairs. Éamonn's expression was cold and distant; as he later wrote to Áine, 'my cold exterior was but a mask. It has saved me these last days.'[35] As always, she was direct with him, saying: 'the Rising was an awful fiasco'. Éamonn replied that 'it was the biggest thing since the rebellion of 1798'.[36]

It was not until Sunday morning, 7 May, that a letter came for Lillie Connolly informing her that she was permitted to see 'the prisoner' in Dublin Castle. She went on Monday morning and brought Fiona with her. She gave her 'word of honour' that she would not tell her husband anything that had happened outside and that she would not bring in anything with which he could take his life. Both Lillie and Fiona were searched by the military before being brought to James, who was in a bed in a room known as 'the Queen's boudoir'. His wound had turned gangrenous and he was very weak, pale and feverish. He had been placed under the care of Mr Richard Francis Tobin, who 'took a strong liking' to him, and passed the days discussing poetry and literature with him. Mr Tobin sent to London to get medicine he had heard of that would stop the spread of gangrene.

People tried to reassure Lillie that the authorities would not execute a wounded man. The family voiced the hope that the British would wait until James was stronger before his trial and that, by then, public opinion would prevent any such execution. Over subsequent days, Lillie was allowed to visit him several times and her spirits lifted. She hoped that her husband might not be shot.

*

Áine decided on Sunday evening that she would visit Sir Charles Cameron at his home on Raglan Road, as Éamonn had requested of her. He was a doctor and head of public health at Dublin Corporation. She asked him if there was anything that could be done to save her husband and he promised to do his best.

Áine and Rónán returned to Drumcondra, where they were staying with Éamonn's sister Ellen and her husband, Jack Casey. That night a soldier on furlough arrived with news of the eldest Kent brother, Company Sergeant William Leeman Kent, who had been posted to Cork the previous March. William too had got caught up in the Rising, guarding Thomas Kent (no relation). Thomas Kent had staged his own armed protest and in the process two policemen were killed. When he was being held awaiting execution, William Leeman was accused of stealing food to give to him. According to the family account, William had purchased the food, but the internal court martial found him guilty of misconduct. Thomas Kent was executed for his actions in Cork during the Rising; Éamonn's brother went to the Front, where he would die on 24 April 1917, the first anniversary of the Rising.

At ten o'clock that same night, it was Áine's turn to return to Kilmainham Jail, accompanied by Richard and Michael Kent, Éamonn's brothers. They were brought to a new cell on the ground floor in the central compound. When Éamonn went over and put his arms around Áine and kissed her, his brothers turned to face the men who were standing guard. When Áine asked him how he was, mentally, he replied that all the rumours of a reprieve had disturbed him. A warder described how, at that final meeting, Áine 'bore up' even after she left her husband's cell; but even at that point she still held out hope of a reprieve.[37] There had been no executions since John MacBride had been shot the previous Friday. As they were leaving the jail, the commandant stopped Richard and told him: 'There is no reprieve; go back and tell your brother.'[38] Áine did not hear this conversation and Richard did not tell her what he had been told.

In his last hour Éamonn wrote to her:

My dearest wife Áine, Not wife but widow before these lines reach you . . . Dearest 'silly little Fanny'. My poor little sweetheart of many years ago. Ever my comforter. God comfort you now. What can I say? I die a noble death for Ireland's freedom. Men and women will vie with one another to shake your dear hand. Be proud of me as I am and ever was of you . . . You have a duty to me and to Rónán to live. My dying wishes are that you shall remember your state of health, work only as much as may be necessary and freely accept the little attentions which in due time will be showered upon you. You will be, you are, the wife of one of the Leaders of the Revolution . . .[39]

In the days after surrender, Agnes Mallin had anxiously watched the papers for the results of the trials. She discussed with her brother-in-law Tom what sentence Michael was likely to get. Agnes talked in terms of years, even twenty years; she never considered a sentence of death.

At his court martial Michael tried to mitigate his sentence by claiming that his role was one of a man following instruction:

I am a silk weaver by trade and have been employed by the Transport Union as a band instructor. During my instruction of these bands they became part of the Irish Citizen Army and from this I was asked to become a drill instructor. I had no commission in the Citizen Army. I was never taken into the confidence of James Connolly. I was under the impression we were going out on manoeuvres on Sunday but something altered the arrangements and the manoeuvres were postponed . . . I had verbal instructions from James Connolly to take 36 men to St Stephens Green and to report to Volunteer Officers there. Shortly after my arrival in St Stephens Green . . . the Countess ordered me to take command of the men as I have long associated with them I felt I could not leave them and from that time I joined the rebellion. I made it my business to save all officers and civilians who were brought in to Stephens Green. I gave explicit orders to the men to make no offensive movements and prevented them attacking the Shelbourne Hotel.[40]

However, there was ample evidence of his true role. Constable John O'Connell stated: 'There is a paper called "The Workers Republic" in which it has been stated that the prisoner is Chief of Staff of the Citizen Army.' In the Rising he was in fact commander of the garrison at St Stephen's Green and the College of Surgeons.

On the night of Sunday, 7 May, a military car came for Agnes and she was told that her husband wanted her immediately. Her brother-in-law Tom got into the car with her. On the journey to Kilmainham he ascertained from a member of the Dublin Metropolitan Police that the sentence was death: 'I spoke to Agnes and said that even if Mike's sentence was death that she should bear up and not make his sentence harder for him.'

Agnes and Tom Mallin were led to a cell and Tom went in first. He saw his brother standing at the back wall. There was very little light. Michael had an old green blanket wrapped around him and he said it was very cold. He had a growth of beard and his eyes appeared to be fixed and glossy. 'He said, "Where is Agnes?" She ran towards him and said, "What is it?" He replied, "Death." She collapsed on the floor.'[41]

Michael's parents were then living in a small house just yards from the wall of Kilmainham Jail. A policeman had arrived at the house, and when Michael's mother saw him, she turned to her daughter Katie and said: 'Mike's time is up.' 'No, that cannot be,' she replied.[42] The family was given permission to visit Michael, so his mother, Katie and his brother Bart all went to the jail. Michael's father was not there as he was working at the new Jacob's Factory in Liverpool at this time.

As Michael wanted to see his children, his mother and sister returned to collect them. Seamus and Seán had been brought back to the city from Chapelizod some days before. Now they were awoken from sleep and told to dress themselves. 'Nothing else was said and though no trace of any tears could be seen on either of the women's cheeks, we knew that something terrible had happened, something that neither woman could bring themselves to tell us.'

As Seamus recounted, 'The jail was in semi-darkness and there were soldiers and police. People spoke in hushed tones. The children could hear the murmur of the rosary.'[43] Joe, the toddler, sat for a while on the last step of the spiral staircase in the main compound of the jail and a soldier gave him sweets.

Among the instructions that Michael gave to Agnes was to burn the wool picture which he had made in India, depicting the flags and drums of the Royal Scottish Fusiliers. Father Michael de Brun, a Capuchin friar who was also in the cell with them, interjected, suggesting to Michael that it was best to have thoughts of charity in his heart and mind as he was about to enter the presence of God. Michael agreed with him and gave a little laugh. Twelve-year-old Seamus said the memory of this stayed clear in his mind, but little else: 'Before the Rising, my father always spoke to me as though I was grown up but now I was just a small boy who had no idea of the ways of the world . . . that I would never see my father again, something I could not grasp or understand.'[44]

During his last hours Michael Mallin put his final thoughts on paper:

My darling wife, pulse of my heart, this is the end of all things earthly; sentence of death has been passed . . . I am prepared but oh my darling if only you and the little ones were coming too, if we could all reach heaven together, my heartstrings are torn to pieces when I think of you, and them, of our manly James, happy go lucky John, shy warm Úna, dady's [sic] girl and oh my little Joseph my little man, my little man. Wife dear wife, I cannot keep the tears back when I think of him, he will rest in my arms no more, to think I have to leave you to battle through the world with them without my help . . . I do not believe our blood has been shed in vain . . . a husband's blessing on your dear head my loving wife, a father's blessings on your dear heads of my children James John Una Joseph my little man my little man my little man, his name unnerves me again all your dear

257

faces arise before me God Bless you God bless you my darlings . . .
Pulse of my heart . . . I feel you will soon be in heaven with me.[45]

Other young men without wives or family were also executed on
8 May: Seán Heuston, the railway worker who had commanded
the Mendicity Institution, and Con Colbert, who had been in the
garrison at Marrowbone Lane.

Despite their friendship, Surgeon Tobin was one of two doctors who
certified James Connolly as fit to stand trial, and on Tuesday, 9 May,
he was tried by Field General Court Martial at the hospital. When
Lillie and Nora came to see him later he did not tell them; he was
very cheerful and talked of the future.

Two days after the court martial, on Thursday, 11 May 1916, a
British officer called to the O'Briens' house at 11 p.m. and asked
Lillie to accompany him. She went with him, thinking that James
'wasn't well, that he had taken a turn for the worst'. She went with
Nora to Dublin Castle by military ambulance. When they entered
the room, James said to his wife, 'Well, Lillie, I suppose you know
what this means?' She said, 'Oh no, Jim,' and she laid her head on
the bed and sobbed.[46] 'But your beautiful life, Jim, your beautiful
life!' He tried to comfort her: 'Wasn't it a full life, Lillie, and isn't this
a good end?' As she continued to sob he said, 'Lillie, please don't cry.
You will unman me.'[47]

Lillie was distraught. She had to be brought away from the room
by the nurse and the young officer who was guarding her husband.
James gave his last statement to Nora to smuggle out. She then told
him that the other leaders had been executed; she recalled that he
was shocked that they had been killed before him. Like all those
executed in the preceding days, James was brought to the stone-
breakers' yard at Kilmainham Jail, but as he was unable to stand, he
was placed sitting on an ordinary kitchen chair and shot dead.[48]

Lillie stood by the window at the O'Briens' home, 'moaning all
the while', and waited. When the sun rose she said to Nora: 'He's
gone, Nora, he's gone, he is gone from us now.'[49] Later she would

write in her Bible: 'There's a sorrow in our hearts, for a voice we loved is stilled; there's a vacancy in our home that never can be filled.'[50]

A few days later, a young soldier, sixteen or seventeen years old, called to the house to see Lillie. He told her he had been part of the firing squad that had killed her husband. He said that before his death James had offered the soldiers forgiveness, describing them as 'brave men doing their duty', but the young soldier was still consumed with shame for having killed such a man. Lillie comforted him by saying that James knew he was a working-class boy, under orders. Once her husband had forgiven him, she told him that he did not need her forgiveness, and that he should not worry any more.

When the postal service resumed, Áine received a letter written by Jim Healy of the House of Commons staff. He wrote that he had only received her letter the day after Éamonn's execution, 9 May, due to the 'irregularity of the post due to the disturbances'. He continued:

> I much regret your sorrow but no such statement was made by Mr Asquith ... I feel that had I received it in time the fact that your hopes had been raised by even a misreport I could have gone to the Prime Minister and pleaded a wife's cause. No husband would have stood indifferent to it. Where love and death are concerned there is no nationality; your arguments as a woman went the whole way. It is my grief that I can only salute you as a widow.[51]

PART THREE
MOURNING

10

Widows' Weeds

In the days following her husband Thomas's execution, Muriel MacDonagh was reportedly ordered to remain at home. It was said that the instruction came from General Maxwell himself as, with her 'sad blue eyes and golden hair', she made such a pathetic figure in mourning clothes that 'her appearance would incite widespread sympathy for the rebels'. Muriel told a reporter that: 'She wished the whole world to know that the authorities never sent her any official notice of her husband's death! "Someone told my little son," she said, "that the soldiers had killed his father – that was very unwise. Now the child screams at the sight of a soldier, and hides his face. He worshipped his daddy. I shall tell him the true story when he grows up."'[1]

Kathleen Clarke's house in Richmond Avenue became a focal point for the families. As the executions continued, so the women came. They came seeking information on their men, and for aid. As Kathleen described it: 'I was so dreadfully sorry for those women . . . many did not know the fate of their men, whether they were dead or alive. Some of them had made the rounds of the hospitals and even the morgues.'[2]

Before the Rising, a plan had been put in place to administer aid to those affected by the fighting, and this job had been assigned to Kathleen Clarke by the Military Council. All commandants in the battalions had drawn up lists of those families who would be in need of help. Kathleen had possession of those lists, but despite her best efforts some information was lost. Sorcha MacMahon postponed her marriage and left her job to assist Kathleen to coordinate the huge relief operation. They worked long hours in the weeks that followed, setting up a network to distribute funds and prioritize those most in need.

For the first twelve weeks the censor refused to allow the printing of notices for the fund because it was called the 'Irish Republican Prisoners' Dependants Fund', so the name was changed to the Irish Volunteers Dependants' Fund and Kathleen became president. She purposely asked the relatives of those executed to become involved, including Áine Ceannt and Muriel MacDonagh, as she knew that even those opposed to the Rising 'dared not say boo to us.'[3] They unashamedly stated that they were 'acting as their dead husbands, sons and brothers would desire.'[4] Later they would incorporate with the Irish National Aid Association, which had also been collecting funds, very successfully, since the cessation of the fighting.

Despite the fact that it had no direct role in organizing the Rising, Sinn Féin, with its political paper and its small membership, became the focus of the Dublin Castle administration and the press. As well as those who had actually taken part, the authorities began rounding up anyone suspected of being involved. The majority were now placed in internment camps in England and Wales: 2,650 were exiled without trial. In Westport, John MacBride's brother Joseph was arrested the day after John was executed. His wife – Maud Gonne's half-sister, Eileen – and her five small children were, like thousands of others, left without an income and with no idea how long this imprisonment would last.

General Maxwell's original plan to execute more men was halted by Prime Minister Asquith in the midst of widespread condemnation. The official figures were that 134[5] who were initially sentenced to death subsequently had their sentences commuted to penal servitude. Among those who publicly criticized the executions was George Bernard Shaw:

My own view is that the men were shot in cold blood, after their capture or surrender, were prisoners of war, and that it was therefore entirely incorrect to slaughter them ... an Irish man resorting to arms to achieve the independence of his own country is doing only what an Englishman will do, if it be their misfortune to be invaded and conquered by the Germans in the course of the present war ...[6]

Áine Ceannt's constant companion, her sister Lily, was not with her during her ordeal, as she was still in prison. There were rumours that Lily was one of seventy-seven women who would be deported to Jamaica to pick oranges. However, she and most of the others were released when General Maxwell, having examined the intelligence reports on those arrested, concluded that they were members of Sinn Féin's Ambulance Society, although in fact no such organization existed. Lily, now aged thirty-eight, was one of those privately described by Maxwell as 'silly little girls'. They were publicly cautioned about their 'behaviour' then and in the future, and released from jail on 8 May. Lily returned home to her sister Fanny, as she still called Áine.

Maxwell did, however, decide that a small number of women warranted further detention. Among those who remained in custody was Nellie Gifford (recorded as Eibhlin), as a sister-in-law of two of the leaders of the Rising and herself a member of the Irish Citizen Army.

To the establishment, the most infamous woman held was Countess Markievicz. Second-in-command at St Stephen's Green and later at the College of Surgeons, she had initially been condemned to death, but her sentence was commuted to life in prison. Her story featured large in the press, as a woman of the Anglo-Irish landed gentry who had turned against her class: 'behind all looms the strange mysterious figure of the Countess Markievicz. Who has played such a prominent part in the late tragic events and has flitted through all the dark pages of Irish discontent and treason of recent years.'[7]

Isabella Gifford claimed that her 'refined and artistic girls' had 'largely been under the influence' of Countess Markievicz, when she was interviewed by a journalist from *Lloyd's Weekly News* in the days following the executions:

> I did not know of my daughter's marriage to Mr. Plunkett until yesterday. I did not even know definitely that they had been engaged, although I heard it stated. I did not ask Grace, and she did not tell me, because she knew I disapproved of the whole thing . . . I first heard of marriage yesterday from Grace herself. I went to see her sister, Mrs. MacDonagh, and while I was there she came into the room. She walked right across to me and held out her left hand, on the third finger of which was a wedding ring. I did not make any remark, but knew she meant she was married.[8]

This made sense of an incident that had taken place on the previous Wednesday night, 3 May, at the Gifford home. There had been a knock on the door and, as the maid had gone to bed, Isabella answered it herself. It was an officer who had been sent to Temple Villas to collect 'Mrs Plunkett'. Isabella informed them they had the wrong address, thinking they were looking for the Countess Plunkett, but they then enquired for Grace Gifford and Isabella told them she was not at home.

Isabella highlighted the loyalist and unionist stance of the Gifford family, telling the *Lloyd's* reporter that one of her sons was home at that time, as part of the Canadian contingent. Claude had given up the legal practice that he had conducted with his father. He had gone to Canada and had enlisted there in the 50th Battalion of the Canadian Overseas Expeditionary Force in June 1915 in Calgary; he had been appointed a lieutenant. Such was the complexity of Isabella's large family that her son was fighting on behalf of Britain and her allies – Liebert was in the Merchant Navy and Edward would later enlist in the American Army – while her daughters were involved in the struggle for Irish independence from the Empire; but she did not elaborate on her family's divided loyalties for the benefit of the readers of the popular illustrated paper.

Isabella also chose not to mention that she had informed Grace, now Mrs Joseph Plunkett, that she was no longer welcome at 8 Temple Villas. Countess Plunkett, in contrast, had sent word from jail to her daughter Geraldine to look after Joe's widow and take her in, so Grace went to Larkfield in Kimmage. Geraldine knew the importance of Grace remaining in the public eye. The jail wedding soon became news all over the world and Grace became the subject of stories, poetry and songs – the young woman as 'maid, wife and widow' all in one night. For many, she was seen as a symbol of the tragedy of the widows, and of the brutality of the executions. Newspaper reporters searching for anyone who would give them an insight into the rebellion were intrigued by the participation of women in combat and in particular by the story of a 'secret wedding ceremony at the dead of night',[9] just hours before the groom was executed.

Six weeks after Joseph Plunkett's death, journalist Eileen Moore visited Grace in the garden at Larkfield. She was one of five correspondents sent to Ireland in June 1916 to bring back uncensored news because, as she described to her readers, 'the mails and cables could not be trusted.' She set out to meet the 'women of the Rebellion and study the human side'. As she reported in Chicago's *New World*, Eileen had 'pictured a desolate stricken widow in black and was prepared for an hour of a broken, sorrowful story when out of the garden came my subject, dressed in white, carrying a kitten and flowers for the house, with a kind and cheerful greeting.' The reporter mused: 'what a bridal night, I thought "what a terrible experience. Her Husband shot at dawn. If she was aware she would have heard the soldiers firing!"'[10]

The story was far more harrowing if Geraldine's account is to be believed. She said that Grace had miscarried at Larkfield in the weeks following Joe's execution; she wrote in her diary that she had seen the foetus in a bucket. Other members of the Plunkett family who heard Geraldine's story said she could not be believed; however, she was the only member of the family in Dublin at that time.

Count Plunkett, now the former director of the National

Museum of Science and Art in Dublin, was among those deported to England for a period of time under the provision of the Defence of the Realm Act. He was accompanied by his wife and his youngest daughter, Fiona, and had to remain under open arrest in a place of his choosing in England. He chose Oxford, as he hoped to read at the Bodleian Library there, but the librarian, who was actually Irish, refused to issue him a ticket as he disagreed with his politics. Of the other Plunkett siblings, Mimi was in America, Moya was in a convent in London, while twenty-three-year-old George and eighteen-year-old Jack were in prison following the Rising.

Just as Éamonn had predicted in his last letter, the O'Brennan sisters and their mother returned to 2 Dolphin Terrace to find it had been looted and ransacked. Tragically, during a raid immediately following the Rising, their neighbours, a mother and daughter, had witnessed soldiers jumping a railing and pointing guns at the Ceannt home, and the younger woman had had a seizure and died.

Áine was now a widow of one of the leaders of a rebellion that had destroyed most of the buildings in the city centre and disrupted the postal system, including the delivery of the 'separation allowance' issued to the wives of serving British soldiers. Many Dubliners believed that the Provisional Government of the Irish Republic, which Éamonn Ceannt had helped create, albeit on paper, had fought against the Empire without the mandate of the Irish people. The family was no longer welcome in the neighbour-hood. They would move in time to Oakley Road where many of their friends lived – so much so that the road became known as 'Rebel Road'.

Éamonn had received an advance in wages during the week before the Rising so that Áine would have some money to sustain her for the duration of the fight; but she now faced a whole new world, with no income and with her mother, sister and son as dependants. Number 2 Dolphin Terrace had also previously been used for Lily's private school. But that life was now in the past. Áine listed the costs of the damage – boards for the broken windows, a new set of dishes, lampshades and the cost of a painter. The military had destroyed their food store: tea and sugar were spilt all over the floor, bayonets had been put through the tinned food. But it was the loss of Éamonn's belongings that affected Áine the most. Valuable pipes that he had bought from a collector had been taken in one of the raids. She immediately set about writing letters to the British military seeking the return of items.

Áine also began to put Éamonn's affairs in order and submitted a claim for two life policies in the name of Edward Kent to the Scottish Amicable Life Assurance Society. It would not be a straight-forward application. The solicitors Beauchamp and Orr on behalf of the assurance society wrote to the advocate general in London to obtain the charges and sentence from the court martial, but these documents were considered by the Army Council to be too sensitive to be supplied for the purpose of a public policy. Over a number of years Áine attended the High Court in what ultimately proved an unsuccessful pursuit of these monies.

The widows were also prevented from reclaiming their husbands' bodies for burial. Lillie and Nora Connolly had gone to Dublin Castle to collect James's body, but they, like the other families, were refused. The bodies had been interred in a mass grave at the military graveyard of Arbour Hill, next to Arbour Hill Prison and Royal Barracks. Some days later they went to claim James's belongings. Nora hoped that they would get her father's uniform, but all they were given was his blood-stained underclothes. Neither did they get his wallet. It contained the first picture that Lillie had ever given him, which he had carried with him for over a quarter of a century.

When Lillie's enquiries came to nothing, she was advised to ask General Maxwell. As Nora recalled: 'She went along. Mama had an extraordinary dignity, though she was so retiring. Maxwell went forward to shake hands with her – the man who had given the order to execute her husband. She just put her hands behind her back. She told him she had come for her husband's wallet and watch, which had not been handed back.'[11] She succeeded in getting back the wallet; her photograph was there along with some documents, but another photograph was missing – Nora dressed in a Volunteer uniform, which she had signed: 'your soldier son'. As a result, the authorities had been looking for Lillie's 'other son' without success.

The seven members of the Connolly family remained living with the O'Briens, aware of the burden they were on their friends. According to Nora: 'We were in dire straits . . . we had no money whatsoever, and no means of getting any. Daddy never had any money to spare: the last few pounds he had in his wallet were taken from him after his arrest.'[12] Individual donations came in to the family, including one from George Bernard Shaw.

Most of the donations were administered through the Volunteers' Dependants' Fund. The allocation of non-specified funding was administered by committee, with internal systems worked out for who would receive which amount. The largest sum was paid to Mrs Pearse and her daughters, who received £1,750, reflecting P. H. Pearse's role as the leader.[13] For widows of the executed leaders an amount of £1,500 per family was invested on behalf of those or the dependants of those killed. They also received one-off grants. It was arranged that Muriel MacDonagh and her two children would receive £250, and Áine Ceannt and her son got the same. Lillie Connolly initially received an instalment of £50 as, according to the records of the Fund, three of her family had jobs.

The widows of the 'Provisional Government of the Irish Republic' were in receipt of more money than those executed who had not signed the Proclamation. As a result, Agnes Mallin was granted just £1 a week.[14] Her circumstances were particularly difficult, as Michael's British Army pension had ceased with his death and, heavily pregnant, she could not work. The shop that the family had run at Emmet Hall did not open again after 1916, and there was very little support and money from her extended family. Agnes's sister Josephine was herself a widow with her own daughter, and she was also looking after their mother, Mary Hickey, who had been paralysed after a fall. Agnes's brother Patrick had died some years previously, leaving a widow and dependants, while her other sister, Mary, had a large family of eight children and was in no position to help.

In his last letter to Agnes, Michael Mallin had asked her not to give her love to another man: 'you are only a girl yet and perhaps it is selfish of me to ask it of you.' Remarriage would have been a great protection for any one of the women widowed so young. Agnes's loss was compounded by the age of her children: Seamus, her eldest, was only twelve when Michael was executed.

In Paris, Maud now made plans to return to her beloved Ireland, writing to Willie Yeats within weeks of John's execution of her desire that Seagan should finish his education there: 'Paris does not suit him and I have always wanted him brought up there. I want that more than ever now – I think Iseult also would be better in Ireland than in France and she has got over her objections to leaving Paris.' It was important for Maud to get Iseult out of France, as there was talk of conscripting women. Emergency passports were available for English subjects for travel from France to England, but none were being issued for Ireland. Iseult travelled to London and met with Yeats. Despite the ongoing war, she and Willie returned to France together to spend the summer of 1916 with Maud and Seagan at Les Mouettes, the house at Colleville-sur-Mer in Normandy. While Maud and her family were in Colleville, Willie again asked Maud, now a widow, to marry him and he was rejected once again. He then asked her permission to marry twenty-two-year-old Iseult. Maud agreed, but Iseult did not give him a clear answer and for some time he remained hopeful of matrimony with Maud's daughter.

During their time at Colleville, another of Maud's old friends was executed for his part in the Rising. Roger Casement was charged with high treason, stripped of his knighthood and hanged in Pentonville Prison on 3 August 1916 for his role in importing German weapons into Ireland. Seagan remembered how he used to be impressed by this 'tall, gaunt figure' on Casement's visits to their flat in Paris, and how he was always enthralled by his conversations with his mother. He in fact knew Roger Casement better than his own father, with whom he had only had written contact.

11

Beginning Again

The first meeting of Cumann na mBan after the Rising was a stormy one. Kathleen Clarke chaired it. A motion was proposed that any woman who had not fought should be expelled and Kathleen called on the members to forget about the failures and get to work, urging them 'let us show the enemy what we can do.'

Cumann na mBan members formed themselves into distribution committees, each with a secretary and a staff assembled to help put a network of distribution in place. For the purpose of distributing funds, they were known as 'visitors' and the women sometimes used prams to distribute the money and any other items required by the needy families. These rounds, often undertaken in the evenings, were highly organized.

Collections on behalf of the Volunteers' Dependants were soon banned by the authorities, however, because, although it was argued that these were collections for charity, they were seen as propaganda, as the images of the men who had been executed were being used on their collecting literature. Cumann na mBan members also organized fundraising concerts and the sale of commemorative material to raise money, and at the same time they were involved in other intelligence work as all the male activists were dead or imprisoned. Áine Ceannt was among those who attended countless meetings to coordinate these activities.

By August, the volume of work undertaken by Kathleen had made her very ill. Well into the later stages of her pregnancy, she suffered a miscarriage. Years later she wrote of this time with chilling brevity: 'My baby was dead and I hoped soon to be.' In fact, she did die for several minutes during the miscarriage, but was revived by the doctors. She described seeing her husband and others who had died in 1916 during this near-death experience and recalled them telling her to go back, as there was work for her to do. When the doctors brought her round, she realized that she had been 'trying to take the easy way out'. She reasoned with herself that she had to take up 'her burden', as she described it, and carry on as well as she could. When her sisters arrived later that day, Kathleen began to cry for the first time since the executions; she said that she cried with the disappointment of not being dead.

Even after her miscarriage, Kathleen continued to work from her sick bed. Her boys were in Limerick, where they were enrolled in school, and there they remained until the end of the summer term, the only males in the Daly household, as Uncle John had died the previous June. Kathleen stayed in Dublin and worked on the fund during the week, travelling down to see her sons at weekends. Her health continued to be problematic and in September she was admitted to a nursing home for a time, suffering from her old ailment, an attack of neuralgia. While she was ill the shop was cleared of over £1,200 worth of stock, and their landlady took possession and leased it to someone else. Kathleen's source of income was gone.

Agnes Mallin's baby girl was born in the Coombe Hospital on 19 August 1916. There were protests outside, as those who opposed the Rising focused their attentions on the families of the leaders; Úna Mallin later described being spat on. Constance Markievicz, who had been in Michael's garrison, asked to be the baby's god-mother and sent a miraculous medal for the infant from Aylesbury jail, where she was being held. The baby was named Maura Constance Connolly Mallin, her middle names given for her famous godmother and for James Connolly. Her godfather was William Partridge, who had served with Michael in the garrison at the College of Surgeons. He too was in prison at the time of Maura's birth. Lillie Connolly acted as proxy at the christening.

Lillie had become a Catholic on 15 August that year. James had been brought up as a Roman Catholic, but had not been practising; yet in his last hour of life he had asked for absolution on his deathbed and received the last rites, and he had asked that Lillie become a Catholic.[1] In deference to his wishes, she went for instruction to Church Street, where she received her baptism with eight-year-old Fiona standing as her sponsor.

Grace had moved from Larkfield as it had to be let out and for a time lived in the Plunketts' house in Fitzwilliam Street. However, Joe's siblings complained that Grace tampered with their possessions, treating them as if they were her own. She told a neighbour, Kitty O'Doherty, who was active in fundraising for the widows and dependants, that she had been forced out and went to live with her instead. When the Countess returned from exile in Oxford, she offered her new daughter-in-law a home, but Grace refused. Josephine Plunkett blamed her daughter Geraldine for coming between her and Joe's widow. It was clear that Geraldine did not approve of her new sister-in-law, although she claimed that, of the Plunkett family, she was the one that liked Grace best. Geraldine's belief was that Grace had been anxious to be married as she had been under the impression that Joe, as the eldest son, was entitled to all the family money. After Count Plunkett and his wife returned to Ireland, Grace would contact her father-in-law on a regular basis and tell him she would kill herself unless he gave her money; after a couple of these calls, according to Geraldine: 'Pa got tired of this after giving her the money the first few times.'[2]

Meanwhile, Muriel went to her brother-in-law Joseph MacDonagh in County Tipperary with the idea that she might move permanently to live in the country. Her mother Isabella wrote to Thomas MacDonagh's sister Mary, the nun Sister Francesca: 'I am really grateful to you for all your kindness to Muriel and her children. I assure you, she is a very difficult person to deal with, and I fear your goodness is not appreciated. As to Muriel settling down in the country, I don't think it at all likely she would content herself there.'[3] When Muriel returned to Dublin, the Plunkett family took over the care of another of the Gifford women: Muriel moved into one of the houses they owned, 50 Marlborough Road, Donnybrook and Mimi Plunkett, having returned from America where she had been since before the Rising, moved in with Muriel and her children.

In accordance with James's last wishes, Lillie Connolly applied for passports for herself and her children in order that they might go back to live in the US. Their application was refused. Nora later wrote that she believed that the British authorities felt that the arrival of Mrs Connolly and her family in America would be 'prejudicial to the interests of the Realm.'[4] However, using an assumed name, Nora managed to get a passport and spent much of 1917 on a propaganda tour telling her story of the Rising. While she was there she met Seamus O'Brien, whom she would marry a few years later.

There was a great appetite in Irish-American circles for news from Ireland. Áine's journalist sister Kit O'Brennan, who had gone to New York in October 1914, was now in demand as a speaker on the Easter Rising. She organized women's pickets at locations such as the White House, demanding recognition for the rights of small nations. Lily warned her sister not to go outside the Irish question. Kit lectured to university students and 'women of leisure'. Áine wrote to her: 'Any information about the martyrs should be highly interesting. We shall send you articles from time to time – which you can embellish if you wish!'[5]

Muriel and Grace's sisters Sidney and Ada Gifford had been living in New York for some time and it is said that, on hearing the news of the Rebellion, Ada had purchased green, white and orange cloth and made an Irish tricolour, waving it from the top of a trolley car as it weaved its way around the city.

Grace also tried to go to America with her sister Nellie, but they too were refused. For the Giffords, it was a difficult time, as their father, Frederick, was dying a slow death, having suffered a stroke.[6] Nellie persisted in getting to America, in late October 1916 going first to a safe house in Liverpool from where she obtained a false passport.[7] Isabella Gifford allowed her to see her father before she left Ireland.

Nellie went to live in Washington shortly after she arrived in America, but soon she went back to New York, where three months later she met Joseph Donnelly, a printer from Omagh, County Tyrone. Joseph had his own printing house, the Donnelly Press, at 164 East 37th Street[8] and his offices also became the centre for meetings of a new Irish society called the Progressive League. Nellie became an organizer for the group and her sister Sidney also played a part in it; between them they managed 'to recruit many new people into the movement.'[9]

Sidney had met a Hungarian, Arpad Czira. The handsome twenty-nine-year-old had been a prisoner-of-war in Russia between 1914 and 1916, but had escaped and fled to America. Sidney gave birth to his son, Finian; however, while the boy was still a baby, Arpad returned to Hungary.[10] Although Sidney claimed there had been a marriage, no record exists. Sidney corresponded with him, but he did not financially support her, and she and her son never saw him again. Henceforth, however, she would use his name and was known as Madame Czira.

Fundraising outside Ireland was very important for the Volunteers' Dependants' Fund, and with this in mind the widows and their children posed for the *Catholic Bulletin* in a series of photographs commissioned by the editor, J. J. Reynolds, for the Christmas 1916 issue. Ever-glamorous, Muriel has a pretty bow in her hair in one photograph, with toddler Barbara standing on the chair which her mother was meant to sit on; she appears not to want to sit still, so her mother holds her from behind, coaxing her to look at the camera, while Don sits on a seat beside them, his feet dangling.

Lillie, Áine, Kathleen and Agnes were also photographed with their children, and Grace was photographed alone. Other widows whose husbands died in the Rising were also included. Hanna Sheehy Skeffington was photographed with her son Owen. Her husband Francis had not taken part in the Rising, but as a pacifist he was on the streets preventing looting when he was picked up by the military and shot without trial. Nannie O'Rahilly's husband Michael was shot in Moore Street during the fighting. She was pictured with her children, including her baby, Rory, who had been born in June 1916 after his father's death. The *Catholic Bulletin* did not include a picture of Maud and Seagan; instead a picture of John's mother, Honoria MacBride, was featured.

The purpose of these photographs was to encourage fundraising for the education of the children. This assistance would bring Agnes more sorrow, however, as it led to the Mallin family being broken up. Agnes remained at home, which was still Emmet Hall in Inchicore, while Seamus, Seán and Úna attended boarding school, their fees and associated expenses paid by the Volunteers' Dependants' Fund. Eight-year-old Úna was provided for at St Philomena's Convent, a girls' boarding school in Kiltimagh, County Mayo, where she was joined for a time by Ina, Moira and Fiona Connolly.[11] St Enda's School was the natural place to send the boys. Rónán Ceannt recorded that he was in class with Seamus and Seán Mallin. Roddy Connolly did not attended St Enda's but instead in the autumn of 1916 went to Blackrock College. Lillie resented being pressurized and refused to comply with demands imposed on her for Roddy's education.[12] She wanted him to take an apprenticeship as an engineer in Belfast, as his father had wished.

Now that she had passed over some of the burden of fundraising to others, Kathleen brought her children back from Limerick to live with her in Dublin on a more permanent basis. Daly was often ill and she was constantly worried about him. Unable to stay in Richmond Avenue where she and Tom had lived together, she rented it out with all their belongings and took a furnished house in the countryside at Dundrum in County Dublin. She tried when possible to keep the youngest, Emmet, with her, as he was only seven, so when she came into Dublin for night-time meetings which required an overnight stay in a hotel on College Green, she would bring him along. On one occasion, she left Emmet alone in the room and, when he started to cry, one of the maids came in. He showed her some postcards, including one of the executions, with the firing party illustrated. The maid asked if it was real and Emmet told her it was not. When his mother returned he told her what he had said to the maid and she scolded him, saying he should not have done so. As he later put it, 'I then realized that I might have inadvertently given information to the enemy.' After that, Kathleen did not bring him with her again. For months afterwards, whenever he went to the cinema with his brother Tom, he pestered him to find out what was written on the screen, fearing that something he had said would be revealed on it.[13]

Fear of informers and spies was a constant for the families. Like many of the other widows, Kathleen was constantly followed by detectives, but this did not deter her from travelling to England to see men who had been rearrested early in 1917 and were being held there under open arrest. Instead of detaining them in prison or in a camp, the British authorities ordered them to live in designated places. Joseph MacBride was one of those who had been released at Christmas 1916 and rearrested in early 1917, with no reason given for the second arrest and deportation. According to Maud: 'Joseph MacBride has again been arrested, though he had taken no part in politics his wife said since he had returned at Xmas after his nine month imprisonment in England – No reason was given re arrest & deportation – he was sent first to Oxford, where having some introduction to the Jesuit fathers he succeeded in getting work . . . most necessary for him, as he has no means & a wife & 5 little children dependent on him . . .'

Joseph had been sent to Oxford along with other Irishmen. Unlike Count Plunkett's experience as a reader, an Irish priest got him work in the Bodleian Library, which meant that he was earning some income for Eileen and ten-year-old twin girls Cleena and Clodhra, nine-year-old Erc, three-year-old Úna and their baby Síle. Then, without 'any alleged reason being formulated', he and ten others were rearrested and 'conducted to a little village in Gloucestershire and left there without any provision being made for them with orders that they were not to move out of a five mile radius'. There was no means of employment. His circumstances were highlighted by his sister-in-law Maud as an example of the injustices being done to the Irish: 'I have always heard that the Germans provide board for deported people though the French & English press complain that it is scanty.'[14]

Joseph MacBride was one of those who applied for assistance in 1917 to the newly amalgamated Irish National Aid and Volunteers' Dependants' Fund – most often referred to simply as the National Aid. He reported that he had no means and that his wife and family were in need of immediate assistance. The new organization took over the offices of the old Irish National Aid Association at 10 Exchequer Street, and it was here that Michael Collins came to work as secretary. Kathleen hired him on 19 February 1917 at a salary of £2 10s a week. He got the job over many other released prisoners who interviewed for it because he was a member of the IRB and being secretary allowed him the opportunity to move around the country 'unmolested', as Kathleen described it, to reorganize the network of newly released prisoners into a cohesive force to fight again. He was in agreement with her that the Rising 'was the first blow' in the fight for Irish freedom.[15] She said that Collins reminded her in many ways of Seán Mac Diarmada.

Speaking on public platforms, attending events and electioneering now became commonplace activities for those widows who wished to take on this public role. In February 1917, when Count Plunkett contested a seat for Sinn Féin in a by-election in North Roscommon against a Home Rule candidate, his daughter-in-law Grace and Kathleen Clarke both campaigned for him. Kathleen recalled that, when she was travelling with the count and his wife during the campaign, they were attacked by a gang with stones and bottles: 'The Countess had her nose cut with a bottle. I got a big stone on the head, which certainly would have split it only for a hard hat I was wearing, off which it bounded. The only injury was done to my feelings; I was mad enough to want to throw stones back.'[16] Despite this hostile reception, Count Plunkett won the seat. In his victory speech he stated that he would not be taking his seat in Westminster. *The*

Times reported that 'A Sinn Féin victory apparently means disfranchisement.'[17]

Arthur Griffith, the founder of Sinn Féin, was released from jail in December 1916 and began reorganizing his party, but his separatist policy for Ireland still included ideas such as a role for the monarchy. On 19 April 1917 Count Plunkett convened a meeting at the Mansion House, calling it an 'Irish Assembly'. Over 1,200 delegates and sixty-eight public bodies attended. They included members of Cumann na mBan, as well as forty-one of Griffith's Sinn Féin clubs. The main objective of this meeting was to gather together a cohesive pressure group to have Ireland's case submitted to the peace conference that would follow the end of war in Europe. Grace and Kathleen were selected to be on the executive, as was Countess Markievicz, who was still in prison. However, only one key position was given to a woman: Count Plunkett's wife, Josephine. She was on the organizing committee, called the 'Council of Nine'.

As prisoners were released, many of whom had lost their jobs, fundraising for their dependants became even more critical. On 20 April 1917 an auction was held of personal items of the executed leaders, as well as items from the survivors, to benefit the Dependants' Fund. Áine donated the piper's outfit Éamonn had worn in Rome when he had played for the Pope in 1908 and his gold fountain pen. Lillie gave a pair of gloves that had belonged to James.

Another commemoration was the placement of a banner on the ruined Liberty Hall, reading 'James Connolly Murdered May 12th 1916'. This in turn became a fundraising postcard, along with the countless memorial cards for those who had been killed and anyone associated with the Rising. Grace appeared on a card, which apparently showed her in the outfit she had worn at her wedding.

The end of April 1917 marked the first anniversary of the Rising and Masses were held in a number of churches in Dublin. They became a focal point for people who wished to support the cause; many young men dated a radicalization of their views to their attendance at the Masses for the dead leaders.[18] The anniversary

Masses were arranged in order of date of death, so the first was for The O'Rahilly, who had been shot during the fighting; it was held in Clarendon Street on 28 April, followed by Masses from 3 to 12 May in Mount Argus, St Peter's in Phibsboro and St Mary of Angels, Church Street.

Following in the footsteps of Grace and Lillie, Muriel converted to Catholicism, making her first communion on 3 May 1917, the anniversary of Thomas's execution. The presence of the widows and their children at these Masses and other events was essential for fundraising and propaganda purposes. Around this time Muriel was photographed wearing Thomas's lecture gown and cap, walking with her sister Grace and holding Barbara's hand. Wearing her dead husband's clothes was perhaps a tangible reminder of him for the tragic young widow.[19]

Grace felt she should be looked after as befitted a widow of a 1916 leader. She was dependent on the money she received from charity to supplement the very meagre income she earned from her cartoons. After 1916 she did unpaid propaganda work on behalf of the movement, on one occasion designing a twenty-foot banner that was placed across a road. She also designed the by-election posters for Sinn Féin candidates.

No longer living in Temple Villas, Grace stayed with her sister Katie or with friends, but she had no fixed abode. She eventually received £500 from her father's estate, although she would often deny this, but from 1916 there was no more support from her mother. She would write angry letters to the Irish National Aid and Volunteers' Dependants' Fund when the weekly remittances were late, threatening to go public if her demands were not met. In one letter, dated 7 May 1917, she wrote that she wanted to hear 'before 10 o'clock tomorrow if there is or is not any money. I think my having to go into the workhouse on the anniversary week of my husband's sacrifice . . .'[20]

In the midst of these anniversaries, Joe McGuinness was elected on 9 May 1917 as a Sinn Féin candidate in a by-election in South

Longford. He was in prison during this time, and his election slogan was 'Put him in to get him out.' David Lloyd George, the new prime minister, was gradually releasing the Irish political prisoners, and in June the last group returned home. Among them was Éamon de Valera, released on 16 June 1917. He had been Thomas MacDonagh's second-in-command and commandant of the battalion at Boland Mills and Bakery. Although the commandants had all been sentenced to death, de Valera was not shot. It was often speculated that this was because he was an American citizen, born in New York, but in reality it was happenstance: his trial was followed by Asquith's announcement that there would be no further executions save those who had signed the Proclamation.[21]

Kathleen Clarke and two of her sisters went to Westland Row station to greet the returning prisoners; 'It was as if all Dublin was at Westland Row,' she remembered. When the train was coming into the platform the excitement was 'fierce', with the ex-prisoners jumping off the train before it stopped. Kathleen watched as wives, mothers and children embraced. She recalled that 'admittance was controlled by the Irish Volunteers, so we were able to be on the platform through their courtesy, even though we had no man of our own to greet.'[22] Emmet remembered being at the barrier with his mother and heard her asking Seán McGarry: 'Who the hell made Paddy Pearse President?'[23] It was her first opportunity to ask one of the men who had been in the general headquarters with Tom if something had happened during Easter Week to change her husband's rank. She would always maintain that Tom was president of the Irish Republic, as indicated by the placing of his name above the other names on the Proclamation. It was Pearse, however, who had read the Proclamation and offered the surrender, and by the end of 1916 people like Maeve Cavanagh, in her book of poetry *A Voice of Insurgency*, were describing him as the commandant general of the IRA.[24]

Áine Ceannt went with her sister Lily to greet the returning prisoners and, when she saw Eoin MacNeill among them, her instinct was to turn away. Immediately deciding that was an unchristian thing to do, however, she turned again, greeting him with '*Fáilte romhat.*' He replied to her in Irish, but she promptly left him.

After all the prisoners had been released from internment camps, Maud wrote to the British Home Office on 30 June 1917 once more seeking permission to go to Ireland, but she was again refused. An old friend of her father was in charge of the passport office and facilitated her in getting passports, but advised her not to travel, saying that she might not get into Ireland. When Maud queried this, given that all the prisoners had been released, including Constance Markievicz, he replied honestly that he thought that the authorities perhaps would not 'want to have two such mad women on the loose in Ireland.'[25]

Six weeks after the prison wedding, Eileen Moore, a journalist from Chicago's *New World* newspaper, visited Grace Plunkett. She had pictured a desolate, stricken widow in black and was prepared for an hour listening to a broken, sorrowful story, when her subject appeared, dressed in white, carrying a kitten.

Left: The Mallin family, photographed for the *Catholic Bulletin*, Christmas 1916, including newborn Maura Constance Connolly Mallin, named after James Connolly and Countess Markievicz.

Middle: The miraculous medal sent by Constance Markievicz to the youngest of the Mallins, born after her father's death. Maura wore this medal for the rest of her life.

Below: The fiftieth anniversary of the Rising. Fr Joseph Mallin, Sr Agnes (Úna) Mallin, Maura Phillips and Fr Seán Mallin, photographed together at Arbour Hill where their father is buried. In his last letter, Michael Mallin requested that his son Joseph, then aged two and a half, become a priest, and his daughter Úna, aged eight, become a nun. Seán also joined the priesthood. Michael believed that if his children entered the religious life they would assist him and his widow in the afterlife.

Left: The Gifford sisters Muriel MacDonagh and Grace Plunkett with Barbara MacDonagh at a public event. This picture was taken in the days before Muriel's tragic drowning in July 1917. In it she appears to be wearing her husband's lecture gown and hat.

Below: Sr Francesca with her nephew and niece, Donagh and Barbara MacDonagh, in the convent garden during the year after they were orphaned.

Above: Presentation dinner for Kathleen Clarke, 1919. Kathleen is in the centre with her sister Madge on her left. Áine Ceannt is second from right. Kathleen was so seriously ill that she was barely able to stand when she attended this dinner in Dublin organized by members of Cumann na mBan to celebrate her release from prison.

Below: Cumann na mBan Convention, October 1920. Countess Markievicz is seen beside Kathleen Clarke and Áine Ceannt is on her right. Áine's small stature is evident in this picture.

Above: 'Margaret Wilson' was the mother of Maud Gonne's illegitimate half-sister Eileen. Maud arranged for her father's lover to take up a position as a governess with the Zakrevsky family in Berezovaya Rudka, in present-day Ukraine. Her child, with a falsified identity, was raised by Maud's nanny.

Below: 'Margaret' with residents, friends and relatives in Kallijärve, Estonia, 1930. By then she had spent almost forty years in exile, never returning to Ireland.

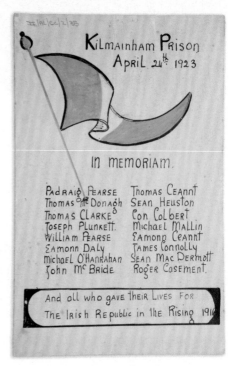

Above: The Irish White Cross was a fund-raising organization for those affected by war in Ireland. It provided funds for families affected by conflict, including children born up to the year 1927.

Above right: Kilmainham Jail commemoration in 1923 for the seventh anniversary of the 1916 executions. This event was staged by Civil War prisoners, including Grace Plunkett, Nora Connolly O'Brien and Lily O'Brennan.

Below: Anti-Treaty members of the Dáil, January 1922. Éamon de Valera is marked as number 2, Countess Markievicz number 13, Cathal Brugha number 16 and Kathleen Clarke number 18.

Above: Maud Gonne MacBride addressing a crowd in O'Connell Street, Dublin, on conditions of prisoners in Mountjoy Jail, 1937. Long after the Civil War ended Maud continued to hold regular Sunday meetings of the Women's Prisoners' Defence League to represent those still being held in jail. Dubliners nicknamed her 'Maud Gone Mad'.

Below: Seán MacBride (centre), Minister of External Affairs, representing Ireland at the Council of Europe, August 1950. He is in conversation with F. H. Boland, Department Secretary.

Above left: Kathleen Clarke and her son Emmet in the 1950s. Having fully recovered from his head injury during the Civil War, Emmet qualified as a doctor in 1950 and obtained a diploma in psychological medicine in 1957.

Above right: Grace Plunkett c.1940.

Below: Áine Ceannt c.1949.

Above: Lillie Connolly with her granddaughters June and Ninel Beech in the back garden of Belgrave Square, Rathmines, before Lillie's death in 1938. Ninel, a reversal of Lenin, was a popular name for those who supported communism.

12

Black Plumes

In the summer of 1917 a fair was held at Peter's Place, Dublin, 'in aid of a special fund to provide a seaside holiday for the children of the men who died for Ireland in 1916.' The event had the 'best Irish-Ireland artists, numerous side shows and endless amusements'.[1] The National Aid committee decided to rent a house for a two-month period for the widows and their children and, after searching for places in Balbriggan and Gormanstown without success, they found an ideal house, Miramar, on the strand at Skerries in the north of County Dublin. It was large enough to accommodate all the families and had a nice garden and a large garage. From the rear of the house there was a view of the Rockabill Lighthouse and Shenick, Colt and Church Islands.

Two women went to clean the house and engage a cook ready for the arrival of the families on 1 July, and 'A card was put in each room so that when the first batch of visitors arrived there was no confusion.'[2] The invitation was accepted by Lillie Connolly, Agnes Mallin, Áine Ceannt, Grace Plunkett and Muriel MacDonagh. Lillie arrived first with three of her family, Ina, Roddy and Fiona. Agnes followed with Seamus, Seán, Úna, Joe and baby Maura. Áine brought Rónán, while Grace Plunkett arrived with her sister-in-law Fiona Plunkett, with whom she had become close. Muriel had been persuaded to go with them, having already that year endured more hardship when five-year-old Don contracted TB and was hospitalized that summer. She arrived with her toddler, Barbara, known by her pet name Babilly.

Everyone had great fun in those first few days. They sang Easter Week songs on the beach. Muriel had brought sparklers and one evening Roddy crowned Áine Ceannt 'Queen of Skerries', but when he placed the sparklers on her hat, it was burnt to a crisp. The children constructed a big sandcastle and placed a Republican flag on top. The Mallin children remembered that the flag was later mounted on a tent on the beach and that the police came and ran away with it. Grace chased after them and got it back, and Muriel said she was going to take it to where it would not be removed so easily. Others later recalled her announcing that she was going to take it to Shenick Island, just off the coast. Indeed, Muriel sent post-cards to Don from Skerries several times a day and in one of them she told him of her plan to swim out to the island.

One story was that Muriel's idea was to plant the Republican flag on Shenick if Éamon de Valera won the East Clare by-election, caused by the death of Willie Redmond – brother of the Irish Parliamentary Party leader John Redmond – who had been killed while leading the Royal Irish Brigade to victory at the Battle of Messines Ridge, at Ypres, on 7 June 1917.

Monday, 9 July 1917 was a fine day. The children were playing on the beach and Barbara was putting shells into an eau de cologne box her mother had given her. 'I must have my own swim, now,' Muriel said, 'as I had only time to bathe Babilly this morning.' Just before going into the water, she asked Ina Connolly to look after Barbara. 'I will not,' said Ina, 'unless you promise not to swim to the island.'[3] Muriel smiled, and said: 'I promise.'

Muriel entered the sea at about 4.30 p.m. Sometime afterwards, the eldest of the Mallin boys ran back to Miramar to tell the adults that Mrs MacDonagh was miles out. At first Seamus was not heeded by the adults in the house, as Muriel was known to be an expert swimmer and had won many prizes for long-distance races. However, Áine, who had been writing letters at the table, felt alarmed and went upstairs to look out of the window. She ran back downstairs and told the others that there was no trace of Muriel and that she could see crowds rushing up the strand.

Ina later recalled that as Muriel swam in the direction of the island, those watching on the shore started to call out to her to come back, but she did not seem to hear them. Her daughter was snatched away from where she had been sitting on the sand and carried to the house. In her hand she was clutching the box that her mother had given her to hold her shells. She would treasure that box of shells for the rest of her life.

Grace acted quickly, sending a boat to Muriel's assistance. It was rowed by Noel Lemass,[4] a young Volunteer who had been in Skerries recovering from wounds he had received in Easter Week, and an English officer who was also visiting Skerries accompanied him. As the boat entered the water, Muriel's cap was visible out near the island, but almost immediately they lost sight of it, and when the boat reached Shenick no trace of Muriel could be found. A yacht in the harbour also made for the island: 'All watched, with straining eyes, the rescuers as they landed on the island. But to the horror of us all they returned to the boats alone. The search proved futile.'[5] Great numbers of people congregated on the island until darkness set in. When the tide receded it was possible to walk on the sand back to the mainland.[6] The locals knew of the cross-currents when the tide was in, making the mile-long swim extremely treacherous.

A wire was sent to Countess Plunkett and during the night anxious friends arrived from Dublin to join the vigil of those awaiting news. At eight o'clock the following morning, 10 July, a policeman called to Miramar to say that Muriel had been found. A Mr Rooney, passing along the strand at about 7 a.m., had spotted her body at the base of the cliffs. He had laid clean straw in his cart and carried her back to the house.

They laid Muriel's body out in Miramar's garage so that a post mortem could be performed. An inquest was held immediately after, issuing a verdict that no water had entered her lungs; death was a result of heart failure from exhaustion. In the midst of all the chaos in the house, Barbara, who had gone looking for her mother, managed to get into the garage and saw her dead mother lying there.[7] For those who witnessed Muriel laid out, 'She looked like a sea goddess. Some seaweed remained in her hair.'[8]

Muriel's body was taken back from Skerries to Dublin. According to the *Irish Times* that day: 'The chapel bell tolled from the moment the remains left "Miramar" until it reached the station. Behind the hearse walked Father Albert, followed by the Volunteers of North Dublin, then came the children from "Miramar" carrying wreaths and near relatives and friends ... the coffin covered with the tricolour was placed on the train and as it steamed out you could hear the sobs and lamentations of the vast crowd that thronged the little seaside station.' The procession went from Dublin's Amiens Street Station through the city before going to Donnybrook, where Muriel's body was to be laid out in her own home.

Following a funeral Mass in the Pro Cathedral on 12 July, Muriel's coffin was carried to Glasnevin cemetery. Don was brought by a nurse to look out of his hospital window. He recalled watching horses with black plumes dancing on their heads, but he did not comprehend until much later that he was actually watching his mother's funeral cortege pass by.[9]

At just five years of age, Donagh MacDonagh and his sister Barbara, who had not even reached her second birthday, were orphans. For many years after, they were to be denied a permanent home. Muriel's older sister, Katie Wilson, herself a childless widow, initially took the children to live with her in Fairview, and it was here that Don came after his release from hospital. TB had distorted his spine and he was left with a curvature in his back.

However, within weeks a dispute erupted over their future. A sub-committee of National Aid was set up 'to enquire into the question of the MacDonagh Minors.' The role of the members of this group was to interpret Thomas MacDonagh's last letter, in which he wrote: 'my beloved wife Muriel, and my beloved children ... My country will then treat them as wards, I hope. I have devoted myself too much to National work and too little to the making of money to leave them a competence.'[10]

On 3 September 1917, Katie received a letter from the executive committee informing her of its existence and that it had been instructed to 'represent the country' on the matter of Thomas and Muriel's children; the future of these children was their remit.[11] Protracted negotiations and threatened legal action would follow this letter. Action was delayed due to the death of the children's grandfather, Frederick Gifford, when the sub-committee decided to wait until his estate was granted probate and the MacDonagh children's eventual bequest determined, before making a decision on the permanent arrangements for their upkeep. Frederick did provide for the children, but although Isabella did have contact with them, she did not play any active role in their upbringing up to her death in 1932.

13

'Mournful Mothers'

With the return from prison of the male activists in the summer of 1917, it was now clear that the nationalist movement was being revived. It was also becoming apparent that women would have no voice or influence in this movement, so a group called the League of Women Delegates was formed from the membership of societies such as the Inghinidhe na hÉireann branch of Cumann na mBan, executive members of Cumann na mBan, the Irish Women Workers Union and women from the Irish Citizen Army. Áine Ceannt was one of the principal members of this group, and chaired their meetings. In June the group met for a second time at Áine's home to consider their response to the news that the 'Council of Nine' was being expanded to include the newly released prisoners and that none of the proposed new members were to be women. They co-opted Countess Markievicz, now out of prison, as a member.

The Sinn Féin Ard Fheis (Annual Convention) in October 1917 was held in the Round Room of the Mansion House. Arthur Griffith stepped aside and Éamon de Valera, victor of the East Clare by-election, became president. The policies of the organization had changed. Áine argued that this be called the First Ard Fheis given that the Sinn Féin organization was so different from the one formed before the Rising, but her objection was overruled and it was called the Sixth Ard Fheis. Kathleen Clarke wrote on her return home: 'Went to the Sinn Féin Convention today and came home disgusted . . . there were many there who had been friends of Tom's but never came near me . . . I had a strong feeling that at least a great proportion of those present and myself were not in sympathy with each other. I felt in quite foreign element.'[1]

When Constance Markievicz objected to Eoin MacNeill being nominated, she was greeted with an angry response. Kathleen backed her, despite being asked by a number of Volunteers not to do so. MacNeill was elected. Kathleen wrote that day:

> Great God to think of it, there was Count Plunkett who lost his eldest son, whose two younger ones got penal servitude, his pension worth 600 to 800 pounds per year gone, and he gets half of MacNeill's vote . . . Countess Markievicz who fought and sentenced to death got 200 less than him . . . Is it any wonder I felt out of sympathy with such a gathering or I felt such an isolated and lonely woman . . .[2]

For months before the convention Arthur Griffith had worked hard to avoid a split. Éamon de Valera had also championed MacNeill in prison on the grounds that he was 'very much a wronged man and had been made a fool by the IRB.'[3] De Valera disputed Kathleen's version of events regarding MacNeill's role in the days leading up to the Rising. Kathleen wrote her reaction: 'de Valera only knew what any officer in the Irish Volunteers knew and no more.' She also wrote down her impression of de Valera that day:

> I hope de Valera will keep it straight, at times, I fear he is too easily influenced and lacks experience. Perhaps, it is that he is young. He is a lovable character, light hearted and boyish and he is getting enough adulation to turn an older and more experienced man's head. I wish I could feel more sure of him. I suppose it is natural, I find it hard to trust new people. Those I had learned to trust are nearly all gone.[4]

The League of Women, now using the Irish form of Cumann na Teachtaire, worked to have women elected on to public boards and on to all institutions within the Sinn Féin organization. At the Sinn Féin Convention the group had a resolution drawn up: 'that the equality of men and women in this organisation be emphasised in all speeches and leaflets.' The resolution was passed. In the end four women were elected to the twenty-four-member Sinn Féin executive: Grace Plunkett, Constance Markievicz, Kathleen Clarke and Dr Kathleen Lynn. Áine Ceannt stepped aside in favour of Dr Lynn, but this did not lessen her participation. As always, she was in the core group of women involved in all nationalist activities.

At the Volunteer Convention two days later Éamon de Valera became president of that organization too. The Cumann na mBan Convention followed. Their constitution stated they were 'an independent body of Irish women pledged to work for the Irish Republic, by organising and training the women of Ireland to take their places by the side of those who are working and fighting for its recognition.' Kathleen and Áine became vice-presidents. A recruiting drive for the organization had already begun following the Rising, and Áine and her sister Lily were among those who travelled around the country recruiting. By 1917 there were one hundred branches and by the following year there were six hundred.

Meanwhile, Maud travelled from Paris to London in mid-September 1917. The Home Office recorded her arrival along with Seagán, Iseult and their cook, Josephine Pillon, accompanied by Willie Yeats. Maud was issued with a notice under the Defence of the Realm Act forbidding her to proceed to Ireland. Iseult had by now turned down Willie Yeats, after which Yeats turned his attentions to George Hyde-Lee, whom he married on 20 October that year.

With all the new developments in the political life of Ireland, Maud was restless to be there. Seagán devised a plan to outwit the detectives who were assigned to follow his mother; he would later describe it as 'a delightful game'. Disguised as an old woman, Maud reached Ireland despite the fact that warnings about her had been sent to all ports, with the direction that she was to be prevented from leaving England. Within days the Home Office was notified that she was in Dublin with her son, who had travelled over after her. The authorities made the decision not to arrest and imprison her at the time, fearing that this would make a martyr out of her.[5] In March 1918, Maud purchased 73 St Stephen's Green, indicating that she was there to stay.

That month Iseult's father, Lucien Millevoye, died in France. Maud herself would never live in France again, and twenty-three-year-old Iseult had stayed on in London. Maud's self-appointed publicity agent, Mary Barry O'Delany, followed the family from Paris to Ireland, collecting a pet parrot and monkey from Iseult in London en route.

On 11 May 1918 sixty-five-year-old Field Marshal Sir John French was appointed the new Lord Lieutenant of Ireland, 'for purpose of military order and combating German intrigue'.[6] Under his governance, the Dublin Castle administration alleged that the Sinn Féin movement was plotting with Germany to start an armed insurrection in Ireland. The 'German Plot', as it became known, was used to justify the internment of leaders from the Sinn Féin organization who were actively opposing the introduction of con-scription. This 'plot' had its origin in a real event when in April Joseph Dowling, a member of Roger Casement's Irish Brigade in Germany, was put ashore in County Clare by a German U-boat.

Republicans were tipped off about the impending internments, allowing some to escape capture, including Michael Collins, who had become central to all military and political activities in his roles as director of organization for the Volunteers, as well as chairman of the Supreme Council of the Irish Republican Brotherhood. Collins told Kathleen Clarke that she was on the list for arrest and advised her to go on the run, but she said she was 'neither temperamentally nor physically fit for such a life.' Consequently, Kathleen was one of 150 people arrested between 16 and 17 May 1918. She was appre-hended in her home on Richmond Avenue, where she had returned with her family some months previously: 'I told the children that I was being arrested by the British who had murdered their father and uncle, and that I did not expect to be back with them until the end of the war.' She told them not to cry, but 'When it came to saying goodbye the youngest, Emmet, was sneaking his handkerchief to wipe away a few tears that had escaped.' Kathleen would not show how heartbroken she was on leaving them.

In total seventy-three Sinn Féin members were deported without charge, including Éamon de Valera, who was held in Lincoln Prison. Kathleen was brought to London and imprisoned in Holloway Jail with Countess Markievicz and Maud Gonne. Maud had been arrested following a dinner with British MP Joseph King, who had come to Ireland to learn about conditions. As Maud recalled, 'we were suddenly surrounded by police in St Stephen's Green and I was arrested. Notwithstanding Mr. King's protest . . . My little Seán ran after the Black Maria in which I was taken and when it reached its destination, with wonderful sense he ran back home, got my big fur coat and brought it to me.'[7] By this time, Maud was using her married name, Maud Gonne MacBride; she ignored those who criticized her for taking John's name.[8] By this time, too, Seaġan had become Seán, the form of his name that he would use for the rest of his life.

Maud, Kathleen and Constance were put in a separate wing of the prison. All the other prisoners had been moved to another part of the jail, leaving many empty cells. In the early days, Kathleen did not really socialize with the other two women, who spent their time together and, at the outset, excluded her. Constance would say to her again and again, 'why on earth did they arrest such a quiet, insignificant little person as you are?' As Kathleen later wrote: 'I was outside their social circle, and had nothing in common with them socially. Madame Markievicz took pains to make me aware of the social gulf between us; it didn't worry me. I walked up and down alone . . . When Madame Markievicz did talk to me in those early days, I sensed a certain amount of patronage in her tone and manner, and that I was not prepared to take from anyone.'[9] Kathleen told Constance that her charge sheet was the same. Over time, and gradually, they became friends as equals.

The separation from her three sons, Daly, Tom and Emmet,

proved extremely difficult for Kathleen. Daly, although he was now sixteen, was 'a frail, delicate boy' who needed 'such care'. For three weeks after her arrest Kathleen had no idea of what had become of them. According to Constance, she was so worried that she neither ate nor slept, consumed with the fear that Tom Clarke's sons would be 'done away with sooner or later'.[10] This idea had taken possession of her mind and it was impossible to persuade her otherwise. The governor of the prison agreed to contact the Dublin Metropolitan Police, who replied that the boys were with their relatives in Limerick. Maud, too, was anxious about her son. She tried to get word to George Russell to put Seán into school; he had not been in a regular school environment since they had left Paris. Years before, Constance had given her daughter, Maeve Alyss, who was born in November 1901, into the care of her mother, Lady Gore Booth, to be brought up in her ancestral demesne of Lissadell in County Sligo. She deemed her prison companions to be 'mournful mothers'.[11]

Over the months in prison, Kathleen pressed for better conditions, including more exercise. She also organized that she and her companions were moved from their cells to a room in the hospital. Prison officials wanted Kathleen hospitalized as she was ill, but she insisted that all three women be accommodated there. Kathleen had lost so much weight that she was granted permission for a weekly food parcel to be sent by her sisters from Limerick.

From August 1918, Hanna Sheehy Skeffington was also imprisoned in Holloway. Her arrival was welcomed by the other women; Kathleen felt it broke the 'monotony' of their lives. Hanna had been arrested in Dublin after being smuggled back in the previous month from America, where she had given over 250 talks at the invitation of the Friends of Irish Freedom. Her talk 'British Militarism as I Have Known It' was later published as a pamphlet and it highlighted the shooting of her husband, the avowed 'pacifist' who had been arrested 'unarmed and unresisting' during the Rising, and shot in Portobello Barracks under the orders of Captain John Bowen-Colthurst, who was later judged insane.[12] Hanna had raised thousands of dollars in the US, which she handed over to Michael

Collins. She had also succeeded in meeting President Woodrow Wilson and presenting him with a 'petition for Ireland's claim to self-determination', compiled by Cumann na mBan. She herself was not a member of either Cumann na mBan or Sinn Féin at this time, but was proud to have entered the White House with the badge of the Irish Republic on her coat. While in prison, she went on hunger strike, as she had done in 1912 in her campaign for women's suffrage. As the widow of a man shot on the orders of a deranged British officer, newspapers speculated that the British government would not want another Sheehy Skeffington tragedy; as a result, she was released.

Willie Yeats took charge of Seán MacBride and brought him to Thoorballylee, near Gort, which he had just refurbished as a house for himself and his new wife, George. Yeats arranged for the village schoolmaster to give Seán tuition in Irish, Latin, arithmetic and algebra. Away from his mother, there was a significant change in the boy, according to his sister Iseult: 'all his illnesses, aches, and pains were long forgotten.'[13] Seán remained with Yeats until 5 September 1918, when he insisted on going to London to campaign for Maud's release. The fourteen-year-old went to the French and American Embassies to request that they use their influence to get his mother out of jail. Maud said they 'received him very nicely' but she did not think they succeeded in doing anything for her.[14]

After several months, some of the women were allowed visitors, though Kathleen refused the conditions laid down by the authorities and so was denied seeing anyone. The countess arranged for her sister Eva to come, Seán and Iseult both came to see their mother. They had taken turns to go to the prison every day since early September to see if they would be permitted visitation rights. Although Seán was allowed to see his mother, the prison officials were highly suspicious of him, as they thought that 'Mrs MacBride' would have taught him 'a secret code' by which she could send political messages.

In prison, Maud was described by Kathleen as being like 'a caged wild animal'. As she believed in auto-suggestion from her days studying hypnotism, she later described how she tried to train her mind to be thin; she 'had to eat normally, yet in three months I lost three stone and became a living skeleton. They got alarmed and the doctor was trying to find the cause.'[15] Kathleen said that Maud 'fell sick or maybe feigned sick, she was such a good actress that you couldn't tell.'[16] Seán wrote to the Home Office highlighting his mother's ill health, while Willie Yeats and the American lawyer John Quinn used their influence to secure her release. As a result of their efforts, Maud was granted temporary release for one week on 29 October to be examined by a Harley Street specialist, who concluded that she had 'pulmonary tuberculosis' and recommended 'open air treatment in a suitable climate without delay'. The authorities decided to release her to a nursing home. Even after her release Seán was in a 'state of agitation' over the way she had been treated and was making 'drastic plans', but in the meantime Maud refused either to remain at the nursing home or return to prison. Iseult had to sign papers accepting her mother into her care.

The prison doctor suggested to Kathleen that she could also appeal for release on the grounds of her health, but she said she would not appeal to the British government for anything.

Maud's influential friends ensured that she stayed out of prison. She and her two children moved temporarily into Willie's apartment in Woburn Buildings, but she did not stay in London long, making her way back to Ireland in November 1918 disguised as a nurse. Constance, still in prison, wrote to her sister Eva: 'Had she leave? I wonder if she'll be sent back. It's very mysterious why they ever took her . . .'[17]

Maud arrived back in Dublin to a city celebrating the end of a war that had seen the deaths of forty-nine thousand Irishmen. The Armistice had been signed on 11 November 1918 and the streets of Dublin were festooned with Union Jacks. The wives of those serving in the British Army held demonstrations outside the Sinn Féin offices and on Armistice night Agnes Mallin and her children, still living in Emmet Hall, next to Richmond Barracks, narrowly avoided an attack. Agnes heard a commotion upstairs and sent five-year-old Joe to see what was happening. There were Irish dancing classes going on in the building and he came down to tell his mother that there were 'girls rolling down a sloping roof'.[18] Just as Agnes realized the building was being attacked, she narrowly missed being hit by a rock as it came flying through the front window. She grabbed her children and left through the back door. The soldiers from the barracks next door were drunk and out of control. When the Mallin family returned to the building the next day the place had been ransacked.[19]

Kathleen and Constance were still in prison when the post-war general election took place. It was the first time all women over thirty could vote and the first time women could stand for election. Hanna Sheehy Skeffington was approached to run, but she rejected the offer as she was offered an unwinnable constituency. Winnie Carney, James Connolly's secretary who had served in the GPO in 1916, did stand for election but was unsuccessful in the Central/East Belfast Victoria District.

Kathleen was disappointed when she did not receive a nomination. Her name had been sent to the Sinn Féin headquarters for ratification for the North City constituency in Dublin where she was then living, but it was withdrawn as she was said to be running in Limerick City, where she was 'sure to be elected'. However, another candidate, Michael Colivet, had been selected there and his literature was already printed. As a result, Kathleen was not put on the ballot paper in either location. Despite being excluded in this election, she remained determined to enter politics and to carry on Tom's legacy.

Sinn Féin returned seventy-three seats. Thanks to their anti-conscription stance during the war, as Irish Parliamentary Party MP T. M. Healy stated, 'The Sinn Féiners won in three years what we did not win in forty.' Those elected included Countess Markievicz, making her the first woman to win a seat at Westminster, but in accordance with Sinn Féin policy she refused to take her seat. The Irish Labour Party had agreed not to contest the 1918 election to allow Sinn Féin an opportunity to focus the vote between themselves and the Home Rule candidates. In Britain, Lloyd George was elected in a coalition with the Conservatives, who were supported by the Unionists. The Unionist Party, led by Sir Edward Carson, saw their MPs rise from eighteen to twenty-six.

Joseph MacBride was elected for the constituency of Mayo West. He too was in prison at the time of the election. While Eileen MacBride was caught up in the political struggles of the day in Ireland, her mother, Margaret Wilson, who had remained in the Ukraine, became ensnared in the turmoil of the Russian Revolution. During the twenty-six years she had been in the Ukraine, she had brought up the four Zakrevsky children and now she was looking after the children of the youngest daughter, Moura, who had been born after Margaret's arrival in Russia over a quarter of a century earlier.

In the spring of 1918, Margaret set out with Paul, aged five, Tania, aged three, and a Swiss escort in a postal coach with false papers to take the children from St Petersburg to Estonia. This treacherous journey could have proved fatal for an English speaker: Germany was still at war with Britain and the German army was now occupying Estonia. The children, however, were brought safely to the home of their paternal grandmother, where conditions were far less grand than in the Zakrevsky household, where Margaret had been waited on by their servants.

A state of lawlessness prevailed in Estonia in the aftermath of the Treaty of Brest-Litovsk, signed on 3 March, which had removed the Baltic States from Russian sovereignty. When the Germans retreated from Estonia in November 1918 the situation did not improve and civil war raged. The children's father, Count Johann von Benckendorff, joined them and their cousin Kira, but Moura herself remained living in St Petersburg (having an affair with a British diplomat) even after her husband Johann was murdered in Janeda in April 1919. Margaret found his body, and thereafter she became both mother and father to the children. Tania later wrote: 'As for my mother we did not have the same intensity of feeling for her as we did for Micky [as the children called Margaret], perhaps [because] she was so little with us as children, and because we very soon realised that we had to share her with other people.'

Back in Ireland, Eileen was facing a prolonged period of unrest, as the conflict that became known as the War of Independence commenced.

14

'Work for Freedom' – The War of Independence

On 21 January 1919 Sinn Féin invited all 105 Irish MPs to a meeting in the Mansion House, Dublin. As expected, the twenty-six Unionist and six Home Rule MPs did not attend. Many of the Sinn Féin TDs (*Teachtaí Dála*) were 'on the run' or in prison. The First Dáil conducted its business in the Irish language. The declaration of independence issued by the 1916 leaders was read out and approved. The members sent a message to the Paris Peace Conference to seek recognition for Irish independence, with Seán T. O'Kelly chosen as the Dáil delegate to attend the conference.

That day also marked the commencement of hostilities in what became known as the War of Independence when a group of Irish Volunteers attacked police in County Tipperary. At the outset such attacks were independent acts, but by April the Dáil had accepted full responsibility for all actions up to that time. The Volunteers were now commonly known as the Irish Republican Army, and this time the fight would take the form of guerrilla warfare, with the groups involved known as 'flying columns'. The role of women was to provide a network of safe houses, as well as a communication system that was utilized by another member of Dáil Éireann, Michael Collins. In his role as director of intelligence he had established a network of spies, and one of his first actions was to coordinate the dramatic escape from Lincoln Prison of Sinn Féin president Éamon de Valera on 3 February 1919.

Still imprisoned in Holloway, Kathleen Clarke's health had gone into rapid decline, culminating in her having a series of small seizures. As there was a real possibility of her dying in jail, she was released on 12 February. Kathleen was so seriously ill that she was barely able to stand when she attended the dinner in Dublin that had been organized by members of Cumann na mBan to celebrate her release. Following that she was cared for in a nursing home in Dublin, unable to continue on to Limerick to be with her boys.

Kathleen was still in the nursing home when Countess Markievicz was released in March. Constance went to visit her there to tell her that she had moved into Kathleen's home. Constance needed a place to put her furniture and pictures. She no longer had her own house, so she had gone ahead and taken four rooms in Kathleen's home. As she told her, she could not think of anyone else with enough space to accommodate her things, some of which were very valuable. Her estranged husband Casimir was in his homeland, her step-son Staskou was in the Polish Army fighting against the Russians, while Maeve, now a young woman of eighteen, was in boarding school in Hampshire. The British authorities had been investigating the possibility of deporting Constance to Poland, but because of the post-war annexing of territories, officials were unable to work out where she should be sent. When Kathleen eventually returned to her home with her sons, Constance was still there, and she continued to live with the Clarkes on and off during 1919. Throughout that period the Clarkes' house on Richmond Avenue was raided often. Kathleen later described how her boys were pulled from their beds as the soldiers searched their home, remembering: 'I think that we had more raids than other people, but those lads never showed the slightest fear, though naturally they must have felt that strain of it.'[1] The main reason for the constant raiding was that Constance was now a member of the unofficial 'Cabinet'.

On 1 April Éamon de Valera presided over the second meeting of Dáil Éireann, which essentially operated as an underground government, or a 'hidden' Dáil. De Valera selected his Cabinet:

Arthur Griffith was made vice-president and minister for home affairs; Michael Collins was minister for finance; Cathal Brugha minister for defence; Count Plunkett minister for foreign affairs; Eoin MacNeill minister for industries; W. T. Cosgrave minister for local government; Robert Barton minister for agriculture; and Countess Markievicz was elected minister for labour. Kathleen recounted:

> When Madame Markievicz was made Minister for Labour she came rushing home to tell me. I asked her how she managed it, as I had noticed that the present leaders were not over-eager to put women into places of honour or power, even though they had earned the right to both as well as the men had . . . She told me she had had to bully them: she claimed she had earned the right to be a minister as well as any of the men, and was equally well fitted for it, educationally and every other way, and if she was not made a minister she would go over to the Labour Party.[2]

Sinn Féin was looking for international recognition for the Irish Republic and Éamon de Valera decided that the best way to achieve this was in America. He departed in June 1919 and remained away for the next eighteen months. During that time he managed to raise considerable sums, but failed to secure a meeting with President Wilson.

Meanwhile, minister for finance Michael Collins was charged with raising a domestic loan through public subscription. The money was to fund the government departments created by Dáil Éireann and to purchase arms. In 1919 Grace, Áine, Agnes and Kathleen took part in a promotional film made by John MacDonagh at St Enda's School. His Irish Film Company had been making *Willie Reilly and His Colleen Bawn* when he was asked by Collins to make a short piece of propaganda to encourage the public to buy bonds. In the film Collins is seen signing the Dáil bonds on what is reputed to be Robert Emmet's execution block. The widows are shown in their finery, slightly awkward as they perform for the camera, purchasing bonds from Collins. It is said that in order to get this film shown some cinema-owners had to be threatened at gunpoint.[3]

The great need was to get arms and ammunition for the IRA and in order to purchase it abroad, gold was required. The Dalys had been storing all the gold coming in from their business and when Collins was informed, he asked Kathleen to carry it back with her to Dublin. She strapped some of it to her chest and hid the rest in her muff; the total value of the gold she was carrying was £2,000. If she was caught, it would mean certain arrest, and indeed she and her party were stopped by soldiers. However, as she was dressed in mourning clothes, like so many of the women who had lost their menfolk on the front, she was not searched. According to Kathleen: 'it was a hair-raising experience, but everyone engaged in work for freedom at that time had scares everyday of the week.'[4]

Throughout 1919 the Royal Irish Constabulary came under constant attack. By the end of that year, many small barracks had been burnt out and the police force was confined to areas with large populations. Cumann na mBan members spearheaded a campaign of boycotting the police. Any members of the force who resigned from the RIC were looked after. Áine Ceannt's home was used, as she described later, as a 'clearing house' for those men. This work was directed by the Hon. Mary Spring Rice, who had been a crew member of the *Asgard* when it brought the arms into Howth in 1914.

Maud joined with Desmond FitzGerald and Bob Brennan, who were running the Dáil's Propaganda Department. They produced a paper, the *Irish Bulletin*, from November 1919 onwards, which was aimed at influencing the international press. Maud was very useful as she had built up a large network of contacts, so many of the foreign press who arrived in Ireland were directed to her house. 'I had considerable experience at publicity,' she wrote, 'having run a news-agency in Paris called l'Irlande Libre.'[5] The *Bulletin* was described by the British authorities as 'the murder gang's publication' in a bid to undermine the entire Republican campaign by taking it out of a political context and describing it as the work of criminals.[6]

Against the backdrop of an ongoing war, home for the MacDonagh children remained their aunt Katie's house in Fairview, until one evening during 1919, when Don was eight years old and Barbara was just four, they were snatched from the house and whisked away in a car driven by a MacDonagh relative. The children were taken to the home of their father's sister, Helen, in Broadford, County Clare. Helen was married to George Bingham, a retired RIC policeman, and their children George, Herbert and Arthur were already grown up, but there were two younger cousins as playmates – Aideen, who was nine years old, and Margaret, who was three.[7] The MacDonaghs attended Broadford National School that year, while their future continued to be debated in Dublin by the committee tasked with the issue of their welfare.

Perhaps things may have been different for the MacDonagh children from the outset if Nellie or Sidney Gifford had been in Dublin, but they were still living in America at the time of the dispute. Nellie and Joseph Donnelly left America in 1920, however, and returned to Ireland to live in Joseph's home place in Omagh. At that point the couple became involved in Donagh and Barbara's welfare and when a final compromise was being worked out for the children in 1920, Joseph Donnelly was named along with John MacDonagh as a trustee for them. Nellie gave birth to his daughter, Maeve, or May, that year, but her relationship with Joseph broke down and she decided to come home to Dublin with her little girl.[8] Joseph Donnelly remained a trustee for the MacDonagh children until Don came of age in 1930.

By March 1920 the war was intensifying, with reinforcements being drafted in on the British side to bolster the regular police force. Dressed in a mixture of the RIC uniform and khaki army trousers, they became known as the 'Black and Tans'. By the end of 1920 it was said that there were over five thousand of them policing the country, often instigating reprisals in places where ambushes had taken place – the burning of Bruff in County Limerick, Balbriggan in County Dublin, Tubbercurry in County Sligo and Trim in County Meath. The system of normal government had broken down.

In August 1920 an officer force known as the Auxiliary Division of the Royal Irish Constabulary was formed, consisting of about fifteen hundred men recruited to combat the Republican forces in Ireland. They were to be a temporary cadet force with the rank of sergeant, and they formed their own hundred-man companies, distributed in the so-called 'hot spots' of Clare, Cork, Dublin, Galway, Kerry, Kilkenny, Limerick, Mayo and Meath.[9]

On the electoral front, as well as establishing the Dáil with its administration system, Sinn Féin obtained control in a number of county and district councils. With the exception of Belfast and Londonderry (known to nationalists as Derry), all the mayors in the country were members of Sinn Féin. On 3 May 1920, Dublin Corporation recognized the authority of the government of the Republic of Ireland, Dáil Éireann, as the duly elected government of Ireland, as Republicans now had the majority vote in the Corporation. Within a short space of time, the majority of corporation and district councils around the country had done the same. Áine worked as acting secretary to the General Council of County Councils. In the municipal elections to Dublin Corporation, Kathleen was nominated by Sinn Féin for two wards, the Wood Quay and Mountjoy Wards, and she was elected to both, becoming one of forty-three women voted into office. Kathleen became 'locum tenens' for the Lord Mayor whenever he was out of town; as she put it: 'I was the only Sinn Féin Alderman always available.'[10]

It was now a considerable risk to one's safety to hold public office. In March 1920, the Lord Mayor of Cork, Tómas MacCurtain, was shot by the RIC and in August that year the city's new Lord Mayor, Terence MacSwiney, was arrested on charges of sedition. He refused to recognize the court and when he was imprisoned he went on hunger strike. Terence MacSwiney died in Brixton Prison after refusing food for seventy-four days. His memorial Mass in London and his funeral in Cork were attended by thousands. Terence left a young wife, Muriel, and their only child, Máire Óg (little Mary). Sir John Lavery, the society artist, painted Muriel MacSwiney's portrait, simply entitling it *The Widow*.[11] Another Muriel, another widow, another pretty young mother, was now feted by the international press. A new generation of Irish widows and Irish martyrs was emerging.

Terence MacSwiney's action in refusing to recognize the British administration highlighted Sinn Féin's policy – the creation of an alternative administration which was now operational in Ireland, including the Dáil Courts or Republican Courts. Áine remembered that it was 'difficult and dangerous to hold arbitrations in secret without the knowledge of the British authorities.'[12] Her cases were held in a dispensary on Dublin's Castle Street, opposite Dublin Castle, the centre of British administration in the capital. Another court was held in Ballsbridge, opposite the Royal Dublin Society, which was occupied at the time by the Black and Tans. Áine also travelled to some of the 'disturbed districts' – areas of Clare, Cork and Limerick. She concentrated on labour disputes in various parts of the country, including Ennis, Drishane and Sixmilebridge in County Clare, Castleconnell in Limerick and Fermoy in Cork.

As a development of this system, supreme, circuit, district and parish courts were set up. The higher courts were heard by a circuit court judge – a qualified lawyer who was paid by the Dáil. Enforcement was carried out by a police force appointed by the courts. Áine recalled that the British authorities were astounded by the success of this illegal police force. She became a trustee of funds collected from fines for breaches of the law.

Kathleen also became involved in administering justice, or arbitration. Like many of the others, she had no legal training but she soon became chairperson of the North Dublin Judiciary. The North City Circuit operated circuit, county and parish courts. Such courts functioned throughout the War of Independence without a break and this was credited to Kathleen. Gradually these courts replaced the existing judicial system: 'They sat in state in empty courts, surrounded by barbed wire and soldiers. And they waited for cases, and none came.'[13] The Dáil Courts ensured that there was a basic maintenance of civic order during the worst of the troubles.[14]

Maud became a judge in the Sinn Féin parish courts, although the details of the cases she presided over are undocumented. She willingly undertook any work that was deemed necessary – hearing cases, propaganda, nursing the wounded. Her house in St Stephen's Green was constantly raided throughout the war, although she had hoped she would be protected by the fact that her neighbours on both sides were Unionists. Maud went when she could to the Glenmalure Valley in County Wicklow, where the family had use of a 'hut' in an isolated spot that Iseult called 'the last in civilization'. It was the last cottage in the glen, where Synge had stayed and based his play *In the Shadow of the Glen*.[15] Staying there gave them some respite from the curfews and raids that took place on a regular basis in Dublin City.

One weekend at the end of September 1920 Seán, who was now studying law at University College Dublin, was contacted by Maurice Bourgeois, who was visiting from Paris on 'a mission from the French Government' looking for material for the Musée de la Guerre. Bourgeois wanted to see Maud, who was in County Wicklow. Seán decided to drive him down. According to Maud, 'all would have been well, if Con [Constance Markievicz] had not heard of the excursion & insisted on coming too.'[16] According to Constance's own account:

> It was very bad luck. I went for a week-end holiday with Sean, and the motor car he was driving kept breaking down all the time . . . Coming back the same thing happened. Engines, horn and lamps all being out of order. The police pulled us up because of the tail lamp not being there: they asked for a permit, he had none, so they got suspicious and finally lit a match in my face and phoned the military. All the King's horses and all the King's men arrived with great pomp

and huge guns . . . I found myself here on remand . . . It sounds like a comic opera, but it's the truth.[17]

The authorities ignored Bourgeois's diplomatic pass and, according to Maud, they 'treated him like a mere Irishman, shut him up . . . without food on a plank bed & refused to let him communicate with his consul . . . He now knows English methods from actual experience which is so much to the good.' He was released after two days, but Constance and Seán were brought to Mountjoy Jail. Maud's real fear was that Seán would be punished 'for being his father's and his mother's son'. She wrote to Willie that she was experiencing 'horrible anxiety' with her son in prison 'for such childish stupidity . . .' She was also concerned that he had missed an exam and she feared 'a whole year's work lost.'[18] During the War of Independence over seven thousand people had been arrested, often without charge.

Maud wrote to Charlotte Despard, sister of the Lord Lieutenant, Sir John French, to ask her to intercede with her brother to have sixteen-year-old Seán released. Charlotte, whom Maud had met in 1917, was a prominent opponent of the British government's policy in Ireland. Now in her seventies and widowed, she was a socialist and a suffragette, and had become president of the Women's Freedom League; she had also joined the India Independence movement and the Irish Self Determination League after its formation in 1919. She had no influence with her brother, standing completely opposed to him as an 'outspoken and uncompromising pacifist'.[19]

Seán was released within days and returned to university. Constance, however, was given two years for having formed Fianna Éireann, a nationalist youth organization, a decade before.

On 1 November, a week after the death on hunger strike of Terence MacSwiney, Kevin Barry, an IRA member who was a medical student at UCD, was hanged for his part in an ambush in Upper Church Street in September in which three British soldiers had been killed. It was the first such execution since the 1916 Rising. The *Irish*

Bulletin issued a 'message to the civilised nations', emphasizing Barry's youth and the fact that British forces captured by the IRA had not been subject to execution.[20] Unknown to his mother, Seán was among a group of students who organized a tricolour to be flown at half mast from the roof of the university. On 2 November the military entered UCD: 'Every male student was searched by the military. It took hours. They didn't search the women only fired off shots to frighten them . . .'[21] Years later Seán wrote: 'Normally one would expect the national university of a country, when one of its students had been hanged, to have reacted. Instead of that, there was virtually no reaction from the student body.'[22]

Later that same month Michael Collins put into action a plan to take out British secret service agents and on the morning of 21 November 1920 eleven intelligence officers were killed. Later that day the British Auxiliaries and Black and Tans responded by driving trucks into Croke Park during a football match between Dublin and Tipperary and opening fire into the crowd. It was reported that of the eight thousand people present, ten men, one woman and three children were killed – twelve were shot, one woman crushed and one man died of shock. A further two hundred people were injured. The *Irish Bulletin* recorded eye-witness accounts that the only firing came from the police and that no member of the force was killed or injured.

In the aftermath of what became known as 'Bloody Sunday', Áine Ceannt came to the attention of the authorities. Nine lorry loads of Black and Tans came to raid her house 'looking for Michael Collins'.[23] Áine, Lily, Rónan and Elizabeth O'Brennan now lived at 44 Oakley Road in Ranelagh. Although Collins was not found there on this occasion, they had in fact sheltered him numerous times; undaunted by the risks, Áine had 'put her home at his disposal.'[24] It was not just Michael Collins. A 'Mr Connor' had lived with them for nine months; this was in fact Robert Barton, who ran his Department of Agriculture from their home. At the outset, the ministers could fit the paperwork of their departments in their pockets, but as time went on the correspondence grew. Áine hid the departmental papers in her home and in other designated hiding places. Robert Barton remained with them until he was arrested in January 1920. Constance also used the house when she was 'on the run'. Despite this, raids on the house, which on occasion used female searchers, found no evidence to warrant any arrests. A surprisingly small number of women were arrested during the War of Independence; Cumann na mBan claimed that by the end of 1921 only fifty women had been imprisoned.

Following these raids, Áine once again looked for the return of items such as her husband's hat, which had been given to her by the commandant of Kilmainham Jail, and a baton that had been among the arms and ammunition landed at Howth six years before. However, when she went to Beggars Bush Barracks to retrieve her possessions, only her child's music case was returned to her.

Kathleen also wrote of raids and the constant possibility of a tragic outcome. On one occasion the raiders ate all their food and on another their Kerry Blue pup was beaten to death, but Kathleen later recalled one particular night with terror: 'I knew real fear for the first and only time. It was a military raid, as usual after midnight, and we were all in bed. When they came into my eldest's son's room they asked his age and examined his face to see if he was shaving and they debated if they would take him. It was then I knew fear, a fear that congealed the blood in my veins.' Daly was sixteen. Over the previous months there had been countless cases of young men being taken and their bodies found on the roadside. Kathleen's family home in Limerick was also targeted on a regular basis and in 1921 the contents of the house were taken out by the military and burnt, including what were described as 'souvenirs of the dead patriots.'[25]

Raids also took place on the Mallin family home, but these were 'civil enough'. Joe Mallin, then aged seven, remembered how impressed he was that his mother, Agnes, remained so 'cool', wrapping his father's ceremonial sword in newspaper when the soldiers were 'only paces away' from them. He recalled the men rifling locked trunks, breaking them open, while his mother asked for permission to get the keys, but she was refused roughly. She managed to retrieve a bank passbook that was taken, but other possessions were not returned.[26]

Maud wrote: 'Life is made hideous with raids & rumours of raids & indiscriminate shootings by the military . . .'[27] Days later she added: 'Things are so bad here, they can't be worse, no one's life or liberty is safe from the military, police or auxiliaries.'[28]

The pre-war plans for Home Rule came to pass in the December 1920 Government of Ireland Act. It provided for two parliaments, one in Belfast and one in Dublin. Ireland would remain a part of the United Kingdom of Britain and Ireland, with the British monarch as the head of state. Sinn Féin ignored the passing of this Act and continued with their alternative administration.

On 10 December 1920, martial law was proclaimed in Cork, Limerick, Kerry and Tipperary, and it was extended to Clare, Waterford, Wexford and Kilkenny in January 1921. On 11 December, Cork city centre was burnt by the Black and Tans. Forty-five businesses were destroyed and in the aftermath four thousand people lost their wages. Éamon de Valera returned to Ireland from America that same month, arriving in the midst of what had become a tumultuous conflict.

That same month an American Commission for Relief in Ireland was organized in New York. Following a call by the editors of the New York *Nation*, this 'committee of 100' had come together, comprising state governors, religious leaders of a number of faiths, newspaper editors and 'prominent citizens' from every state in the Union. Its activities were non-political and non-sectarian; funding came from the Catholic Church in America, the Jewish community, the American Red Cross and the Society of Friends. In November and December 1920 and in January 1921 the American Commission held public hearings in Washington DC. They approached the British ambassador to give evidence; while declining to take part in the commission, he told it he would do nothing to hinder the inquiry and no reprisals would be taken against any witnesses.

During 1921 a delegation from the American Commission visited Ireland on a fact-finding mission and documented the costs of two years of unofficial war. The number of shops and houses destroyed was calculated at approximately two thousand, while another fifteen hundred had some form of damage. The Commission noted that the economy of rural Ireland was under siege: it was estimated that forty creameries alone were ruined, while thirty-five were partially wrecked.

The Commission decided that the American relief should be distributed by the White Cross, which had just been formed in Ireland. The organization would be administered by a committee made up of dignitaries from secular and religious communities, and would be directed from Dublin, with parish councils distributing the funds. Maud and Kathleen both became members of the Standing Executive Committee. Kathleen (who was a member of the General Council at the outset) joined the organization to ensure that there would be no overlapping with the National Aid and Volunteers' Dependants' Fund, which was still operational.

An estimated hundred thousand people benefited from the new fund. From the middle of 1920, some ten thousand Catholic workers in Belfast, who had been prevented from working due to sectarian issues, sought the support of the White Cross for themselves and their dependants, numbering about twenty thousand.[29] Other areas, such as Lisburn, Bangor, Dromore, Banbridge and Newtownards, were also affected and were supported by the work of the organization.

Lillie Connolly was among those who accepted White Cross funds, although in 1920 she had refused the Irish Transport and General Workers' Union's offer of a pension in honour of James. She had replied to Thomas Foran, an official of the union: 'I am glad and proud that the union has put on record its appreciation of his value to it but I do not see how I can allow it to accept any responsibility for me or my family now that he is dead. To accept your bounty . . . would not be acceptable to the dignity and honour of the position I occupy as his wife.'[30]

*

313

During the most violent phase of fighting, Nellie Donnelly and Maeve travelled back from Omagh to Dublin with Sidney, who had finally managed to get back to Ireland with her son Finian and had landed in Belfast on 2 April 1921. Sidney would have returned sooner, but she had needed a false passport to get home and it was difficult to 'obtain' one that listed a child of a similar age to her own. Finally she 'borrowed' a passport that listed a nine-month-old baby, although Finian was by then a boy of four. Despite this obvious discrepancy, she managed to get on the ship with her son. When she arrived in Liverpool, she talked her way on to a ship leaving for Belfast, but she was in such a state of nerves when she arrived in Belfast without incident that she left her trunk on the ship.[31]

When Sidney (now Madame Czira to some, but always 'John Brennan' to others) got back to Dublin she immediately joined her old friends in their political activities and became involved with the White Cross.[32] Of the other Gifford sisters, Grace was still producing publicity for the Republican movement but was not active in any military activities. Katie had stood unsuccessfully for the municipal elections in 1920 and throughout the War of Independence worked for Michael Collins raising the Dáil Loan.[33] Ironically, it was Nellie, the only sister who took part in the Rising, who did not become involved in active politics again.

In 1921 Charlotte Despard returned to Ireland, where she and Maud became companions, working with a common aim. They undertook a fact-finding mission in war-torn County Cork, and they also met with Cleeves Factory workers in Limerick following the destruction of their workplace by the Black and Tans. Charlotte's status as the sister of the Lord Lieutenant allowed them access to restricted areas, although by the summer of 1921, when she took up permanent residency in the country, her brother was no longer in this position.

They visited Balbriggan in County Dublin in the aftermath of its sacking on 20 September, when the Black and Tans left many homes and businesses destroyed, including a hosiery factory, resulting in the loss of employment for 120 factory workers and a further 300 who produced work for the factory in their homes. Charlotte and Maud were photographed looking at the ruins by W. D. Hogan, a commercial and press photographer whom they employed to accompany them to these locations. His photographs were made available to the American Commission on Ireland and appeared in its report on the War in Ireland. In one photograph Maud is identified as one of the 'victims of the Imperial British Forces', the caption describing her as 'Madame MacBride, husband executed'.[34] The fact that by 1916 she and John had been estranged for more than a decade did not need to get in the way of such a good story, and the statuesque woman in widows' weeds was painted as a victim too.

In his own way Maud's son was also using his lineage to gain status in the IRA. Seán, now seventeen years old, spent much of his time preparing defences for prisoners. His role was very junior – collecting statements, gathering evidence and finding witnesses. On one occasion he was asked to assess the evidence of prisoners to ascertain who should be rescued from jail. One of the prisoners whom he thought was safe and left behind was subsequently executed. This made 'a deep impression' on him, showing how unreliable the judicial system could be in regard to capital punishment.

Seán was also on active service. In March 1921 he was involved in his first major military operation for the IRA, an ambush in Sandwith Street in Dublin. His small unit ended up in a position where Black and Tans were firing directly at him and his friend Leo FitzGerald: 'I realised our position was untenable and I said, "Look Leo, we'd better go back; we should get into the lane at the back of the house and see what we can do." I got no response from Leo. I put my hand out to shake him. My hand was full of hot blood and I realised that he was dead.' Years later he wrote: 'I remember this occasion very clearly. It made a deep impression on my mind. This was the first time that I had been really that close to death.'[35] Even then Maud did not know Seán was a member of the IRA.

Despite his youth, Seán directed a number of ambushes on Black and Tan patrols. He dressed in a yellow waistcoat, believing that if he were ever captured he would be able to convince the military that he was a foreign journalist. The son of another 1916 leader, seventeen-year-old Seamus Mallin, became an adjutant for Seán MacBride. This was often retold, as was the fact that at this time Seán had on one occasion hidden in the Mallins' loft, at a house named Loyola on the South Circular Road.[36]

Seán's military ability was recognized by Michael Collins and others, and he was asked to 'step up' activities in the IRA in Counties Wicklow, Wexford and Carlow, as these were the only counties that still had operational RIC stations.[37] The idea was to have an area that was dormant suddenly becoming active. Seán set up his own 'flying column' in Wicklow, using Glenmalure as a base. It was his belief that, with organization, a strong unit could easily be built up in the eastern coastal area.

He was in County Wicklow undertaking this task on 9 July 'when I learned that a Truce had been declared. My immediate reaction was one of considerable annoyance. I had a feeling that this was quite wrong, that we were on the way to really make things hotter.' The truce signed in Dublin stated that from twelve o'clock on 11 July 1921 'active operations of our troops will be suspended'.[38]

The catalyst for the truce had been a conciliatory speech by King George V at the opening of the Belfast parliament in June 1921, calling for 'an end to strife'. Two days after the speech, on 24 June 1921, *The Times* declared that this was the 'moment for a Truce'.

Maud wrote to Willie Yeats from Dublin on 27 July 1921:

> the truce is a great relief to everybody, but no one as far as I can see is very confident as to settlement. We all distrust the English Govt so much that until we see the jails & internment camps opened & the ships carrying away the English forces we cannot believe in the peace however much we may hope for it . . . Still the truce is satisfactory. & I can go to bed without stockings on & Seaġan can sleep at home.

She felt that now that there was a truce, the Irish Army could no longer be referred to as a murder gang.

In this letter, politics and what Maud described as 'her work' came before mention of a 'horror' that had just been visited upon her family. 'The reason for my delay in answering your letter was that besides my usual work I have been much taken up with my poor Iseult. Her baby got ill about two months ago . . . It died of meningitis three days ago.'[39]

Two years previously Iseult, then aged twenty-five, had entered into a relationship with aspiring poet Francis Stuart, who was then only seventeen, although Iseult thought he was nineteen.[40] They had married in London in April 1920, but the union was disastrous from the start. Maud wrote to Willie in June 1920: 'knowing this horrible life Iseult has prepared for herself, I have refused to quarrel with them, for Iseult will need all the help & support her friends can give her.' Although the relationship deteriorated quickly, Iseult became pregnant. The Stuarts' unstable and unsettled lives were lived out between Wicklow, a flat in Dublin and periods spent staying with their relatives in both Ireland and England.

Iseult's baby, Delores, was born on 6 March 1921; her death at just four months old was a tragic mirroring of Maud's own life, for meningitis had also taken her baby son Georges thirty years before. Maud wrote of Delores to Willie: 'We buried it in a very beautiful place . . . The tiny grave is among the roots of a very old yew tree.'[41] The following month she wrote of Iseult, with a discernible detachment: 'Poor Iseult is still very sad & very broken at the loss of her baby. She misses it terribly but she is very brave & charming as usual.'[42]

15

'A Divided People'

Following the truce in the summer of 1921, Lloyd George sent a letter to Éamon de Valera asking for a meeting with him and James Craig, the first prime minister of the Parliament of Northern Ireland, established by the Government of Ireland Act in 1920, which had set up the six counties as a separate province. De Valera agreed in July to attend 'the Irish Peace Talks'. Count Plunkett and Arthur Griffith also formed part of the delegation. However, the proposals were 'unacceptable' to Éamon de Valera and the other delegates. Áine also recorded her dissatisfaction with them.[1] The delegation returned home.

Following the rejection of the British peace proposals that July, a new delegation of plenipotentiaries was selected to negotiate a peace settlement in October. Neither Kathleen Clarke nor any of the other female TDs was selected. (Kathleen had been elected as a TD in an election held in May 1921; there had been no ballot as all candidates had been unopposed.) Women were included as secretarial staff to travel to London, including Áine's sister Lily, while Seán MacBride went as Michael Collins's aide-de-camp. Collins and Arthur Griffith headed up the delegation after President Éamon de Valera refused to go. Kathleen recalled: 'He gave his reasons but they were not very clear ... One of his reasons, I thought, was that if the plenipotentiaries made a mistake, or agreed to do something of which he did not approve, he would not be involved, but would be there as head of the nation to correct their mistake or repudiate their actions.' When the selection was made, Kathleen overheard an exchange between de Valera and Griffith in which she heard de Valera say: 'You know, Griffith, we must have scapegoats.'[2]

Seán MacBride was tasked with arranging a 'quick getaway' for Michael Collins if things did not work out in London, though during the three months of negotiations his main occupation was to carry despatches between Dublin and London. He stayed with Collins and his men at Cadogan Gardens; however, he often went to Hans Place, where the politicians were staying, to play chess and bridge. He later wrote that he was amazed by the amount of drinking that Collins did, commenting that he thought that 'such behaviour was a bad influence on the delegation.' He claimed he was 'rather revolted by it', but it did not stop him from joining in and he drank a 'good deal with them.'[3] Seán did not have to put an escape plan into action, but was sent by Collins on a mission to Germany to negotiate an arms deal, although he was instructed to hold off its conclusion until after the Treaty was negotiated.

As the Peace Treaty was being concluded in London, in early December Kathleen Clarke was awarded the Freedom of her native Limerick City 'in recognition of her steadfast fidelity to the Republic'.[4] The same honour was to be bestowed on Eoin MacNeill and Éamon de Valera; MacNeill was conferred alone, but de Valera arranged for himself and Kathleen to be conferred together on 6 December. On the train returning to Dublin the next day, Kathleen was asked to join de Valera and his party in first class, and when they arrived at Ballybrophy station they bought the Dublin evening papers which gave the first news of the agreement just signed in London. As Kathleen recalled: 'Cathal Brugha handed the papers to de Valera. He read them and said to Cathal "If they have signed, they must have got all we demanded."'[5]

When he heard the actual terms of the agreement, Éamon de Valera issued a 'Proclamation to the Irish People', which stated that he could not recommend the acceptance of the Treaty to Dáil Éireann or to the people. Amongst the Treaty terms were that Ireland would hold Dominion status within the Empire; the head of the Irish Free State would be a British monarch, represented by a governor general; and members of parliament would have to swear an Oath of Allegiance.

Before the Dáil was due to meet on 14 December to discuss the issue, the IRA was divided. Many people followed Michael Collins, who was also president of the IRB and that organization came out in acceptance of the terms. Seán MacBride later wrote: 'I don't think that the IRB itself had very much influence on the treaty; as far as I was concerned, I regarded them as being an older generation living in the past a bit. They were not facing the realities of that day's struggle.'[6]

As the Dáil convened to debate acceptance, Kathleen was left stunned by the exchanges between former comrades. De Valera opened the discussion by attacking the plenipotentiaries for signing the Treaty without first consulting Dublin. Griffith said they had not exceeded their instructions. Kathleen was determined that when she spoke during the debates that there would be 'no harsh words'. She got her opportunity on 22 December:

> I rise to support the motion of the President to reject this Treaty. It is to me the simple question of right and wrong. To my mind it is a surrender of our national ideals . . . Arthur Griffith said he had brought back peace from England, and freedom to Ireland . . . if this Treaty is ratified, the result will be a divided people; the same old division will go on; . . . and so England's old game of divide and conquer goes on.[7]

Grace Plunkett wrote to the papers that, while she acknowledged the past contributions of both Arthur Griffith and Éamon de Valera to win the Republic, she urged her readers to reject the Treaty.

Between 22 December and 3 January 1922 the Dáil was in recess, with the vote on the acceptance of the Treaty to take place after that. During the Christmas break TDs found that public opinion in their constituencies had come out strongly in favour of acceptance, with the result that many deputies who may have rejected the Treaty decided to support it. Consequently, on 7 January 1922 the Dáil approved the acceptance of the Treaty by 64 to 57. Éamon de Valera resigned as president of the Irish Republic and led the Anti-Treaty members, including Kathleen, out of the Dáil. Kathleen later wrote: 'had I been in his place, law or no law, I would not have resigned, they might have voted me out but then I would go down fighting.'[8] On 14 January 1922 the Pro-Treaty members of the Dáil and the four Unionists elected by Trinity College met to appoint Michael Collins as head of the Provisional Government, allowing him to appoint a Cabinet that would oversee the transfer of power during the next twelve months.

Lillie Connolly's son Roddy had followed his father's path to socialism in the years since James's execution, having joined the Socialist Party of Ireland in 1917. As editor of the *Workers' Republic*, he wrote that the Treaty was 'a repugnant collaboration between British imperialism and Irish capitalism.' Roddy had been active during the War of Independence and as a supporter of the Bolsheviks in the Russian Revolution he had made two visits to Moscow. On one of these trips he attended the Third Congress of the Communist International, where he had talks with Vladimir Lenin and told him that the IRA rank and file was winnable to communism. To this end he was given permission for the formation of an Irish Communist Party. As the leader of this newly formed party, James Connolly's only son was the first party leader publicly to oppose the Treaty.

Maud saw the Treaty as 'a tremendous step forward'. Her son disagreed: Seán thought that they would have got more if they had waited, and later said that, at the time, many people believed that its acceptance was a ploy by Collins to allow the IRA to regroup. Seán and his mother agreed to disagree, and from this point on they chose not to exchange political views. Seán offered his services to de Valera, telling him that he would help him in any way he could, and he joined a 'Republican Headquarters' that was set up in Suffolk Street. Iseult and her husband Francis Stuart also opposed the Treaty.

In January 1922, Maud and Seán returned separately to Paris to attend the Irish Race Conference, an international gathering of people of Irish descent, which had been organized for some time. Maud represented the Irish Free State at the request of Arthur Griffith and Seán was on the opposing side as a general organizer for Éamon de Valera and the Anti-Treaty Republicans. The timing of the Conference, given the complex and fractured political situation in Ireland, meant that the possibilities for a lobby group of Irish people of all nationalities to support the cause of Irish independence were rendered negligible. The Irish Free State had no funds to continue international committees or gatherings. Seán had more immediate concerns, as he had to borrow money to pay for accommodation and meals for his stay in Paris, in contrast to his mother, who was there as a legitimate representative of the Irish Free State.

Maud returned home to undertake humanitarian work on behalf of families who had fled from rioting in Belfast in the aftermath of the formation of the Irish Free State. Partition had been in place since 1920, but it was envisioned that the Boundary Commission, which was formed following the Anglo-Irish Treaty, would ultimately demonstrate that the creation of the Province of Northern Ireland (six of the existing thirty-two counties on the island of Ireland) would prove economically unviable. In the early months of 1922, however, there was the immediate and ongoing problem of the nationalists who had made their way south. Maud witnessed 'women half demented and children sick with terror'.[9] She went to Arthur Griffith seeking help, but none was forthcoming, as Griffith blamed the IRA for encouraging the refugees to come to Dublin. He again sent Maud to Paris to publicize the formation of the Irish Free State. While she was there she also highlighted the plight of the victims from the North, despite it being against Irish Free State policy.

At their convention on 5 February, Cumann na mBan became the first organization to vote against ratification of the Treaty, by an overwhelming 419 votes to 63. In their view, the agreement represented the loss of the Republic that had been proclaimed in 1916 – a Republic that offered women an Ireland of equal opportunities. The Cumann na mBan executive, which included Áine Ceannt, circulated their branches, outlining that at their convention the organization had reaffirmed its allegiance to the Republic of Ireland and therefore rejected the Articles of Agreement signed in London on 6 December 1921. The executive stated that all monies from the branches that were against the resolution would have to be forwarded to them, as 'these monies were collected to uphold the existing Republic and it would be an indictable offence for any person to devote them to a purpose other than this.'[10]

With the ratification of the Treaty, the White Cross now felt that its main work was over. The managing committee decided to allocate the remaining money to the care of children orphaned as a result of the struggle, and the Children's Relief Association was formed to administer the funds; provision was also made for people disabled during the fighting. The first meeting of the Association took place on 6 February 1922. At the outset Kathleen Clarke was honorary secretary, but she declined to continue in the role, although she remained a member of the council. She was replaced in April by Áine Ceannt, who began a huge administration exercise in collating all the information on the orphans. As a paid position, this became Áine's full-time job, operating from an office in Room 7, 27 Dawson Street, from that August.[11]

In May 1922, in an effort to avoid civil war, Collins and de Valera decided on an 'agreed election' in which successful Pro- and Anti-Treaty candidates would create a coalition government. However, on 14 June, shortly before the election, Collins repudiated the pact. At the general election two days later there was widespread approval of the Treaty, with a majority of Pro-Treaty Sinn Féin members being elected, including Joseph MacBride, who was once again re-elected unopposed. For his family and many other Irish people, it was hoped that this was a chance to return to the peacetime existence that they had enjoyed six years earlier.

All the women in the second Dáil chose the Anti-Treaty side and lost their seats, including Kathleen. Those thirty-five Anti-Treaty Sinn Féin members who were elected refused to recognize the Dáil and did not take their seats. A Dáil committee chaired by Kathleen tried to work out a diplomatic resolution, but failed.

In April, those who supported the Anti-Treaty side, anticipating civil war, occupied strategic buildings. Known by the Irish Free State as 'Irregulars' (in contrast to the regular soldiers of the state), they made the Four Courts their headquarters.

It was now six years since the executions. In May 1922 the relatives of the 1916 leaders received letters requesting their attendance at a Mass in Kilmainham Jail which the brigade adjutant of the Dublin City Brigade of the IRA had organized. The Mass, by Canon Magill, was held on the morning of 8 May, Michael Mallin's anniversary; Agnes subsequently kept her copy of the letter. The jail was disused at the time, but it would soon be made ready again, this time for prisoners opposing the Irish Free State.

16

Civil War

By June 1922, after all pacts and deals had failed, civil war had become inevitable. Hostilities began at 4 a.m. on 28 June, the IRA having refused to surrender when Free State forces started bombarding the Four Courts – using artillery borrowed from the British military. Maud was still in Paris when she read of the attack on the Four Courts; as her son Seán was among the IRA forces there, she made arrangements to travel back to Dublin. The attack lasted until 30 June, when the Republican forces surrendered the Four Courts. Seán was among those arrested but Maud, having just arrived home, was unaware of this and began searching the hospitals for her son.

Peace negotiations were being brokered by a group of women, the Women's Peace Committee, representing the different sides. Maud joined the committee, representing herself as neutral. The women:

> . . . spoke of the sufferings of the people and need for peace and got the usual sort of answers from Griffith, Collins and Cosgrave. Maud asked would they let the Republicans evacuate without giving up arms – Griffith said no, they must give up their arms. Maud said that they certainly would not do, and that it would be better to let them go with their arms than to shell the city. Griffith said the lives of all the ministers were in the greatest danger.[1]

The Women's Peace Committee demanded that the Dáil be recalled and framed a peace proposal – a cessation of hostilities to be agreed by the Dáil – but on Monday, 3 July it was rejected by Collins, Cosgrave and Griffith.

On the same day the women were pleading their case, government troops attacked Republican positions in O'Connell Street and elsewhere. Roddy Connolly was in the Wood Printing Works when hostilities began, editing the *Workers' Republic*. Armed with a revolver, he went to the Four Courts to offer his services and was sent to the fighting in O'Connell Street. Kathleen's boys were not involved in the fighting, but she volunteered at a first-aid station at the Gresham Hotel. Grace reported to a first-aid station at Tara Hall, as did Nora and Ina Connolly.[2] One of the other women there, Rosamond Jacob, recalled:

> A Trade Union place called Tara hall, full of girls making bandages. They showed me how, and I worked there till dinner time. Two wounded civilians were brought in to be attended to in the next room ... There was a lot of firing in the streets and a tremendous explosion once that broke the glass in one window. Some of the girls were the C. Na mB [Cumann na mBan] type that loved the whole thing in a horrible way.[3]

Áine Ceannt also reported to Tara Hall along with other members of Cumann na mBan, describing later how she worked there until lunchtime, when she received instructions to set up a 'base hospital' in her own neighbourhood of Ranelagh, in Cullenswood House, the building that Pearse had first used as St Enda's School. She purchased first-aid equipment in anticipation of casualties and a bloody fight that never materialized. In her account of those days there is no mention of sixteen-year-old Rónán.[4]

Having discovered that her son was in Mountjoy Jail, Maud had a row with the government representatives, as she was 'not being allowed to see Sean in Mountjoy, or even send him in a clean shirt'.[5] She went to the prison, but was refused admittance.

Anti-Treaty forces continued to occupy buildings, including the Gresham and Hammam Hotels, holding out until the 5 July, when the buildings were set alight by Irish Free State troops and evacuated. Cathal Brugha refused to surrender and was among those shot dead during the week of fighting.

On 12 July 1922 the Council of War appointed Michael Collins commander-in-chief of the National Army. On the same day, Maud was one of the speakers at a peace meeting at the Round Room in the Mansion House, addressing, in the words of Rosamond Jacob, 'great crowds of women, but none of them apparently keen on peace.'[6] They were in the minority as the Irish Free State restored order in the capital.

Outside Dublin, the province of Munster was declared a republic, with Anti-Treaty supporters in the majority. The National Army attacked the Republican strongholds in the south of the country. After fighting in Dublin ceased, Roddy Connolly was instructed to go to Clonmel in Tipperary, one of the areas with a concentration of Anti-Treaty IRA. He brought a letter of introduction to the IRA leadership there from Liam Lynch, leader of the Republican forces, urging that the fight be continued in the country. Over the next few weeks, the Irish Free State Army managed to take over Limerick, Waterford, Tralee and Cork City. From that point on, guerrilla war continued in the countryside. Michael Collins was shot dead in an ambush in west Cork on 22 August.

The weeks of fighting saw mass arrests of Anti-Treaty forces, but no information about those held was supplied by the prison authorities or the government. No visits were allowed. Maud joined the crowds of women outside prison gates all over the country looking for news of their missing sons, husbands, wives and daughters. In August 1922, along with Charlotte Despard and other women from outside Mountjoy Jail, Maud was instrumental in starting an organization called the Women's Prisoners' Defence League, affectionately known as 'the Mothers'. According to Maud: 'Terrifying stories . . . of the beating and torture of prisoners for information circulated.

The constant sound of firing in the jail and the wounding of prisoners made the need of a Prisoners' Defence League obvious and urgent.'[7]

Qualification for membership of the league was to have a relative in jail and to pay a halfpenny a week. A committee was appointed, with Charlotte Despard as president and Maud as secretary, and the first meeting was held in the Round Room of the Mansion House. The league organized services such as attendance at court cases and provision of food to those in custody – especially important for those who came from the country and had no relatives to look after them; it also published lists of prisoners and distributed leaflets concerning conditions in state jails.

On 9 September 1922 the new Dáil met, but Republicans stayed out of the chamber. With the deaths of both Michael Collins and Arthur Griffith the previous month, W. T. Cosgrave now became chairman of the Provisional Government. On 15 October a Special Emergency Powers Act was passed, imposing martial law and setting up special military courts with the power to impose the death penalty on those found in unauthorized possession of arms.

Relatives of some of the men executed in 1916 got together and wrote an open letter to Cosgrave:

When in 1916 the Government of the day executed those who had surrendered after the Easter Week fight, the heart of Ireland was stirred at the infamy of executing men whom they held were prisoners of war. Sixteen having been tried by secret court martial, were condemned to death and executed; many others including the present Chairman of the Provisional Government were also condemned to death, the sentence after being commuted to penal servitude for life . . . Friends at the time trying to comfort us bereaved ones said they are better off dead than doing penal servitude for life but the release the following year proved how foolish was this state-ment . . . We would ask the present Chairman WT Cosgrave to reflect on the effect those few words had on him, 'death commute to penal servitude for life' . . . Let the men who are at the moment in

Power think twice before they order the execution of any man who is a prisoner in their hands . . .'[8]

One of those listed to be executed was Agnes Mallin's eldest son, Seamus. Agnes had been aware of her son's stance from the time that the Treaty was rejected. He was now nineteen years old, and had been living at home whilst studying for an engineering degree at University College Dublin. When their house was raided by Irish Free State troops Seamus would hold seven-year-old Maura to avoid being searched. His brother Joe, then aged ten, remembered Seamus showing him his gun.[9] In October 1922 Seamus was one of four men arrested following an attack, with bombs and revolver fire, on a lorry of Irish Free State troops on the South Circular, near his home. Each of the four was found to be in possession of a loaded revolver.

The case of the four men, Joseph Spooner, Patrick Farrelly, John Murphy and a 'youth called Mallin' came to a lawyer, Cahir Davitt (son of Michael Davitt, founder of the Land League), for consideration. He later recalled: 'Mallin was much the youngest of the four and was a student at University College Dublin. The charge against him was of being in possession of a revolver without lawful authority'. According to Davitt, there was no evidence that Seamus Mallin had been involved in the attack on the lorry: 'I seized upon it as a pretext for advising against the confirmation of the sentence in his case on the ground that, having regard to his youth, the court in the absence of such evidence might have seen fit to impose a less sentence than that of death. I advised that the sentence should be committed to one of penal servitude.'[10]

Following the submission of this document, Davitt was asked to attend a meeting of the Army Council, where he was closely questioned about his reasons for advising against the death sentence for Seamus. He recalled: 'I could only reiterate what I had said in writing and adhere to what I had already advised. I was given no clue as to whether my advice was going to be accepted.'[11]

On 30 November, Seamus Mallin's fellow prisoners Spooner, Farrelly and Murphy were executed. Seamus's sentence was commuted to penal servitude. Cahir Davitt wrote: 'I thought at the time that it was solely due to my advice, but I was told years after that it was mainly because he was the son of Michael Mallin executed in 1916.'[12] News of the reprieve came to Agnes in the form of a smuggled letter delivered by Seamus's cousin Lily Thewlis, a member of Cumann na mBan, who was herself later arrested and taken to Kilmainham Jail.

Within months there were thousands of prisoners in jails around the country. As former friends turned captors, it was all too easy to identify those who were involved. From November 1922 onwards women, mainly members of Cumann na mBan, were arrested in large numbers. Lily O'Brennan was imprisoned after a six-hour raid on the Republican headquarters in Suffolk Street, Dublin.[13] Nora Connolly O'Brien was also arrested that month. She and her husband Seamus spent their first wedding anniversary in different parts of Mountjoy Jail. Nora was later transferred to Kilmainham Jail. While she was there she was allowed no communication with her mother. Nora later recalled: 'She had been in great difficulties about our house. A Trustee Fund had been set up for the widows of the men executed in 1916 and the Trustees plan was to assist my mother in setting up a boarding house. She was very simple minded about such things and while I was in prison she did not have me to advise her.'[14] Lillie moved back to her childhood village of Rathmines; her new home was a red-brick-over-basement house overlooking Belgrave Square.

On 6 December 1922 the Dáil passed the Irish Free State Constitution Bill and the Irish Free State officially came into existence. Two days later, in retaliation for the shooting of Seán Hales, a TD for Cork, on the instructions of the Cabinet four imprisoned men were selected for execution, each from a different part of Ireland. One of them, Rory O'Connor, was Seán MacBride's cell mate. Seán recalled that he too was ordered to dress, but then was told that he was to stay. There had been a rumour that men were being deported to the Seychelles, so Seán sewed money into Rory's belt as it could be useful to him out there. When the news came that Rory had been executed, Seán and his fellow prisoners were 'shocked, hurt and pained.' He thought that there was 'personal enmity of certain members of the government towards Rory O'Connor.' Many years later he would relive those days:

> I carefully folded Rory's blankets neatly in a corner . . . I used to do this every day. I kept them there that way for some days . . . Several days passed by and then I decided I might as well use some of Rory's blankets. It was cold at night. I remember having a funny feeling that in a way that I shouldn't use them . . . but then arguing with myself, well, he's gone after all, and I am sure he would like me to use them.[15]

The Irish Free State government increased the powers of the military courts and issued a statement that any person found in possession of 'a plan, document for the purpose of being prejudicial to the safety of the state or national forces' would be executed. By January 1923 over fifty Republicans had been executed and prisoners incarcerated in such numbers that they were held in jails in the towns of Athlone, Carlow, Athy, Carrick-on-Shannon, Cork, Dundalk, Kilkenny, Limerick, Naas, Navan, Portlaoise, Sligo, Tipperary, Thurles, Waterford and Westport, as well as being detained in army barracks such as Wellington, Portobello and Beggars Bush. Camps were set up in the Curragh – Tintown and Hare Park – and other prisoners were held in Kilmainham and Mountjoy Jails and workhouses such as the North Dublin Union.

Although women gained certain privileges as political prisoners detained without trial, they were not permitted to receive visitors. Their guards were armed and several women were injured while in prison. There was always the threat that a woman would be executed, as government-sanctioned executions continued throughout this period.

In January 1923 the government banned the Women's Prisoners' Defence League. Charlotte Despard wrote at this time: 'Possibly if we had held our tongues things would have been even worse than they were. But we knew the agitation has kept up the courage of our boys and girls in prison.'[16]

The widows, who had become symbols of the Republican cause, were particularly vulnerable to harassment, raids and arrest. Grace Plunkett was arrested on 6 February 1923. A party of Free State soldiers ransacked her sister Katie's house at Philipsburgh Avenue, looking for guns and other incriminating items. As well as Katie Wilson – who in the style of the time called herself by her Irish name, Cáit Bean Mhic Liam – Grace, Nellie and Sidney were all there, as were the children Maeve and Finian. Although Grace was never a member of Cumann na mBan and the 'mere sight of a gun would cause her to faint',[17] such was her association with the Republic that she was the focus of attention, and she and Katie were arrested and brought to Kilmainham Jail on the very first day it was made ready for prisoners. Almost seven years on from Easter Week, Grace found herself incarcerated in the place where she and Joe had been married, and where Joe had been shot.

Two weeks later, on 21 February, Kathleen Clarke was in Suffolk Street at the 'Republican Headquarters' when it was raided by the Criminal Investigation Division (CID); she was arrested but released the next day. It is surprising that she was not held for longer, as at this time her shop on Amiens Street was 'a known centre of Irregular communication.'[18]

Agnes Mallin had been working at two jobs, as a night nurse and also as a school truancy officer. Around this time, she became very ill, experiencing symptoms that appeared to relate to overwork – tiredness, loss of weight, loss of appetite, elevated temperature and a stiff and painful back. On 9 February 1923 Seamus Mallin wrote to his mother from Hut 21 at Hare Park Camp, the Curragh. He had been prohibited from writing for a month, but now he told her that he was concerned about her health, given that she was working two jobs: 'perhaps it is for better you did not get this permanent position. One never knows. Besides the last time your health suffered very much and after all your health is of more importance than all the positions in Europe.'[19]

*

Áine Ceannt noted to her imprisoned sister that they had had three raids during one month alone. The house where her seventy-two-year-old mother and her teenage son Rónán lived had been ransacked by men with faces blackened to avoid recognition, but on one occasion Áine recognized one as a man who had served in Éamonn's battalion during the Rising. Writing to her sister Lily, who had been in prison since the previous December, Áine described how the soldiers smashed windows, ate the family's food and maliciously destroyed furniture, including a marble washstand, a wardrobe, a chest of drawers and other belongings. During one raid, as she told her sister: 'I believe they dressed up in your clothes and jazzed in my bedroom. I thought the dining room ceiling would come down . . . when ten people take possession of your house and eat everything in it – by order they said, it does not encourage one to spend money.'[20]

These raiders of the Free State Army thought nothing of taking items that had once belonged to Éamonn or destroying his wife's few keepsakes. During one raid they disfigured Éamonn's photograph beyond recognition. As Áine wrote to her sister at the time: 'when the Black and Tans raided they did not destroy it . . . All the etchings of the seven signatories were torn down and torn to pieces, in fact anything pertaining to that period was particularly mutilated. However we are still alive'.[21]

During raids on Maud's home at 73 St Stephen's Green, letters and poems from Willie Yeats were destroyed, as were mementoes from her children. After one raid Maud decided to leave her city-centre location and, with Charlotte Despard, she moved to Roebuck House in the south County Dublin countryside. The house had extensive grounds, outbuildings and a walled garden, and they had plans to utilize it for work to assist those in need as a result of the war. It was said of the refuge they established there that, if one managed to get past the unwelcoming dogs, 'any person could walk in and ask for dinner or asylum for life.'[22]

On 10 April 1923 Maud was arrested, along with Iseult, for

painting banners for 'seditious demonstrations' and producing anti-government literature.[23] Their arrival in Kilmainham Jail caused some commotion, as Maud had brought her lap dog with her. One of her fellow inmates recorded in her diary: 'Early this morning we could see Maud walking majestically past our cell door leading on a leash a funny little lap dog which answered to the name that sounded like Wuzzo Wuzzo.'[24] Along with ninety-one other women, Maud immediately went on hunger strike. Seventy-eight-year-old Charlotte Despard stayed at the prison gates in protest, later describing: 'Oh the bitter cold and the <u>length</u> of those nights.'[25] The hunger strike was used as a weapon to obtain concessions. Although no women actually died in prison at this time, a number did die from the effects of their imprisonment some time after being released. Willie Yeats contacted W. T. Cosgrave to protest that Maud, who was now fifty-seven, could not be expected to 'stand the strain as the younger women.'[26] She was released on 30 April after twenty days on hunger strike.

Iseult, whose husband Francis was in Mountjoy Jail at the same time, remained incarcerated. On the very day that her mother was released, Iseult was one of seventy prisoners taken from Kilmainham to the North Dublin Union, located beside Broadstone Station, which was known as Tig na mBocht (House of the Poor) as it had once been a workhouse. When the prisoners were being moved they protested and resisted, and in the process many were injured. Before her arrest Maud had written to Willie, who had been made an Irish Free State senator, threatening that if he did not denounce the government she would renounce his society for ever. However, she sought his assistance that May to check with the authorities whether Iseult had been injured in the fracas. Willie found that the lorry journey to the North Dublin Union had made Iseult ill, but he assured Maud that she was otherwise well and he was continuing to work to secure her release.

On 10 May 1923 the Republican leader Liam Lynch was fatally wounded in County Tipperary. He was replaced as chief of staff by

Frank Aiken, who called a ceasefire on 24 May. Éamon de Valera issued a statement: 'Soldiers of the Republic, Legion of the Rearguard, the Republic can no longer be defended successfully by your arms. Further sacrifice would now be in vain . . .' None of the women was consulted about the ceasefire.

While Iseult was released on 11 May, the ceasefire did not bring about the general release of prisoners, although freedom could be achieved if one signed 'The Form' – an undertaking not to take up further arms against the Irish Free State. All the remaining prisoners were issued with a detention order under the Public Safety Emergency Powers Act 1923, as the minister of defence Richard Mulcahy stated that: 'public safety would be endangered by the prisoner being set at liberty.'[27]

The political landscape was changing; on 27 May, three days after the ceasefire, the Cumann na nGaedheal party was founded by the Pro-Treaty members of the Dáil, and in August the first general election under the Irish Free State saw the new party winning sixty-three seats, Anti-Treaty candidates forty-four seats, as well as seats for Independents, the Labour Party and Farmers Party. Joseph MacBride, standing for Cumann na nGaedheal, was elected for Mayo South. Those forty-four elected representatives who now went under the Sinn Féin banner refused to take their seats and met as if they were in fact members of the Dáil, but as Kathleen described: 'No one, outside the four walls of the room we met in, acknowledged this as a government, not even our own supporters.'[28]

That same month, a barrister named Alex Lynn brought a case of *habeas corpus* on behalf of Nora Connolly O'Brien. He proved that her arrest had been unconstitutional as the Act under which she was being held had not been signed, and so he obtained her release.

Grace Plunkett was eventually released on 30 August 1923.[29] Katie was not freed at the same time and at first Grace told the authorities that she refused to go without her sister, but despite this initial protest she left the jail before her. Katie was very influential in the prison structure as head of the Cumann na mBan Prisoners' Committee and was held until 29 September.

Agnes Mallin's agony over her son Seamus had not ended after he was removed from the execution list. By October of 1923 tension was at an all-time high in the prisons and camps because of conditions and with no release in sight. In mid-October a mass hunger strike by three hundred prisoners began in Mountjoy Jail. It soon spread to other prisons, and within days 7,033 Republicans were on hunger strike, including Seamus and his comrades in Hare Park Camp in the Curragh. Previously, the Free State government had passed a motion outlawing the release of prisoners who were on hunger strike, with the result that two men who took part in this strike died. The IRA command ordered the strikes to end on 23 November. Seamus was on the strike for twenty-eight days.

During her son's imprisonment Agnes's health worsened and she was taken into hospital. The true nature of her years of ill health was finally revealed. Her symptoms, so long appearing to arise from the strain of work, were now diagnosed as TB of the spine. Surgeon Stokes of the Meath Hospital suspected that, while she could have had it from childhood, the condition may have been triggered by the trauma of her husband's execution. Dr Stokes removed a bone from her leg and inserted it into her spine, a technique that had been discovered to work during the First World War.

While Agnes was in hospital, Maura was brought to St Enda's, where her brother Joe was still a pupil. She was the only girl in the school. The first day Agnes got out of bed was the day that Maura made her first Holy Communion.

For a time the operation gave Agnes back her mobility, but she could not work as she had before. With no employment, her eldest son in prison and her other children too young to earn a wage, she suffered greatly. Money was a constant worry, but when she complained she was told by Thomas Farren, the trade union official appointed to be her trustee following the Rising, that she should manage her budget.[30] Seamus Mallin was finally released in 1924, having been imprisoned for nearly two years.

There was no work in the Irish Free State for the newly released prisoners, however. At Roebuck, Maud and Charlotte set up a jam factory and introduced the making of shell ornaments to provide employment. Even though the vast majority of prisoners had been released by 1924, Maud continued to hold regular Sunday meetings of the Women's Prisoners' Defence League to represent those still being held. They gathered for a time in the ruins of the Gresham Hotel in O'Connell Street, but the league was a proscribed organization, so when they were inevitably prevented from meeting in one place they simply set up elsewhere. Maud and Charlotte Despard, who by this time was eighty years old, were out in all weathers. It was not surprising that Dubliners viewing these old ladies, week after week, protesting the rights of political prisoners, nicknamed them 'Maud Gone Mad and Mrs Desperate'.[31]

17

Aftermath

Áine Ceannt stood *in loco parentis* to a whole generation of Irish orphans. As secretary of the organization now called the Irish White Cross Children's Relief Association, one of her tasks was to visit each child in turn in their homes. In 1923 she made her first tour of inspection, travelling to Belfast, as the White Cross did not recognize partition: 'Boundaries, religion, nor politics interfered with the work.' Her job would take her on many occasions throughout the thirty-two counties of Ireland, with the exception of Cavan, where there were no children to be assisted by the association.

By January 1925 the association was looking after the welfare of 723 children. Áine resigned as vice-president of Cumann na mBan and from the standing committee of Sinn Féin that year to concentrate on her ever-expanding role in the White Cross, which had extended its maintenance to children who had 'lost a breadwinner' during the Civil War. It was also decided that the need of some families was so great that children born after the conflict should also be included.[1] Where Áine deemed a family to be living in insanitary conditions, causing them illness, she was able to arrange for a house to be bought for them by the association, with repayments taken care of by the children when they began working. It was also her job to assist the children in deciding on a career and to encourage them to enter commercial colleges, nursing, apprenticeships or to undertake rural domestic science. Many of the children were supported up to the age of twenty-one or until marriage. To encourage 'thrift', payments were often made in Free State Saving Certificates. Áine also made recommendations for special medical treatment, glasses or sanatorium treatments. Monies continued to be sent to those who had emigrated to England, Scotland and America.

Some families had been assisted under the Army Pension Act of 1923 and no longer required assistance, but financial help from the White Cross and other agencies, such as the National Aid and Volunteers' Dependants' Fund, kept many from destitution, including the Mallins. They, with trustees acting as guarantors, first rented a house at 105 Ceant's Fort in Mount Brown,[2] then later were assisted in the purchase of Loyola on the South Circular Road. As Michael Mallin had been killed in the course of his duty, in July 1924 Agnes was allocated an award from the Army Finance Office, receiving an allowance for the education of the three youngest children, Úna, Joe and Maura.

Maud continued working on the council of the White Cross, as did Kathleen, who never ceased her work for the widows and dependants in the National Aid. In 1924 Kathleen agreed to travel to the US to fundraise for the NAVDF. She was delighted with the opportunity to go to America to visit her son Daly, who by this time had been in Los Angeles for three years. As an American born in the Bronx, he had been able to obtain a passport, but Kathleen travelled on false papers via Canada. She had speaking engagements in New York and Washington, but there was not much enthusiasm, as she later recounted, because of the split over the Treaty.

Although she enjoyed seeing her eldest son, Kathleen was anxious to get home to her youngest, fifteen-year-old Emmet. Some time previously he had been injured by a military motor car, which had knocked him from his bicycle and he hit his head. The effects were not physical but mental, and they had worsened over the two years following the accident. By 1924, on doctor's orders, Kathleen had to take him out of his boarding school, Mount St Benedict in Gorey, County Wexford. However, she could not send him to day school in Dublin either; as she wrote in March 1925: 'he cannot go through the street unaccompanied he is unable to attend day school so I am compelled to have a private teacher for him . . .'[3] She engaged a Mary Duffy to give him private tuition at home during 1924 and 1925.

During these years Lillie Connolly's life was filled with the activities of her extended family, which now included the first of her grandchildren – Roddy had married Jessica Maidment and their son James Lenin Maidment (Seamus) was born on 1 November 1923. Lillie's mothering extended to her sons-in-law, who addressed her as 'mother' in the Irish language, '*a mháthair*'. After their release from prison, Nora Connolly O'Brien and her husband Seamus lived at the top of her mother's house in Belgrave Square. When the superintendent of 'E' Division came to interview Lillie for her military pension, he noted that she was in 'comfortable circumstances'. Although she qualified under the terms of the Army Pension Act, the money was slow in coming and in February 1924 William O'Brien wrote on her behalf to Richard Mulcahy, then minister of defence, saying Mrs Connolly had 'found it difficult to make ends meet during recent years and at the present moment is rather embarrassed for the want of some ready money.'[4]

The army pension meant that Lillie had assistance in paying for the education of her youngest child, and by 1924 Fiona was the only one of the Connollys eligible. She was then at school in North Great George's Street. When she finished there the following year she travelled to France to attend the Institute of St Marie in Cette, Hérault, although her fees were not covered for this. Nor were the costs of the final year of medicine for Moira in 1926. Her 'exceptional ability' was noted, and she sat her finals in January 1926.

At the Sinn Féin Ard Fheis in March 1926, Éamon de Valera proposed that the party would enter the Dáil if the Oath of Allegiance were abolished. This motion was defeated. De Valera consequently left Sinn Féin, taking many followers with him, including Kathleen. In May 1926 she became a founder member of Fianna Fáil, the so-called 'Soldiers of Destiny'. In order to join the new party, she had to resign from Cumann na mBan. She was elected to the National

Executive of Fianna Fáil, later writing of this period: 'Building up a new organisation without funds was hard work; I know I put every ounce of energy and enthusiasm I possessed into it, and up to a certain time believed in de Valera.'[5]

Kathleen was re-elected to the short-lived Fifth Dáil in June 1927 as a Fianna Fáil member for the Dublin constituency. However, the Fianna Fáil deputies did not take their seats because the Oath was still in place. Cumann na nGaedheal lost sixteen seats in this election. Joseph MacBride was among those defeated and, aged sixty-five, he retired from politics. Before his departure from the Dáil he voiced the opinion that it was 'perfect nonsense' that his nephew Seán was still on the run.[6]

Seán had been wanted by the authorities ever since escaping from custody in 1923. On 26 January 1926 he had married Catalina Bulfin (known affectionately as Kid) at 6 a.m. in University Church, Dublin, in a ceremony that, because Seán was on the run, was supposed to be a 'great hush, hush secret. But there were, nevertheless, about two or three hundred people at the church, at six o'clock in the morning.' They lived for a time in Paris, but Kid became pregnant so she travelled back to Ireland and moved in with her mother-in-law in Roebuck House. She continued to live with Maud following the birth on 24 November 1926 of a baby daughter, Anna.

Six weeks earlier, Maud had become a grandmother again when, on 5 October, Iseult gave birth to her second child, a son called Ian. Iseult moved to Laragh Castle in County Wicklow, where she mostly lived alone as Francis occupied himself with his various pursuits. Seán was also an often-absent father. He came back to Ireland at the request of Andy Cooney, who asked him to resume his IRA duties, but this did not signal a resumption of family life, as he was returning to become involved with a proscribed organization. Kid and Anna stayed living with Maud at Roebuck. Maud's income would continue to provide for them all. Seán's 'public occupation' was in the jam factory that his mother and Charlotte Despard had set up there.[7]

In the mid-summer of 1927 Seán was in Brussels getting equipment for the jam factory. While he was there he read in *Le Soir* an article under the heading: 'Man responsible for the 77 executions in Ireland assassinated.'[8] Kevin O'Higgins had been a member of the Cumann na nGaedheal Cabinet during the period of the Civil War, and was part of the Cabinet that had sanctioned the '77' official executions, most notably that of Rory O'Connor, who had been best man at O'Higgins's own wedding. On 10 July 1927 O'Higgins had gone to early Mass with his usual bodyguard in Booterstown when members of the IRA took the opportunity to assassinate him. Seán was amongst those arrested as a suspect, although he was out of the country when the assassination took place. A Special Powers Act had been passed that allowed for a special court that could impose the death penalty on those found in possession of illegal weapons. It also allowed the Irish Free State authorities to hold Seán for an indefinite period. He later wrote that he was the only political prisoner in Mountjoy Jail at that time.

The other change that came about following the assassination of Kevin O'Higgins was that legislation was enacted to force Fianna Fáil into the Dáil. The Electoral Amended Act meant that candidates for the Dáil or Seanad (Senate) would have to swear that, if elected, they would take the Oath of Allegiance. As a result, on 11 August Fianna Fáil deputies entered the Dáil. Kathleen did not want to take the Oath, but she was persuaded and reluctantly agreed to do so 'in the best interests of Ireland'.[9] In the September 1927 election that followed, she lost her seat. The following year she was elected as one of six Fianna Fáil senators to the Free State Seanad. De Valera had asked her to step aside for Mrs Pearse, but she refused; she felt that he was testing her to see if she was 'the pliable type'. Kathleen got enough votes to be elected to the Seanad for the maximum period of time, nine years.

Agnes Mallin's respite from illness following her operation was short-lived. It was not possible to operate again and she was told that she would need bed rest for a year. In the autumn of 1927 she was being cared for by a Miss Balfe on Strand Street in Skerries, hoping that the curative powers of the sea air would restore her. It was where she and Michael had spent their holidays in the early years of their marriage. In September 1927 she wrote that she 'would be there some time'. The network of Republican women came to her aid. Úna Stack[10] took in Joe and Maura to live with her for a period and it was these women who arranged for Agnes eventually to be back at home, with a woman who had worked in St Enda's School coming to care for her.

Eleven-year-old Maura was also her mother's carer; she did not go to school, but Margaret Pearse tutored her. At the time of Agnes's second illness, her elder daughter, Úna, also refused to return to finish her schooling in Mayo, where she had been since she was eight years old. Instead she went to the Loreto Convent in Bray, County Wicklow, a train journey away from Dublin City and her mother. There Úna excelled in her studies, particularly in music. Joe, at St Enda's, was also a talented musician, a fluent Irish speaker and outstanding at Gaelic Games.

In 1927 Agnes's second son, Seán, left school in Carlow and joined the Jesuits, beginning his training at Tullabeg, Rahan, in County Offaly. It was Joseph whom his father had asked to enter into religious life, writing: 'be a priest if you can.' In his last letter Michael had also written to Agnes: 'if you can I would like you to dedicate Úna to the service of God'.[11] He had believed that if two of their children were in religious life, they could help him in the afterlife; in his final hours he wrote: 'so that we may have 2 to rest on as penance for our sins and try and do this if you can pray to our Divine Lord it may be so.'[12] While she was finishing her education at the Loreto Convent in Bray, Úna Mallin took the decision to enter the order, and she eventually left Ireland to undertake her novitiate. She travelled to Castilleja de la Cuesta, just outside Seville in Spain, where a community of Irish Loreto nuns had recently established a school and convent with the mission to help 'disadvantaged women and children'.

Agnes continued to suffer. In October 1928 she wrote to the

minister of pensions that the 'very serious illness which I suffered and which still affects me considerably is a direct result of 1916' and she pointed out that she was 'the only widow of all of the executed leaders of Easter week not in receipt of an increased pension.'[13] She visited W. T. Cosgrave in her quest for more money, and she asked him why she was considered a lesser widow, less worthy because Michael had not been part of the Provisional Government of the Irish Republic. The circumstances of her widowhood were outlined: she had no private income and had been totally dependent on Michael; she was the mother of five, the eldest aged twelve when her husband died. Furthermore, her subsequent physical problems meant that she was unable to work. The reply she received stated that section 4 (2) made provision for the dependants of those who had signed the Proclamation; due to the wording of the Act, there was no power to increase Agnes's allowance.

The economic depression that followed the Wall Street Crash affected Ireland badly: agricultural exports declined, factories closed and there was widespread unemployment. Work was particularly hard to find for those who, like Seamus Mallin, had opposed the state and been imprisoned. After he qualified as an engineer, unable to find employment in Ireland, Seamus went to Venezuela in search of work. Before his departure, he made an appeal to a member of the Dáil that his family's omission from the pension award would be reviewed. On 9 March 1929, Dr James Ryan replied to him that, despite the family's arguments, the pension 'cannot be granted'. Education costs were allowable, but when Agnes wrote asking for additional funding for books, travel and maintenance, she was refused.

After Seamus went to Venezuela, Agnes was admitted to hospital in Dún Laoghaire. She was now permanently bedridden, as she described when she wrote once more to the officials. As time passed her pleas became more desperate and she wrote over and over again: 'Please let me have the cheque . . . I am ill and want the money.'[14]

Joe was still boarding at St Enda's and Maura joined him there again for a while, before being sent to Bray where her sister had been at school. Maura said she always regretted being away from her mother when she was in Bray in 1929, for during that three-month period Agnes was left without any of her children. Maura insisted she be transferred as a day pupil to the new Loreto Convent in Crumlin when it opened in 1930 and she was one of the first pupils at that school.

Harassment of known Republican families continued in the post-Civil War period. Roebuck House was raided frequently. Maud wrote to a friend in December 1928: 'Yesterday morning I was awoken by a man in a trench coat and clutching a gun and crawling under my bed.'[15] Seán was never recorded as being present during these raids; he was constantly on the move. In 1929 he was arrested again, along with five other men, in Pallas, County Offaly. He was held in Mountjoy Jail for six months before being tried under the Treasonable Offences Act. He defended himself and the jury found all six men not guilty. Around the same time, following suspicions of jury intimidation, a Juries Protection Act was passed.

By the early 1930s Seán MacBride was adjutant general of the IRA and was recorded in this period by the authorities as their travelling organizer. He was arrested again in Kerry in 1931 and accused of illegal drilling, but the judge deemed him and his fellow accused to have 'been too far away from the drilling party to be guilty of the charge.'[16]

Despite her advancing years, Maud continued to organize meetings and parades and street painting, as part of the Political Prisoners Committee, to highlight conditions for those in jail. She also arranged and took part in deputations to Dublin Corporation and the Red Cross. She produced and distributed lists of Republican prisoners and prisoners-of-war, writing in one pamphlet in July 1930: 'Even long term prisoners are made to exercise in silence, six feet apart, round and round the asphalt rings behind high walls . . . The awful prison monotony injures the brains of a number of prisoners, and every lunatic asylum in Ireland holds some of the victims of the Free State prison system.' She believed that the 'General conditions in Irish prisons are bad and antiquated. None of the prison reforms adopted in other countries have penetrated the Free State.'[17] There were no lectures or educational classes, except for those who were illiterate. Political prisoners were treated as common criminals.

In 1931 Roebuck House was raided numerous times. On the eleventh occasion that year, seventeen detectives took part in the raid, in which books, papers and furniture were damaged. Charlotte still remained living there and working for the Women's Prisoners' Defence League until it was disbanded in 1932, after which she left Dublin to live in Belfast for her final years. Maud became a grandmother again when Iseult had another baby girl, Katherine, who became known as Kay. Iseult's marriage was still troubled, as Francis had numerous affairs and lived away from her for long periods of time. Seán also often lived apart from his wife and children due to his involvement with the IRA. By 1932 he was having talks with Éamon de Valera to see if the IRA and Fianna Fáil could be united, but the talks came to nothing.

In May 1931 Agnes Mallin and fourteen-year-old Maura made the arduous trip to Spain to be there for Úna's profession. Arrangements were made for them by Margaret Pearse, and entailed taking a boat to Holyhead, followed by a train to London and then a boat to Gibraltar, from where they went on to Seville. Agnes recorded their trip, noting that she found it frightening. When they finally arrived in the convent in Spain, she wrote: 'I entered our room – someone said Mamie, Mamie [*sic*] – and next I was in the arms of dear Una – then I felt overcome – I cried so much the Nuns brought some wine.'[18] On her profession, Úna became Sister Agnes. During this visit, her mother fell in the garden of the convent and was so immobilized that for the boat trip back she had to be confined to bed. Maura knew that it was 'all happening over again.' The exertion of this trip accelerated Agnes's decline.

Once home she was confined to her bed again in Dún Laoghaire.

She wrote: 'I fear the night . . . Everyone here is very kind here. Very kind yet it is my head that is the trouble.' She was suffering with pressure in her head that made her feel 'weak and very strange'. She prayed that she would get well again, writing in August 1931: 'I Know God will leave [me] with you all.' Later she wrote: 'If God takes me from you my Own Darling Children (which I pray and hope he won't) please don't fret. God will mind you all. My own heart's pulse Maura . . .'[19]

In the summer of 1931 Agnes was moved from Dún Laoghaire to the Meath Hospital. She wrote how foolish she had been to have worked as hard as she did and her diary records that she would give any worldly thing to regain her health: 'When God restores me to health I will indeed be a different person.' Seamus had wanted her to go to the south of France, but she had refused and now she regretted this: 'it might have saved me this. It might not. God alone knows.'[20] On another day she wrote that she was having nightmares, including one that she was dying and that Seamus was there: 'I put out my arms to him'. But of course she knew he was not there. Once she was overheard saying she knew she would never see her eldest son again.

By autumn 1932 it was clear that Agnes Mallin was dying. Joe had now left school and spent time at home as his mother's companion and helper. When it became clear she had only weeks to live, her second son, Seán, who was still a novice at St Stanislaus College in Tullabeg, County Offaly, also came home to 86 South Circular Road to be with her as the end drew near during the last days of September. He slept on a chair in her room and remained there for her final days.

On the evening of 29 September Agnes died of broncho-pneumonia, with an associated illness from which, it was noted, she had suffered for seven years. She was fifty-six. She had written some time previously: 'I leave house and furniture Loyola South Circular Road to my three children Seamus, Joseph and Maura.' Úna and Seán, having entered religious life, had no need of these things. Agnes left some money in the Munster & Leinster Bank, and she asked Maura to 'put it to the purpose I save it for a bungalow – the dream.'[21]

Agnes Mallin's body lay overnight in St James's Church in James' Street, Dublin. Her funeral, on 2 May in Clonsilla, was attended by representatives from the Irish Republican Army, Cumann na mBan, Clann na nGaedheal (Girl Scouts), Citizen Army veterans, and the Workers' Union of Ireland, as well as from the Loreto Convent at Crumlin and St Enda's School. The coffin, draped in a tricolour used by the Irish Citizen Army in 1916, was carried to the grave by members of the Citizen Army and other 1916 veterans. Two of her children were not there: Seamus, in exile in South America, could not be contacted, and Úna, as she was in an enclosed order, was not allowed home.

A new Army Pension Act came into being in December 1932. Its announcement brought an application from an unlikely source: Maud applied for monies as John's widow. When her claim was processed in 1933, the attorney general stated that the late application did not affect the award. Maud's separation was not raised as an issue and the pension was granted. In 1938 she was given an increased allowance as per the Pensions Act, 1937.[22]

In the years following her release from prison in 1923, Grace had stayed apolitical. She continued to work as an artist and two volumes of her work were published in 1929 and 1930. She always struggled with money. In filling out her form for pension entitlements, she wrote to Irish Free State officials that she was prepared to emigrate to London in a few weeks unless she received a pension. In 1924 she was eventually awarded £90 a year, which she protested was half that given to the widows of the other leaders of the Rising. Her complaint prompted the response from the board that £90 was the maximum allowable to the widow of an officer, but Grace expressed dissatisfaction that her pension was less than that received by the children of Arthur Griffith. She wrote that her husband would have been president or a minister had he not been executed and the pension she was receiving was an insult to the seven signatories, including her husband.[23]

When her mother Isabella Gifford died on 15 January 1932 Grace was excluded from her will, as were her sisters Nellie and Sidney. Isabella's reason cannot just have been their politics, as Katie was a beneficiary. The Gifford siblings living outside Ireland – Ada, Claude, Liebert and Edward Cecil – all received an inheritance. Gabriel was excluded, as he had been in his father's will; his mother stated that he had got his inheritance before going to America. Grace's twin, Edward, known by his second name Cecil, had kept in touch with his mother. He had enlisted in the US Army in Michigan in 1917 during the First World War, a year after the Rising, as part of the Medical Corps. After his discharge in 1919 he worked as a cook, then enlisted again in 1921, only to be discharged again as the army was reducing numbers. Suffering from poor health, he was immediately accepted at the Grand Rapids Veterans Home in Michigan, although his ailments were not combat-related, and he died there, aged forty-four, in December 1932.[24]

During the 1920s and into the 1930s Grace had been trying to get her share of Joe's money and also a statement of accounts for the Plunkett estate. Joe had made a will, but it was pre-nuptial and only had one witness to the signature. Grace decided to take Count and Countess Plunkett to court and appointed a Mr Rice as her senior counsel, but eventually the Plunketts decided to settle out of court.[25] The estate was heavily encumbered, and Grace was awarded just £700. The judge, Justice Johnston, observed: 'I am very glad that the Countess has seen her way to take over these assets and pay off this young woman.'[26] By then the 'young woman' was in fact forty-seven years of age.

Éamon de Valera returned to power following the 1932 general election, which saw Fianna Fáil overtaking Cumann na nGaedheal. During his time in office, as well as being president of the Executive Council, he also took on the external affairs portfolio and set about dismantling some of the terms of the Treaty agreed a decade earlier. In 1933, de Valera removed the Oath of Allegiance, and in 1936, following the abdication of King Edward VIII, the

Constitutional Amendment Act removed the role of the monarch in domestic matters, at the same time reducing the role of governor general, the representative of the monarch in Ireland. The External Relations Act left Ireland with two heads of state – a president in domestic matters and the British monarch in foreign affairs. That year de Valera also abolished the Senate. Kathleen noted that 'I was out of the only paid job I ever got.'[27] She also commented that, of the six Fianna Fáil senators, all were given paid positions except her.

Bunreacht na hÉireann, the constitution of Ireland, was adopted by referendum on 1 July 1937. It replaced the Free State Constitution of 1922 (part of the Treaty settlement) and the Irish Free State became known as Éire. The new constitution was criticized as being limiting to the rights of women, with article 41.2, which made reference to the woman's 'life within the home', considered particularly unacceptable. Despite objections, de Valera refused to remove it. Kathleen wrote of it: 'I think it is up to every Irish woman to see that no man or group of men rob us of our status enshrined in the Proclamation.' In protest, she resigned from the local Fianna Fáil Cumann – the Tom Clarke Cumann, named after her husband – although she did not resign from the Fianna Fáil executive. She continued to attend the executive meetings but, as she recounted, she was not very popular as she asked lots of questions.

The IRA was declared an illegal organization in June 1936, during Seán MacBride's time as its chief of staff. His period in this position was fraught with difficulties and he was replaced, then later resigned because he disagreed with the IRA's bombing campaign in England. He resumed his legal studies and was admitted to the Bar in November 1937. From then on he represented Republicans without asking monetary compensation.

Over the years, Lillie Connolly had kept in contact with the poor of Pimlico, the area in the Liberties where she had lived in the harshest of conditions. Her 'new found comfort' did not lead her to forget 'her own struggles of former years.' Her grandson Seamus remembered her: 'She had a great sense of charity and wanted to repay the debt.'[28]

During the 1930s Lillie watched the changing fortunes of her large extended family. Nora and her husband Seamus did not have a family; they remained interested in politics and worked with the Labour Party.[29] Ina had married Archie Heron, whom she had known since the days in Belfast when he had been in the Fianna. They worked in England in these years and had a son, Seamus, born in 1921. Aideen had married Hugh Francis Ward in 1919 and moved to County Kildare; she had three daughters and a son and, as always, remained outside politics. By 1937 both Moira and Fiona were living in England. Moira was a doctor and had married Richard Clyde Beech. Fiona became Mrs Deegan; she later remarried and had a son, Roderic Wilson.

Roddy's wife, Jessica, died prematurely in 1930 as a result of septicaemia following an operation. Their two sons, Seamus, then aged seven, and Ross, aged three, came to live with Lillie. Roddy was still active in a number of political movements. By 1934 he was involved in the Labour League Against Fascism, and the following year he was central to the establishment of the Republican Congress, which advocated that 'a Republic of a united Ireland will never be achieved except through a struggle which uproots capitalism on its way.' He was arrested in January 1935 and imprisoned for protesting against a company union at O'Mara's bacon shops in Dublin and their employing of 'scab labour'. While in jail Roddy organized political lectures. Arrested again later the same year at a protest over the sacking of a tram-worker, he argued for the formation of an 'Irish labour defence league'.

Roddy got married again, on 27 December 1937, to schoolteacher Peggy Stafford, who was ten years his junior. The ceremony took place in her native Glasgow,[30] but Lillie was unable to attend, as by this time she was bedridden. Her last public event, towards the end of 1937, had been a children's dancing festival organized by the Labour Youth Movement.

Lillie Connolly died on 22 January 1938. She was seventy-one years old. The *Irish Times* said of her: 'Throughout her life the late Mrs Connolly appeared but rarely in public. She was of the most retiring and modest disposition, home-loving and devoted to the welfare of her family.'[31] She was given a state funeral, with her cortege led by members of the Workers' Union Band and two hundred veterans of the Irish Citizen Army. Her love of children was reflected by a wreath simply inscribed 'from the children of Belgrave Square'.

During the 1930s Maud had been writing her memoirs, which were finally published by Gollancz in 1938. *A Servant of the Queen* covered her life story up to 1904. She was planning a second volume, but it was never published. The autobiography was part fictionalized in order to protect the identity of her father's lover, Margaret. Even as Maud wrote this story, Margaret was still alive and still in exile. She died on 24 June 1939, aged seventy-five, at Kalli Jarv and was buried in Charlottenhof (now Aegviidu) Cemetery in Estonia.

Willie Yeats died the same year in Menton, France, and was buried abroad due to the political situation in Europe, although his body was brought back to County Sligo some years later.

In 1939 Kathleen Clarke became the first female mayor of Dublin. Her first action was to remove the royal portraits from the Mansion House, including one of Queen Victoria: 'I felt that I could not sleep in the house until she was out of it.'[32] She refused to wear the mayor's chain, as it had been presented to the city by William of Orange. Just as she assumed office the Fianna Fáil government introduced the Offences Against the State Act. Kathleen never compromised her Republican stance and clashed with the Fianna Fáil party over the draconian new legislation. A change of leadership in the IRA meant that a new phase of activity began, with a bombing campaign in Britain. Kathleen was the leader of an unsuccessful campaign to reprieve Peter Barnes and James McCormack, IRA members responsible for a bombing in Coventry, but all representations failed and they were hanged in England on 8 February 1940.

That same spring, six IRA activists began a hunger strike when one of their members was put into the criminal section of Mountjoy Jail. Jack Plunkett, Joe's brother, was one of those who went on strike. Kathleen wrote to Éamon de Valera opposing his handling of the affair, pointing out: 'had a little tact and common sense been used, the cause for the hunger-strike would not have arisen . . .'[33] De Valera replied to her: 'The Government regrets that men should lose their lives on hunger-strike. They do not will the death of anybody, but they have a public duty to perform and they must perform it or allow indiscipline and disorder so to grow that it might eventuate in serious bloodshed and, in the critical position of the present day, lead perhaps to the loss of what the community has so far achieved by great effort and great sacrifice.'[34]

As the strike entered its fifty-fourth day, Tony Darcy from Galway died, while Jack McNeela from Mayo lasted only one day longer, dying on 19 April.

Seán MacBride represented McNeela's family at the inquest, where he told Gerry Boland, minister of justice, that he was placed 'in the dock as far as the Irish people were concerned.' Later Boland described this encounter as 'one of the worst experiences I have ever had.'[35]

During the Second World War, known in Ireland as 'The Emergency', the country remained neutral. Several German agents landed in Ireland and in May 1940 Iseult was arrested for assisting a German, Herman Görtz, who had parachuted into the country. Earlier he had met with her husband, who was lecturing in Berlin, and Francis Stuart had given him Iseult's address. She was found not guilty in July. Iseult did not see her husband for another eleven years.

During the war the Irish government, fearful of a Nazi invasion, began to intern IRA members. As Francis was associated with the Nazi regime, and as Maud and her family had a close friendship with the German ambassador and his family dating from before the war started, suspicion naturally fell on Seán. At this point he was taken in for questioning and found to have incriminating material in his possession, but he was not detained. The authorities got assurances from him that he would not become involved with the Germans. Ultimately, the expected Nazi invasion of Ireland did not take place.

Seán continued as legal counsel representing Republicans in cases being tried in the new military courts operating under the Emergency Powers (Amendment) No. 2 Act. He failed to save Patrick McGrath, an IRA member sentenced to death for killing a policeman. Kathleen also opposed this execution and pleaded for mercy for McGrath. On the day of his execution she ordered that all the blinds in the Mansion House be lowered and that its flag fly at half-mast. As she later wrote: 'as a member of the government's political organisation this was a dreadful thing to do, but then I had to do what I thought was right.'[36]

Year on year, the deaths continued, some by execution, some by hunger strike. In 1946 Maud wrote about one hunger striker, Seán McCaughey, to the editor of the *Irish Times*: 'Those unable to serve can *demand* nothing; therefore, I, who am almost 80 and bedridden, make my *last* request . . . I make it to the people of Ireland and to the Government: Let no more young lives be sacrificed to uphold an old British rule of Victorian origin; be speedier than death in releasing the young McCaughey . . .'[37]

Seán McCaughey, an IRA activist from Northern Ireland, had been held in solitary confinement for three of his five years in Portlaoise Prison. He had been showing signs of 'nervous strain' and 'paranoia.'[38] This had been his punishment for refusing to wear prison uniform, instead just wearing blankets. McCaughey eventually went on a hunger and thirst strike, but the government still refused to grant him political status. He died on 11 May 1946. At the inquest, Maud recorded that Seán MacBride was able to get the prison doctor to admit that he would not 'treat a dog as the prisoners had been treated.' In the strange interconnected web of the Easter widows, Maud wrote to Muriel and Thomas's daughter Barbara, now Mrs Redmond, reflecting back to her work in the Amnesty Association some sixty years before: 'The brave young men are getting the same terrible sentences that Tom Clarke and his comrades got last century.'[39]

Kathleen Clarke had begun to write her memoirs in 1939, fulfilling a promise to one of the priests who attended the executions, who had said, 'I think you know more than anyone alive about the Rising and all connected with it.' She wanted to tell the truth, and she was concerned that in writing what she remembered she would cause 'disillusionment'. While she wrote over the next number of years, she remained active on the boards of a number of Dublin hospitals, and in this capacity she managed to arrange the return of one of Tom's prison comrades from a mental asylum in England to spend his last years in Ireland. She was also involved with the National Graves Association, which organized the preservation of graves and monuments and the creation of new ones to honour those who had died for Ireland.

In June 1941, Kathleen announced that she would not seek re-election and resigned from Fianna Fáil. However, she entered into politics again a few years later as a candidate for Clann na Poblachta (the Republican Family), a new party established by Seán MacBride in Dublin in July 1946 on the ticket of radical reform and the abolition of partition. Seán was elected in a County Dublin by-election in October 1947, but in 1948, when Éamon de Valera called a snap election, the new party was ill prepared and fielded too many candidates. Kathleen, at the age of seventy, was one of them. She was unsuccessful, although she maintained links with the party.

Clann na Poblachta, however, managed to win ten seats and joined with other parties in the Dáil to form the Inter-Party Government to oust Fianna Fáil. Maud walked into Dáil Éireann on the arm of her son to see him take up his seat as a deputy. After the election, he became minister for external affairs. In December 1948, while he was in office, the Inter-Party Government repealed the External Relations Act and severed the country's link to the Commonwealth, and Éire became a founding member of the Council of Europe. Seán MacBride, acting on behalf of the government, refused to join the North Atlantic Treaty Organization (NATO) as long as the six counties remained a part of the United Kingdom.

Seán was also a member of the government when, on Easter Monday 1949 at the General Post Office in Dublin, the Republic of Ireland was formally proclaimed, albeit without the six counties that formed the province of Northern Ireland.

Áine Ceannt, too, continued to work for those in need, and was a founder member of the Irish Red Cross, serving as honorary treasurer of the society from its inception in 1939 until 1947. In 1941 she oversaw the closure of the Irish White Cross Children's Relief Association office on Dawson Street, but continued to work from her home. As the 1940s drew to an end, she supervised the winding up of the organization and began to write the story of its twenty-seven-year existence, published when the association finally came to a close in 1948. Its chairman, James Webb, wrote of Áine's contribution: 'One cannot imagine what the Children's Relief Association would have been without Mrs Ceannt. It would only be fair to say that SHE was the Association. We, the Council attended for an hour or so when necessary, but Mrs Ceannt was there all the time – administering, mothering, guiding and admonishing – year after year – with wisdom, knowledge and sympathy.'[40]

Grace Plunkett still worked as an artist through these years, living alone in a flat on Nassau Street next to Trinity College. She applied for a pension in her own right in 1942. Previously the amount she received had been upped to £180 a year and in 1937 to £500, a considerable sum at the time. She never remarried or had any of her own children – yet she claimed to have applied for the pension on the basis that she had nine dependants, although these were not identified. Was she claiming her sisters Nellie, Sidney and Katie, as well as her nieces Maeve and Barbara and her nephews Don and Finian? It seems unlikely to include her brother Gabriel in America, nor his only child, a daughter named Geraldine, who appears to have had little contact with her aunts in Ireland. Nor is it likely to include her sister Ada, who had no family. Grace had taken some interest in her brother Claude's son, Eric, an engineer by profession who was also an artist. He had left Ireland to study in Rome in 1920 and held a one-man show of his paintings in the Wertheim Gallery in London in 1937. After travelling extensively, he eventually ended up in Morocco working for Radio Africa.[41]

Grace's special favourite was her nephew Donagh, Muriel and Thomas's son, so perhaps in the nine she had been including his two children. Don had studied at University College Dublin, the Sorbonne in Paris and King's Inn, Dublin, before being called to the Bar in 1935. He married Maura Smyth in 1934; tragically, she drowned in her bath during an epileptic fit in 1939, leaving him with two small children, Iseult and Breifne. By 1941, Donagh was a district judge on the Western Circuit, as well as a poet and play-wright. That year, he was appointed a district justice in Wexford.

Donagh remarried in 1943, to his sister-in-law Nuala, and he had two children with her, Niall and Barbara. He had great success with his play *Happy as Larry* in post-war London and from the 1940s onwards published several volumes of poetry; he was also a popular broadcaster. His sister Barbara married the Abbey actor Liam Redmond and had four children, Helen, Dara, Muriel and Lucille.

Maeve Donnelly and Finian Czira both remained unmarried, living with their mothers. Maeve contributed to the household from her work as an assistant secretary at Arks Advertising Agency and Finian worked as a photographer and a projectionist, as well as mending film at Paramount Reuters office in Middle Abbey Street.

Grace's sisters struggled to maintain employment. Katie was involved in the National Radio Station 2RN, but lost this job, it is thought, because of her political beliefs. She eventually found work, like many Republicans, at the Hospital Commission, responsible for the Irish Sweepstakes. In her later years she also taught French in a technical school. Sidney worked as a journalist and wrote extensively on the revolutionary period, but her income was sparse and she was often in financial difficulties as she continued to support the

Women's Prisoners' Defence League and 'Save the German Children' during the war. Nellie was the secretary of a 1916 Club, and began corresponding with the Department of Education, proposing an exhibition of 1916 relics to coincide with the 31st International Eucharistic Congress, to be held in Dublin in 1932. She requested that the National Museum host the exhibition and, despite some concerns about space and finance, a small space was agreed and Nellie set about sourcing objects for display. She was completely disillusioned when, after she had done all the organization, the exhibition was taken over by the National Museum. She wrote: 'I am not required and will not even be permitted to write a book on same. Apparently, we 1916 people – the women anyhow – will not be given any encouragement.'[42]

The Military Pension Board refused Grace's application for a pension in her own right, finding that she was already in receipt of a considerable state pension: 'She realises that she has no claim and states that the only reason she put in a claim under the Act was that she had been induced . . . to do so.' The board concluded, following an interview in February 1942, that as 'a recipient of such a large pension she would not be entitled to a second pension from public funds'.[43] The same interviewer stated that 'this lady does not have any service which could be regarded as qualifying service for this act.'[44]

In 1948 Áine Ceannt buried her sisters Kit and Lily O'Brennan – tragically they both died in the same month of May, Kit on the 12th and Lily on the 31st. The only indication of Áine's grief was how she struggled to organize a gravestone for their burial place in Deansgrange Cemetery, and never succeeded in erecting it in her lifetime.[45] The loss of Lily, in particular, was grievous. She had been Áine's companion since childhood, lived with her during her marriage and in her long widowhood. Moving from Ranelagh, the sisters had spent Lily's final years living together with Rónán in Dundrum, County Dublin. Now Áine and Rónán were there alone.

In May 1949 Áine gave a lengthy Witness Statement of eighty

pages, recounting her life and her involvement in Ireland's struggle for independence, to the Military Bureau. Part of her interview was recorded and in it her voice is clear and her delivery strong. In 1937 she had applied for and received a pension of £500 per annum as the widow of one of the signatories of the Proclamation, which was made tax-free under the 1949 Act.

However, when Áine became eligible to apply for a pension based on her own contribution, her interview with the official from the Department of Defence was unsuccessful. She felt her answers had not reflected her role, so afterwards her son Rónán contacted the office with a detailed statement of his mother's activities, explaining that she had not seen herself as being involved in 'military' work, rather in 'political' work. Following the submission of her own contribution from the Rising onwards, however, she was granted a pension 'for full service to September 1923'. This was most welcome extra money, but by the start of the new year in 1952 she had received nothing and it was causing her some anxiety. She had become ill in those last months, so a friend of the family wrote asking for the pension to be processed quickly, but to no avail.

Áine Ceannt died in February 1952. Afterwards Rónán wrote to the Department of Defence saying: 'on her death bed she was troubled in her mind' and he described how she referred to the non-payment of this pension several times 'shortly before she lapsed into unconsciousness preceding her death'. To her son in his bereavement, it seemed a 'discourtesy to her'. The official reply was that the required notification had not come from revenue, and the anonymous Civil Servant wrote: 'it is very much regretted that the amount in question could not have been released.'[46]

Following his mother's death, Rónán suffered greatly in his bereavement, and wrote to Máire Walker, better known by her stage name Máire Nic Shiubhlaigh, who had been out in the Rising in Jacob's Factory with Thomas MacDonagh and John MacBride. She had known his mother from the time they had been in Cumann na mBan together and they had remained friends. Rónán wrote on the black-bordered mourning paper:

Maire, from time to time, for years past, I wonder if mamy [*sic*] was, in a way, disappointed in me for not having shown myself as fine a man as my father was. I had never had the courage to ask mamy and she never gave me any special reason for my idea, but, yet, she may, deep down, have felt I was a bit of a failure. I'd rather know the answer to that question than be kept in ignorance, so if mamy ever spoke of the matter, will you please tell me what [she] said even if it's hard to hear? Please remember I am not looking for words of praise and suchlike but just to be told the truth. Whilst I haven't exactly got an 'inferior complex', at the same time I have no great sense of my own importance and it won't do me any harm to know the truth . . . Therefore, it might have seemed to hear that my lack of forcefulness etc, as compared with my father's courage was a bit of a 'let-down', shall we say. Anyhow, tell me, if you know . . .[47]

It is undocumented how Máire responded to him, but his mother had written in her last will and testament: 'to my devoted son – my blessing and thanks for all his goodness to me.'

When Rónán was ten years old, his father's last words to him when he left him that day in Dolphin's Barn were 'Look after your mother.' The solicitor, who never married, lived for the next thirty-six years doing just that, being the man of the house. Now, at forty-six, he was alone in the world.

In 1952 Maud, in her eighty-sixth year, was dying. She had suffered on and off with TB, which had taken her mother, grandmother and sister – but she lived on into old age, outliving Willie Yeats and Joseph MacBride (who had died on 1 January 1938), although Eileen was still living in Mayo.

Knowing that his mother would soon pass away, Seán asked his sister Iseult, who had been suffering ill health herself, to come and stay at Roebuck with them as the end drew near. She and her mother would talk endlessly of the past, Maud in her bed while Iseult sat on the old rocking chair beside her. Iseult was always in a haze of cigarette smoke. In a surviving letter written to Maud in 1952, Iseult talked of John MacBride:

> My Lady Heart, These days, you live so much in the past and close
> to the people that you knew in the old days, that it is important to
> help you to retain a clear image of them . . . Even John MacBride, I
> am able to see now as someone rather pathetic because you were so
> much the wrong person for him and his whole life became cast in the
> wrong mould for him. He was physically brave but in other ways a
> very weak character. He wasn't a good man, but in different circum-
> stances and with different people he might have been . . .[48]

Maud died with her family around her on 27 April 1953. One of
her last acts was to ask for Georges's bootees. She held them at the
end, and they were placed in her coffin. Within the year, Iseult herself would be dead.

Following Maud's death, of the seven widows only Grace and
Kathleen remained. Throughout the 1940s Grace had been unwell
with heart problems. Those who remember her say she was gaunt
and frail, but she tried to keep working and continued to draw.
Grace Plunkett died alone on 13 December 1955, aged sixty-seven,
in a flat in South Richmond Street, where she had moved a short
time before. Grace, who had stayed away from direct involvement in
military activities, was given a burial with full military honours, the
coffin draped with the tricolour and the Irish Army firing shots over
her grave. She was buried as Joe's widow and, despite the strain with
her in-laws over her entitlement to the family money, she is interred
as a Plunkett, in the family plot in Glasnevin Cemetery.

Donagh MacDonagh wrote of his aunt in the *Irish Press*, saying
how one of his memories of his childhood in Clare was hearing a
ballad: 'I loved Joe Plunkett and he loved me. He gave his life to set
Ireland free.' It was not the first or the last song written about Grace,
but in 1955 her nephew wrote: 'What Ireland will remember longest
is the scene at Kilmainham prison where she married, by the light of
two guttering candles, the young man who was to be executed in a

few hours . . . Now she is dead but as long as Ireland has a history she will be remembered.'

Now Kathleen was the final widow living. At the age of eighty-eight, she attended the government commemoration on the fiftieth anniversary of the Easter Rising in 1966 and was conferred with an honorary degree of laws by Éamon de Valera in his role as chancellor of the National University of Ireland. He was also at this time president of Ireland. In 1967 Kathleen opened a Fenian exhibit in Kilmainham Jail, which was being set up as a museum to honour the memory of those who had been executed there in 1916.

From the mid-1960s onwards Kathleen spent extended periods staying in Liverpool, where Emmet, her youngest son, lived. Emmet, who had recovered from the brain injury caused by the accident with the military car during the Civil War, had become a doctor of medicine in 1950. He attained a diploma in psychological medicine in 1957 and worked as a consultant psychiatrist. He married a Mayo woman, Ellen Mullaney, whom he had met in England. They married in Dublin in April 1955. Emmet was the only one of Kathleen's three sons to have children – Edward Emmet James Clarke, born in 1957, and Thomas John Daly Clarke, born in 1958.

Kathleen lived long enough to see the 'disturbances in 1969' in Northern Ireland turn into what became known simply as 'the Troubles'. In her autobiography she had written that she was 'left with one hope, that the bitterness resulting from the difference of opinion on the question of the Treaty' would be allowed to die and that Irish men and women would 'stand together as unbreakable on the abolition of partition of our country and the complete freedom from foreign domination of our thirty-two counties, as they did before the Treaty split them.'[49]

Kathleen was interviewed that summer by William J. Heaney of the *Nenagh Guardian*.[50] When asked if she would like to live her life over again, she simply replied that she 'wouldn't like to go through all the sorrow again', but she went on: 'I've never regretted marrying Tom Clarke. He wanted the Rising, and even though I knew it meant tragedy I worked with him.' The pain of her bereavement was still strong, even after fifty-three years; when the interviewer asked her what had happened after the Rising, her answer was simply: 'I lost a baby, that's the first thing I did.'

She was described in the article as 'astonishingly agile' and, despite being almost totally deaf, her memory for details was sharper than that of 'many a woman half her age'. Independent, she lived alone in Dollymount with her dog Sherry. She had been told by her doctor since 1968 that she was not to live alone, and she spent a lot of time in Liverpool with Emmet and his family, but would not give up her Dublin home: 'I come and go and stay as long as I like.' The Clarkes' shops were long gone and Kathleen struggled to live on her 'tiny' pension. She described herself as 'still working', making all her own clothes as she had done since the age of twelve. Needlework and writing occupied her time. Her focus was to get her book of 'her recollections' published.

In 1971 Emmet got a call from a Dublin nursing home to tell him his ninety-three-year-old mother was dying. Kathleen's daughter-in-law Ellen travelled over immediately. As a nurse, Ellen recognized the cause as starvation.[51] Ellen nursed her back to health. As soon as she was well enough she brought Kathleen and her dog Sherry with her to England, and she remained living in Liverpool.

In August 1971 Kathleen read about the introduction of internment without trial in Northern Ireland; and, on 30 January 1972, following the anti-internment march organized by the Northern Ireland Civil Rights Association, thirteen men died at the scene in Derry's Bogside. There were many other casualties that day, one of whom subsequently died from wounds. Kathleen's grandson Emmet remembers that she was sad but not surprised by this new Bloody Sunday.[52]

Kathleen was given life membership of the Irish Centre in Liverpool and went there quite often to meet with people from home, but she was not to live long. Kathleen Clarke died at 'the home of Dr Emmet E. Clarke' on 29 September 1972, at the age of ninety-four. Her body was brought back to Ireland and she was given a state funeral in the Pro-Cathedral, Dublin, on 3 October. She is not buried with Tom, but on the other side of the city in Deansgrange Cemetery. There is no list of her achievements on her headstone; instead, on it is written in the Irish language: Chaitlin Ui Chleirigh, Baintreach, Tomáis S Uí Cléirigh, a básaíodh i mBaile Átha Cliath, Bealtaine 3 1916 [Kathleen Clarke, widow, Thomas J Clarke, died in Dublin, 3 May 1916].

And so in death, as in life, Kathleen wanted her memory to be linked with Tom's. It is said that she did not like to be called Kathleen Clarke, preferring to be referred to as Mrs Tom Clarke. For her long widowhood of over fifty years, her focus had been on preserving his memory and legacy. To the end she never wavered in her claim that he was President of the Irish Republic proclaimed at noon on Easter Monday, 24 April 1916.

Epilogue
The Heroic One

Father Joe Mallin only once saw his mother cry. It was sometime in the early 1920s. He remembered one day coming upon her silently weeping while washing at the sink. He recalled that it was a bright day and that it must have been a May morning, the anniversary of his father's execution on the eighth day of the month. He remembered leaving the room without being noticed to tell his younger sister Maura that their mother was crying. They did not disturb her.

Agnes never talked to them about their father's execution. Joe said she 'didn't want a dark and sad shadow hanging over their lives, that they would have as normal a family life as possible.'[1] Years later, Maura would remark on this, telling me that her mother never cried; she would just sigh. She never shared her sadness with them. 'She was too good for that,' Maura would say.

I have been writing this book, on and off, for twenty years now. I could not have completed it without the recently released Witness Statements and the Military Pension Archives, which gave validity to the upset that Maura felt about how the state treated her mother. Because her father had not signed the Proclamation as a member of the Provisional Government of the Irish Republic, his family was left in dire poverty, and she believed this also contributed to her mother's early death.

As Maura told me many times in the last years of her life, 'I always thought that my mother was the heroic one; she was the one left behind'.

Author's Note

When I first heard some of the stories of the 'Easter Widows' in the early 1990s, I could scarcely believe them: they sounded like fiction rather than fact. At first I was not sure this story could be written. Did the documentation survive? Was there enough first-hand material to tell it using the women's own words?

In 1994, I was told that Rónán, son of Áine Ceannt, had accidentally burned all the family papers that he intended to bring to the National Library of Ireland (NLI). I believed the material was lost until, about twelve years later, a student brought my attention to a listing that had just appeared on the NLI's website. It was Collection List No. 97, compiled by Dr Brian Kirby, in association with the National Committee for History, and was described as 'a collection of the political and personal papers of Éamonn Ceannt, of his wife Áine and of her two sisters Lily and Kathleen O'Brennan'. This collection contained the letters and information to tell their story.

The Tom and Kathleen Clarke archive came up for sale in 2006. I was able to examine the entire archive before it was sold, as I wrote the overview essay for the Adams Auction Rooms catalogue. I knew there had been some papers – Kathleen had said in her memoir that she just had her memory and the few documents that she had managed to preserve from military raids – but when the material came up for sale I was surprised by the extent of it, and particularly by the love letters between her and Tom. It gave me a real sense of discovery to be the first reader outside the family circle to be given access to them, albeit for the preparation of their sale. Looking at them before they got to an archive, to be reading them alongside Tom's prison letters, was a privilege. The love letters have been published, nearly in their entirety, in Gerard MacAtasney's *Tom Clarke: Life, Liberty, Revolution*, and are now preserved in the NLI. However, some of the supporting material is now dispersed for ever, as it was sold in different lots to private collectors and is therefore no longer in the public domain. The starting point for me, as for so many others, was Kathleen's memoir, *Revolutionary Woman*, published in 1991, edited by her grand-niece Helen Litton – a book which Helen aptly described as 'the voice of Kathleen Daly Clarke – forthright, outspoken and passionate . . .' Re-reading this work alongside those letters gave me a completely different look at this period, and Kathleen's voice is a key part of this book.

Lillie Connolly's story was the easiest to research, because of the wealth of material written about their upbringing by her daughters Nora and Ina. The countless works on James himself, while invaluable, proved very difficult to condense into a 'romance' chapter. Retired Brigadier General James (Seamus) Connolly, Lillie's grandson, was so helpful with his family stories; even as I write this, I wish I could do more research following our recent conversations.

The holdings for Thomas and Muriel MacDonagh are substantial, and the NLI holds the first-hand material needed to tell their story, placed there by their descendants. These papers facilitated my research into their lives, alongside the literary biographies of Thomas MacDonagh, which gave a lot of useful information.

The NLI was also a treasure house for Grace Gifford. Her love letters from Joe Plunkett are among their holdings, as well as Grace's wonderful scrapbook, in which she records and corrects much of the misinformation about her wedding (debunking some of the stories and, alas, some of the famous song lyrics). Joe's grand-niece Honor Ó Brolcháin has done wonderful work on her grandmother's papers and, together with the Plunkett family archive, was another key source for this book, as was Anne Clare's book *Unlikely Rebels*, based on Nellie Gifford Donnelly's papers.

Maud Gonne MacBride, John MacBride and their son Seán MacBride have all had biographies written about them. There are volumes of letters between Maud and W. B. Yeats, and also between her daughter Iseult and the poet; Maud's granddaughter Anna MacBride White gave me access to her family papers and to images I have been so grateful to have been able to utilize here. The Fred Allen papers in the NLI were a wonderful source for John's voice. I regret not being able to access Emory University's collection of Maud's papers on the divorce – but again the challenge was to keep their 'romance' chapter to a manageable length.

Over the years I met the children of these women – Dr Emmet Clarke, Maura Phillips and Father Joseph Mallin, and so many of their grandchildren. I was given access to the Mallin papers, Agnes Mallin's diaries and Michael's love letters to her, which allowed their story to be told for the first time. I am very grateful for the trust placed in me by the Mallin and Phillips families.

Over time I was given access to precious family papers, photographs and personal recollections not to be found elsewhere. During those years they also gave me their friendship, they showed an interest in my family. Sadly, most of them have passed away over the last two decades without seeing my completed work.

It is unbelievable to me that Joe Mallin, the curly-haired toddler described in his father's last letter as 'my little man, my little man', the child of whom he wrote with anguish in his final hours 'I cannot keep the tears back when I think that he will rest in my arms no more', is the same person who has lived to read my words, my take on his story. People talk about living history – I have been fortunate enough to be able to have that experience. Thank you to all those descendants who let me do just that.

Mayo, August 2014

Notes

For publication details of books and articles listed in these notes, see Bibliography, page 417.

Throughout the notes, the following abbreviations are used for writers and recipients of letters:

AH/AM	Agnes Hickey/Mallin
AO'B/AC	Áine (Fanny) O'Brennan/Ceannt
EC	Éamonn Ceannt
GG/GP	Grace Gifford/Plunkett
JC	James Connolly
JM	John MacBride
JP	Joe Plunkett
KD/KC	Kathleen Daly/Clarke
LR/LC	Lillie Reynolds/Connolly
MG/MMD	Muriel Gifford/MacDonagh
MGM	Maud Gonne MacBride
MM	Michael Mallin
TC	Tom Clarke
TM	Thomas MacDonagh
WBY	William Butler Yeats

The abbreviation NLI is used for the National Library of Ireland.

Notes for Chapter 1

Details of the lives of Tom and Kathleen Clarke (*née* Daly) are primarily taken from the following sources: Kathleen Clarke, *Revolutionary Woman, 1878–1972: An Autobiography* (ed. Helen Litton); Thomas J. Clarke, *Glimpses of an Irish Felon's Prison Life*; Louis Le Roux, *Tom Clarke and the Irish Freedom Movement*; Gerard MacAtasney, *Tom Clarke: Life, Liberty, Revolution*. Other details are drawn from letters and papers in the Tom and Kathleen Clarke papers, NLI; and in Sinéad McCoole, *The Thomas Clarke Archive*, contained in the Independence Catalogue, seen by the author in its entirety before being included in the 'Independence Sale', Adam's Auction House, Dublin, 19 April 2006.

1   Kathleen Clarke, *Revolutionary Woman, 1878–1972: An Autobiography*, (ed. Helen Litton), p. 24.

2   An Amnesty Association was founded in 1869 to campaign for the release of Fenian prisoners held since the failed rebellion of 1867. In the 1890s it was revived in Ireland and a branch was also established in Liverpool in 1892 as the Amnesty Association of Great Britain.

3   Helen Litton, *16Lives: Edward Daly*, pp. 14–15.

4   Edward Daly married Catherine O'Mara of Ballingarry, County Limerick, in January 1873. Litton, op. cit., p. 18.

5   Kathleen Clarke, op. cit., p. 19.

6   Ibid.

7   Ibid.

8   Thomas J. Clarke, *Glimpses of an Irish Felon's Prison Life*, pp. 4–5.

9   Thomas Clarke Archive.

10   Thomas J. Clarke, op. cit., p. 2.

11   Thomas Clarke Archive.

12   Thomas J. Clarke, op. cit., p. 62.

13   www.carrigallen.com contains information on James Clarke of Errew, Carrigallen, Co. Leitrim. James's place of origin is given incorrectly as Galway in P. S. O'Hegarty's introduction to *An Irish Felon's Prison Life*. According to the 1840s OS map of the village of Clonmel, at the time when James served there was a military barracks in the village itself; it is not clear, however, whether the jail at which Michael Palmer was employed was in Clogheen or Clonmel. Le Roux, *Tom Clarke and the Irish Freedom Movement*, states that when James was transferred back to England he was posted to Hurst Park and that this is where Tom was born, but two documents in the Thomas Clarke Archive refer to Tom's birthplace as Hurst Castle.

14   Census of Ireland 1911 stated that she had had eight children, four of whom were living. The author has surmised that they were born in Natal (no documentation sourced), given the gap between the birth of her first children in 1858 and 1859 and the two children born in Ireland after 1865.

15   When he retired he was admitted as an Out Pensioner of the Royal Hospital, Chelsea. His Chelsea Pension Certificate, 23 March 1869, 'Independence Sale', Lot 363.

16   Thomas Clarke Archive.

17   Louis Le Roux, *Tom Clarke and the Irish Freedom Movement*, p. 23.

18   Gerard MacAtasney, *Tom Clarke: Life, Liberty, Revolution*, p. 34.

19   Thomas J. Clarke, op. cit., p. 62.

20   MacAtasney, op. cit., p. 40.

21   Thomas Clarke Archive.

22   TC to KD, 15 April 1901; quoted in MacAtasney, pp. 177–8.

23   TC to KD, 23 July 1905; ibid., p. 182.

24   TC to KD, 18 August 1905; ibid., p. 186.

25   MacAtasney, op. cit., p. 58.

26   TC to KD, 11 September 1905; quoted in MacAtasney, p.186.

27   TC to KD, 28 June 1907; ibid., p. 192.

28   TC to John Daly, 28 June 1907; ibid., pp. 61 and 192.

29   Ibid., p. 193.

30   Kathleen Clarke, op. cit., p. 33.

31   Mike McCormack, historian, Ancient Order of Hibernians, in the Brookhaven Archives, Suffolk County, New York. In June 1907 Tom talks about sending the deeds to convey the property to the Dalys. In 1909, with John Daly's agreement, he instructed James Reidy to sell the properties, but they remained unsold in 1911. Madge was paying the instalments on the mortgage. TC to James Reidy, 3 January and 16 April 1909; quoted in MacAtasney, pp. 237–9.

32   MacAtasney, op. cit., p. 62.

33   TC to James Reidy, 27 December 1907; quoted in MacAtasney, p. 257.

34   MacAtasney, op. cit., p. 65.

35   Ibid., p. 63.

36   TC to KC, 14 January 1908; quoted in MacAtasney, p. 197.

37   TC to KC, [January 1908]; ibid., pp. 198–9.

38   TC to KC, 18 January 1908; ibid., p. 202.

39   TC to KC, 5 March 1908; ibid., p. 209.

40   TC to KC, 8 February 1908; ibid., p. 205.

41   TC to KC, March 1908; ibid., p. 213.

42   TC to KC, 14 May 1908; ibid., p. 224.

43   MacAtasney, op. cit., p. 65.

44   TC to James Reidy, 3 January 1909; quoted in MacAtasney, p. 235.

45   TC to KC, March 1908; ibid., p. 213.

46 This is normally given as 1910. This information comes from his death certificate, March 2004.

47 TC to John Daly, 27 December 1910; quoted in MacAtasney, p. 243.

48 TC to Joe [McGarrity], 8 December 1913; ibid., p. 270.

49 Le Roux, op. cit., p. 120.

50 MacAtasney, op. cit, p. 84.

51 Kathleen Clarke, op. cit., p. 60.

52 Ibid., p. 71.

53 MacAtasney, op. cit., p. 72.

54 Kathleen Clarke, op. cit., p. 77.

55 Thomas Clarke Archive.

56 Kathleen Clarke, op. cit., p. 70.

Notes for Chapter 2

Details of the lives of Maud Gonne and John MacBride are primarily taken from the following sources: Nancy Cardozo, *Lucky Eyes and a High Heart: The Life of Maud Gonne*; Maud Gonne MacBride, *A Servant of the Queen*; Elizabeth Keane, *Seán MacBride: A Life*; Margaret Ward, *Maud Gonne*; interviews by the author with Anna MacBride White and from the MacBride family papers. Letters are largely quoted from A. Norman Jeffares, Anna MacBride White and Christina Bridgwater (eds), *Letters to W. B. Yeats and Ezra Pound from Iseult Gonne: A Girl That Knew All Dante Once*; Anna MacBride and A. Norman Jeffares (eds), *The Gonne–Yeats Letters, 1893–1938: 'Always Your Friend'*. Letters from Maud Gonne to Kathleen Pilcher (*née* Gonne) taken from the Conrad Balliet papers, No. 771, Box 1, Robert W. Woodruff Library, Special Collections, Emory University. Quotations from the MacBride divorce case and other details of the couple's marriage are from John MacBride's own handwritten account of his life in his Notebook and also his Draft Statement to the court; from the Transcript of Proceedings, *MacBride v MacBride*; and from 'A Handwritten Account, *MacBride v MacBride*, Observations of the Evidence of the Petitioners Witnesses', all from the Fred Allen papers, NLI MSS 29,816 to 29,821.

1 Elizabeth Coxhead, *Daughters of Erin: Five Women of the Irish Renaissance*, p. 19. While researching her book in the early 1970s, Coxhead recalled: 'I have talked with several who remembered her prime. The verdict was always the same: "The most beautiful person I ever saw."'

2 Louis Botha, Commandant General B. Viljoen, wrote to John

MacBride: 'Hereby we have much pleasure in expressing our deepest gratitude toward you and your Irish Brigade for all the military services rendered to us during the past twelve months in which we were engaged in a war against Great Britain. We appreciate very highly the assistance, which you have so sincerely rendered to us during the war. We wish you and your men a hearty farewell on your return voyage.' John MacBride's own testimony of his past life, Transcript of Proceedings, *MacBride v MacBride*.

3   Liamy MacNally, 'Major MacBride', *Mayo News*, 27 July 1910. This brother became a sheep farmer in Australia.

4   'A Handwritten Account, *MacBride v MacBride*, Observations of the Evidence of the Petitioners Witnesses'.

5   Notebook compiled by John MacBride, Fred Allen papers.

6   MGM to WBY, 25 March [1901]; Anna MacBride and A. Norman Jeffares (eds), *The Gonne–Yeats Letters, 1893–1938: 'Always Your Friend'*, p. 139.

7   Nancy Cardozo, *Lucky Eyes and a High Heart: The Life of Maud Gonne*, 1978, p. 206.

8   Records of the Holy Trinity Church, Paddington, London, accessed on www.findmypast.co.uk. She died in Tunbridge Wells. There was a curl of blond hair belonging to this baby among Maud's possessions along with her mother's letters. Information from Anna MacBride White.

9   He was appointed military attaché to the court of Emperor Franz Joseph of Austria, followed by a posting as assistant military attaché in Romania, where he was awarded a Romanian War Medal. After that he was sent to Bosnia and was awarded the Austrian War Medal. He was appointed lieutenant colonel in September 1878. In 1879, due to an injury to his foot, he was not posted abroad and lived in London during this period. According to Anna MacBride White, from family correspondence it appears that his daughters spent six years in various locations in England, until Thomas Gonne was posted to India and it was decided that they would reside in the south of France.

10   England, Wales and Scotland Census 1881, sourced via findmypast.co.uk.

11   In Maud's version of the story she claimed she was sixteen. She was actually nineteen.

12   His death certificate notes unknown fever. *The Times*, 3 December 1886, reported typhoid fever, 'a disease that has for some time past claimed many victims there. The unsanitary condition of the barracks has

for a long time been represented to the military authorities.'

13   Maud's autobiographical account was that they met in 1887 in Royat, Auvergne, in the mountains in central France, where she was taking the cure to avert the tuberculosis that had killed both her mother and her maternal grandmother. Anna MacBride White, however, suggested that she may have met him before her father died. Interview with the author, 2005.

14   This portrait was first entitled *New Pet*. It was painted in 1890 and exhibited in the Royal Hibernian Academy in 1891. Now in the collection of the National Gallery of Ireland.

15   Card from the 2nd Collection Félix Potin, undated. Author's collection.

16   They never divorced. They were photographed together as late as 1910. Margaret Ward, *Maud Gonne: A Life*, p. 16.

17   He died on 31 August, aged nineteen and a half months. Information from Anna MacBride White. She also stated that his parents were not listed on his death certificate.

18   Maud Gonne MacBride, Witness Statement 317, Bureau of Military History, 5 September 1949.

19   The baptismal certificate of Eileen Constance Wilson, baptized 10 November 1886 by Rev. Berry, St Matthias Church, Hatch Street, Dublin. Sourced on www.irishgenealogy.ie. However, there is evidence to suggest that the child's real name was Daisy. In her book Maud calls her Daphne. Daisy Wilson registered the death of Mary Anne Meredith in 1902. They were both living at Stanley House, Netley Street, Farnborough, Hampshire. If for the first number of years the child was using the name Daisy Wilson, she may be the 'Daisy Wilson, aged 4, birthplace Ireland, visitor, William and Ellen Hoar in Godalming, Surrey', Census 1891. With thanks to Paul Turnell for this research. Maud says her father never saw the child, as he was dead when 'Mrs Robbins' came out of hospital, as she was six weeks old. The baby was in fact four months old when he died. Other information in Maud's autobiography is incorrect and fictionalized.

20   Maud Gonne MacBride, *A Servant of the Queen*, pp. 49–53.

21   Tania Alexander, *A Little of All These: An Estonian Childhood*, pp. 17–18. It has been suggested that Margaret Wilson had been the Gonnes' governess. Maud, her sister and their cousin Edith M. Browning, along with Mary Ann Meredith, did attend a school run by a Margaret Wilson in Torquay, in Devon, in 1881. However, this Margaret Wilson continued to live on in Devon, as illustrated by Census entries for 1891 and 1901,

while the other Margaret Wilson was in Russia with the Zakrevsky family.

22   'Eileen Constance Wilson, 14, adopted daughter'; Census 1901, sourced at findmypast.co.uk.

23   For this and other journalism, see Karen Steele, *Maud Gonne's Irish Nationalist Writings 1895–1946.*

24   A. Norman Jeffares, Anna MacBride White and Christina Bridgwater (eds), *Letters to W. B. Yeats and Ezra Pound from Iseult Gonne: A Girl That Knew All Dante Once*, p. 7.

25   Maud says *American Sun.*

26   Later, conscious of this name in public, Iseult changed it to 'Moura', a name she continued to call Maud all her life; *Girl That Knew All Dante*, p. 9.

27   MGM to WBY, 10 February [1903], *Letters*, pp. 166–7.

28   MGM to Mme Avril, undated, NIL, MS 10,714.

29   Gonne MacBride, op. cit., pp. 318–19.

30   JM to Emmie MacBride; quoted in *Letters*, p. 167.

31   Death certificate of Mary Ann Meredith, Hartley Wintney, 1902.

32   Iseult Stuart to MGM, 1952. The year before Maud's death, Iseult wrote to her mother that 'I still can't see any good in Eileen Wilson; she still appears to me an incredibly nasty piece of goods and I can still laugh with unrepentant amusement when I rushed at her and rubbed half a pound of butter in her hair saying: Now you can get me punished without having to tell a lie about me.'; *Girl That Knew All Dante*, op. cit., pp. 156–7.

33   *Girl That Knew All Dante*, p. 13.

34   Ibid.

35   He made mention of this ring at the divorce proceedings, stating that Maud retained it.

36   Scrapbook relating to birth of Seagan MacBride, seen and noted by the author, 1994.

37   The memoir of a traveller to Westport described: 'Outside the town I saw some land and cattle and I discovered that they were the property of Joseph [MacBride] . . . In a word the MacBrides are like a basis of energy in the midst of a desert of human hopelessness.' Elsewhere he states that you could not find 'two brighter healthier, more intelligent or better looking men . . . than Joseph and his brother [Patrick]'. Michael McCarthy, *Priests and People in Ireland*, pp. 182–3.

38   Census of Ireland 1901.

39   MGM to WBY, [August/September 1902], *Letters*, p. 157.

40 In Russia, her mother was now looking after Zakrevsky's grandchildren, Paul and Titiana von Benckendorff, the two children of his youngest daughter, Moura, born in 1893. She was also looking after their cousin Kira von Englehardt. Margaret never returned to Ireland; her one-year sojourn in Russia turned into a lifetime. She corresponded with her daughter, but through all those years she never saw Eileen again.

41 MGM to WBY, [August/September 1902], *Letters*, p. 157. Maud misleadingly described it as a 'charming cottage'.

42 Information provided by Mary MacBride Walsh, grand-daughter of Eileen and Joseph, 2013.

43 Anthony J. Jordan, *The Yeats-MacBride-Gonne Triangle*, 2000, p. 52.

44 MGM to WBY, [January 1905], *Letters*, pp. 186–7.

45 Jordan, *Yeats-MacBride-Gonne Triangle*, p. 52.

46 JM to John Daly, 5 December 1903; quoted in Anthony J. Jordan, *Major John MacBride, 1865–1916*, 1991.

47 MGM to WBY; quoted in *Yeats-MacBride-Gonne Triangle*.

48 Letter R. Barry O'Brien to MGM, 1 January 1905; copy, Fred Allen papers.

49 MGM to WBY, [January 1905], *Letters*, pp. 184–7.

50 *Letters* pp. 203–4.

51 Maitre Crouppi, *Letters*, p. 191.

52 MGM to WBY [January 1905], *Letters*, pp. 189, 190 and 203.

53 'A Handwritten Account, *MacBride v MacBride*', p. 37.

54 *Letters*, p. 207.

55 Ibid., p. 204.

56 She later changed her name to O'Delaney to sound more Irish. She moved to Paris from Ireland in 1883 to commence life as a freelance journalist for Irish, American and French newspapers. Information from Anna MacBride White.

57 MGM to WBY, [November 1905], *Letters*, p. 216.

58 Ibid.

59 Francis Stuart, *Black List, Section H*, p. 33.

60 Information from Anna MacBride White.

61 MGM to WBY, 8 August [1906]; quoted in Anthony J. Jordan, *Willie Yeats and the Gonne-MacBrides*, p. 111.

62 *Girl That Knew All Dante*, pp. 17–19.

63 Information from Anna MacBride White.

64 MGM to WBY, [November 1905], *Letters*, pp. 214–15.

65 'The MacBride Divorce Case', *The Times*, London, 8 August 1906.

66   *Girl That Knew All Dante*, pp. 18–19.

67   'The MacBride Matrimonial Case', *The Times*, 31 January 1908.

68   MGM to John Quinn, 25 March 1908; cited in Elizabeth Keane, *Seán MacBride: A Life*, p. 18.

69   MGM to WBY, [January 1908], *Letters*, pp. 252–3.

70   Anthony J. Jordan, *Clara Allen*, www.academia.edu/4469164/clara_allen.

71   This was a friendly society with a weekly subscription that provided welfare for members. One of its objectives was Irish independence. It was at its height in 1914, with branches in Ireland, Scotland and elsewhere; members wore a uniform.

72   Jordan, *Major John MacBride*, p. 100.

73   St Enda's School Prospectus, 1910–1911, Jackie Clarke Collection, Ballina, Co. Mayo.

74   MGM to WBY, [December 1914], *Letters*, pp. 352–3.

75   MGM to John Quinn; quoted in Cardozo, p. 300.

76   MGM to WBY, 26 August [1914], *Letters*, pp. 347–8.

77   MGM to John Quinn; quoted in Cardozo, p. 300.

78   MGM to WBY, [April 1914], *Letters*, p. 372.

79   MGM to John Quinn; quoted in Cardozo, p. 307.

Notes for Chapter 3

Details of the lives of James and Lillie Connolly (*née* Reynolds) are primarily taken from the following sources: Lorcan Collins, *16Lives: James Connolly*; Ina Connolly Heron, 'James Connolly: A Biography', published in eight instalments in *Liberty*, the journal of the IGTWU; Nora Connolly O'Brien, *Portrait of a Rebel Father*; Ruth Dudley Edwards, *James Connolly*; C. Desmond Greaves, *The Life and Times of James Connolly*; Samuel Levenson, *James Connolly: A Biography*; Austen Morgan, *James Connolly: A Political Biography*; Carol Murphy, *Lillie Connolly: Her Life and Times*; Donal Nevin, *James Connolly: A Full Life*; and South Inner City Community Development Association (Siccda), *Ladies of the Liberties*. Letters from James Connolly to Lillie Reynolds and others taken from the William O'Brien papers, NLI, MS 15,570; and those from James Connolly to Winifred Carney from the Cathal O'Shannon papers, Irish Labour History Museum and Archives. Details of the early days of the Irish Republican movement taken from Nora Connolly O'Brien, *We Shall Rise Again*; Uinseann MacEoin, *Survivors: The story of Ireland's struggle as told through some of her outstanding living people . . .* Further details relating to the Connolly family and the Easter Rising 1916 taken from Witness Statements given by Nora Connolly

(WS 286) and Ina Connolly (WS 919), held in the Military Archives, Cathal Brugha Barracks, Dublin; and from documents in the Kilmainham Jail Collection, 15 LG 1C 26 21.

1   C. Desmond Greaves, *The Life and Times of James Connolly*, p. 22.

2   Ina Connolly Heron, 'James Connolly: A Biography, Part 1 – The Early Years', p. 18, refers to her grandfather moving from Scotstown, Ballybay, Co. Monaghan. In a local song, Annalore is named as James Connolly's birthplace.

3   Lillie's daughter Nora Connolly stated that her mother was from Carnew, Co. Wicklow (MacEoin, *Survivors*, p. 183); other family sources say Rathdrum. The Census of Ireland, 1911, records her brother John (Johnny) Reynolds's birthplace as Rathdrum. In addition see Reynolds family research undertaken by S. Reynolds (descendant of George Reynolds, Lillie's brother) of Faversham, Kent, available on www.rootsweb.ancestry.com.

4   That he was no longer in the army has not been substantiated by documentation as his army records are untraced, but James Connolly himself said that this was the case in the *Workers' Republic*, 15 July 1899, quoted in Nevin, *James Connolly: A Full Life*, p. 9. Nora suggested that 'they had planned to leave Dublin; he to be demobbed in Aldershot (although he never went through this formality) and Lillie was en-route to a job in London' (MacEoin, *Survivors*, p. 184). The suggestion that he was going to Aldershot ties in with the records of the 1st Battalion King's Liverpool Regiment, which many biographers have believed to have been his regiment.

5   Greaves, op. cit., p. 23.

6   JC to LR, 7 April [1889]. See also Greaves, op. cit., p. 24, for his interpretation of dating as April 1889.

7   Connolly Heron, 'The Early Years', p. 20.

8   JC to LR, undated; quoted in Donal Nevin, *James Connolly: A Full Life*, pp. 721–2.

9   JC to LR, [17 April 1889]; ibid., p. 720.

10   JC to LR, undated; ibid., p. 722.

11   JC to LR, [undated, 1889?]; ibid., pp. 721–2.

12   JC to LR, [17 November 1889], ibid., p. 722.

13   Ibid., p. 723.

14   JC to LR, [undated], William O'Brien papers, NLI MS 13,911.

15   JC to LR, undated [1890]; ibid., p. 725.

16   Ibid.

17   Connolly Heron, 'The Early Years', p. 20.

18   Quoted in Nevin, p. 39.

19   In April 1895, the first election of its kind, Connolly contested the St Giles Ward and got 14 per cent of the vote.

20   Greaves, op. cit., p. 53.

21   Connolly Heron, 'The Early Years', p. 20.

22   Greaves, op. cit., p. 56.

23   Nevin, op. cit., p. 48.

24   Margaret had married William Armstrong St Clair Douglas, a tobacco-pipe maker. She died in childbirth on 4 January 1900 in Scotland. According to family research undertaken by S. Reynolds of Faversham, Kent, it does not appear that the child survived, as in a later Census record William Armstrong St Clair Douglas is living as a boarder. Source: www.rootschat.com.

25   Nora Connolly O'Brien, *Portrait of a Rebel Father*, p. 18.

26   Siccda, *Ladies of the Liberties*, p. 93.

27   Connolly O'Brien, op. cit., p. 25.

28   Nora Connolly always used the Irish version Aġna for her sister Ina.

29   Connolly Heron, 'The Early Years', p. 19.

30   Nevin, op. cit., p. 88.

31   According to Austen Morgan, *James Connolly: A Political Biography*, p. 43, that summer of 1897 the family moved to 71 Queen Street. He does not cite his source for this information.

32   Connolly Heron, op. cit., p. 20.

33   Siccda, op. cit., p. 95.

34   Connolly O'Brien, op. cit., p 45.

35   Connolly O'Brien, op. cit., p. 34.

36   Samuel Levenson, *James Connolly: A Biography*, p. 164.

37   Connolly Heron, op. cit., p. 21.

38   Nevin, op. cit., p. 178.

39   Ibid., pp. 169–70.

40   Ibid., p. 196.

41   JC to Daniel O'Brien, 3 October 1902; quoted in Nevin, p. 200.

42   JC to LC, [undated].

43   Uinseann MacEoin, *Survivors*, p. 187.

44   Levenson, op. cit., p. 107.

45   Quoted in Nevin, p. 209.

46   JC to Jack Lyng, 15 May 1903; quoted in Nevin, p. 216.

47   JC to William O'Brien, undated [August 1903]; ibid., pp. 217–18.

48   Ina Connolly Heron, Witness Statement 919.

49   Levenson, op. cit., pp. 115–16.

50   Greaves, op. cit., p. 149.

51   JC to Jack Mulray, June 1905; quoted in Nevin, p. 218.

52   JC to J. C. Matheson, 27 December 1905; ibid., p. 248.

53   Connolly O'Brien, op. cit., p. 516.

54   Greaves, op. cit., p. 165.

55   Connolly Heron, 'James Connolly: A Biography, Part 2 – The Search for Roots', p. 23.

56   Connolly O'Brien, op. cit., pp. 96–7.

57   JC to Jack Mulray, 7 May 1905; quoted in Ruth Dudley Edwards, *James Connolly*, p. 45.

58   Connolly O'Brien, op. cit., p. 108.

59   He had previously written a number of pamphlets, including *Erin's Hope* in 1897 and *The New Evangel Preached to Irish Toilers* in 1903.

60   United States Federal Census, 23 April 1910, Bronx Assembly District 33. Once again James Connolly states he is born in Ireland. Thanks to Paul Turnell for sourcing this.

61   Nevin, op. cit., p. 317.

62   JC to William O'Brien, 5 July 1909; ibid., p. 315.

63   Jackie Clarke Collection, Ballina, Co. Mayo.

64   Connolly O'Brien, op. cit., p. 109.

65   LC to Mr Foran, 10 August 1920, William O'Brien papers.

66   Nevin, op. cit., p. 379.

67   According to the *Freeman's Journal*, 1 October 1906: 'The circumstances under which Mr. Larkin was convicted and sentenced, in June last, are still fresh in the memory of the public who take an interest in Labour disputes and their consequences, and the announcement that he is to be released on 1st October causes no surprise . . . it was strongly felt at the time of the trial that although technically he had broken the law he had been guilty of no moral turpitude, that the sentence was altogether disproportionate to the office, and that, in fact, it ought not be allowed to stand.'

68   JC to William O'Brien; quoted in Nevin, p. 381.

69   Ibid., 20 September 1910.

70   Connolly O'Brien, op. cit., p. 110.

71   Nevin, op. cit., p. 380.

72   Connolly Heron, 'James Connolly: A Biography, Part 3 – The Return of the Wild Geese', p. 18.

73   Connolly O'Brien, op. cit., p. 116.

74   Connolly Heron, 'The Return of the Wild Geese', p. 19.

75   Margaret Ward, *Maud Gonne: A Life*, pp. 98–100. A programme of providing hot meals was introduced first in several Dublin schools, run by women volunteers, and finally in September 1914 the Act was extended to the whole of Ireland.

76   JC to John Leslie; quoted in Nevin, p. 389.

77   According to family research by S. Reynolds of Faversham, Kent, George would have sixteen children in total.

78   Connolly Heron, 'The Return of the Wild Geese', p. 22.

79   JC to R. J. Hoskin, 14 June 1911; quoted in Dudley Edwards, p. 88.

80   Connolly Heron, 'The Return of the Wild Geese', p. 20.

81   Connolly Heron, 'James Connolly: A Biography, Part 4 – Belfast: Early Battles and Consolidation', p. 14.

82   Connolly O'Brien, op. cit., p.137.

83   Helga Woggon, *Silent Radical – Winifred Carney, 1887–1943: A Reconstruction of Her Biography*, p. 15.

84   Ina Connolly Heron says Peter was her father's brother ('The Early Years', p. 18); other sources give him as James's uncle.

85   Ibid., p. 18.

86   Ibid.

87   Connolly Heron, 'Belfast: Early Battles and Consolidation', p. 19.

88   Pamphlet for Belfast Municipal Elections, January 1913, transcribed by the James Connolly Society, 1997.

89   JC in *Forward*, 4 October 1913; quoted in Nevin, p. 479.

90   Woggon, op. cit., p. 13.

91   Connolly O'Brien, op. cit., pp. 141–2.

92   Ibid., p. 146.

93   MacEoin, op. cit., p. 190.

94   Connolly Heron, 'James Connolly: A Biography, Part 5 – The General Strike', pp. 47–8.

95   Joe McGowan (ed.), *Countess Markievicz: The People's Countess*, p. 22.

96   Elizabeth Coxhead, *Daughters of Erin*, p. 90.

97   McGowan, op. cit., p. 24.

98   Nevin, op. cit., p. 552.

99   JC to LC, 1 January 1914.

100   Connolly Heron, 'The Early Years', p. 23.

101   Connolly Heron, 'James Connolly: A Biography, Part 6 – We Serve Neither King Nor Kaiser, But Ireland', p. 19.

102 Nevin, op. cit., p. 602.

103 O'Donovan Rossa Souvenir Pamphlet, 1915.

104 JC to Winifred Carney, 21 December 1915.

105 Woggon, op. cit., pp. 15–16.

106 JC to Winifred Carney, 1 December 1915.

107 Ibid., 5 December 1915.

108 JC to William O'Brien, [undated]; quoted in Nevin, p. 506.

109 Connolly Heron, 'The Early Years', p. 23.

110 Connolly Heron, 'James Connolly: A Biography, Part 7 – Final Preparations', p. 23.

111 JC to Winifred Carney, 22 December 1915.

112 Count Johann Heinrich, Graf von Bernstorff (1862–1939) was ambassador to the United States and Mexico from 1908 until his recall on 3 February 1917. The German embassy in Washington was involved in espionage against Britain and America.

113 MacEoin, op. cit., p. 196.

114 Quoted in Connolly Heron, 'We Serve Neither King Nor Kaiser, But Ireland', p. 23.

115 Nora Connolly O'Brien, Witness Statement.

116 Woggon, op. cit., p. 16.

117 Connolly Heron, 'Final Preparations', p. 24.

118 Connolly O'Brien, op. cit., p. 138.

119 Ibid., p. 279.

120 Margaret Skinnider, *Doing My Bit for Ireland*, pp. 78–9.

121 Fiona Connolly papers, Marx Library, London.

Notes for Chapter 4

Details of the lives of Éamonn and Áine Ceannt (Edward and Fanny Kent, *née* O'Brennan) are primarily taken from the following sources: William Henry, *Supreme Sacrifice: The Story of Éamonn Ceannt*; and Donagh MacDonagh, 'Pen Portrait of the Seven Signatories – Éamonn Ceannt: Maker of History and Myth' published in the *Irish Press*. Letters and other documents relating to the Ceannt and O'Brennan families are taken from the collection of personal and political papers of Éamonn and Áine Ceannt and of Kathleen and Lily O'Brennan held in the NLI, MS 13,069 and 41,479; and from correspondence of Éamonn Ceannt, Rónán Ceannt and other documents held in the Allen Library, Dublin. Further details of Éamonn Ceannt and the Easter Rising 1916 are from the Witness Statement given by Áine Ceannt (WS 264), held in the Military Archives, Cathal Brugha Barracks, Dublin.

1   William Henry, *Supreme Sacrifice: The Story of Éamonn Ceannt, 1881–1916*, pp. 19–20.

2   EC to AO'B, 12 December 1903.

3   Joyce left North Richmond Street in early 1893 when he was offered free education at Belvedere; Richard Ellmann, *James Joyce*, Oxford, 1983, p. 33.

4   Henry, op. cit., p. 10.

5   He was a Colour sergeant major, 1st Royal Dublin Fusiliers, #6425. He died in action in France, 24 April 1917. Records of Irish War Dead.

6   Donagh MacDonagh, 'Pen Portrait of the Seven Signatories – Éamonn Ceannt: Maker of History and Myth', *Irish Press*, 9 April 1956, p. 6.

7   Minutes of the Irish Pipers' Club, Dublin, 1900–1904, Allen Library, Allen B1.

8   EC to Rev. K. Fielding, 7 June 1902, Allen Library, MS 13,069–70, Folder 1.

9   Áine Ceannt, Witness Statement 264.

10 EC to AO'B, 1 April 1904.

11 Áine is most often used as a direct translation of Anne.

12 EC to AO'B, 30 June 1903.

13 Account of Éamonn Ceannt written by his brother Richard Kent, April 1917; copy given to the author by Richard's daughter Moira, November 1995.

14 EC to AO'B, 31 March 1904.

15 EC to AO'B, 9 April 1904.

16 MacDonagh, op. cit., p. 6.

17 EC to AO'B, 30 June 1903.

18 EC to AO'B, 10 and 11 June 1903.

19 EC to AO'B, 4 December 1903.

20 EC to AO'B, 12 December 1903.

21 EC to AO'B at St Joseph's South Circular Road, Kilmainham, St Stephen's Day, 1903.

22 EC to AO'B, Christmas Eve, 1903.

23 EC to AO'B, St Stephen's Day, 1903.

24 Ibid.

25 Éamonn's ideas, if he was being serious, were outdated. Officially the Married Women's Property Act 1882 allowed women to hold their own property.

26 EC to AO'B, 5 May 1904.

27 EC to AO'B, 14 February 1904.

28   EC to AO'B, 17 March [1904].

29   EC to AO'B, 1 April 1904.

30   A ring worn to protect the more valuable ring from being lost.

31   Unidentified typescript by 'Maire', who knew EC from 1899, in the Ceannt–O'Brennan papers.

32   This same year was a difficult one, as Éamonn's brother James Kent, known as Jem, who had been suffering from TB, died aged twenty-nine.

33   Áine Ceannt, Witness Statement.

34   Census of Ireland 1911 records the number of children born alive. The Ceannts record one child.

35   Timothy O'Neill, 'Wine and Gold', unpublished MS, Allen Library.

36   Draft text of his lecture on 'The Bagpipes', delivered 30 January 1912 at National Museum of Ireland; Ceannt–O'Brennan papers.

37   Áine Ceannt, Witness Statement.

38   MacDonagh, op. cit., p. 6.

39   Henry, op. cit., p. 28.

40   Ceannt–O'Brennan papers.

41   EC to Uí Raghallaigh, 10 November 1913 (copy), Ceannt–O'Brennan papers.

42   'The Fourth Battalion', *Dublin Brigade Review*, 1939; William Henry Collection. Éamonn Ceannt's Volunteers membership card, December 1913–April 1914, is amongst documents held at the Allen Library (Box 181).

43   Handwritten account of this period in the Ceannt–O'Brennan papers.

44   'The Fourth Battalion'.

45   Áine Ceannt, Witness Statement.

46   Kit was active in such organizations as the Friends of Irish Freedom and the American Association for the Recognition of the Irish Republic. For additional information on Kathleen Brennan's work in the US for the Irish Republican movement, see Catherine M. Burns, 'Kathleen O'Brennan and American Identity in the Transatlantic Irish Republican Movement', in *The Irish in the Atlantic World*, (ed.) David T. Gleeson.

47   Prospectus for St Enda's School 1910–1911, published by Dollard, 1910. Jackie Clarke Collection, Ballina, Co. Mayo.

48   PC 166, Box 5, Folder 1, Allen Library; copy in William Henry Collection.

49   Gerard MacAtasney, *Seán Mac Diarmada: Mind of the Revolution*, p. 104.

50 Áine Ceannt, Witness Statement.

51 Ceannt–O'Brennan papers.

52 Áine Ceannt, Witness Statement.

53 Henry, op. cit., p. 46.

54 Áine Ceannt, Witness Statement.

55 James Connolly to EC, 23 April 1916, Allen Library, Box 105, B6.

56 Extracts from the diary of Michael Kent, brother of Éamonn Ceannt, courtesy of William Henry.

57 Áine Ceannt, 'Éamonn Ceannt the Soldier', in *Wolfe Tone Annual*, Special 1916 Number, Dublin: Brian O'Higgins, undated.

58 Áine Ceannt, Witness Statement.

Notes for Chapter 5

Details of the lives of Michael and Agnes Mallin (*née* Hickey) are primarily taken from the following sources: Brian Hughes, *16Lives: Michael Mallin*; Seamus Mallin, 'Commandant Michael Mallin', published in *Inniú* (in Irish; typescript of English translation by Michael Mallin, Seamus's son, in author's collection); 'The Late Mrs Mallin – A Story of Sacrifice', published in *An Phoblacht*; and from the letters of Michael Mallin to Agnes Hickey, held in a private collection. Other details are drawn from Witness Statements given by Thomas Mallin (WS 382) and James O'Shea (WS 733), held in the Military Archives, Cathal Brugha Barracks, Dublin; Brian Hughes, 'A Splendid Type of the Dublin Tradesman', MPhil thesis, Trinity College Dublin; Noel McDermott, 'Solving the Mallin Mystery', in *Red Banner*; letters from Michael Mallin to his parents John and Sarah Mallin, quoted in Piaras F. Mac Lochlainn, *Last Words: Letters and Statements of the Leaders Executed after the Rising at Easter 1916*; the records of the Royal Scots Fusiliers (including the Long Service Record of Michael Mallin; and 'The Ublan Pass', in *Royal Scots Fusilier*) held at the Public Records Office, Kew, No. 774553; records held in the Kilmainham Jail Collection; interviews with Fr Joseph Mallin and Maura Phillips (*née* Mallin) and letters from Fr Joseph Mallin to the author, 1995–2014.

1 Michael makes reference to the fact that Agnes's father had knowledge of a frontier station, implying that he had served with the British Army, although this has not been confirmed from any other source.

2 The deaths of the other three children are undocumented, possibly because sometimes children who died before they were a year old were not registered.

3   MM to AH [undated].
4   Agnes's correspondence does not survive. Most of it was lost when Michael lost his kit bag on the Tirah expedition; letter from MM to AH, 27 September 1900.
5   MM to AH, 19 January 1896.
6   MM to AH, 22 February 1901.
7   MM to AH, 11 April 1896.
8   MM to AH, 9 May 1898.
9   MM to AH, 21 March 1897.
10   MM to AH, 9 May 1898.
11   MM to AH, 9 August 1897.
12   MM to AH, 7 December 1897.
13   MM to AH, 20 October 1897.
14   MM to AH, 19 December 1897.
15   MM to AH, 7 December 1897.
16   MM to AH, 12 December 1901.
17   MM to AH, 1 March 1898.
18   MM to AH, 23 March 1898. His pay book lists Marksman 1st Grade 1895; Marksman 1896–8; Marksman 1899; and Marksman 2nd Grade 1900–02; Kilmainham Jail Collection.
19   MM to AH, 1 March 1898.
20   MM to AH, 23 March 1898.
21   MM to AH, 9 May 1898.
22   MM to AH, 1 June 1898.
23   MM to AH, 15 June 1898.
24   MM to AH, 12 July 1898.
25   The *Irish Citizen*; quoted in Brian Hughes, 'A Splendid Type of the Dublin Tradesman', MPhil thesis Trinity College Dublin.
26   MM to AH, 7 September 1898.
27   MM to AH, 31 August 1898.
28   Anne Fagan, 'Profile – The Thewlis Sisters – Lily and Cissie', *Chapelizod Chat* (Culture, History, Activities and Traditions), Issue 2, February 1995.
29   MM to AH, 21 September 1898.
30   MM to AH, 5 October 1898.
31   MM to AH, undated [1898].
32   'She always spoke with appreciation of the work of surgeons and doctors and I think she would have considered being a Doctor – not easy in those days'; Father Joe Mallin to the author, 24 August 2008.
33   MM to AH, 22 November 1898.

34 MM to AH, 30 November 1898.

35 MM to AH, 4 January 1899.

36 MM to AH, [undated].

37 MM to AH, 8 November 1899.

38 MM to AH, 8 January 1899.

39 MM to AH, 14 November 1900.

40 MM to AH, 24 July 1900.

41 MM to AH, 21 August 1900.

42 MM to AH, 10 October 1900.

43 MM to AH, 24 July 1900.

44 Census of England and Wales 1901, return from the Lunatic Asylum at the Strang in the Parish of Bradden, Isle of Man. Later known as Ballamona Hospital, in the 1890s it had approximately 200 inmates. It was demolished in 1998.

45 MM to AH, 1 August 1900.

46 MM to AH, 21 August 1900.

47 MM to AH, 14 November 1900.

48 MM to Mrs Hickey, 7 November 1900, in the possession of Kevin McConnell, a relative of Agnes Hickey; copy given to author 1996.

49 MM to AH, 22 February 1901.

50 MM to Mrs Hickey, 24 May 1901; quoted in Brian Hughes, *Michael Mallin*, p. 33.

51 MM to AH, 21 August 1900, Chirat. This ring was shown to the author when it was in the possession of the late Maura Phillips (*née* Mallin), *c.*1994. It was subsequently stolen.

52 MM to AH, 19 April 1901.

53 MM to AH, 14 June 1901.

54 MM to AH, 1 November 1901.

55 Thomas Mallin, quoted in Hughes, 'A Splendid Type of the Dublin Tradesman'.

56 MM to AH, 25 December 1901.

57 MM to AH, 24 May 1901.

58 MM to AH, 23 January 1902.

59 MM to AH, 28 March 1901.

60 MM to AH, 8 April 1902.

61 MM describes the sword thus in a letter to AH, 31 August 1898. In the aftermath of the Rising he told her to destroy the wool picture; see Seamus Mallin, 'Commandant Michael Mallin', in *Inniú*.

62 MM to AH, 21 November 1902.

63 His Long Service Record states that he served 13 years and 59 days.

64 MM to AH, 5 January [1903].

65 MM to AH, envelope dated 9 January 1903.

66 MM to AH, 17 February 1903.

67 MM to AH, 18 January 1903.

68 Certificate of marriage of Michael Mallin to Agnes Hickey, 26 April 1903; quoted in Hughes, 'A Splendid Type of the Dublin Tradesman'.

69 24 June 1906, Agnes (Úna) Mallin, Military Pension Record.

70 From the time he married he worked in College Green. Catherine Rossiter (*née* Mallin), Military Pension Record.

71 Indenture of Bartholomew Mallin, Allen Library, Box 200, File A, Pack M.

72 James O'Shea, Witness Statement 733. The first recorded meeting took place at the home of Mr Richard P. Fortune, 3 Dame Street, Dublin, on 15 February 1908, when four boys were enrolled in the Wolf Patrol of the 1st Dublin Troop. A plaque marks the location of the house, now demolished, on the plaza next to Dublin's City Hall. The 2nd Dublin formed the following week at 5 Upper Camden Street. www.scouts.ie.

73 Leon Feddersen to MM, 21 September 1908, private collection.

74 Mallin, op. cit.

75 It is commonly recognized that James Joyce's cinema, The Volta, was probably the first opened in Dublin, in 1909. Michael's venture must have been roughly contemporaneous with this.

76 Mallin, op. cit.

77 Ibid.

78 James O'Shea, Witness Statement.

79 MM to AM, 7 May 1916, Kilmainham Jail Collection.

80 Hughes, 'A Splendid Type of the Dublin Tradesman'.

81 Mallin, op. cit.

82 R. M. Fox, quoted in Hughes, *Michael Mallin*, p. 74.

83 Father Joseph Mallin to the author.

84 Hughes, *Michael Mallin*, pp. 80–1.

85 William Partridge, quoted in Hughes, *Michael Mallin*, p. 84.

86 James O'Shea Witness Statement.

87 Hughes, *Michael Mallin*, p. 91.

88 James O'Shea Witness Statement.

89 *Workers' Republic*, 27 May 1915; quoted in Hughes, 'A Splendid Type of the Dublin Tradesman'.

90 Mallin, op. cit.

91 Ibid.

92 Maeve Cavanagh, quoted in Hughes, 'A Splendid Type of the Dublin Tradesman'.

93 Mallin, op. cit.

94 Hughes, 'A Splendid Type of the Dublin Tradesman'.

95 Frank Robbins, Witness Statement, 585.

96 Mallin, op. cit.

97 James O'Shea Witness Statement.

98 Ibid.

Notes for Chapter 6

Details of the lives of Joe and Grace Plunkett (*née* Gifford) are primarily taken from the following sources: Anne Clare, *Unlikely Rebels: The Gifford Girls*; Honor Ó Brolcháin, *16Lives: Joseph Plunkett*; Marie O'Neill, *Grace Gifford Plunkett and Irish Freedom: Tragic Bride of 1916*; and Geraldine Plunkett Dillon, *All In the Blood: A Memoir of the Plunkett Family, the 1916 Rising and the War of Independence*; and 'Joseph Plunkett and His Friends', published in the *Irish Press*. Quotations from letters from Joe Plunkett to Grace Gifford are from the Grace Plunkett papers, NLI, MS 21,590–3. Further details are taken from Witness Statements given by Grace Plunkett (WS 257) and Dr Charles MacAuley (WS 735), Military Archives, Cathal Brugha Barracks, Dublin. Information on the Abbey Theatre, Theatre of Ireland and Irish Theatre Company is drawn from documents in the Kitty McCormack Archive, held in the Jackie Clarke Collection, Ballina, Co. Mayo; from William J. Feeney, *Drama in Hardwicke Street: A History of the Irish Theatre Company*; and from Máire Nic Shiubhlaigh, *The Splendid Years*. Information regarding the lives of members of the Gifford family in North America are from the Ellis Island Archives and public records of New York and Quebec.

1 JP to GG, 7 January 1916.

2 While Patrick Cranny had fathered seventeen children, only four sons and a daughter survived to adulthood.

3 George Plunkett, *Botticelli and his School*, London: George Bell & Sons, 1900.

4 Joe's sister Moya (christened Mary Josephine) was born in 1889 when Joe was one year old; another sister, Geraldine, followed in 1891; a brother, George, in 1894. The youngest girl, again named for her mother, Josephine Mary, but always known as Fiona, was born in 1896; and finally another boy, John (but known as Jack), was born in 1897.

5 Geraldine Plunkett Dillon, *All In the Blood*, p. 47. In her autobiography

Geraldine said that by the age of six she knew she hated her mother. Her account of her upbringing is scathing in relation to her mother, whereas her father is always depicted in a sympathetic light. She says that he was rarely around to see what was happening and would not interfere with his wife as he believed she knew what she was doing. Nevertheless, he must have been somewhat aware of what was going on and never chose to change it.

6   Plunkett Dillon, op. cit., p. 52.

7   The school was forced to close two years later due to the irregular practices there.

8   Plunkett Dillon, op. cit., p. 82.

9   JP to TM, NLI, MS 10,999/3.

10 TM to JP, NLI, MS 10,999/2.

11 Plunkett Dillon, op. cit., p. 94.

12 Geraldine Plunkett Dillon, 'Joseph Plunkett and his Friends', *Irish Press*, 5 May 1936.

13 MG to TM, 28 October 1911, NLI, MS 44,320/2.

14 There are records of a Samuel Burton leasing a tower house known as Tomra Castle (also given as Trumnera/Tromroe/Tromrath) in the barony of Ibrickan, in the parish of Kilmurry, *c*.1660. Frederic Burton was born in his grandfather Edward William Burton's home, Cliften House, Corofin, Co. Clare in 1816. See Alan Hayes (ed.), *The Years Flew By: Recollections of Madame Sidney Gifford Czira*, p. 7.

15 Robert Burton was in Carlow when the Irish potato crop failed and a million died from starvation and diseases. It was said that her father learned the Catholic rite for the dying so he could administer it and ease the people into death with some dignity when the Catholic priest was not available. He was survived by his children: Francis Charles Burton (later colonel, 2nd Bengal Lancers); Clara M. Griffin; Hannah Burton; Emily Burton; Alfred Burton (who was clerk in Holy Orders like his father); Mary Burton; Fanny E. Burton; and Henry Bindon Burton (who worked in banking). Information from the headstone of Sir Frederic William Burton, along with the inscription erected by his nephews and nieces, with additional information supplied by the Burton family.

16 Information from family photographs quoted in Anne Clare, *Unlikely Rebels: The Gifford Girls*, p. 15, suggests that her brothers, who are unnamed and said to have been doctors, were in London and Buenos Aires. She states from the family papers that the boys attended Trinity College Dublin, where one studied law and the others medicine. (This

information appears to contradict information on the headstone in Mount Jerome Cemetery; see note 17.) Hannah, Emily and Mary remained unmarried and when they were unable to live off their investments became nurses. Hannah later became matron of an English hospital.

17 Clare, op. cit., p. 54, refers to the fact that J. M. Synge, the playwright and friend of Jack B. Yeats, learned Irish from a man called Mícháil on the Aran Islands.

18 Grace Plunkett Scrapbook.

19 Catalogue entry by Kenneth McConkey in *Orpen and the Edwardian Era*, p. 72.

20 Family information quoted in Clare, op. cit., p. 16.

21 McConkey in *Orpen and the Edwardian Era*, p. 72.

22 The *Shanachie* only had six issues, 1906–07; issues in the NLI. In Lady Lavery's Scrapbooks (private collection) there are a number of her hand-painted cartoons, but there is no record of how she acquired them. The largest collection of her work is in the NLI Prints and Drawings Department, from the Joseph Holloway Collection.

23 Robert Hogan and Michael J. O'Neill (eds), *Joseph Holloway's Abbey Theatre: A Selection from His Unpublished Journal 'Impressions of a Dublin Playgoer'*, p. 13; Entry: 21 October 1901.

24 The original watercolour and ink on board is in the Joseph Holloway Collection, NLI Prints and Drawings Department, PD 2159 TX (16) 37. The cartoon entitled 'Edward Martyn, having a week of it in Paris' shows the bachelor resisting the temptations of a French damsel. Pen and ink on paper, Hugh Lane, Dublin City Gallery Collection.

25 Máire Nic Shiubhlaigh, *The Splendid Years*, pp. 13–19.

26 Advertisement, *The Times*, 27 October 1910; quoted in William J. Feeney, *Drama in Hardwicke Street: A History of the Irish Theatre Company*, p. 37.

27 Feeney, op. cit., p. 40.

28 Anonymous critic, *The Times*, November 1911; quoted in Feeney, p. 39.

29 *Freeman's Journal* dated in pen '9-5-13' (this is an error, as it states on the Notice for the play that it took place on 10 May 1913 and, as the article states 'last night', it should read '11-5-13'); from the Kitty McCormack Archive.

30 Feeney, op. cit., p. 40.

31 Evelyn Gleeson and her niece Catherine (Kitty) McCormack, a textile designer, and Nora FitzPatrick worked there. Kitty and Nora were

keenly interested in the theatre. Kitty often acted under the name of Catia Nic Cormac. Joe Plunkett had known Kitty since 1902, when at the age of twelve she had moved with her mother Constance and siblings Eddie, aged thirteen, and Grace, aged four, to live with their aunt Evelyn Gleeson at Runnemede, Sandyford Road, Co. Dublin. The Plunketts attended an art class there which was given by Elizabeth (Lolly) Yeats, who at that time was working with the Dun Emer Guild before leaving with her sister Lily to set up the Cuala Industries. Joe and his sister also had classes with Nora FitzPatrick, who taught Joe and Gerry bookbinding.

32   Plunkett Dillon, *All In the Blood*, p. 135.

33   Ibid., p. 131.

34   Ibid., p. 139.

35   Not to be confused with the Columba Press, an independent Catholic publisher established in 1985.

36   Thomas MacDonagh had sold the press when he went to live in Grange House Lodge in 1912. Information supplied by Patrick Hawe. The printer Mr Latchford would set the poems on the linotype and Joe printed them on handmade paper; Plunkett Dillon, *All In the Blood*, p. 136. The NLI has a copy signed by Joe Plunkett, which he numbered 11, stating that thirteen copies were printed on 31 December 1913.

37   Joe had come from a long line of those who protested against injustice and fought for their beliefs. He was proud of his ancestral link to Archbishop Oliver Plunkett, who had been martyred, accused of planning a French invasion of Ireland in 1678.

38   Letter from JP to Aidan McCabe, 4 April 1914; quoted in Plunkett Dillon, p. 247.

39   *Irish Review*, Vol. 4, No. 42, September–November 1914.

40   The letterhead of the Irish Theatre Company stated it was founded in 1914, because on 1 November 1914 the first staging of Edward Martyn's *The Dream Physician* had taken place in 40 Upper O'Connell Street. Plunkett, Martyn and MacDonagh were listed as managers; Thomas's brother John MacDonagh is given as stage and general manager.

41   JP to Columba O'Carroll, 13 September 1915; quoted in Honor Ó Brolcháin, *16Lives: Joseph Plunkett*, p. 331. According to his family, he never intended to send these letters; they acted as a kind of therapy. However, the arrival of Columba to see him on his return may suggest otherwise.

42 Columba married Dudley Heathcote but discovered afterwards that he was not divorced; Plunkett Dillon, *All in the Blood*. She next married Evan Guest, eighteen years her junior, in Penang, Malaya, in September 1935; *Singapore Free Press*, September 1935. They were divorced in 1952. Columba died on 1 December 1955; sourced via www.thepeerage.com/p7085.htm.

43 Grace Plunkett, Witness Statement 257.

44 JP to GG, 28 November 1915.

45 Grace Plunkett, Witness Statement.

46 JP to GG, 29 November 1915.

47 JP to GG, 2 December 1915.

48 Gifford Plunkett, Witness Statement.

49 Plunkett Dillon, op. cit., p. 196.

50 In another hand '2 December 1915' is written, but this is incorrect; it would be 2 a.m. on the 3rd.

51 JP to GG, 2 December 1915.

52 JP to GG, 4 December 1915.

53 JP to Aidan McCabe, 5 December 1915; quoted in Ó Brolcháin, pp. 345–6.

54 JP to GG, 15 December 1915.

55 JP to GG, 26 December 1915.

56 JP to GG, 19 January 1916.

57 Ibid.

58 JP to GG, 1 February 1916.

59 JP to GG, 7 February 1916

60 JP to GG, 8 February 1916.

61 JP to GG, 13 February 1916.

62 Contained with Letters November 1915–April 1916, Grace Plunkett papers.

63 Plunkett Dillon, op. cit., p. 174.

64 JP to GG, 13 February 1916.

65 Holloway's Diary (1824:490); quoted in Feeney, p. 125.

66 Grace Plunkett, Witness Statement: 'it was she was aware a very secret thing, he was bound by oath.'

67 Information from Máirtín MacSiúrtáin, research on F. R. Sherwin, supplied to the author 1997.

68 Grace Plunkett, Witness Statement.

69 Ó Brolcháin, op. cit., p. 363.

70 Dr Charles MacAuley, Witness Statement 735.

71 Gifford Plunkett, Witness Statement; quoted in Ó Brolcháin, p. 370.
72 JP to GG, Easter Sunday 1916.

Notes for Chapter 7

Details of the lives of Thomas and Muriel MacDonagh (*née* Gifford) are primarily taken from the following sources: Anne Clare, *Unlikely Rebels: The Gifford Girls*; Johann Norstedt, *Thomas MacDonagh: A Critical Biography*; Alan Hayes (ed.), *The Years Flew By: Recollections of Madame Sidney Gifford Czira*; Donagh MacDonagh, 'Pen Portrait of the Seven Signatories: A Poet and Scholar Died', published in the *Irish Press*; Marie O'Neill, *Grace Gifford Plunkett and Irish Freedom: Tragic Bride of 1916*; and Edd W. Parks and Aileen Wells Parks, *Thomas MacDonagh*. Letters and other documents are from the Thomas MacDonagh papers, NLI, MS 10,843–52; the MacDonagh family papers, NLI, MS 44,318–24; and the Gifford family papers, including an account of Thomas MacDonagh by George Bingham, all NLI, MS 20,646. Information on the Abbey Theatre, Theatre of Ireland and Irish Theatre Company is drawn from documents in the Kitty McCormack Archive, held in the Jackie Clarke Collection, Ballina, Co. Mayo; and from William J. Feeney, *Drama in Hardwicke Street: A History of the Irish Theatre Company*.

1 John Brennan, *Irish Times*; quoted in Edd W. Parks and Aileen Wells Parks, *Thomas MacDonagh*, p. 26.
2 Alan Hayes (ed.), *The Years Flew By: Recollections of Madame Sidney Gifford Czira*, p. 19.
3 Grace Plunkett Scrapbook, NLI, MS 21,593.
4 On his marriage certificate Frederick Gifford stated that his father was Surgeon William Gifford (see irishgenealogy.ie/churchrecords). Family research undertaken by Lucille Redmond (granddaughter of Muriel Gifford) and posted on rootsweb, however, states that the Royal College of Surgeons has no record of this man, which suggests he either practised outside Ireland or had no academic qualifications.
5 Information from Gifford family papers quoted in Anne Clare, *Unlikely Rebels: The Gifford Girls*, p. 15. In the Census of Ireland 1901 Frederic gives his place of birth as Dublin. In 1911 he simply states born in Ireland.
6 Isabella's actual birthdate is unrecorded, but from information on ages given in the Census of Ireland 1901 and 1911 it appears that the year was 1848. A son, John George Burton, born to the couple in November 1848, died aged five months in March 1849. He is buried in Kiltennel, County Carlow.

7 Information from Thor Ewing, descendant of H. Bindon Burton, who married Isabella's cousin Fanny Burton. They lived for a while close to the Giffords and their children knew their Gifford cousins. Later, when such associations became difficult as a result of their involvement in the Rising, information on her cousins was hidden in a private drawer. These mementos included an obituary of Muriel and a copy of Grace's Madonna painted on the wall of Kilmainham Jail.

8 Hayes, op. cit., p. 10.

9 According to Hilary Pyle, Gabriel Paul Gifford exhibited in London as well as in the United States; see *Irish Women Artists*, p. 162.

10 Her sister Katie, who had been working in Germany, having qualified as a 'teacher in language', had just married Walter Harris Wilson and was living in Wales. Gabriel had moved to the US to work as an artist, where his sister Ada and brother Edward joined him. Liebert joined the British Merchant Navy; he would settle in Canada. Frederick was in London.

11 Hayes, op. cit., p. 33.

12 Nine children is the number given by his nephew, son of his sister Eleanor. The first three died as infants. Their surviving children were Mary Josephine, Thomas, John (known as Jack, b.1880), James (known as Jim) and Joseph (known as Joe), and a younger sister Helen (known as Nell/Nellie), who was later Mrs Bingham. George Bingham, Account of Thomas MacDonagh.

13 Quoted in Parks, p. 5.

14 Ibid., pp. 4–5.

15 Johann Norstedt, *Thomas MacDonagh: A Critical Biography*, p. 27.

16 Thomas MacDonagh, *Poems: A Selection by His Sister*, Talbot Press, [undated].

17 Quoted in Parks, p. 7.

18 Copy in the Jackie Clarke Collection.

19 Parks, op. cit., p. 9. The cottage, Fermoy, stood on a street later renamed MacDonagh Terrace.

20 Quoted in Parks, p. 10.

21 Norstedt, op. cit., p. 45.

22 Ibid., p. 47.

23 *The Golden Joy*, published by O'Donoghue & Co., 1906. Signed to Joseph MacDonagh; Jackie Clarke Collection. A copy in the collection has the year of publication corrected to 1907 in the hand of Thomas MacDonagh.

24 Norstedt, op. cit., p. 47.

25 Parks, op. cit., p. 11.

26 *Bean na hÉireann,* November 1908, p. 4; Kilmainham Jail Collection. Mrs Bloomer was the housemistress in St Enda's in 1910. NLI, MS 8,903/1.

27 Parks, op. cit., p. 13.

28 *Bean na hÉireann,* Vol. 1, No. 1, Samhain November 1908.

29 TM to Dominick Hackett, 5 November 1908; quoted in Norstedt, p. 60.

30 Nannie (also known as Nora) Dryhurst (1856–1930), writer and translator. Among the works she translated was one from Russian. She wrote for the *Daily Chronicle* on history and also contributed to Irish publications. She was an expert in Scottish folklore and Celtic literature. She had an affair with Henry W. Nevinson, journalist and writer, over many years.

31 Parks, op. cit., p. 18.

32 TM to MG, 7 August 1909.

33 MG to TM, 14 September [1911].

34 Mary MacGuire Colum, *Life and the Dream,* pp. 174–5.

35 Thomas must have kept the ring, as it was amongst Muriel's possessions and has passed by descent to their granddaughter Muriel MacAuley. It has been described by a jeweller as 'smoked', its dull hue suggesting that it was retrieved from a fire. Interview Muriel MacAuley with the author, 1994.

36 Parks, op. cit., p. 26.

37 MG to TM, February 1910. According to Donagh, their son, theirs was a whirlwind courtship during which they exchanged two, three, four letters a day, not all of which have survived.

38 TM to Mrs Bloomer, 17 June 1919, NLI, MS 8,903/1.

39 Parks, op. cit., pp. 23–5. According to Geraldine Plunkett, Thomas had studied art in Paris for two years; *All In the Blood,* p. 108. Norstedt, op. cit., p. 68, however, states that he could not paint. There is no documentation to suggest that he was in France for a period of two years, nor any evidence of his artistic ability.

40 Donagh MacDonagh, 'Pen Portrait of the Seven Signatories: A Poet and Scholar Died', p. 4.

41 Quoted in Parks, p. 25.

42 Quoted in Norstedt, p. 80.

43 MacDonagh, p. 4.

44 MG to TM, 28 October 1911.

45 MG to TM, 17 October 1911, written on paper *High Court of Justice.*

46 TM to MG, 8 October 1911.

47   MG to TM, [undated] October 1911.

48   MG to TM, 9 November 1911.

49   MG to TM, 16 November 1911.

50   MG to TM, 19 October 1911.

51   MG to TM, 14 October 1911.

52   MG to TM, 2 October 1911.

53   MG to TM, 21 October 1911.

54   MG to TM, 25 October 1911.

55   MS 44,338/6. This has a date of 21 November 1911 and may be a more finished version of the poem.

56   MG to TM, 28 October 1911.

57   MG to TM, 9 November 1911.

58   MG to TM, 10 November 1911.

59   MG to TM, 16 November 1911.

60   TM to Dominick Hackett and Jack MacDonagh, 11 November; quoted in Parks, p. 28.

61   Ibid.

62   MG to TM, [November 1911].

63   MG to TM, [undated].

64   MG to TM, 16 November 1911.

65   MG to TM, 23 November 1911.

66   MG to TM, 2 November 1911.

67   Quoted in Parks, p. 29.

68   MG to TM, 28 October 1911.

69   MG to TM, 28 October 1911.

70   MG to TM, [December 1911].

71   TM to MG, 2 January 1912

72   Quoted in Parks, p. 29.

73   TM to MMD, 26 December 1912.

74   Quoted in William J. Feeney, *Drama at Hardwicke Street, A History of the Irish Theatre Company*, p. 46.

75   TM to MMD, Rotunda Hospital; letter dated 28th, but on the envelope it is dated [30] September 1912.

76   George Bingham (nephew of Thomas MacDonagh, son of his sister Eleanor) states that the Sligo link was confirmed by later research; Bingham's account of Thomas MacDonagh. Thomas recorded that his family had lived in Sligo as far back as the fifteenth century, according to a letter quoted in Parks, p. 1; however, this source is not documented.

77   MMD to TM, [December 1912].

78   Ibid.

79   TM to MMD, 26 December 1912.

80   TM to MMD, 30 November 1912.

81   TM to MMD, 5 December 1912.

82   TM to MMD, 25 December 1912.

83   TM to MMD, 28 December 1912.

84   TM to MMD, 29 December 1912.

85   TM to MMD, 4 February 1913.

86   TM to MMD, 15 February 1913.

87   Parks, op. cit., p. 46.

88   *Freeman's Journal* dated in pen '9-5-13' (this is an error, as it states on the Notice for the play that it took place on 10 May 1913 and, as the article states 'last night', it should read '11-5-13'); from the Kitty McCormack Archive.

89   TM to MMD, [January 1913].

90   Parks, op. cit., p. 32.

91   MMD to TM, envelope dated 7 November 1913.

92   MMD to TM, envelope dated 9 November 1913.

93   MMD to TM, envelope dated 10 November 1913.

94   MMD to TM, envelope dated 11 November 1913.

95   MMD to TM, envelope dated 12 November 1913.

96   TM to MMD, 1 November 1915; quoted in Norstedt, p. 118.

97   Quoted in Norstedt, p. 120.

98   Norstedt, op. cit., p. 119.

99   MMD to TM, 5 March 1914.

100   Quoted in Norstedt, p. 41.

101   TM to MMD, [1914].

102   Quoted in Norstedt, p. 46.

103   This is suggested by Frank Pakenham Longford and Thomas P. O'Neill, *Éamon de Valera*, p. 21.

104   *The Troth* by Rutherford Mayne had been translated by Liam O'Domhnaill. *The Revolt*, a French play by Villiers de l'Isle Adam, was translated by Teresa Barclay. *The Phoenix on the Roof* by Eimar O'Duffy and *The Swan Song* by Anton Chekhóv were in Marian Fell's translation.

105   Norstedt, op. cit., pp. 120–1.

106   Thomas MacDonagh, 'The Irish Volunteer in 1915', *O'Donovan Rossa Funeral Programme*, Dublin: Sign of the Three Candles, 1954, p. 8.

107   TM to Dominick Hackett, NLI, MS 22,934.

108   Quoted in Norstedt, p. 124, note 16.

109 Marcus Bourke in *The Irish Sword* (1968) suggests that MacDonagh was coopted as he was a colleague of Eoin MacNeill in UCD. He was a go-between for Patrick Pearse during the change of plans in Easter Week.

110 James Stephens, *The Poems of Thomas MacDonagh*, p. xi.

111 Áine Ceannt, Witness Statement 264.

112 Muriel MacDonagh's Statement, undated newspaper article, Gifford family papers.

113 Ibid.

Notes for Chapter 8

Details of events in the week of the Rising are primarily taken from the following sources: Brian Barton, *From Behind a Closed Door: Secret Court Martial Records of the 1916 Easter Rising*; Anne Clare, *Unlikely Rebels: The Gifford Girls*; Kathleen Clarke, *Revolutionary Woman*; John Cowell, *A Noontide Blazing: Brigid Lyons Thornton – Rebel, Soldier, Doctor*; Piaras F. Mac Lochlainn, *Last Words: Letters and Statements of the Leaders Executed after the Rising at Easter 1916*; Paul O'Brien, *Shootout: The Battle for St Stephen's Green, 1916*; and from Witness Statements given by Áine Ceannt (WS 264) and Thomas Mallin (WS 382), held in the Military Archives, Cathal Brugha Barracks, Dublin.

1 William G. Wylie, prosecution council, unpublished memoir; quoted in Brian Barton, *From Behind a Closed Door: Secret Court Martial Records of the 1916 Easter Rising*, p. 35.

2 R. M. Fox, 'Nora Connolly', in *Rebel Irishwomen*, p. 108.

3 Ina Connolly Heron, Witness Statement 919.

4 Testimony of Mrs Allen, 8 Spenser Villas; quoted in Barton, p. 226.

5 Dr Anthony MacBride married Elizabeth Mooney, 26 April 1916. Her brother Henry Mooney was best man. Anthony Jordan, *Clara Allen*; sourced at www.academia.edu/4469164/clara_allen.

6 Testimony of John MacBride; quoted in Barton, p. 228.

7 Piaras F. Mac Lochlainn, *Last Words: Letters and Statements of the Leaders Executed after the Rising at Easter 1916*, p. 99.

8 Testimony of John MacBride; quoted in Barton, p. 226.

9 Kathleen Clarke, *Revolutionary Woman*, p. 79.

10 Áine Ceannt, Witness Statement 264.

11 Her name is given variously as McMahon and MacMahon; John Cowell, *A Noontide Blazing: Brigid Lyons Thornton – Rebel, Soldier, Doctor*, p. 54.

12   Thomas Mallin, Witness Statement 382.

13   Nora and Éamonn Dore married in 1918.

14   Clarke, op. cit., p. 84.

15   Mac Lochlainn, op. cit., p. 38.

16   Charlie McGuire, *Roddy Connolly and the Struggle for Socialism in Ireland*, p. 15.

17   She did not make public the contents of this; Mac Lochlainn, op. cit., p. 38.

18   Clarke, op. cit., p. 82.

19   Donal Nevin, *James Connolly: A Full Life*, p. 656.

20   Handwritten account by Fiona Connolly, undated; Fiona Connolly papers, Marx Library.

21   Clarke, op. cit., pp. 82–3.

22   Áine Ceannt, Witness Statement.

23   Quoted in Anne Clare, *Unlikely Rebels: The Gifford Girls*, p. 159.

24   Clarke, op. cit., p. 83.

25   Áine Ceannt, Witness Statement.

26   JP to GG, 29 April 1916.

Notes for Chapter 9

Details of events in the days following the Rising are primarily taken from the following sources: Brian Barton, *From Behind a Closed Door: Secret Court Martial Records of the 1916 Easter Rising*; Kathleen Clarke, *Revolutionary Woman*; Anne Clare, *Unlikely Rebels: The Gifford Girls*; Nora Connolly O'Brien, *The Unbroken Tradition* and *We Shall Rise Again*; William Henry, *Supreme Sacrifice: The Story of Éamonn Ceannt*; Piaras F. Mac Lochlainn, *Last Words: Letters and Statements of the Leaders Executed after the Rising at Easter 1916*; Seamus Mallin, 'Commandant Michael Mallin', published in *Inniú*; Geraldine Plunkett Dillon, *All In the Blood: A Memoir of the Plunkett Family, the 1916 Rising and the War of Independence*; and from Witness Statements given by Áine Ceannt (WS 264), Thomas Mallin (WS 382) and Sergeant Michael T. Soughley (WS 189) held in the Military Archives, Cathal Brugha Barracks, Dublin.

1   *Sinn Féin Rebellion Handbook*, Dublin: Fred Hanna Ltd, 1917, p. 4.

2   Piaras F. Mac Lochlainn, *Last Words: Letters and Statements of the Leaders Executed after the Rising at Easter 1916*, p. 53.

3   Nellie Gifford Donnelly papers; quoted in Anne Clare, *Unlikely Rebels: The Gifford Girls*, p. 161.

4   Máire Ní Shiubhlaigh, *The Splendid Years*, p. 184.

5   Kilmainham Jail Collection.

6   Kathleen Clarke, *Revolutionary Woman*, p. 83.

7   TC to KC, 30 April 1916; quoted in Mac Lochlainn, p. 42.

8   Nora Connolly O'Brien, *The Unbroken Tradition*, New York, 1918, p. 171.

9   Ina Connolly Heron, 'James Connolly: A Biography, Part 8 – A Full Life and a Good End', *Liberty*, p. 15.

10   Connolly O'Brien, *The Unbroken Tradition*, p. 172.

11   Connolly O'Brien, *Portrait of a Rebel Father*, p. 312.

12   Clarke, op. cit., p. 87.

13   Áine Ceannt, Witness Statement 264.

14   Honor Ó Brolcháin, *16Lives: Joe Plunkett*, p. 399.

15   Mac Lochlainn, op. cit., pp. 31–2.

16   Kilmainham Jail Collection.

17   Clarke, op. cit., pp. 91–6.

18   Madge Daly, quoted in Clarke, p. 232.

19   Sergeant Michael T. Soughley, Witness Statement 189.

20   Quoted in Brian Barton, *From Behind a Closed Door: Secret Court Martial Records of the 1916 Easter Rising*, p. 147.

21   Geraldine Plunkett Dillon, *All In the Blood: A Memoir of the Plunkett Family, the 1916 Rising and the War of Independence*, p. 231.

22   Donagh MacDonagh, quoted in Barton, p. 130.

23   Plunkett Dillon, op. cit., p. 31.

24   *Lloyd's Weekly News*, 7 May 1916.

25   Geraldine later wrote that Grace had a letter from an ex-fiancé, whom she calls 'Moore', in the weeks following the Rising, who wrote to congratulate her on the birth of a son. Grace wrote back to him that it was not true she had had a baby. There is no other documentation on her having had a fiancé. Plunkett Dillon, op. cit., p. 247.

26   Plunkett Dillon, op. cit., p. 227.

27   R. M. Fox, *Rebel Irishwomen*, p. 78.

28   Connolly O'Brien, *Portrait of a Rebel Father*, p. 316.

29   Barton, op. cit., p. 215.

30   Anthony J. Jordan, *Major John MacBride, 1865–1916*, p. 124.

31   Ibid., p. 127.

32   EC to AC, 4 May 1916; quoted in Mac Lochlainn, pp. 134–5.

33   EC to AC, 5 May 1916; ibid.

34   EC, 7 May 1916; ibid., p. 136.

35   EC to AC, 8 May 1916; ibid., p. 141.

36   Áine Ceannt, Witness Statement.

37   'My poor wife saw me yesterday and bore up – so my warden told me – even after she left my presence'; statement, 7 May 1916, quoted in William Henry, *Supreme Sacrifice: The Story of Éamonn Ceannt*, p. 127.

38   Henry, op. cit., p. 122.

39   EC to AC, 2.30 a.m., 8 May 1916.

40   Court Martial Papers, Michael Mallin, Public Record Office, Kew, W071/353 22758.

41   Thomas Mallin, Witness Statement 382.

42   Seamus Mallin, 'Commandant Michael Mallin', in *Inniú*.

43   Ibid.

44   Ibid.

45   Original letter, Kilmainham Jail Collection.

46   Mac Lochlainn, op. cit., p. 191.

47   Connolly Heron, 'A Full Life and a Good End'.

48   Military Archives file WS 1,019, Bureau of Military History, comprises a memoir made in early 1953 by the Rt Hon. Sir Alfred Bucknill, retired Lord Justice of Appeal, who had been deputy judge advocate general of the British forces in Ireland in 1916. There was a record of an interview he had with the Irish ambassador in London on 4 February 1953, who told the story of the chair and that it might possibly still be extant, saying that the back of the chair was badly damaged by the bullets.

49   Connolly O'Brien, *We Shall Rise Again*, p. 39.

50   Information from Carol Murphy, 1996.

51   Henry, op. cit., p. 128.

Notes for Chapter 10

Details of events are primarily taken from the following sources: Anne Clare, *Unlikely Rebels: The Gifford Girls*; Anna MacBride and A. Norman Jeffares (eds), *The Gonne–Yeats Letters 1893–1938: 'Always Your Friend'*; Seán MacBride, *That Day's Struggle: A Memoir 1904–1951* (ed. Catriona Lawlor); Geraldine Plunkett Dillon, *All In the Blood: A Memoir of the Plunkett Family, the 1916 Rising and the War of Independence*; Witness Statement given by Áine Ceannt (WS 264), held in the Military Archives, Cathal Brugha Barracks, Dublin; documents held in the Ceannt, O'Brennan and Plunkett family papers, NLI.

1   Eileen Moore, *Catholic Press*, Sydney, NSW, 1916.

2   Kathleen Clarke, *Revolutionary Woman*, p. 120.

3   Ibid., p. 137.

4   Caoimhe Nic Dháibhéid (2012), 'The Irish National Aid Association

and the Radicalisation of Public Opinion in Ireland, 1916–1918', *The Historical Journal*, 55, pp. 705-729. DOI: 1017/50018246X12000234.

5 Lily Conlon, 'Cumann na mBan and the Women of Ireland 1913–1915', in *Kilkenny People*, p. 35.

6 George Bernard Shaw, quoted in Anna MacBride and A. Norman Jeffares (eds), *The Gonne–Yeats Letters 1893–1938: 'Always Your Friend'*, p. 377.

7 *Lloyd's Weekly News*, 7 May 1916; in Grace Plunkett Scrapbook, NLI, MS 21,593.

8 *Lloyd's Weekly News*, 7 May 1916; in Kilmainham Jail Collection, quoted in full in Sinéad McCoole, *Guns & Chiffon: Women Revolutionaries and Kilmainham Gaol*, p. 33.

9 Headline from *Lloyd's Weekly News*, 7 May 1916; in Kilmainham Jail Collection.

10 Eileen Moore, 'Maid, Wife and Widow on her Wedding Day', *New World* (Chicago), 6 October 1916; in Grace Plunkett Scrapbook.

11 Nora Connolly O'Brien, Witness Statement 285.

12 Uinseann MacEoin, *Survivors: The story of Ireland's struggle as told through some of her outstanding living people . . .*, p. 205.

13 Nic Dháibhéid, op. cit., has argued that the amount of the awards was to do with the prestige of the executed men, with some of the families being overlooked. Con Colbert's invalided sister got £300, while Seán Mac Diarmada's family got £100 in late 1917, when it was made known that in his last days Seán had expressed a wish that his nephew should be looked after.

14 Pearse's elderly mother got £250. Mrs O'Hanrahan, whose son Michael was executed, was given £100, as he had provided for his family and of his three sisters two had lost their work following the Rising. Mrs Heuston, the separated mother of Seán Heuston, was given £5. Seán, a former rail worker, was executed for his role as commandant of the small battalion at the Mendicity Institute. He had been the family wage-earner. Sometime later it was recorded that £70 was raised in Limerick for Mrs Heuston's sole use.

Notes for Chapter 11

Details of events are primarily taken from the following sources: Anne Clare, *Unlikely Rebels: The Gifford Girls*; Geraldine Plunkett Dillon, *All In the Blood: A Memoir of the Plunkett Family, the 1916 Rising and the War of Independence*; Witness Statement given by Áine Ceannt (WS 264) in the Military Archives,

Cathal Brugha Barracks, Dublin; papers of the Ceannt, O'Brennan, Plunkett and Gifford families held in the NLI; Military Pension Records; Kilmainham Jail Records; letter from Emmet Clarke to the author, 1995; and the author's interview with Maura Phillips (*née* Mallin), 1995.

1   Annie P. Smithson, quoted in Siccda Heritage Centre, *Ladies of the Liberties*.

2   Geraldine Plunkett Dillon, *All In the Blood: A Memoir of the Plunkett Family, the 1916 Rising and the War of Independence*, p. 254.

3   Isabella Gifford to Sister Francesa, 21 June 1916, dh.tcd.ie/letters1916/diyhhistory/190.

4   Uinseann MacEoin, *Survivors: The story of Ireland's struggle as told through some of her outstanding living people . . .*, p. 144.

5   Rónán Ceannt to Kathleen O'Brennan, 14 January 1917; Catherine M. Burns, 'Kathleen O'Brennan and American Identity', in *The Irish in the Atlantic World*, p. 179.

6   He died on 19 September 1917.

7   Maeve Donnelly, daughter of Nellie Gifford Donnelly, interview with the author, 1994.

8   He printed James Connolly's *Labour in Irish History* in 1919.

9   Anne Clare, *Unlikely Rebels: The Gifford Girls*, pp. 213–14.

10 Arpad Czira (1887–1964) returned to his native Hungary, but the area in which he lived was annexed by Romania. He got married in the mid-1920s to a painter, Stima Erzsebet. They had one son, who still lives in Szatmarnemeti. Arpad was deputy mayor of Satu-Mare, northern Transylvania, Romania, in 1932 through the so-called temporary committee. He confessed to his son on his deathbed that he had had a son in America. With thanks to Larisa Sioneriu and Tamas Sarandi for this information.

11 Caoimhe Nic Dháibhéid, in 'The Irish National Aid Association and the Radicalisation of Public Opinion in Ireland, 1916-1918'. The three daughters are not identified, but by age profile Moira and Fiona would have attended. Ina was younger than Aideen, but it is unclear which of them attended.

12 Charlie McGuire, *Roddy Connolly and the Struggle for Socialism in Ireland*, p. 18. It is often stated Dr Tobin paid for Roddy's education, but according to his biographer there is no evidence to suggest this, although Roddy did maintain a friendship with the doctor into later life.

13 Letter from Emmet Clarke to the author, 25 March 1995, in which he

said he had never mentioned this incident to anyone before.

14 Anna MacBride and A. Norman Jeffares (eds), *The Gonne–Yeats Letters 1893–1938: 'Always Your Friend'*, p. 389.

15 Kathleen Clarke, *Revolutionary Woman*, p. 138.

16 Ibid., p. 144.

17 *The Times*, 8 February 1917; quoted in M. Rast, 'Tactics, Politics and Propaganda in the Irish War of Independence, 1917–1921', MA thesis, Georgia State University, 2011.

18 Nic Dháibhéid, op. cit.

19 A newspaper photograph of Muriel with her sister Grace and toddler Barbara was dated to July 1917 when it was reproduced in the *Irish Independent*, 22 March 1966. As Muriel died that month it was probably printed in the newspaper at the time of her death; from the clothing and the age of the child it has to date between May and July of that year.

20 GP to D. O'Connor, 7 May 1917; in Irish National Aid Association papers.

21 According to Judge William Wylie reviewing the list, General Maxwell enquired if de Valera was important, and as Wylie replied in the negative his life was spared; quoted in Tim Pat Coogan, *De Valera: Long Fellow, Long Shadow*, p. 78.

22 Clarke, op. cit., p. 144.

23 Information supplied to the author by Emmet Clarke, 1995.

24 The poem 'Patrick Pearse, Commandant General IRA' was written on 23 October 1916; in *A Voice of Insurgency*, privately printed, 1916.

25 MGM to WBY, *Letters*, p. 391.

Notes for Chapter 12

Details of events are primarily taken from the following sources: Lily O'Brennan, 'Leading a Dog's Life in Ireland', NLI, MS 15,602–03; interviews by the author with Muriel Maculey and the late Iseult MacGuinness, granddaughter of Muriel MacDonagh; and the archives of *Skerries News* and the *Irish Times*.

1 Flyer for the *Aeridheacht Mor*, Sunday, 22 July 1917, IR 914109 N2. A second one was planned for 29 July but postponed to 1–2 September.

2 Lily O'Brennan, 'Leading a Dog's Life in Ireland'.

3 Ibid.

4 Brother of Seán Lemass, later Taoiseach of Ireland.

5 O'Brennan, op. cit.

6   Elizabeth Balcombe, 'Day of the Drowning', *Skerries News*, Vol. 18, No. 3, 2007.

7   Iseult MacGuinness, daughter of Donagh MacDonagh, to the author, 1995.

8   O'Brennan, op. cit.

9   Iseult MacGuinness to author.

10   Thomas MacDonagh's last letter, 2 May 1916.

11   John Gore to Katherine Wilson, 3 September 1917, Thomas MacDonagh papers. The committee consisted of Alderman Corrigan, John Gore, Mr Nesbitt and P. T. Keohane.

Notes for Chapter 13

Details of events are primarily drawn from the following sources: Nancy Cardozo, *Lucky Eyes and a High Heart: The Life of Maud Gonne*; Kathleen Clarke, *Revolutionary Woman*; Elizabeth Keane, *Seán MacBride: A Life*; Margaret Ward, *Maud Gonne: A Life* and 'The League of Women Delegates & Sinn Féin', *History Ireland*; Witness Statements given by Áine Ceannt (WS 264) and Maud Gonne MacBride (WS 317), held in the Military Archives, Cathal Brugha Barracks, Dublin; Military Pension Records; letter from Father Joseph Mallin to the author, 1995; and the author's interview with Maura Phillips (*née* Mallin), 1995.

1   Kathleen Clarke, autobiographical notes, 5 October 1917; typed and given to the author by Emmet Clarke.

2   Ibid.

3   Kathleen Clarke, *Revolutionary Woman*, p. 148.

4   Clarke, autobiographical notes.

5   Elizabeth Keane, *Seán MacBride: A Life*, p. 32.

6   Margaret Mulvihill, *Charlotte Despard: A Biography*, p. 1.

7   Maud Gonne MacBride, Witness Statement 317.

8   Nancy Cardozo, *Lucky Eyes and a High Heart: The Life of Maud Gonne*, p. 324.

9   Clarke, *Revolutionary Woman*, p. 160.

10   Ibid., p. 157.

11   Constance Markievicz to Eva Gore Booth, 22 June [1918]; quoted in Constance Markievicz, *Prison Letters of Countess Markievicz*, p. 180.

12   Margaret Ward, *Hanna Sheehy Skeffington: A Life*, p. 215.

13   A. Norman Jeffares, Anna MacBride White and Christina Bridgwater

(eds), *Letters to W. B. Yeats and Ezra Pound from Iseult Gonne: A Girl That Knew All Dante Once*, p. 107.

14   Maud Gonne MacBride, Witness Statement.

15   Ibid.

16   Elizabeth Coxhead, *Daughters of Erin: Five Women of the Irish Renaissance*, p. 67.

17   Constance Markievicz to Eva Gore Booth, 4 December [1918], quoted in Markievicz, p. 189.

18   Father Joseph Mallin, letter to the author, 10 May 1995.

19   Ibid.

Notes for Chapter 14

Details of events are primarily taken from the following sources: Áine Ceannt, *The Story of the Irish White Cross 1920–1947*; Kathleen Clarke, *Revolutionary Woman*; Anne Clare, *Unlikely Rebels: The Gifford Girls*; Albert Coyle, *Evidence on Conditions in Ireland*; A. Norman Jeffares, Anna MacBride White and Christina Bridgwater (eds), *Letters to W. B. Yeats and Ezra Pound from Iseult Gonne: A Girl That Knew All Dante Once*; Anna MacBride White and A. Norman Jeffares (eds), *The Gonne–Yeats Letters 1893–1938: 'Always Your Friend'*; Seán MacBride, *That Day's Struggle: A Memoir 1904–1951*; Witness Statements given by Áine Ceannt (WS 264), Maud Gonne MacBride (WS 317) and Sidney Czira (WS 909), held in the Military Archives, Cathal Brugha Barracks, Dublin; Military Pension Records; and the records of Cumann na mBan, Kilmainham Jail Collection.

1   Kathleen Clarke, *Revolutionary Woman*, p. 168.

2   Ibid., p. 170.

3   Kevin Rockett, Luke Gibbons and John Hill (eds), *Cinema & Ireland*, Routledge Library Editions: Cinema, 1987, pp. 19–20.

4   Clarke, op. cit., p. 176.

5   Maud Gonne MacBride, Witness Statement 317.

6   Mike Rast, 'Tactics, Politics, and Propaganda in the Irish War of Independence 1917–1921'.

7   Helen Bingham Nyberg Military Pension Record. Helen had married Daniel Bingham in 1897. He retired from the RIC in 1909. After his death in 1926 Helen, then fifty-one, departed for America with ten-year-old Margaret, as three of her children were then living there. In New York she married again to a man ten years her junior, Edward Nyberg, but three years later, in 1942, she died aged sixty-seven.

8   Joseph Donnelly supported his daughter until she was twelve. He

remarried (during Nellie's lifetime) and had another daughter.

9   F. P. Crozier, *Ireland For Ever*, quoted in Rast, op. cit., p. 110.

10   Clarke, op. cit., p. 172.

11   Painting in the collection of the Crawford Art Gallery, Cork.

12   Áine Ceannt Military Pension Record.

13   Albert Coyle, *Evidence on Conditions in Ireland*, p. 245.

14   Mary Kotsonuris, in *The People's Courts – Ireland's Dáil Courts 1920–1924*.

15   It is unclear how Maud came to have Synge's cottage. Later the same cottage was in the possession of Dr Kathleen Lynn, who gave it to the An Óige for use as a youth hostel.

16   MGM to WBY, [October, 1920]; in Anna MacBride and A. Norman Jeffares (eds), *The Gonne–Yeats Letters 1893–1938: 'Always Your Friend'*, pp. 413–14.

17   Constance Markievicz, *Prison Letters of Countess Markievicz*, p. 251.

18   MGM to WBY, [Thursday, October, 1920], *Letters*, pp. 413–15.

19   Margaret Mulvihill, *Charlotte Despard: A Biography*, p. 116.

20   Rast, op. cit., pp. 118–19.

21   *Letters*, p. 417.

22   Seán MacBride, *That Day's Struggle: A Memoir 1904–1951*, p. 23.

23   Áine Ceannt, Witness Statement 264.

24   Áine Ceannt Military Pension Record.

25   Clarke, op. cit., p. 187.

26   Father Joseph Mallin to the author, 10 May 1995.

27   MGM to WBY, 22 October [1920], *Letters*, p. 416.

28   MGM to WBY, [November 1920], *Letters*, p. 417.

29   Irish White Cross Report, p. 27.

30   LC to James Foran, William O'Brien papers; quoted in Siccda Heritage Centre, *Ladies of the Liberties*, p. 117.

31   Sidney Czira, Witness Statement 909.

32   According to her military pension application, she was involved with the White Cross from April 1921 until March 1922.

33   Sinéad McCoole, *No Ordinary Women: Irish Female Activists in the Revolutionary Years 1900–1923*, p. 169.

34   Albert Coyle, *Evidence on Conditions in Ireland*, pp. 60–1.

35   Seán MacBride, op. cit., pp. 27–31.

36   Micheál Mallin, son of Seamus Mallin, interview with the author, 27 January 1995.

37   Seán MacBride, op. cit., p. 34.

38 *Irish Bulletin*, 9 July 1921; quoted in Mike Rast, 'Tactics, Politics, and Propaganda in the Irish War of Independence, 1917–1921', p. 143.

39 MGM to WBY, 27 July [1921], *Letters*, p. 426.

40 A. Norman Jeffares, Anna MacBride White and Christina Bridgwater (eds), *Letters to W. B. Yeats and Ezra Pound from Iseult Gonne: A Girl That Knew All Dante Once*, p. 116.

41 MGM to WBY, 27 July [1921], *Letters*, p. 426.

42 MGM to WBY, 24 August 1921, ibid.

Notes for Chapter 15

Details of events are primarily taken from the following sources: Kathleen Clarke, *Revolutionary Woman*; Anne Clare, *Unlikely Rebels: The Gifford Girls*; Elizabeth Keane, *Seán MacBride: A Life*; Charlie McGuire, *Roddy Connolly and the Struggle for Socialism in Ireland*; Margaret Ward, *Maud Gonne*; and Military Pension Records.

1 Áine Ceannt, Witness Statement 264.

2 Kathleen Clarke, *Revolutionary Woman*, p. 188.

3 Elizabeth Keane, *Seán MacBride: A Life*, p. 39.

4 The casket presented to her was sold at the 'Independence Sale', Adams Auction Rooms, Dublin, 12 April 2006, Lot 330. This information is inscribed on the wooden presentation casket, which also has the dates 1916 and 1921 carved on it.

5 Clarke, op. cit., p. 190.

6 Seán MacBride, *That Day's Struggle: A Memoir*, p. 54.

7 Peace Treaty Debates, 22 December 1921; Dáil Éireann, Vol. 3, p. 141.

8 Clarke, op. cit., p. 193.

9 Margaret Ward, *Maud Gonne: A Life*, p. 131.

10 Circular, Cumann na mBan, 14 February 1922.

11 Áine Ceannt, *The Story of the Irish White Cross 1920–1947*, pp. 27–9.

Notes for Chapter 16

Details of events are primarily taken from the following sources: Anne Clare, *Unlikely Rebels: The Gifford Girls*; Andro Linklater, *An Unhusbanded Life: Charlotte Despard – Suffragist, Socialist and Sinn Féiner*; Anna MacBride and A. Norman Jeffares (eds), *The Gonne–Yeats Letters 1893–1938: 'Always Your Friend'*; Sinéad McCoole, *No Ordinary Women: Irish Female Activists in the Revolutionary Years 1900–1923*; Rosamond Jacob diaries, 22 April–7 August 1922, held in the NLI, MS 32,582; Witness Statement given by Cahir Davitt, Judge, Dáil Courts

(WS 993); Women's Prisoners' Defence League pamphlet, copy in author's collection; and Military Pension Records.

1   Rosamond Jacob diaries, 22 April–7 August 1922.
2   Uinseann MacEoin, *Survivors: The story of Ireland's struggle as told through some of her outstanding living people* . . ., p. 211.
3   Jacob diaries, op. cit.
4   Áine Ceannt Military Pension Record.
5   Jacob, op. cit.
6   Ibid.
7   The Women's Prisoners' Defence League, undated pamphlet, private collection; copy in author's collection.
8   Undated draft of letter, unsigned, UCDA, P13/72.
9   Father Joseph Mallin, interview with the author, May 2005.
10   Witness Statement, Cahir Davitt, Judge, Dáil Courts, Bureau of Military History, Witness Statement, 993.
11   Cahir Davitt, Judge, Dáil Courts, Witness Statement.
12   Ibid.
13   *Poblacht na hÉireann, War News*, No. 90, 11 November 1922.
14   Siccda Heritage Centre, *Ladies of the Liberties*, p. 118.
15   Seán MacBride, *That Day's Struggle: A Memoir 1904–1951*, pp. 69–72.
16   Andro Linklater, *An Unhusbanded Life: Charlotte Despard – Suffragist, Socialist and Sinn Féiner*, p. 224.
17   Grace Gifford Plunkett Military Pension Record. Her file states 'She had done none of the service which could be regarded as qualifying service under the act'.
18   Kathleen Clarke Military Pension Record.
19   Seamus Mallin to AM, 9 February 1923; copy in author's collection.
20   AC to Lily O'Brennan, 3 April 1923; O'Brennan papers.
21   Ibid.
22   Linklater, op. cit., p. 227.
23   Charlotte Fallon, MA thesis, University College Dublin; quoted in Sinéad McCoole, *No Ordinary Women: Irish Female Activists in the Revolutionary Years 1900–1923*, p. 118.
24   Hannah Monihan's diary; ibid.
25   Linklater, op. cit., p. 225.
26   Charlotte Fallon, *Éire*, Vol. 2, 1987; quoted in McCoole, p. 118.
27   Quoted in Anne Clare, *Unlikely Rebels: The Gifford Girls*, p. 240.
28   Katherine Clarke, *Revolutionary Woman*, p. 208.

29   Elsewhere it is given as 13 August. Interview with interviewing officer,
      19 January 1942, Military Pension Records.
30   Interviews with Maura Phillips (*née* Mallin), 22 January 1995, 2 April
      1995 and 19 April 1999.
31   Anthony Bradley, *Imagining Ireland in the Poems and Plays of W. B. Yeats:
      Nation, Class, and State*, p. 88.

Notes for Chapter 17

Details of events and of the lives of the protagonists and their families are
primarily taken from the following sources: Áine Ceannt, *The Story of the Irish
White Cross 1920–1947*; Anne Clare, *Unlikely Rebels: The Gifford Girls*;
Kathleen Clarke, *Revolutionary Woman*; Anna MacBride and A. Norman
Jeffares (eds), *The Gonne–Yeats Letters 1893–1938: 'Always Your Friend'*; Seán
MacBride, *That Day's Struggle: A Memoir 1904–1951*; Sinéad McCoole, *No
Ordinary Women: Irish Female Activists in the Revolutionary Years 1900–1923*;
Caoimhe Nic Dháibhéid, *Seán MacBride: A Republican Life 1904–1946*; Siccda
Heritage Centre, *Ladies of the Liberties*; Military Pension Records; Records of
the Political Prisoners Committee, held in the Kilmainham Jail Collection;
letters from Father Joseph Mallin to the author; and interviews by the author
with Maura Phillips (*née* Mallin), and with Emmet Clarke.

1   It was decided that no child born after 1 June 1924 would be eligible for
      maintenance. So many applications were being rejected on this ruling,
      however, that the date was changed to 1 June 1926, then again, after an
      examination of its resources, it was extended to 1 June 1927. Report of
      the Meeting of the White Cross, 1 September 1936, p. 16.
2   The older spelling is Ceant's Fort, as opposed to the modern Ceannt's
      Fort. In an interview with Judy Rogerson, Dundrum (Cumann na
      mBan), in 1995 she stated that the National Aid bought this house for
      the Mallins, but Maura Philips (*née* Mallin) stated to the author in an
      interview on 19 April 1999 that they rented it and that National Aid
      trustee Thomas Farren had to be a guarantor.
3   Kathleen Clarke Military Pension Record.
4   William O'Brien to General Mulcahy, 6 February 1924, and interview,
      15 February 1924; Lillie (Lily) Connolly Military Pension Record.
5   Kathleen Clarke, *Revolutionary Woman*, p. 210.
6   Elizabeth Keane, *Seán MacBride: A Life*, p. 50.
7   Caoimhe Nic Dháibhéid, *Seán MacBride: A Republican Life 1904–1946*,
      p. 79.

8   Seán MacBride, *That Day's Struggle: A Memoir 1904–1951*, p. 100.

9   Clarke, op. cit., p. 211.

10   Winifred (Úna) Gordon married first an RIC officer who died during the First World War. In 1935 she then married Austin Stack, whom she had sheltered during the War of Independence. During the Civil War she was imprisoned in Kilmainham Jail for her opposition to the Treaty.

11   Maura Phillips (*née* Mallin), interview with the author, 2 April 1995.

12   MM to AM, 8 May 1916; Kilmainham Jail Collection, 17 LR IB 24 16.

13   Agnes Mallin Military Pension Record.

14   Ibid.

15   Nic Dháibhéid, op. cit., p. 88.

16   Ibid., p. 94.

17   Political Prisoners' Committee Circular, No, 14, July 1930; Kilmainham Jail Collection.

18   'Mammy's Notebook 1, Trip to Seville', 1930, private collection.

19   Agnes Mallin, Diary 2, 1931, private collection.

20   Ibid.

21   Ibid.

22   Maud Gonne MacBride Military Pension Record.

23   She was turned down under the conditions of the Pension Act, 1936. Grace Plunkett Military Pension Record.

24   Information sourced by Paul Turnell: register of the National Homes for Disabled Soldiers, at www.ancestry.co.uk.

25   Thomas Clarke Archive.

26   *Irish Press*, 2 March 1935; in Anne Clare, *Unlikely Rebels: The Gifford Girls*, p. 267.

27   Clarke, op. cit., p. 217.

28   Siccda Heritage Centre, *Ladies of the Liberties*, p. 120.

29   They remained in the Labour Party until 1939 when the objective of a Workers' Republic was removed from the constitution, at which point Nora and Seamus retired from the party.

30   Charlie McGuire, *Roddy Connolly and the Struggle for Socialism in Ireland*, p. 167. There were five children from this marriage: Rory (born 1939), Margaret (born 1941), Maura (born 1943), Frank (born 1945) and John (born 1947).

31   Siccda Heritage Centre, op. cit., p. 120.

32   Clarke, op. cit., p. 222.

33   Thomas Clarke Archive.

34   Ibid.

35 Nic Dháibhéid, op. cit., pp. 144–5.

36 Clarke, op. cit., p. 224.

37 Nancy Cardozo, *Lucky Eyes and a High Heart: The Life of Maud Gonne*, p. 400.

38 Nic Dháibhéid, op. cit., p. 197.

39 Cardozo, op. cit., p. 398.

40 Ceannt, *The Story of the White Cross*, Foreword.

41 Clare, op. cit., p. 273.

42 Nellie Gifford Donnelly Military Pension Record.

43 Summary of sworn evidence, 19 January 1942, Grace Plunkett Military Pension Record.

44 Ibid.

45 Áine left a sum of money for this purpose in her will, but the headstone was erected after her death by a member of Éamonn Ceannt's battalion; see www.gonebutnotforgotten.ie.

46 Áine Ceannt Military Pension Record.

47 Dave Kenny, 'The Son Also Rises', *The Magazine*; at www.writing.ie.

48 A. Norman Jeffares, Anna MacBride White and Christina Bridgwater (eds), *Letters to W. B. Yeats and Ezra Pound from Iseult Gonne: A Girl That Knew All Dante Once*, pp. 156–7.

49 Clarke, op. cit., p. 226.

50 'Some Reminiscences of Mrs. Tom Clarke', *Nenagh Guardian*, 14 October 1972, p. 10.

51 Emmet Clarke, son of Edward Emmet Clarke, interview with the author, 13 March 2014.

52 Emmet and Tom Clarke, information supplied to the author, 2014.

Notes for Epilogue

Details are taken from letters from Father Joseph Mallin to the author; and from interviews by the author with Maura Phillips (*née* Mallin).

1 Seán Coughlan SJ, interview with Father Joseph Mallin, 2013; recorded online.

Bibliography

Books

Alexander, Tania, *A Little of All These: An Estonian Childhood*, London: Jonathan Cape, 1987

Barton, Brian, *From Behind a Closed Door: Secret Court Martial Records of the 1916 Easter Rising*, Belfast: Blackstaff Press, 2002

Bradley, Anthony, *Imagining Ireland in the Poems and Plays of W. B. Yeats: Nation, Class, and State*, Basingstoke: Palgrave Macmillan, 2011

Burns, Catherine M., 'Kathleen O'Brennan and American Identity in the Transatlantic Irish Republican Movement', in David T. Gleeson (ed.), *The Irish in the Atlantic World*, Columbia, SC: University of South Carolina Press, 2010

Cardozo, Nancy, *Lucky Eyes and a High Heart: The Life of Maud Gonne*, Indianapolis, Ind: Bobbs-Merrill Company, 1978

Ceannt, Áine, *The Story of the Irish White Cross 1920–1947*, Dublin: Sign of the Three Candles, 1948

Clare, Anne, *Unlikely Rebels: The Gifford Girls*, Dublin: Mercier Press, 2011

Clarke, Kathleen, *Revolutionary Woman, 1878–1972: An Autobiography* (ed. Helen Litton), Dublin: O'Brien Press, 1991

Clarke, Thomas J., *Glimpses of an Irish Felon's Prison Life*, Dublin & London: Maunsel & Roberts, 1922

Collins, Lorcan, *16Lives: James Connolly*, Dublin: O'Brien Press, 2012

Colum, Mary Maguire, *Life and the Dream*, New York: Doubleday & Company, 1947

Conlon, Lily, 'Cumann na mBan and the Women of Ireland 1913–1915', *Kilkenny People*, 1969

Connolly O'Brien, Nora, *Portrait of a Rebel Father*, Dublin: Talbot Press, 1935

Connolly O'Brien, Nora, *We Shall Rise Again*, London: Mosquito Press, 1981

Coogan, Tim Pat, *De Valera: Long Fellow, Long Shadow*, London: Random House, 1993

Cowell, John, *A Noontide Blazing: Brigid Lyons Thornton – Rebel, Soldier, Doctor*, Blackrock, Co. Dublin: Currach Press, 2005

Coxhead, Elizabeth, *Daughters of Erin: Five Women of the Irish Renaissance*, Gerrards Cross: Colin Smythe, 1979

Coyle, Albert, *Evidence on Conditions in Ireland*, Washington DC: American Commission on Ireland, 1921

Dudley Edwards, Ruth, *James Connolly, in Gill's Irish Lives* (series), Dublin: Gill & Macmillan, 1981

Feeney, William J., *Drama in Hardwicke Street: A History of the Irish Theatre Company*, Cranbury, NJ: Associated University Presses, 1984

Fox, R. M., *Rebel Irishwomen*, Dublin: Talbot Press, 1935

Gonne MacBride, Maud, *A Servant of the Queen* (ed. A. Norman Jeffares and Anna MacBride White), Chicago, Ill: University of Chicago Press, 1995

Greaves, C. Desmond, *The Life and Times of James Connolly*, London: Lawrence & Wishart, 1961

Hayes, Alan (ed.), *The Years Flew By: Recollections of Madame Sidney Gifford Czira*, Galway: Arlen House, 2007

Henry, William, *Supreme Sacrifice: The Story of Éamonn Ceannt*, Cork: Mercier Press, 2005

Hogan, Robert, and O'Neill, Michael J., *Joseph Holloway's Abbey Theatre: A Selection from His Unpublished Journal 'Impressions of a Dublin Playgoer'*, Carbondale, Ill: Southern Illinois University Press, 1967

Hughes, Brian, *16Lives: Michael Mallin*, Dublin: O'Brien Press, 2012

Jeffares, A. Norman, MacBride White, Anna, and Bridgwater, Christina (eds), *Letters to W. B. Yeats and Ezra Pound from Iseult Gonne: A Girl That Knew All Dante Once*, Basingstoke: Palgrave Macmillan, 2004

Jordan, Anthony J., *Major John MacBride, 1865–1916*, Westport, Co. Mayo: Westport Historical Society, 1991

Jordan, Anthony J., *The Yeats-Gonne-MacBride Triangle*, Westport, Co. Mayo: Westport Books, 2000

Jordan, Anthony J., *Willie Yeats and the Gonne-MacBrides*, Anthony J. Jordan, 1997

Keane, Elizabeth: *Seán MacBride: A Life*, Dublin: Gill & Macmillan, 2007

Kotsonuris, Mary, *The People's Courts – Ireland's Dail Courts 1920–1924*, privately published, 2013

Le Roux, Louis, *Tom Clarke and the Irish Freedom Movement*, Dublin: Talbot Press, 1936

Levenson, Samuel, *James Connolly: A Biography*, London: Martin Brian and O'Keefe, 1973

Linklater, Andro, *An Unhusbanded Life: Charlotte Despard – Suffragist, Socialist and Sinn Féiner*, London: Hutchinson, 1980

Litton, Helen, *16Lives: Edward Daly*, Dublin: O'Brien Press, 2013

Longford, Frank Pakenham, Earl of, and O'Neill, Thomas P., *Éamon de Valera*, Boston, Mass: Houghton Mifflin, 1971

MacAtasney, Gerard, *Tom Clarke: Life, Liberty, Revolution*, Dublin: Merrion, 2012

MacAtasney, Gerard, *Seán Mac Diarmada: Mind of the Revolution*, Manorhamilton, Co. Leitrim: Drumlin Publications, 2004

MacBride, Anna, and Jeffares, A. Norman (eds), *The Gonne–Yeats Letters 1893–1938: 'Always Your Friend'*, London: Hutchinson, 1992

MacBride, Seán, *That Day's Struggle: A Memoir 1904–1951* (ed. Catriona Lawlor), Dublin: Currach Press, 2005

MacDonagh, Thomas, *Poem: A Selection by His Sister*, Dublin: Talbot Press, 1925

MacEoin, Uinseann, *Survivors: The story of Ireland's struggle as told through some of her outstanding living people . . .*, Dublin: Argenta Publications, 1980

Mac Lochlainn, Piaras F., *Last Words: Letters and Statements of the Leaders Executed after the Rising at Easter 1916*, Dublin: Kilmainham Jail Restoration Society, 1971

Markievicz, Constance, *Prison Letters of Countess Markievicz*, London: Virago, 1987

McCarthy, Michael, *Priests and People in Ireland*, Dublin: Hodges Figgis, 1902

McConkey, Kenneth, *Celtic Splendour: An Exhibition of Irish Paintings and Drawings*, London: Pyms Gallery, 1985

McConkey, Kenneth, *Orpen and the Edwardian Era*, London: Pyms Gallery, 1987

McCoole, Sinéad, *Guns & Chiffon: Women Revolutionaries and Kilmainham Gaol*, Dublin: Stationery Office, 1997

McCoole, Sinéad, *No Ordinary Women: Irish Female Activists in the Revolutionary Years 1900–1923*, Madison, WI: University of Wisconsin Press, 2003

McGowan, Joe (ed.), *Countess Markievicz: The People's Countess*, Sligo: Countess Markievicz Millennium Committee, 2003

McGuire, Charlie, *Roddy Connolly and the Struggle for Socialism in Ireland*, Cork: Cork University Press, 2008

Morgan, Austen, *James Connolly: A Political Biography*, Manchester: Manchester University Press, 1988

Mulvihill, Margaret, *Charlotte Despard: A Biography*, London: Pandora, 1989

Murphy, Carol, *Lillie Connolly: Her Life and Times*, Workers' Party International Women's Day Lecture, Dublin: Citizen Press, 2006

Nevin, Donal, *James Connolly: A Full Life*, Dublin: Gill & Macmillan, 2005

Nic Dháibhéid, Caoimhe, *Seán MacBride: A Republican Life 1904–1946*, Liverpool: Liverpool University, 2011

Nic Shiubhlaigh, Máire, *The Splendid Years*, Dublin: James O'Duffy & Co., 1955

Norstedt, Johann, *Thomas MacDonagh: A Critical Biography*, Charlottesville, Va: University Press of Virginia, 1980

O'Brien, Paul, *Shootout: The Battle for St Stephen's Green, 1916*, Stillorgan, Co. Dublin: New Island Books, 2013

Ó Brolcháin, Honor, *16Lives: Joe Plunkett*, Dublin: O'Brien Press, 2012

O'Neill, Marie, *Grace Gifford Plunkett and Irish Freedom: Tragic Bride of 1916*, Dublin: Irish Academic Press, 2000

Parks, Edd W., and Parks, Aileen Wells, *Thomas MacDonagh*, Athens, Ga: University of Georgia Press, 1967

Plunkett Dillon, Geraldine, *All In the Blood: A Memoir of the Plunkett Family, the 1916 Rising and the War of Independence* (ed. Honor Ó Brolcháin), Dublin: A&A Farmar, 2006

Ryan, Meda, *Michael Collins and the Women in His Life*, Dublin: Mercier Press, 1996

Skinnider, Margaret, *Doing My Bit for Ireland*, New York: Century Co., 1917

South Inner City Community Devolopment Association (Siccda), *Ladies of the Liberties*, Dublin: Siccda Heritage Centre, 2002

Steele, Karen, *Maud Gonne's Irish Nationalist Writings 1895–1946*, Dublin: Irish Academic Press, 2004

Stuart, Francis, *Black List, Section H*, London: Penguin, 1982

Taillon, Ruth, *When History Was Made: The Women of 1916*, Belfast: Beyond the Pale Publications, 1996

Ward, Margaret, *Hanna Sheehy Skeffington: A Life*, Dublin: Attic Press, 1997

Ward, Margaret, *Maud Gonne: A Life*, London: HarperCollins, 1993

Woggon, Helga, *Silent Radical – Winifred Carney, 1887–1943: A Reconstruction of Her Biography*, Dublin: SIPTU, 2000

Articles

Ceannt, Áine, 'Eamonn Ceannt, the Soldier', *Wolfe Tone Annual*, Special 1916 Number, Dublin: Brian O'Higgins, undated

Connolly Heron, Ina, 'James Connolly: A Biography', *Liberty* (eight instalments), Dublin: March–October 1966

MacDonagh, Donagh, 'Pen Portrait of the Seven Signatories', *Irish Press*, April 1956: 'Éamonn Ceannt – Maker of History and Myth'; and 'A Poet and Scholar Died' (Joe Plunkett)

MacNally, Liam, 'Major MacBride', *Mayo News*, 27 July 1910

McDermott, Noel, 'Solving the Mallin Mystery', *Red Banner*, No. 48, June 2012

Mallin, Seamus, 'Commandant Michael Mallin', *Inniú*, [1996]; unpublished English translation by Michael Mallin

Moore, Eileen, 'Maid, Wife and Widow on her Wedding Day', *New World* (Chicago), 6 October 1916

Plunkett Dillon, Geraldine, 'Joseph Plunkett and His Friends', *Irish Press*, 5 May 1936

Ward, Margaret, 'The League of Women Delegates & Sinn Féin', *History Ireland*, Autumn 1996

'The Late Mrs Mallin – A Story of Sacrifice', *An Phoblacht*, 7 March 1932

'The Uhlan Pass', *Royal Scots Fusilier*, 1928, Vol. 1, No. 3

Newspapers and journals

Bean na hÉireann, Vol. 1, No. 1, Samhain November 1908

Lloyd's Weekly News, May 1916

Skerries News, Vol. 18, No. 3

The Times: 3 December 1886, 8 August 1906, 31 January 1908, 27 October 1910, November 1911, 8 Febuary 1917

Other documents
National Library of Ireland Collections:

Tom Clarke and Kathleen Clarke papers

Fred Allen papers, MSS 29,816–21: John MacBride, handwritten account of his life; Transcript of Proceedings, *MacBride v MacBride*; 'A Handwritten Account, *MacBride v MacBride*, Observations of the Evidence of the Petitioners Witnesses'

William O'Brien papers, MS 15,570: letters from James Connolly to Lillie Reynolds and others

Ceannt–O'Brennan papers, MS 13,069

O'Brennan, Lily, 'Leading a Dog's Life in Ireland', unpublished MS

Gifford family papers, MS 20,649

Grace Plunkett papers, MS 21,590

MacDonagh family papers, MS 44,318–20

Thomas MacDonagh papers, MS 10,999
Bingham, George, Account of Thomas MacDonagh, MS 20,646
Rosamond Jacob diaries, 22 April – 7 August 1922, MS 32,582

Other family papers
Allen Library, Dublin: documents relating to the Ceannt family; 'Wine and
   Gold', unpublished MS by Timothy O'Neill
Ceannt family record in the William Henry papers, private collection
Letters from Maud Gonne to Kathleen Pilcher (*née* Gonne), in the Conrad
   Balliet Papers, No. 771, Box 1, Robert Woodruff Library, Special
   Collections, Emory University, Atlanta, Ga
Letters from James Connolly to Winifred Carney, in the O'Shannon papers,
   Irish Labour History Museum and Archives, Dublin
Letters from Michael Mallin to Agnes Hickey, unpublished collection
MacBride family papers
O'Brennan family papers, University College Dublin
University of Limerick, documents and letters relating to Tom Clarke

Historical documents
Census of Ireland: 1901, 1911
England, Wales and Scotland Census: 1881, 1891, 1901; available at
   www.findmypast.co.uk
Cumann na mBan: documents relating to the organization
Jackie Clarke Collection, Ballina, Co. Mayo
Kilmainham Jail Collection, Dublin: original documents and objects relating
   to the Easter Rising 1916 and to political prisoners 1916–1924
Kitty McCormack Archive: programmes, play bills and other documents
   relating to the Abbey Theatre, the Theatre of Ireland and the Irish Theatre
   Company, held in the Jackie Clarke Collection
Military Pension Records
New York passenger arrival records from the Ellis Island Archives
Witness Statements given by Áine Ceannt (WS 264); Ina Connolly Heron (WS
   919); Nora Connolly O'Brien (WS 286), Cahir Davitt (WS 993), Grace
   Gifford Plunkett (WS 257), Dr Charles MacAuley (WS 735), Thomas
   Mallin (WS 382), James O'Shea (WS 733), Sergeant Michael T. Soughley
   (WS 189): all held in the Military Archives, Bureau of Military History,
   Cathal Brugha Barracks, Dublin
Women's Prisoners' Defence League, undated pamphlet; copy in the author's
   collection

BIBLIOGRAPHY

Academic studies

Hughes, Brian, 'A Splendid Type of the Dublin Tradesman', MPhil thesis, Trinity College Dublin, 2008

Caoimhe Nic Dháibhéid (2012), 'The Irish National Aid Association and the Radicalisation of Public Opinion in Ireland, 1916–1918', *The Historical Journal*, 55, pp. 705-29. DOI: 1017/50018246X12000234.

Rast, Mike, 'Tactics, Politics, and Propaganda in the Irish War of Independence 1917–1921', MA thesis, Georgia State University, 2011

Picture Acknowledgements

All unacknowledged images are from the author's collection.

First plate section
Kathleen Daly and Tom Clarke: both photographs courtesy of Helen Litton.
Maude Gonne: courtesy of the Library of Congress, Washington DC.
Iseult Gonne: courtesy of Anna MacBride White.
'Three Irish Irreconcilables in Paris', from the *Tatler*: courtesy of Anna MacBride White.
Lillie Reynolds, during her courtship with James Connolly: courtesy of Seamus Connolly.
Frances O'Brennan, later to become Áine Ceannt: courtesy of the National Library of Ireland.
The photographs exchanged by Agnes Hickey and Michael Mallin during their courtship: both photographs courtesy of Kilmainham Jail Museum, Dublin; 17PC–1B52–07b and 07a.
Young Ireland, William Orpen's portrait of Grace Gifford: private collection; courtesy of Pym's Gallery, London.
Muriel Gifford in 1911: courtesy of Kilmainham Jail Museum, Dublin; 17PC–1B53–05.
Muriel and Thomas MacDonagh with their baby son Donagh, 1913: courtesy of Kilmainham Jail Museum, Dublin.

Second plate section
The ruins of the GPO, Dublin: courtesy of the National Museum of Ireland.
Major John MacBride under arrest: courtesy of the Allen Library, Dublin.
Lillie Connolly with her daughter Fiona, the morning after her husband's execution: courtesy of Seamus Connolly.

PICTURE ACKNOWLEDGEMENTS

Third plate section

Grace Plunkett, photographed six weeks after her wedding: courtesy of Kilmainham Jail Museum, Dublin; 17PC–1B52–01.

The Mallin family, Christmas 1916: courtesy of Kilmainham Jail Museum, Dublin; 17PC–1B52–07.

Fr Joseph Mallin, Sr Agnes (Úna) Mallin, Maura Phillips and Fr Seán Mallin on the fiftieth anniversary of the Rising: courtesy of Maura Mallin.

Muriel MacDonagh and Grace Plunkett with Barbara MacDonagh, shortly before Muriel's death: courtesy of the Allen Library, Dublin; 17PC–1B53–05.

Sr Francesca with her nephew and niece, Donagh and Barbara MacDonagh: courtesy of Kilmainham Jail Museum, Dublin; 19PO–1A33–29.

Presentation dinner for Kathleen Clarke, 1919: courtesy of Kilmainham Jail Museum, Dublin.

Cumann na mBan Convention, October 1920: courtesy of the Military Archives, Dublin; BMH-CD-216-3.

'Margaret Wilson', mother of Maud Gonne's half-sister Eileen: courtesy of the Jäneda Museum, Estonia.

'Margaret' with residents, friends and relatives, Kallijärve, Estonia, 1930: courtesy of the Jäneda Museum, Estonia.

The Irish White Cross: courtesy of the Allen Library, Dublin.

Kilmainham Jail commemoration 1923 for the seventh anniversary of the 1916 executions: courtesy of the Allen Library, Dublin.

Anti-Treaty members of the Dáil, January 1922: courtesy of the Military Archives, Dublin; IE-MA-CP-A-0863.

Maud Gonne MacBride addressing a crowd in O'Connell Street, Dublin, 1937: courtesy of the LIFE picture collection/Getty Images.

Seán MacBride, Minister of External Affairs, at the Council of Europe, August 1950: courtesy of Anna MacBride White.

Kathleen Clarke and her son Emmet in the 1950s: courtesy of the Daly papers, University of Limerick, Glucksman Library.

Grace Plunkett, c.1940: courtesy of Kilmainham Jail Museum, Dublin.

Áine Ceannt, c.1949: courtesy of Kilmainham Jail Museum, Dublin.

Lillie Connolly with her granddaughters June and Ninel Beech, 1938: courtesy of the Marx Memorial Library, London.

Index

424